The Body Politic

Corporeal Metaphor in Revolutionary France, 1770–1800

Mestizo Spaces
Espaces Métissés

V. YT. Mudimbe
EDITOR

Bogumil Jewsiewicki
ASSOCIATE EDITOR

The Body Politic

Corporeal Metaphor in Revolutionary France, 1770–1800

Antoine de Baecque

Translated by Charlotte Mandell

STANFORD UNIVERSITY PRESS
STANFORD, CALIFORNIA

*The Body Politic: Corporeal Metaphor in
Revolutionary France, 1770-1800* was originally
published in French in 1993 under the title *Le Corps
de l'histoire: Métaphores et politique (1770-1800)*
© 1993 Calmann-Lévy

Assistance for the translation was provided by the
French Ministry of Culture.

Stanford University Press
Stanford, California

© 1997 by the Board of Trustees
of the Leland Stanford Junior University

Printed in the United States of America

CIP data appear at the end of the book

to Sylvie

Acknowledgments

Michel Vovelle has guided me in history with acuity and good humor. I want to thank him for the attention that he has devoted to this work and for his constant encouragement. Likewise, the warm friendships of Monique Vovelle, Danielle Le Monnier, Marie-Claude Baron, François Garnier, Corinne Michaud, and Paule and Georges Miraval were especially dear to me. Without the response and advice of Roger Chartier, Serge Daney, Lynn Hunt, Mona Ozouf, Jacques Revel, and Daniel Roche, this research would never have been completed. Finally, these studies were enriched by the many suggestions of Philippe Bordes, Ladan Boroumand, Christian-Marc Bosséno, Maïté Bouyssy, Olivier Coquard, Annie Duprat, Ouzi Elyada, Yann Fauchois, Frank Géorgi, Marc Grinsztajn, Patrice Gueniffey, Jacques Guilhaumou, Ran Halévi, Carla Hesse, Valérie-Noëlle Jouffre, Thierry Jousse, Ewa Lajer-Burcharth, Laura Mason, Régis Michel, Philippe Minard, Hervé Paturle, Jean-Baptiste Rauzy, Sylvie Robic, Yannick Séïté, Pierre Serna, Pascal Simonetti, Nicolas Weill, and Frédéric Worms. I should like here to express my gratitude to them all.

A. de B.

Contents

Translator's Note   XV

Introduction. The Body of History   1

    Metaphor as a Historical Tool . . . 1   The Three Body Politics: Embodying the State, Narrating History, Peopling Ceremonies . . . 7   The Text of the Revolution: A World in Representation . . . 13   In Praise of the Complex Source: For a Heterogeneous Reading of History . . . 15   The Spider's Strategy: Toward a Nonquantitative Serial History . . . 18 A Writing of History: Live Quotation and Analogical Montage . . . 20

PART I. The State-Body: Metaphor of the Transition of Sovereignty

  1. The Defeat of the Body of the King: Essay on the Impotence of Louis XVI   29

    The Ceremony of the Royal Sex . . . 31   The "Scrutation" of the Sheets: A Chronicle of Intimacies in the Royal Bed . . . 39 The Opposite of a Birth, or The Writing of the Furtive Gaze . . . 45 From the "Flaccid King" to the "Right" of Man . . . 51 Political Use of the Impotence of the King . . . 56   The "Gaiety" of Varennes, or The Misadventures of the Pig-King . . . 63

2. Sieyès, Doctor of the Body Politic: The Metaphor of the
Great Body of the Citizens   76

*Antisocial Disease, or The Body and the Orders . . . 79   The
"Admirable Edifice" of Political Incorporation . . . 86   How
Politics Speaks of Recovery: The Constitution of the Sovereign
Body of the Nation . . . 96   The Diffusion of a Political
Philosophy by Metaphor, or Birth of the Giant People . . . 102
Dividing the Territory: A "Skeleton" and "Muscles" for a New
Nation . . . 106   The Debate of the* Départements: *In Search of
the Organic Units of the French Body . . . 113   The Discourse of
the Federations: A Body Joined Together by the
Revolution . . . 122*

PART II. The Narrative-Body, or History in Fiction

3. Regeneration: The Marvelous Body, or The Body Raised
Upright of the New Revolutionary Man   131

*How a Word Enters into Politics: Regeneration of the Faithful,
Regeneration of Wounds, Regeneration of the French
People . . . 132   Imagining the Revolutionary Homo
Novus . . . 137   Regeneration, or The "Alphabet for
Children" . . . 146*

4. The Monsters of a Fantastic Aristocracy, or How the
Revolution Embodies Its Horrors   157

*Iscariot: The Story of a "Narrative-Body" . . . 160   Imagining
the Aristocratic Conspiracy: Spaces and Images of Teratological
Intertextuality . . . 166   The Paper Monster: The Fictional Body
of Political Event . . . 175*

5. David, or The Struggle of Bodies   183

*Under the Clothes, Bodies Laid Bare: The Line of Ideal
Beauty . . . 187   From Ideal Beauty to Ideal Politics:
Regeneration of a Concept . . . 191   From* Ataraxia *to*
Parenthyrsis: *Bodies Consumed by Low Pathos . . . 198*

**PART III. The Body as Spectacle: The Flesh of
            Political Ceremony**

6. The Great Spectacle of Transparency: Public Denunciation
    and the Classification of Appearances   209

    *Space Made Transparent: The Parisian Press of
    Denunciation . . . 217   Clear-sightedness, Rite of an Absolute
    Democracy . . . 225   Reading the Body . . . 233*

7. The Bodies of the Political Carnival   247

    *The Festival of Laughter, or The Need for Artifice . . . 249
    The Three Forms of Political Laughter: "The Wars of Epigrams,"
    Grotesque Travesties, Blasphemous Outbursts . . . 254
    The Battle of the Carnival . . . 269*

8. The Offertory of the Martyrs: The Wounded Body
    of the Revolution   280

    *The Ceremony of Wounds . . . 282   Narrative, Exhibition, and
    Simulacrum of the Tragic Body . . . 287   From the Cult of the
    Great Martyrs to Everyday Wounds: The Bodily Makeup of
    Terrorist Discourse . . . 297*

Conclusion. A Few Bodies to End (the Revolution)   309

    *The Terror, or The Club of Hercules . . . 310   Leaving the Terror:
    Can the French Colossus Be Pacified? . . . 314   The Body of
    Liberty: Prophecy of a Completed Revolution . . . 320*

Notes   327

Index   359

Illustrations are gathered between pages 182 and 183.

Translator's Note

In a way, the hardest part of this book to translate was the title. The French title literally rendered would be something like "The Body of History: Metaphors and Politics (1770–1800)." The author himself (who kindly read the opening pages of my translation, and offered useful suggestions and emendations) proposed the present title. The reader should be warned that the word *corps* is of very wide semantic range in French, just as its literal equivalent "body" is in English. Unfortunately, the ranges are not identical. This failure of neat symmetry sometimes makes a trenchant and memorable title in French (*corps-état*, for example) come out rather flat ("state body") or circumlocuitous (the state as a body). As a result, the reader will have to put up with a mixture of literal translations and "explaining translations"; I have included the French whenever I thought any confusion might arise. *Corps* also enters overtly into many other words—corporation, corporeal, corpulence, for example—not all of which can be translated using some version of "body." The reader should be aware too of the pervasive play on the word *histoire*, which of course means "history," but also "story." While the latter meaning is usually specified in the French text by *récit*, *conte*, and so on, one is never remote from the "story" in "history."

In the hope of providing helpful information to the reader, I have chosen to be somewhat inconsistent in citation of titles in the references. When the text cited has been published in English, I have tried to give the English title if possible. Page citations correspond to the French original used

by de Baecque. Titles of eighteenth-century texts are translated, whether
or not any modern translation (or even edition) exists. The pamphlet titles
are often witty (if scabrous) and verbally adroit, and therefore called out
for translation so the English-using reader—who has, after all, bought or
borrowed a translation—will not miss the fun.

I would like to thank Odile Chilton for her help, as invaluable as it was
cheerful. I am also grateful to the reference facilities of the Harvard University libraries, the Boston Public Library, and the Bard College library,
especially Jane Hryshko of the last named for her help in finding, almost
instantaneously, various elusive texts. Gloria Monti at Yale referred me to
Cynthia Markins-Dieden, who helped me understand de Baecque's discussion of Godard. To all these and others, including my husband, Robert
Kelly, I offer the thanks so natural in this desperate art of translation.

The Body Politic

*Corporeal Metaphor in
Revolutionary France,
1770–1800*

The Body of History

> The metaphor is that strategy of discourse by which language rids itself of the function of direct description in order to attain the mythic level where its function of discovery is freed.
>
> —Paul Ricoeur, *The Rule of Metaphor.*

> When a painter from the Far East paints a flower, he changes his nature. At least he strives to do so. He makes himself into a flower, then into that particular flower in front of him. The rendering should be the result of a knowledge of being by being. Likewise, it seems to me, the sole interest of criticism consists in trying to accomplish the creative act in reverse: starting with the metaphor, to discern and disclose what caused it to come into being.
>
> —Jean Douchet, *L'Art d'aimer.*

I first encountered the "body" of history while working on a political cartoon from the autumn of 1789 called "The Patriotic Fat Remover," printed in Paris at the time of the nationalization of the clergy's wealth. In this engraving, an obese prelate is pressed into a "physiological machine" activated by a revolutionary soldier: pieces of gold fall into the "national treasury" as the ecclesiastic loses weight. In the background are two spindly, emaciated priests, "their fat removed" in keeping with the title of the picture. The correspondence in this illustration between the flesh of the body and its political significance offers a possible reading of hundreds of caricatures printed between 1789 and 1791. However, it soon came to my attention that the image of the "patriotic fat remover" transforming flesh into money also enables us to understand something much larger, for corporeal images were at the very center of the metaphoric language used to describe the revolution in progress.

Metaphor as a Historical Tool

From the fall of 1789 on, the caricature was no longer the only document in which it was possible to observe the "political intent" of representations of the body: the tale of the Revolution itself is strewn with these metaphors that "paint a picture" of political principles and events, metaphors that deliberately sought readers' eyes and imagination. This tale was told, from 1788 onward, in the totality of writings that wove the "discourse of the Revolution about itself," in the thousands of texts, pamphlets, announcements, opinions, accounts, treatises, and journals that contemporaries, faced with the proliferation and sheer multiplication of pages, have referred to under the generic term "little pamphlets." The only thing that linked these texts with their diversity of authors, genres, and avowed goals was the day-by-day commentary on political events. If there does exist a textual reality of the Revolution, this is where it is found; this is likewise where the body of history lies.

We are mistaken in thinking of revolutionaries as men of abstraction. It would be more correct to say that they thought abstractly by means of metaphor and that they gave to their comprehension of the individual, and of the human community, and even the universe, the figure of the human body. Their language, even at its most philosophical and legalistic, was charged with these images. The Abbé Sieyès, to take the example of someone highly suspected of "metaphysics," conceived of his ideal legislative system—necessarily abstract since it was only mental projection—in terms of pure geometry: "I imagine the Law in the center of an immense globe; all the citizens, without exception, are at the same distance upon the circumference, and all occupy equal places." This symbol of perfection traced by the bodies of all citizens joined together in a circle is the quintessential metaphor with Sieyès, but similar images are found throughout the pamphlets, giving body to the story of the Revolution. Bernardin de Saint-Pierre, for example, could give such bodily form to the spectacle of truth: "We would not see the light of the sun if it were not intercepted by bodies, or at least by clouds. It escapes us in the absence of any atmosphere and blinds us at its source. The same is true for truth; we would not grasp it if it did not fix on perceptible events, or at least on metaphors and comparisons that reflect it; it needs a body to reflect it," he wrote in the preface to *The Indian Cottage* of 1791. The text of the pamphlets is the body that reflects the revolutionary event; it proposes perceptible metaphors that, by themselves, allow the tale of the Revolution to take shape and to happen in the mind of writers and of readers. All the descriptions, inventions, denunciations, relationships, and accounts dealt with by these texts aim at giving a face to heroes and to traitors, a body to ideas, a physiognomy to history.

The first aim of my research consisted in seeing this "body." This vision is not easy: the polysemy of these five letters [*corps*, body] is truly disconcerting at the end of the French ancien régime. The *Encyclopédie*, while devoting more than ten pages to the entries "corporation," "corporeity," *corps*, even "incorporation," finally had to admit that, in the words of the Chevalier de Jaucourt, "It is impossible to demonstrate the existence of bodies [*corps*]." The problem is not that philosophy renounces its materialist approach to the universe of forms, but that this polysemy risks dissolving the meaning of the word into an infinity of metaphors and a multiplicity of definitions. To enumerate them would be tedious. The *Encyclopédie*, however, did not dodge the task. From "Corporal" ("liturgical term, sacred cloth used during the Mass and spread beneath the chalice for the respectful placement thereon of the body of Our Lord Jesus Christ") to "Corpulence" ("anatomical term, shape and fullness of the body"), it gave its verdict on the theological, political, social, metaphysical, physical, chemical, medical, literary, juridical, architectural, military, handicraft, and anatomical meanings of the word. In this encyclopedic survey, we no doubt retain the first meaning of the "body" at the end of the ancien régime: it is a word that says everything, a word whose range of meaning was never so extensive and that was taken to its extreme not just by the social and professional structure of old France but also by the legacy of a political order ensuing from a religious interpretation of the universe, by philosophical and political debates, and by scientific research. The language of the end of the eighteenth century seems stretched between different acceptations of this word that can, by itself, describe each individual of the kingdom, physically, medically, from head to foot; unite the many communities, all these people, these tradesmen, these merchants, these administrators for whom it is allowed, by letters of patent duly registered, to assemble and "form a corporate body"; or, finally, to take on the French system in its entirety, a political, religious, monarchic model of organization of the state and of society.

Metaphors of the body are thus amenable to contradictory interpretations. This was particularly true at the end of the eighteenth century, and on this ambivalence revolutionary discourse would play. On the one hand, a tendency to transparency would try to put an end to all the confusion of bodies that fragmented the old French society into so many privileges, restrictions, and areas of shadow. On the other hand, there was a desire to employ the word in an extended range of meaning, to exploit the word's

incomparable power of evocation and persuasion. The "body" is truly a pivotal word: it can deal with the political, social, and cultural organization of
the ancien régime while telling of itself anew and fashioning a narrative of
its own origins, of its "coming into the world." At the end of the eighteenth
century, the metaphor of the body tells the condition of one political system, its death, and then the birth of another. This book itself is continually
confronted with the danger of dissipating the symbolic meaning of a word
that ends up hiding as much as it reveals: the omnipresence of the representation of the body and the multiplicity of its registers risk dissolving the
historic object studied into the infinity of its fragments and its uses.

Despite the dangers of possible confusion, I remain persuaded that one
must "risk the metaphor,"[1] as much in the questions a historian poses to
past societies as in the historian's own writing. That is to say, one must ask
a question that goes to the foundation of interpretation and of criticism, a
question that illuminates one of our ways of knowing: how do humanity and
society choose to "represent themselves by metaphor," how do they find
forms, specific objects in front of which they say to themselves either in a
burst of imagination or in conformity: "*That* is me"? One must rethink, in
some way, the reasons for the "ontological vehemence"[2] of metaphors of
a historic moment. For me as a historian, this question of representations
has consisted of seeking the chief bodily images brought back or invented
by writers at the end of the eighteenth century to talk about society as
it was in the very process of evolving, of changing at a dizzying rate—an
abruptness that precisely named the images or symbols that were capable
of fixing in the mind the terms of a particular narrative of events, one that
invents the everyday and at the same time transforms it into a terrible or
marvelous adventure.

Metaphors of the body thus offer networks of themes and references that
constitute a coherent narrative of historic fracture and fill the chasm hollowed out by 1789 in the traditional chronicle of the monarchy. These metaphors were able simultaneously to describe the event and to make the description attain the level of the imaginary. The deployment of these bodily
topoi—the degeneracy of the nobility, the impotence of the king, the herculean strength of the citizenry, the goddesses of politics appearing naked
like Truth, the congenital deformity of the aristocrats, the bleeding wound
of the martyrs—allowed political society to represent itself at a pivotal moment of its history. This is the trail I mean to follow in proposing a history
of these unique bodies. It is a matter of describing a historical moment

through the right metaphors, what Serge Daney and Jean-Luc Godard persist in calling the "art of montage," a way of placing the metaphors of a historic time in correspondence in order to describe it better.

This "montage" opens up two "metaphorical categories," two definitions of what a "metaphor" is. The metaphor is a narrative form of history; it is also a way of knowing history. These two approaches for me are embedded within each other: shedding light on the narrative forms used in the political account of an event leads to a better understanding of the history of that event. It is not only the interpretation of ideas, the commentary on values, or the counting of the economic indicators of a society, but also the study of its forms of narrative, sometimes the most out of place, the most trivial or the most surprising, that allow the seeker to obtain historical knowledge. In this sense, metaphors appear in their first historical form, namely, "telling about oneself": to say "That is me" is first and foremost to construct a narrative of the self, whether as an individual or as a community (before 1789, I was a sick, suffering body; but now I am a cured body, on my feet again, free in my movements, brought back to life). In addition, metaphors are the second historical form, namely, "knowing oneself." One must pass through the forms of a narrative in order to reach knowledge: the ontological vehemence of "That is me" brings into play a formidable ontological introspective method of knowing (before I was sterile, that's how I know the truth of the evil from which the state suffered, embodied by its king at the end of the ancien régime; from now on I am fertile, that's how I know the truth of the new power, that of the National Assembly in 1789, capable of giving birth to a French national body ordered and organized by the multiplicity of its laws).

If this metaphor of the body is so powerful at the end of the eighteenth century, it is precisely because it, better than any other, succeeds in *connecting* narrative and knowledge, meaning and knowing. Thanks to a representation—that of the human body—it allows the association of three registers of discourse about society. First, individuality: the body is the unit of living individuality. All the scientific research in the Age of Enlightenment contributed the category of the *alive* to this reading: that which possesses a composite body is alive. Scholars from Buffon to Bichat chose the human—sometimes animal—body, rather than the soul, as the proper matter for their studies and experiments, in order to calibrate the grid through which they read the microcosm and the macrocosm.

In the same way, the second level of metaphoric discourse, the human

community, the organism that reunites all individualities, is also represented as a bodily whole. To introduce this human entity into a logic of
corporeal understanding is at once to make the management of the community—either as history, or as organization of a society or a state—comparable to the scientific management of the body. Different individuals are
cells, different human associations are organs, which those responsible (for
history, for society, for the state) set in order and regulate, like doctors.
The metaphor of the body offers to politicians and men of letters alike the
illusion of an organic ordering of the human community, an illusion that
thus gives them a scientific claim to observe it and organize it. Finally, each
body moves in a universe of bodies: the idea of a body is essentially pluralistic, so that the corporeity of society is placed at one and the same time
in conjunction with the singular individual-body and with the pluralistic
universe-body, in homogeneous and complex relationships. And these relationships are not only those of membership, of size, and of inclusion but
also of representation, of analogy. From these graduated scales of bodily
imagery, both meaning and, even more important, knowledge are elicited.

Judith Schlanger has lucidly summarized the advantages of organic
thinking as applied to political and social organization: "Because the organism is a representation founded on analogical correspondence, it communicates both information and meaning simultaneously."[3] The universe, the
human community, and the individual all take on meaning through bodily
analogy and, at the same time, thanks to historic context, become the
means to knowledge as objects of knowledge for those scholars who have
chosen to explore the body rather than the soul. Narrative and knowledge
are closely interwoven in these (ana)logical and scientistic politics, as if men
of politics and men of letters could, at that exact moment, write a metaphorical narrative of social upheavals with the very weapons of knowledge,
the body having become, through exploits of taxonomies, experiences, and
dissections, the first level of knowledge of individuals and community. The
great architect of these three macrocosms is no longer so much divine as
it is natural: it is the body. This body, through systems of analogies, summons to itself both the metaphors of a narrative about society and also the
ways by which different macrocosms can be known.

To be a historian of representations consists then of paying attention to
the creative intelligences of these analogical forms in each society, of this
discourse by metaphors, whether in speech, in print, or in image, put into
place by politicians and men of letters. It also consists of paying attention to

the ways in which these forms are apprehended, listened to, read, and seen by the public. These two approaches of narrative forms taken together are like a path toward knowledge—not because these forms reflect the truth of the individual or the community but because they *are* a truth, with that same ontological vehemence that anyone uses in choosing the metaphors that tell one's story and guide one's thinking.

This book should be understood as an attempt to clarify, through three possible registers of the metaphoric narration of history (the state-body, the narrative-body, the spectacle-body), the way in which the revolutionary moment chose to represent itself or to represent the other, its opposite: the cured man facing the sick man, the regenerated man facing the deformed aristocrat, the supervising man facing the supervised man. But I think this way, these ways, these representations that border the tale of the Revolution, must also be seen or conceived as ways of knowing, interpreting, and thinking about the history of the revolutionary event, exactly as the body, at the end of the eighteenth century, was at once a form of political representation *and* a scientific scale of knowledge. Then an entire tradition of reason separated representation from knowledge, form from content, spectacle from theory, illustration from interpretation. Yet, to illustrate is to interpret: to choose the right metaphors, describe them, clarify the tale, is to propose an interpretation of history, a way of thinking, a way of knowing. That is also why the *object* of this book (its content, if you like) is inseparable from the *way* in which it was written (its form, if you like), just as the knowledge of history is inseparable from the representation of it. First, I will set forth the object of the book: metaphors faced with the political event. Second, I will detail the method of this book: the interpretative montage of metaphors, the analogical bringing together of different representative supports. The object and method of the historian, knowledge and the representation of this knowledge, are the two indissociable subjects of this book: history is made in the very account of research, and the history book shows history in the process of writing itself, just as a film is always a tale of its own filming.

The Three Body Politics: Embodying the State, Narrating History, Peopling Ceremonies

Revolutionaries, by representing themselves as a political community united in one single body, used the metaphor of the state-body to go from one regime to another: such is the first line of research that I tried to trace and that I retrace in Part I of this book. This transition leads from the "body of the king" to the great "body of citizens." It has already been said, and seems obvious today, that the end of a political representation of the state corresponded to the death of the body of the king. Similarly, with the execution of Louis XVI, we often speak of the culmination of a process of desacralization. Though one might be skeptical about this last word, the bodily representation of the power of the king played a fundamental role in the ancien régime. One single body perpetuated itself from Bourbon king to king, embodying the continuity of the state, a body in which all subjects could recognize themselves and in which everyone recognized their sovereign.

This body had a double function: it imposed a stable, continuous, unique, central presence (the incarnation of absolutism), and it imposed the king, through substitution (by means of his image, the multiple portrayals of his profile, the story of his fame), on each Frenchman. The body of the king, as Louis Marin has written, was a representation in the two exact meanings of the word: intensifying a presentation ("re" in its acceptation of intensification) or simulating it ("re" in its acceptation of substitution). The king's body kept this double function until the reproductive capacity of this presence was placed in doubt by echoes from the royal bed, then proclaimed as "null and imbecilic" by rumor, texts, and images (which went beyond the closed society of the court), and was finally put to use by revolutionary politics, whether Royalist, Republican, or Feuillant. That is why I study the transition of the sovereignty of the body from the king to the nation by following the words and images proliferating in several registers and genres that, starting with the marriage in 1770, delineated the "impotence" of Louis XVI.

Through these multiple references to royal impotence, traced, with the most meticulous detail, over twenty years, we can witness a political transfer of seminal power. The king, incapable in licentious—and then political—imagination of fathering even one heir, and thus of engendering the state, leaves this power to the revolutionary *homo novus* who, by the intermediary of his representatives and of his "right" as a man, creates laws and institutions, creates a sovereign nation. This story of royal impotence leads to the flight to Varennes, after which people laughed noisily at the impotence of the monarch, who, in pamphlets, newspapers, and caricatures, became a grotesque circus pig, a "gelded fattened animal."

How could the power of this new body of the nation be fashioned, and then represented? I try to follow that process through the texts of the Abbé Sieyès, who, like a number of political commentators in the course of the winter of 1788–89, began with the representation of the "antisocial disease" paralyzing the French body and went on to establish a program of cure in two phases. First, radical intervention: to rid the great citizen body of its privileged excrescences, tumors eating away at the French organism. That involves denying the discourse of the orders and striking at the root of the evil: only the Third Estate embodies the sovereignty of the national body.

Second, the philosopher must give life to the great citizen body and to the assembly of representatives, the double body of modern political representation having assumed, by an explicit transfer of bodily metaphors of power, the oldest instruments of royal majesty. This novel body of the new France very quickly finds its symbols, its illustrations, its exempla, in revolutionary discourse. Sieyès himself initiates this metaphorical diffusion by applying a "language of the body" to the description of the ideal organization of the country that is then relayed by proposals for reform of institutions, powers, and French space issued by numerous revolutionary administrators. An essential moment in the beginnings of the Revolution, this reformed system is embodied in the discourse on the new departmental division of France, beginning in the autumn of 1789, then in the organic language of the Federates in the spring of 1790. The "body of France" is carried by the festivals and processions of the Federation that multiply until they all join together in the great Parisian ceremony of the Fourteenth of July. Placing the center in contact with the periphery, activating a circulation of the vital forces of the nation, the new France is divided into living, unprecedented cells to unite itself better into a regenerated organism.

In the course of Part II of this book, I try to show how the political narrative used metaphors of the body to tell about the Revolution as it was being born, then enlarging, then being fought. According to the words of the writer Joseph-Antoine Cérutti, an ardent defender of the embodiment of persuasive speech, it is a question of "giving a body to ideas to throw them, alive, into the mind of the reader"—in other words, to convince readers, observers, and witnesses to adhere to the narrative of the Revolution. To my thinking, that best defines the role of the writer and of the journalist from 1789 on: to use a language that was embodied at the time of the rich controversies of the ancien régime, a language loaded with multiple techniques of persuasion infinitely elaborated, and to transform it into a revolutionary language, a new language able, because of its metaphors, to take charge of the tale of historic rupture. If the discourse of the Revolution so quickly and efficiently snatched up its own tale of origins, it is because it knew how to inherit an art of embodied speech, which reached it in all its metaphorical—theological, medical, scientific, political, poetic—richness, thanks to the intermediary of the republic of letters of the ancien régime.

This transition does not occur without an upheaval of the political language shaped by writers involved in a severe struggle, at the time of the "war of the little pamphlets," aiming to control the production of persuasive metaphors. Thus I examine the two principal ways of convincing or frightening by political words (the language of the "marvelous" and that of the "terrible"), studying these two possibilities through two omnipresent metaphors of the body from 1789 on: regeneration and monstrosity. The first bears the birth of a New Man; the second engenders the hydra of the aristocratic plot. But both answer essential questions. How was the emotional discourse of the revolutionary event put into place? How, at a time of sudden political mutation, could one tell one's own story, the ideals and fears where the dreams and anxieties of a new society take root? These questions are clarified by the struggle of narrative-bodies: a process of exaggeration of discourse carried out between 1789 and 1791. It is in fact these two archetypal figures—the New Man and the aristocratic man—embodied by the pamphlets' rhetoric of the body, including the discourses of assemblies and images alike, that now carry the tale of the Revolution, that make it "fictionalized," transforming History [*Histoire*] into stories [*histoires*] through metaphoric imagination.

Part III, "The Body as Spectacle: The Flesh of Political Ceremony," illustrates, through the study of certain rituals, this transition of one bodily representation of political society into another. The tale of the Revolution, its omnipresent metaphors, now finds a scene where bodies appear in flesh and bone. This stage is decisive: the body is not only a metaphor for the world, it is also a spectacle given for us to see, most often during festivals that punctuate the ceremonies of the Revolution. For ceremony must bring bodies to the gaze of all citizens: that is what embodies, in the almost daily political practices of the Revolution, the new regime. The omnipotence of the public gaze is essential, for it places bodies in the space of political transparency. This is one of the major axes of my research: how does the body politic forged by metaphors of discourse propose the transparency of its real spectacle? In this space of transparency is established a possible, if not compulsory, reading of the body.

This reading is offered during political celebrations that I study in two ceremonial forms: the ritual of laughter and the ritual of tears. The festival of laughter has its apogee between February and June 1791; the ceremony of tears is the most expressive in the year that leads to the assassination of Marat, in July 1793, at the installation of the laws of Prairial Year II, inaugurating the Reign of Terror. The carnival imprints its mark on the development of the former; the murdered bodies of Republican martyrs guide the latter. Through these two possible bodies of the political spectacle, another chronology of the Revolution is brought to light, one that wanted to break with the beliefs of the old world. This was done by laughing at traditional bodies in blasphemous outbursts in grotesque pamphlets, and by miming, in words, a street carnival forbidden by the Parisian municipality: the body of the pope burned in effigy during a burlesque procession in May 1791; the body of the king portrayed as a greedy, impotent pig at the end of June after Varennes; power abused on Mardi Gras 1791 during the "war of laughs." This spectacle of laughter is not a light comedy but punctuates its lively ripostes with attacks on the body. Even if it transfers in part the violence of the street into a burlesque of discourse and ritualized gestures, it does not leave individuals unharmed.

A few months later, attacks on the body became real (assassination in Paris and war on the frontiers), and the organism that is threatened is that of the Republic itself, which now organizes the inspection of its own wounds through a very controlled, expressive ritual. The great political decisions, such as giving the order for the Terror in September 1793 or the putting into effect of the Reign of Terror in Prairial Year II, are thus carried out in the name of the wounds of the martyrs, presented to the citizens' gaze during funerals worthy of baroque pomp or during multiple processions of war wounded returning from the front. This murdered body is never handed over in innocence to the gaze of the political spectator: by means of concentrating on its wounds, presented as those of the great body of the Republican state, it captures the violence of brutal, anarchic populist repression, the kind that took place in the beginning of the Revolution, from the massacres of July 1789 to those of September 1792. Intense emotion leads to political decision: the inauguration of the Terror, the vengeance organized by the murdered Republican body against its murderers.

The story of this "Republican body," symbolized by the figure of the

colossus of popular sovereignty, Hercules armed with his terrible club, culminates in the fragmentation of organic elements. This tale occurs in the
conclusion of this book: the fusional energy demanded by the Terror to
unite the national body, faced with its obsessive enemies, into one great
indivisible whole ends up by turning against the very limbs of the body.
Then, after Thermidor, the metaphor of sovereignty, that colossus forged
by Sieyès in 1789, must again be taken up, and softened: its movements
made gentler, its outbursts contained, the functions in its body of government (the brain) separated from those of action (the limbs), functions that
had been fused together by the urgency of the Terror. This attempt, conceived by the doctors and politicians of the Directory, is completed, then
replaced, by the success, definitive at the time, of the representation of the
Republic as the body of a woman, Liberty herself, usually depicted as wise
and serene, that symbol that the Revolution bequeathes to the Republicans
of the nineteenth century.

Searching for the "body of history," I came across three forms of political representation. First, the metaphorical representation of the body as an
anthropomorphic symbol of the political system—the transition of sovereignty from the body of the king to the great citizen body. Second, the metaphorical representation of the body as a tool of discourse for persuasion; for
this, I investigated the embodied tale of the revolutionary epic. Third, the
representations offered in public ceremonies—the spectacle of the body
evolving, with precise rituals, into the space of political transparency. My
method was to review these different types of corporeal representation, arranged according to a particular chronological order (from the marriage
of the Dauphin Louis in 1770, to the initiation of the Reign of Terror in
Prairial Year II, then to the Brumaire coup d'état, Year VIII), and to follow
a particular set of themes (from the impotence of the king to the glory of
the martyr, from the regenerated colossus to the degenerate monster, from
imagination to laughter, then to tears). This is the story of the Revolution
that I want to offer: the transition to sovereignty, the tale of its own epic, the
creation of a space of absolute transparency that imposed itself as the scene
of Terror, then the disappearance of the colossal metaphor of the sovereign
people as an organism (no doubt too much linked to the awful memories
of the period of the Terror) that gives way to another symbol—the embodiment of Liberty with the lineaments of a proud woman, who expresses the
certainty of having successfully completed the revolutionary adventure.

If this work does not always succeed, since the story of the Revolution, having proliferated into many possibilities, has today become untellable in its unity, it is nonetheless the body of history, laid bare like the classical allegory, that I wanted to show. For in this political form, this *forma* in the Latin sense of a "configuration" allowing the world to be seen and understood, one can read surprising tales and behold edifying spectacles.[4]

The Text of the Revolution: A World in Representation

While trying to see the body of history, I set in the heart of this book an image generated by the proliferating registers of metaphor. The material in which these metaphors are principally inscribed is no less rich and complex: the thousands of pamphlets making up the political commentary on the revolutionary event. These texts, which form the primary source of this work, are quite difficult to define and delimit. Their appearance is banal: generally eight or sixteen pages *in octavo* printed carelessly on bad paper, most often without a cover or binding, but heralded by a title suitable for attracting credulous readers, a title in which, besides descriptions of all the political events, are promised confessions, revelations, and denunciations of all the conspiracies driving the course of the Revolution. This universe created by the writing of pamphlets is like what could be called a "world of representation"[5] where politics are exhibited as overt actions and at the same time reinvented in order to reveal to the reader the secret, inevitably hidden meaning of any event. In both cases, the narrative, overflowing with portraits, details, atmospheres, unfolds on a conventional political canvas: conspiracy, corruption of power, revolt, purification of public morality, France regenerated. These are the master fictions of narrative, the forms of representation, which are the "eyes" through which the reader is to understand this universe of alliances and rivalries knotted around power, the framework on which political events become fiction.

Thus a paradox animates all these texts. How do these literally "un-believable" narratives compel belief, constructed as they most often are out of excess, invented sources, and pretended confessions? What these pamphlets put into play is a very particular kind of accreditation of political narrative, close, in the forms of support used, to the caricature. Of course, recognizing the person or the power being portrayed is most important, but the distancing of falsity is absolutely necessary for these texts to be effective and get read. The pamphlet of the revolutionary narrative relies on an openly oversignified reconstitution of the plausible. In this distancing, between the realist mode (the display of politics) and the caricatural play (its reinvention), the writing unfurls and the representations are born. This operation is ambivalent: it does not require the reader's faith. It has nothing to gain or lose by mobilization even though it never stops calling to action, to vigilance or to violence; yet it shamelessly presents readers with the procedures of a writing of the false mimicking the true, pulling them into a game of unveiling, guiding their gaze by means of images of the political world. The reader knows that the descriptions are re-composed, or invented, but takes pleasure in this reconstitution precisely because it stems from mime, from a literary genre in a recognized code, one taken over by its spirit of complicity. Because adherence to all the details of the text is not required, belief in the foundations of the narrative—those representations that organize the immediate writing of the story—can take shape.

Moreover, this writing of the false with a claim to being real has its effects doubled by the law of sequence that rules over the serial publication of the pamphlets. There are polemical series: one text launches an attack, another follows it up, some try to reply to it. Networks of a paper war are formed whose heralds would be the Orléans Royalist coterie, the Fayettist writers, the "friends" of the king, the "atelier" of Mirabeau, the gang of "Neckerists." There are thematic series: around a concept, an event, or a person, a common fund of largely inherited imagery can very quickly form (anticlerical, for example) or carry forward images of historic rupture, of the Golden Age rediscovered. Journalists and writers borrow from this common fund, but they also nourish and renew it. The revolutionary pamphlet, often anonymous as it is, is usually a stranger to notions of literary correctness. Its writing operates by excess, by successive, multiform borrowings and outrageously bombastic reappropriations rather than by explicit citations. Finally, there is the series of news reports, which appears because the only chronology of this literature of the moment is that of the Revolution itself, or a Revolution lived from day to day, in which "circumstances" make the pamphlet.

If these texts have something to tell and to proclaim, and seek to make narrative from political upheaval, they still answer only to the multiplication of microevents that mark off the rapid course of the history to which they are linked. You will never find, even through all the pullulation of the prophets, one single, unique text that suspends or even anticipates the course of events. It is not so much the "individual book" or the "exemplary book" that counts as the effects of the writing, which plays both with borrowings from fashionable genres and with the complicity of readers to fashion representations of politics. It is also the incremental pressure of the series itself, forming polemical networks, thematic networks, and networks of facts.

The practical politics of writing and reading carried along by the swell of pamphlets are an integral part of the French democratic culture born in the first months of the Revolution. Writing and reading the commentary on the event plays a part in learning democratic life, bearing witness to a space suddenly opened to all eyes. The desire, manifested by an endlessly increasing number of readers, to know *everything*, including the most absurd, about the intimate details of power is in fact the first mainspring of a communal, democratic political life. Each political figure knows from then on that he not only has to justify his conduct but that he must also watch carefully the "image" that he creates. In this sense, the pamphlets of the Revolution are almost a prophetic sign of the modern "mediatized" world, so much do they succeed in putting into circulation an unequaled number of narratives, anecdotes, and representations of power. It is this modernity of discourse, this power given to words of "making an image" from politics, of making visible a universe of abstract principles or of what was behind the scenes, that I wanted to set in the center of my work. What pamphlets offer to the researcher is a subject of the first order, a means offered to writers and politicians of the Revolution of describing themselves as a community turned upside-down by history: a political self-representation. "Self" designates the intense reflexive work of the period on itself. "Representation" summons imaginary forms that bring to focus the diverse perceptions of political society, forms of reference that bind the group together (the New Man, the conspiracy, the martyr) and forms that legitimize instances of judgment and allow members to be included within the body of the Revolution, or to be radically excluded. "Political" designates the prioritized field on which, almost exclusively (so much were society and culture seen from a political perspective), these forms of representation are written.

In Praise of the Complex Source: For a Heterogeneous Reading of History

These pamphlets offer an anchorage—the revolutionary text—for this book, and an object of study: a political self-representation abounding with metaphors of the body. Starting from the pamphlets, I tried to offer a way to write history. From the six thousand pamphlets that circulated through Paris between August 1788, when Louis XVI called for "opinions and advice" on the convocation of the next Estates General (thereby opening a way toward freedom of the press), and the summer of 1791, when the municipal police and the National Guard imposed strict control over printed matter after the Republican agitation that was crushed by the repression of 17 July—from these three fine years of political shorthand, I analyzed two thousand texts.

Yet as soon as one enters into this universe, one takes the risk of getting lost in an immense continent where only a few reliable points of orientation exist, where each text, in itself, has only a fragmentary interest. It is a perplexing, even discouraging, otherness. But faithful to Robert Darnton's intuition, "when we cannot get a proverb, or a joke, or a ritual, or a poem, we know we are on to something,"[6] I had to persevere. Read and reread. Group these readings into a series. Bring these particular series of events closer. Try to recognize authors and strategies of persuasion. Establish the effects of these texts on reading and readers. Isolated, a pamphlet is weak; grouped together with its written siblings, it gains in thickness; brought close to the warmth of an "event," this family of writings fills with sense. Offered to readers, these writings can illuminate a way of telling about and understanding the world. Thus a piece of historical writing emerges. It is intertextual, since none of these texts has a unique personality and since they plagiarize each other and answer each other to such a point that a purely descriptive report and a pornographic chronicle can get confused, but above all it is intercontextual.

The pamphlet, or rather the series of pamphlets, never gained an autonomous life. Its universe is not closed; it welcomes and breathes otherness in, mixes it up, then sends it back to another "other thing." The pamphlet is often only an impure mediation, a necessary element, seething with culture, that causes passage from something to something else. These "other things" are never reducible to simple expressions. Sometimes they are the speeches that had been exchanged the day before in a National Assembly; sometimes they are the bedsheets of a king used to watch for signs of his virility. Sometimes it is the private life of a politician; sometimes it is a massacre that parades with severed heads on the ends of stakes. But the pamphlet is never just a commentary on one particular event; it refers us also to another source of information. A series of pamphlets is inseparable from a concomitant series of engravings, from a picture, from the gestures at a ceremony, from a scholarly work that it popularizes. The series of texts foregrounds some event, some personage, some ritual, that can only be understood in connection with other sources. Thus the complex source takes shape—as if, in order to gain in depth, the historical object had to pass through sometimes convergent but usually divergent mirrors that reflect the dense matrix of the sources. The product of these bursts of visions is neither simple to interpret nor devoid of questions.

Two by no means negligible problems arise. Gathering together (for example) thirty or so eight-page pamphlets, some political cartoons, two handsome mezzotints, the scholarly writings in three volumes of some prestigious author, a painting by a master of a few hundred standing deputies who are raising their hats to salute a king, and what might turn out to be stains of sperm on a bedsheet—in other words, the actual substance of these multiple cross-sources—creates disarray. But to go without (visible) transition from the body of the king to a monster invented by a pamphlet, from the New Man to the corpse of Marat, is inelegant. I believe that by placing myself in the space of the revolutionary text, and then carefully enlarging the gaze, little by little, toward other heterogeneous sources, it is possible to preserve a coherence of interpretation.

In fact, it is even necessary. We must understand Jacques-Louis David's painting through the monsters that cartoons or texts caused to be born at the same instant in the public imagination. We must understand the thinking, metaphysical as it seems at first glance, of Emmanuel Sieyès, by reading the most trivial, the most violent, or the most anecdotal anonymous pamphlets that surrounded his *Essay on Privileges*. These texts, these obviously diverse sources, are a challenge to the reader. Will it be possible to unify these writings, these images, these accounts of rituals into one continuum of meaning, yet keep its multiform aspect, retain its particular genres, its abundance of authors, and submit it to the same interpretative gaze of the historian? To read at the same time a juridical treatise and a lampoon of injuries ad hominem, a political memoir and a pamphlet of fantastic prognostications, is certainly a risky game, but, conducted with great precautions (keeping in mind, for example, what is specific to each genre), it quickly becomes extremely suggestive and elicits important meetings. It seems to me that even if all sources are not born free and equal among themselves, they do have a *right* to the same consideration, a *right* to be fused into one heterogeneous whole and be offered to the interpretative gaze. The mystery preserved then is homage to the capacity for invention of writers of the past, and the will to penetrate it, even a little, mobilizes the interpretative imagination of the researcher of today.

To read the historical text in that way requires a bold approach to sources, made "dense" by the intersection of the assembled works. It forces one to think about the connection from source to source, the ill-managed coherence, the "inter," which, in the end, remains the first condition of historical work: *inter*pretation. The scholar, to use the categorizations of Michel de Certeau, escapes from the "explanation of History" to reach a far richer land of uncertainty: the reading, or readings, often concurrent but parallel, of historical texts mixed—almost fused—around one particular historical object. Interpretation is the thread, or link, that guides the historian through the mixture of sources in all their heterogeneity. The historian's work thrives on this fundamental dissonance. This approach finally resembles what could be called a "nonquantitative serial history," a heterogeneous series of contextual fabrics sewn together by the interpretative gaze, by which a shape is given to one unique, nonquantifiable historical object. The particular case is put back into the center of the story (a "nonquantitative history"), but from the perspective of a hermeneutics working with a series of heterogeneous sources (a "serial history"). Each particular object chosen by the historian becomes an interpretative machine that ingests series of information drawn from multiple, diverse, and contradictory sources.

The Spider's Strategy: Toward a Nonquantitative Serial History

In methodological terms, this nonquantitative serial history necessitates anchoring the reading of the historic text in all the diversity of its possible sources. The text is placed in the situation of being read *with*: with pictures, with reports of ceremonies, with police archives—historical registers for a long time neglected not in their specificity but in their interaction. The reconstitution of this interpretative fabric becomes valid only in all its complexity and, without neglecting any thread of reading, is capable of making a kind of hermeneutic moment occur in historiography. This might come close to approaching a dream once expressed by Gadamer in *Truth and Method*, that of the search for an "authentic meaning" of the text in which the "unity of a heterogeneous whole" becomes the true hermeneutic object,[7] that "whole" born in the multitude of connections established between the different registers of texts, images, representations, and cultural practices, connections that call for interpretation and thus engender the historical object. The hermeneutic interest does not reside in the fullness of the historical object itself, but in the multiplication of threads of interpretation twined around this object, taking into account the heterogeneity of the sources likely to illuminate it. That is naturally why I persist in choosing limited historical subjects, ones that we might think anecdotal or laughable. After all, what are we to make of Louis XVI's genitals, or the wounds of Republican martyrs? But once these are offered to fruitful interpretation, mysterious, pervading different registers of texts or images — obscure and limited at first glance — they oblige the researcher to take deep cross-sections that reveal the heart of the sufferings or troubles of a society. To probe the wounds of martyrs is to penetrate into the Revolution; to investigate the impotence of the king is to understand the crisis of credibility of an entire political system thanks to the study of the numerous metaphorical shifts that propagated that representation.

My project consists of weaving an interpretative fabric around these historical microsubjects in a constant movement of come-and-go between chosen bodies and diverse sources that shed light on them from unforeseen angles. I would like this fabric to be as closely knit as possible. When it is submitted to this test, the body of the object studied best conserves its resistance to the scrutiny of the historian and thus reveals itself at its richest. The "historical test," in this sense, should try to saturate its object with intelligibility. We must make an effort to think positively of this saturation, something we could compare to a kind of interpretative wager. The researcher acts like a gambler: betting that the wager will be returned augmented by reflection, hoping that the form of the object will be the most inextricable possible — and that the very obstacles deliberately imposed on the act of scrutiny will be additional motivation of the desire to interpret. The ideal of this avid researcher in interpretation is nothing other than the metaphor of a spider that weaves its web, playing with corners and nooks to capture the prey it wants to catch in flight and ensnare in the threads that it secretes before devouring it.

Yet how can we conserve the life of this captured, ingested object? Flesh, which should not be cruelly omitted, is here the business of a writer of history. Hermeneutic strategy does not seem thinkable to me except in connection with bringing back to life the texts that it strives to interpret. This strategy must of course function according to the macabre sequence of devouring the object as a means of bringing it back to life. The web is a death trap from which life comes. The historical narrative that follows from it, like the creature that lives in its web, is an embodied writing, an ultimate presence of life. *How to give a body to hermeneutic writing?* It is certainly a disturbing problem at which the historian leaps.

A Writing of History: Live Quotation and Analogical Montage

There is a film auteur who "quotes" particularly well, and I mention him here without any further ado to help me organize my toolbox. One sequence in a film by this auteur, Jean-Luc Godard, that I like very much is a trivial event in the middle of *A Woman Is a Woman*. In a small apartment near the Porte Saint-Denis, a lovers' spat degenerates into a war of quotations. "Monster [*Monstre*]," Angela shouts. "Go . . . Fuck off [*Eva . . . Te faire foutre*]," Emile answers. Slight lull, time for these intimate enemies to gather some quotation ammunition. "Peruvian mummy [*Momie péruvienne*]," the man continues. "Crook [*Filou*]," replies the woman, before the furious lover definitively wins the contest thanks to an "All women . . . to the stake [*Toutes les femmes . . . Au poteau*]" with the most persuasive effect. The lights go out.

Why include such a methodological reference? First because the argument is serious. During the entire sequence Angela and Emile keep the solemn mask that suits a potential breakup. Second, because the whole argument is silent. These serious insults are spoken with lips sealed. The book, the printed text, speaks in this mystery. It is by means of titles of novels snatched from the couple's little library that the argument got going. Words are not said, they are shown—a distancing that is essential in this modern art that is the cinema for Jean-Luc Godard. This distancing, in fact, masterfully rediscovers the titles used in silent movies. The quotation functions literally here: Godard shows the covers of books as he would once have inserted titles showing the dialogue, thus giving the modern life of his film the leisure to be reflected in a mirror inherited from the cinema when it was just beginning. The quotation assumes an essential power of recollection: it brings back into the present of the film the entire silent, textual past of the cinema.

Again, why include such a methodological reference? Because that film moment seems to me a model both of understanding and of writing for a historian of textual practices. Godard takes an inventory of the library of an ordinary young couple in the beginning of the 1960's. Some fashionable books (Claude Mauriac's *All Women Are Fatal*, for example) are mixed with a travel guide to South America; some great classical French novels, with subliterary best-sellers that are looked down on but make a strong impression by the number of copies sold and by their counterculture imagination, like the *Séries noires* written by Antoine Dominique (author of the popular sequel *Gorilles* and *Au poteau*) and *Simenon des ruisseaux* among others; and finally some "philosophical works" in which the word *foutre* [fuck] resonates scandalously.

A profile of the reader also emerges, made clear by the film's synopsis: "Angela and Emile like Dashiell Hammett, the *Séries noires*, escapist novels, and *Marie-Claire*." This investigation finally leads to a serious argument — a way to shed light on the intellectual origins of an armchair revolution. What Godard invents here is a diversion, a softening of the conventions of violence by literary quotation. No slaps, no broken dishes, no separation — and no hint whatever of a crime of passion — in this argument. Not even emotion: just some closed faces and an exchange of printed quotations. Through the distancing of insult, this paper war allows the bodies of the two protagonists (Anna Karina and Jean-Claude Brialy) to be introduced into a process of civilization that Godard calls "modern cinema." By the intermediaries of actors and books, cinema should imitate the real war of couples, by transferring, or distancing, it to a war of quotations. Thus the quotation has the power of life: it embodies the argument by absorbing the physical battle of the couple into the titles on book covers.

Why include such a methodological reference? Because Godard, by thus joining the "power of recollection" with the "power of life" through the presence of texts integrated into his cinema, practices what I call the "live writing of the quotation." Through the gift of the book, even if here it turns out to be a poisoned present, Godard activates the narrative of the film. By insulting Angela, Emile literally offers her a story. The book is also present on the screen through its thickness, the color of its cover, the graphics of its title. The director does not approach the quotation as a pedant, or even as a scholar, but by filming its flesh. The flesh of a literary quotation in the cinema is the thickness, the color, the graphics that reveal the naked book, which Godard shows without false modesty, knowing how to confer on the quotation a function of "f(r)iction gears"[8] along with the printed embodiment of the wars between the lovers. No sooner has an attentive observer understood the literary insults than they disappear from the screen; one can scarcely notice the authors of the books and probably never looked up the novels destined to be abruptly cited one after another.

From this use of subliminal quotation, I want to elicit a manner of writing: if Godard quotes with so much resonance, it is because he quotes in his own style, willfully confusing quotation marks with italics. In his text, Godard succeeds in erasing the scars that usually highlight the integration of the quotation with the substance of a film: the "as so-and-so says" or the "voice-over" of some literary commentary on the action. He has not, like a thief of words, rubbed out these scars but has embedded them so deeply in the substance of his film that the flesh of the body of cinema closes back on itself. The scar still exists, but it is hidden inside, showing through for example only during a freeze-frame. Never does it stop the personal narrative: it prefers to trouble it from within, to renew its attack from the inside. With Godard, quotation marks have become italics. The "words of another" taken from a text, the finished sentence (which is exactly what quotation marks surround), here make themselves into words of the self, which is the mark of the omnipotence of a writer emphasizing an expression by italics. Emile and Angela argue with each other by borrowing the titles of others' books, but never has the cinema invented more personal insults. Godard has brought about in his own way what a few years later Michel de Certeau will identify as "reading-as-pilfering."[9]

I too dream of mitigating the tyranny of "quotation scars": the specific kinds of graphics (indented text, reduced leading of lines, composition in recognizable blocks), the obligatory conventions (introduce the quotation, conclude the quotation, comment on the quotation), and the precautions of usage (shorten the quotations in the body of the actual text, avoid overlong excerpts, gather them into notes or appendixes). While remaining within the community of historians and thus respecting the indispensable reference marks of the critical gaze (quotation marks defining the limits of the quote, source references for original texts), I would like to loosen up the rules. I would like to reject typographically distinctive setting of quotations and to integrate even substantial excerpts into the body of the narrative. This writing-by-quotation aims not only at materially putting the text of the time back into the heart of the interpretative work (what, with Godard, I have called the "power of recollection") but also wants to be seen as the mark of vitality of the narrative (what, in *A Woman Is a Woman*, I called "power of life" borne by the art of the quotation). Quotation is the memory and the blood of historical writing, the almost physical proof of the historian's attention to the subject, the living cogwheel, finally, of the hermeneutic machine. Any concern with the form of historical writing is usually neglected and sometimes scorned — why should historians take pains about their own narratives when they already have to handle the narratives of others, namely, the people being studied? And isn't a concern with the form of writing a sign of compromise, almost a selling-out to that eternal enemy of history, fiction? On the contrary, it is my belief that concern with the very form of historical writing is essential.

It is not a question here of a simple return of a fashion, what some have called the "return to narrative,"[10] but rather an urgent responsibility to link interpretation with the writing of history, so that the past narrative and the present text are put in constant connection — a connection, here, of a fictional nature, since the narratives taken into account in this book tell History as a story. One must, the historian thinks, practice this writing. One must, in some way, know how to submit oneself to the attempt to create fiction starting from the texts studied: to draw from what endlessly threatens to corrupt one's gaze a strength of inspiration that will allow one to renew the imagination and increase the desire to interpret. In the present instance, I think it is essential that (thanks to the power of quotation) my discourse on the metaphor is itself charged with the metaphors it describes, while it is at the same time aware of this "community" of language — not by "ontological naïveté," some degree of belief in the truth of metaphorical language that would trap the historian, but by "contamination by fiction," a way of reviving the movement of interpretation by the shared experiment of a kind of narrative in its most intimate recognition. It would involve defining the work of the historian of the texts of the past as an experiment in critical fiction. It is a way of bringing the "complicity with . . . creative subjectivity" into balance with the "panoramic gaze" of historiography.[11]

The "live writing of quotation" is the first mark of my historical narrative. The second I investigate in a particular "movement" of writing, a link between heterogeneous sources and the different objects of history studied. "How . . . are we . . . to proceed?" asks Walter Benjamin at the outset of his *Origin of German Tragic Drama*.[12] He sets the researcher, the (rather unique) "graduate student" that he was, face to face with the "panorama of ideas." Then he questions himself on the "way of writing ideas": "Are we to assemble all manner of examples, . . . that is to say occurrences and events which are said to create the [same] impression, . . . and then ana-

lyze inductively what it is that they all have 'in common'?" Another possibility is the "deductive method": "Whereas induction reduces ideas to
concepts, . . . deduction does the same by projecting them into a pseudo-
logical continuum." Both induction and deduction equally deny the ability
to narrate the origins of baroque drama. But Benjamin does not give up.
Neither inductive nor deductive, his writing gaze will be other: "Only by
approaching the subject from some distance and, initially, foregoing any
view of the whole, can the mind be led, through a more or less ascetic apprenticeship, to the position of strength from which it is possible to take
in the whole panorama and yet remain in control of oneself. The course of
this apprenticeship is what had to be described here."

This apprenticeship is above all a call to humility, as if Benjamin dreaded
two shortcomings: suffocating under the weight of "facts and events" and
being sidetracked by preexisting judgments. Not to accumulate proofs and
not to add references are his two answers to "how not to regress." As for the
"how to proceed," an answer is found in a process of writing that is simple,
all things considered: the "description of the world of ideas." Benjamin
raises this to the condition of analytical method: "To execute this description it is necessary to treat every idea as an original one. For ideas exist
in irreducible multiplicity." What Benjamin succeeds in "executing," in
treating head-on, is juxtaposition (the irreducibility of each idea) and connection (continually pursuing the same process of bringing closer). A form
of reasoning that thinks both of the irreducible and the connection, a *connected juxtaposition*, must follow what the inductive and deductive methods
advocate (logic that explicates by concentration or by generalization of the
meaning—what Benjamin calls "pseudo-logic"). For Benjamin, as he says
explicitly at the end of his "Epistemo-Critical Prologue," it is above all a
matter of giving a movement to thought through writing, of "making a gust
of wind," of stripping the tree of the knowledge of its leaves: a movement
that can take an idea, irreducible in itself, on which writing has paused and
transport it suddenly toward another, sometimes distanced by thousands
of prejudices but the abrupt juxtaposition of which seems then, under the
pen and the thought, gifted with a creative spark. It is an analogical process quite close to a "writing by metaphors" that Benjamin defines in place
of the "pseudo-logical" procedure.

Godard, who shows by the inner scars of live quotation how to give blood
to the narrative, grants moreover to the "and" a function strangely close to
Benjamin's "connected juxtaposition": analogical collage of ideas, of two

irreducible images producing meaning. That is what I try to apply to my work as a historian: quotation confers memory and life to the interpretative machine. Benjamin brings an analogical movement to the "how to proceed to make a historical narrative." The "connected juxtaposition" of Benjamin along with the "and" of Godard are models of narrative for me. Between each historical object, there should be no "thus" or "because." The "and" should call forth juxtaposition, unforeseen or unexpected "discord-accord" from which the wish to make a connection is born. The wish for "and" gives rise to the "movement of metaphor," the desire to go from one form to another, the movement to *inter*pret. These two elements, blood and movement, are the vital force of writing and make a connection between historical objects.

The studies that follow, illustrating the plan of this work, try to define a historical object by examining a method and a way of writing. The historical object is a political self-representation, that of a revolutionary society seen and described by its actors themselves by means of metaphors of the human body. A "nonquantitative serial historical" method: the historical hermeneutics that I would compare here (for I believe as much in the evocative power of metaphors as in the theorizing of what will always be the "practice" of the historian) to the strategy of a spider weaving its web between heterogeneous sources in order to capture its prey, the particular case. Finally, I have chosen a way of writing: citing texts, many and diverse, that give the strength of life and of memory to this book, and confronting their dissonances by the analogical movement of interpretation.

PART I

The State-Body: Metaphor of the Transition of Sovereignty

1. The Defeat of the Body of the King

Essay on the Impotence of Louis XVI

How did the king lose his body? Historians have approached this question by examining the death of Louis XVI, the political and symbolic breakup in the Revolution, that transition from royal dignity to Republican severity. Most often, they placed in the center of their picture the ceremony of the execution on 21 January 1793, studied along with the archives of the trial in the Convention. Others have worked out more original studies, before the guillotine (political cartoons or songs, for instance) or after it (the opening of the Saint-Denis tombs). All have shared the same conclusion: the defeat of the body of the king represents a major caesura or gap in the French system of political representation. When it is compressed into the period from the king's capture in Varennes to his execution in January 1793, this process seems abrupt and brutal.

I would like to follow another trail here, one that may seem anecdotal but that is actually of great importance. It too leads to the turning point of Varennes, but has its origins long before it, almost twenty years before the Revolution: the story of the impotence of the king. For if a multitude of historians concur in seeing in the weakness of character and in the indecision of Louis XVI one of the causes of his ruin, there is some interest in understanding why, among the king's contemporaries, this characteristic was embodied in the tale of his bodily impotence. One does not occur without the other. This "other" is often evoked without anything being said explicitly, merely an occasion for innuendos in history books; now it must be brought out in the open. For this somewhat uncertain story accompanies the discrediting of royal dignity: it is, paradoxically, one of the exemplary metaphors for the transition from the body of the king to the Hercules of populist sovereignty. It is an essential tale for two reasons: mainly, it begins even before the actual reign of Louis XVI, replacing the process of the bodily defeat of the king in a more nuanced chronology than the single break after Varennes, and moreover, it brings together images and symbols of royal majesty that are finer and more precise than the mere signs connected with the convenient, commonly used concept of the "desacralization" of the king.

Precision of the study, on this point, is essential. When one is interested in these rumors, one must see them being born from bodies and bedsheets, coming to settle in pictures or words, changing registers, passing from gossip to pamphlets, from court joke to street rumor, from customs to politics, from the clinical to the lewd, then from licentiousness to laughter. One should also advance cautiously from the body of archives to the body of texts, from songs to pictures. The story of the impotence of the king, spread out chronologically over more than twenty years, unwinds its sources and its representations over numerous registers of interpretation. It was from the outset a body confronted with its procreative function, the primary function in a hereditary monarchy. As such, it was a body scrutinized by all the kings of Europe, adversaries or allies, by their doctors as well as their spies. This reputation for impotence was certainly not a radical innovation: Louis XIV and Louis XV were both described as impotent. The end of the former's reign became an object of sarcasm; for some cruel chroniclers, he lost military power and sexual power. The latter became the unfortunate hero of songs and the plaything of his Mme Dubarry:

> Look at this King among Kings
> Kneel before a strumpet,
> She who once for a shilling bit
> Would have been your mistress;
> Watch him make a hundred tries
> At lechery beside her,
> To get the springs to work
> On his rusty old device.
> All in vain has he recourse
> To this high priestess—
> Right in the midst of his discourse,
> He falls back into weakness.[1]

But back then it was a matter of old men who were already fathers and grandfathers, an impotence traditionally attached to the image of the "elegant old child." Louis XVI is haunted by this degraded image of an "inactive vigor" from his youth, from the moment of his marriage, which went unconsummated for a long time. While the symbolism of the Bourbons abounds with emblems of fertility and burgeoning, this king dawdles for more than eight years before giving a child to France, and more than eleven years pass before a crown prince is born. That is nothing, one might say, compared to the twenty-two years of the infertile marriage of Louis XIII and Anne of Austria between 1616 and 1638. But then it was not so much the impotence of the king that was called into question as the little taste the monarch had for the flesh and for "*la créature* [woman]," and above all the queen's sterility: four successive false pregnancies made the king in fact despair, and brought him to think seriously about divorce. Moreover — and this is a fundamental point — if Louis XIII's distaste for his wife, if his entirely platonic love for Marie de Hautefort and Louise de Lafayette, if his friendships for a few favorites (De Luynes, Barradat, Claude de Saint-Simon, or Cinq-Mars), if all these commotions were of public notoriety in the court of France, never did the figure of the impotent king enter a *political discourse* against Louis XIII, let alone against the monarchy. Of course the long sterility of the couple was commented on, followed closely by ambassadors and courtiers, and made the subject of innumerable schemes and suppositions, but it was not used by political rhetoric anxious to attack the royal majesty through the degradation of his seminal potency. That is not the case with Louis XVI: in this sense, the contrast between the wedding ceremonies of 1770, adorned with rituals, odes, and symbols celebrating the bodily potency of the monarch, and the rumors of impotence that follow makes up a game of rumors, anecdotes, and reproaches suitable for undermining the body of the king.

The Ceremony of the Royal Sex

On 19 December 1778, a few hours after the birth of his first child, Louis XVI writes to Monseigneur de Beaumont, Archbishop of Paris: "Dear cousin, my very dear Wife and Companion the Queen, has just given me a precious token of her love by the birth of a Daughter of whom she was successfully delivered today. This visible mark of protection that Providence grants my marriage, makes me hope for the complete accom-

plishment both of my wishes and those of my People by the birth of a
Dauphin; it is to ask that of Providence, and to thank it for the blessings it
has already given me, that I write you this letter, to convey to you my wish
that you have the *Te Deum* sung in the Metropolitan Church of my good
City of Paris, at a date and time that the Grand Master of Ceremonies will
communicate to you on my behalf." [2]

By placing the birth of a royal child under the protection of Divine
Providence, Louis XVI is doing nothing new. The *Te Deum* "given as an
offering of thanks for the birth of the Princess of whom the Queen was
delivered," sung on Saturday 26 December 1778 in Notre-Dame, accompanied by the versicles *Benedicamus Patrem et Filium* and *Fiat manus tua*,
by the prayers *Pro gratiarum actione* and *Pro Rege*, along with the antiphon
Domine, Salvum fac Regem, enters into the tradition of royal births. This
ceremony answers to the prayers said on the subject of the queen's pregnancy during the summer, and calls for speeches and sermons "on the fortunate delivery of the Queen and on the duties of her subjects." Prayers, *Te
Deum*, and sermons are not confined to Notre-Dame: they launch a series
of celebrations that last for many weeks, from Paris to Versailles, from
foreign embassies to provincial towns. These ceremonies make up the religious underpinning of a rejoicing that invariably, whatever the region or
season, brings with it a "feast" and then a pyrotechnic "fireworks display."
The church, the meal, and the illuminated square or lake are the three
obligatory stages of the ceremony for a royal birth.

But the first ceremonial place is the bedroom of the queen herself and
her "bed of travail." The birth is public. Louis XVI records the facts of it
very meticulously in his *Journal*: "The Queen went to bed at eleven o'clock
without suffering anything; at half past midnight, she began to suffer, and
at one-thirty, she rang. Mme De Lamballe and the maids of honor were sent
for; at three o'clock, M. De Chimay came to look for me, the Queen was
still in her great bed; half an hour later, she went onto her bed of travail.
Mme De Lamballe sent out to alert the royal family, and the princes and
princesses who were at Versailles, and sent pages to M. the Duc d'Orléans,
Mme the Duchesse de Bourbon, and Mme the Princesse de Conti who were
at Saint-Cloud. The Queen's pains abated, she walked about the room until
almost eight o'clock, then laid herself back on the bed of travail. There
were in the room the royal family, the princes and princesses of blood, the
maids of honor, and Mme de Polignac; in the great chamber my family,
that of the Queen and the high visitors; the game room and the gallery
were for everyone else. We entered when the obstetrician alerted us; the

Queen was delivered at eleven-thirty of a girl. . . . The sublieutenant of the Queen's service guards left immediately to announce the birth to the body of the city that had assembled at the news of her labor."[3]

If there is such a crowd, it is undoubtedly due to a twofold expectation: they hoped for the birth of a dauphin, an event that hadn't occurred for almost fifty years in the court of France, and they were anxious to put an end to eight years of waiting for the royal couple. That is where the "Providence" invoked by the king intervenes: his marriage is finally rewarded by God, before it is recognized by the people and the European courts. Sterility, divine punishment, is dismissed. This solace, which makes up for the disappointment of the birth of a girl, is at the heart of the speeches and sermons of the church: "Louis the Procreant" is a chosen one of God. "And so, the two spouses, like Zachary and Elizabeth, walked in the ways of the Lord. Deprived for many years of the worthy object that would form their consolation, yet without any remission in the pursuit of righteousness, their union suffered no alteration, and they waited in humble submission on the decree of the Almighty. It is imperative, Christian listeners, that such a conduct be universally followed by those who have embraced the state of matrimony. Do we not see every day alliances ruined when it does not please God to make them fertile? Faithfulness wronged, reciprocal disgust, overwhelming scorn, injurious suspicions, scandalous ruptures, and excessive debauchery, that is how we revolt against Heaven, by taking vengeance on ourselves. Learn, men of flesh and blood, that only those who walk continuously in the paths of virtue can count with certainty on the gifts and satisfactions of Divine Mercy. If today Providence crowns the desires of Their Majesties, it is in recompense for their faithfulness tested and proved,"[4] declares Father Tardiveaux in his church in Coueron, near Nantes. The church plays its traditional role here: it recalls humility to the king, "man of flesh and blood," faced with God, and in return consecrates the majesty of his glory. It alone makes a connection between fertility and Providence, thus placing the heredity of the throne under divine protection: "His race, said the Lord, will be forever, and his throne will be like a sun in my presence."[5]

Another traditional register of royal fertility is abundance. The king procreates, the king nourishes: these two propositions are inseparable. Father of a family, the monarch becomes the father who feeds the kingdom. The royal family and the ordinary French family share in the same prosperity that the songs surrounding the birth of the dauphin, in October 1781, cleverly emphasize:

> If the King is everyone's father,
> The Queen's our mother too;
> Rejoice, boys, let's rejoice
> To see a little brother given to us.
> . . . Don't be afraid, father dear,
> To see your tribe increase,
> The good Lord will provide,
> Make Versailles swarm with them!
> If we had a hundred Bourbons more,
> There's bread and fame enough for all.[6]

In this sense, the celebrations of birth are particularly awaited occasions of gaiety and feasts. At every "family celebration," as Louis XVI calls it in his *Journal*, there must be a banquet. The prosperity of the king, enriched by the power of procreation, implies an abundant table. This was never better furnished than at the Parisian celebration hailing the birth of the dauphin. On 21 and 23 January 1782 the most important celebration of Louis XVI's ancien régime reign took place in Paris. Organizing the first day, the three decisive stages of ceremonies of royal birth took place: Mass in Notre-Dame, which the royal couple attends after a "slow, majestic procession" across the capital; the great banquet at the city hall; then the "fireworks and illuminations" on the Seine, facing the Hôtel de Ville, where a reviewing stand had been raised.[7]

The city's meal is linked with the king's; this is emphasized by a studied game of looks. On one hand, the royal banquet is public, a kind of transfer of the Palace of Versailles to Paris and its people, gathered at the traditional "grand banquet [*souper au grand couvert*]" that the courtiers of the palace so admired: "In the dining room of the Hôtel de Ville, the king's table, including seventy-eight place settings, will be surrounded by a balustrade, and the public will be able to enter and circle around without stopping, in order to procure for everyone the liberty of enjoying such an august and magnificent spectacle. They will be able to make the round of the table many times if the length of the meal allows it." On the other hand, after the fireworks display, the Parisians are invited to eat, since "it is envisaged building many dining rooms at the outer limits of Paris where saveloy sausage, bread, and refreshments will be provided, and where they can dance."

"Joy of the stomach and joy of the heart"[8]: thus does a plan for celebration sum up these ceremonies of royal marriage and birth, a meeting of two "gaieties" manifested by the ritual succession of table and fire. These pyrotechnic games play an ever larger role, reaching the point where the Parisian ceremonies of January 1782, while taking care to avoid fatal crushes (the marriage celebration of the dauphin, in 1770, imprinted itself on people's memories by leaving almost two hundred dead on the pavement), offer three "spectacles of structures of light" in two days. First, on 21 January, an "illumination on the water" that represents the "temple of Hymen" where one can see "illuminated allegorical compositions" played on pedestals built on the Seine, "groups of children carrying flaming torches" and "the goddess France receiving the Dauphin from the hands of Hymen, accompanied by Peace and Abundance." Immediately after these presentations, the fireworks are set off facing the royal enclosure. Finally, on 23 January, accompanying the masked ball and the "abundantly served buffets"—all in the same places as before—one last pyrotechnic spectacle takes place. Torches and fireworks are here as much the visible marks of the flame that animates each subject for his king as the symbols of the powerful fertility of the sovereign: the main theme of the illuminations of the temple of Hymen consists of "a mud of gold from which a lily of flames arises."

Surrounding the celebrations, punctuating them with words and rhymes, a deluge of odes and verses rains down on the sovereign on these happy occasions. These pieces are often repetitive and academic. However, they should be read, since they say a lot about the "fertility symbolism" that traditionally surrounds the monarch. This symbolism begins to be employed with the marriage in May 1770 of Louis-Auguste, Dauphin of France, to Marie-Antoinette, Archduchess of Austria, and becomes established on different registers, from the most direct—the "fucking king [*roi fouteur*]"—to a catalogue of the most conventional allegories. The dauphin, under the eyes of his grandfather Louis XV, is placed in the heart of this symbolism with many levels of comprehension. Elaborate drinking songs promise a fruitful destiny to the young sixteen-year-old:

> Down at Versailles
> They're waiting for the Princess;
> God makes the nuptials,
> She'll get fucked and fucked some more;
> And how her spouse
> Will make her moan.[9]

It is a destiny that must unite the house of France with that of Austria, the Family Contract read with a jovial and benign bawdiness:

The German and the French
   Long ago
Killed each other for their kings;
Fighting is a rotten thing
Screwing is more pleasant.
The Frenchman and the German lady
   Quite content
F—— together often;
They're going to make it legal
To mate the lily with the eagle.[10]

All the traditional patterns of symbolism take on the task of representing the long-awaited abundant vigor of the future king. The biblical pattern draws its sources from numerous excerpts of the Old Testament in which the Almighty promises seed and fertility to the just: "Blessed is the Lord who will fulfill . . . the promise he once made to Abraham about Sara [Genesis 17:16]: 'I shall bless her, I shall make her greatly fertile; I shall give thee a son, born of her.' May [Mme the Dauphine] be, in the enclosed garden of her palace, like a vine abundant with fruit! May her children, like fine olive groves, surround her table! Alleluia! Alleluia!"[11] The mythological pattern revisits the countless love affairs of the Olympian gods, of which we need only cite this touching scene from the *Dream or horoscope of the future childbirth of Marie-Antoinette of Lorraine* written a few weeks before the queen's second delivery: "Pomona, goddess of gardens, followed by Love and by the god Hymen, to mark the fortunate fertility of the House of Bourbon, is preceded by a troupe of Nymphs who are carrying baskets of vine branches that they continuously strew on the steps around the royal Cradle. From all sides of the enclosure, our August Sovereign Lady can be seen reposing on a bed of roses. . . . Finally, to the right of the royal Cradle is our August Master, blessed by Jupiter and Juno, who lets his joy burst forth in showing to his tender wife, with a satisfied air and full of gratitude, the gift that he has just received from the Gods."[12]

In this double biblico-mythological symbolic network, we readily recognize the emblems of the monarchy. They are mainly in groups of three, each one corresponding to some Bourbon vigor: the phoenix, the bird rising again from its ashes; the sun, fertile star; and the lily, rich in signification. The phoenix is one of the most important symbols of dynastic hereditary continuity. It is mostly linked to royal births and deaths, first appearing during the reign of Louis XVI in 1774, then at the death of the

"Well-Beloved," and again in 1781 on the occasion of the birth of the dauphin. The sun, too, connotes royal continuity, just as much as the fame and
brightness of Louis XIV. But the star that is born again every day is equally
a token of natural fertility: the sun is at the center of the symbolism that
celebrates the marriage of 1770. The portrait of the young Louis-Auguste
is illumined by it:

> One gives to plants their useful burgeoning,
> The other assures his people of a gentle existence.
> Just as the star of day fertilizes the earth,
> May he become the father of numerous heirs!
> May he be a God favorable to our ample harvests! [13]

From the star to the harvest, the symbolic register of abundance and
vigor proposes a fruitful garden. The gardener king is clearly an apt metaphor for a sovereign not only useful to his people but also fecund in flesh.
In 1767, King Louis XV had had a large number of engravings distributed representing "Monseigneur the Dauphin trying his hand at the plow."
Naturally this image of the "monarch-laborer" is to be found again in the
praises of the princely couple of 1770: "Pressed under a fertile hand, the
plowshare of Triptolemus regained its splendor." [14] In the garden worked
and sown by the dauphin—the sexual references are explicit—abundance
will reign. In this domain, versifiers rival each other in cleverness, but not
invention. The poets again take up one of the oldest symbols of French
royalty: the lily. Yet its whiteness, together with its constant association
with Mary—particularly in paintings of the Annunciation—connote virginity in traditional iconology. The next step, then, would be to attribute
the births of Marie-Antoinette to some miracle of Immaculate Conception;
that step was crossed only by the pamphleteers, who did not deny themselves this excess. But the poets of royal praise know how to extract all the
essence from this traditional flower of monarchy:

> The goddess with a hundred voices, from your ancient stem,
> O Bourbons, announces a young shoot. [15]

Offering bouquet upon bouquet to the young couple, the poets lavish
compliments—indirect, of course—on the imposing, fecund virility of the
future king. In one composition of allegorical medallions, Louis-Auguste
"holds a lily and an oak branch heavy with acorns, to mix the symbols of
royalty and fecundity," while at his feet "flows a beautiful, lively fountain,
emblem of a happy, numerous progeny. Two children bathe there and raise

their little arms, a sign of the young princes to come."[16] Another composition attributes a flower and a metrical compliment to each prince, while Marie-Antoinette is seen offering the lily, that "beautiful white lily that is the King of flowers, and in which she will suddenly recognize the image of her august husband."[17] The compliment that follows this gift forms a portrait of this "lily-husband":

> This charming lily, young Dauphine,
> Seems to rejoice in adorning your beautiful breast.
> For you Flora and Love have made it blossom,
> And France destines it for you.
> Its bearing, its strength, its freshness
> Portray your husband's fine qualities.
> Its pure and shining whiteness
> Tells the vigor of your future children.

This virile portrayal is paired with an equally explicit description of the female flower, the "rose-wife":

> For a bouquet, Your Highness, accept this single rose.
> It comes from a far clime,
> And for you alone it has opened out.
> Cultivate it with your august hand
> And each day it will acquaint your eyes
> With some new treasure of blessing and of charm.
> The tender shoots you will see born from it
> Will make it a hundred times more beautiful to you.

Concluding his bouquet, the poet compares the marriage of 1770 to "a lily and a rose intertwined."

The union of Louis-Auguste and Marie-Antoinette causes symbols of generation and fertility to gush forth around the body of the (future) king: rarely before had one read or seen so many charms surrounding a king's sex. Plans for the celebration also overflow with them—the temple of Hymen, for instance, planted in the Place Louis XV and bearing this rural decorative motif on its third façade: "From the powerful trunk of the tree let rise a thick green branch, garnished with leaves, having a hollow knot in which should be seen a bird making its nest, and the male, carrying wisps of straw, calls to his little ones to feed them."[18]

This unrestrained interlocking of fertility symbolism is very characteristic of the Bourbons. Louis-Auguste is the final beneficiary of it; in a sense,

he could almost be seen as the result of it: "There sometimes exist illustrious families destined to give to the universe the example of a chain of
original qualities, as rare as they are precious to humanity. It is a river that,
arising from a pure, fertile source, flows across immense tracts of country
in order to bring them the tribute of its salutary waters. The more it advances, the more majestic and peaceful it is."[19]

The wedding of 1770, favoring the proliferation of such symbols, is an
important stage in the life of the body of the dauphin. The nuptial ritual
confirms the "ceremony of the royal sex" displayed in festivities, odes, and
engravings. Marie-Antoinette arrived in Strasbourg on the seventh of May.
For a week, in Saverne, Nancy, Bar-le-Duc, Châlons, Reims, and Soissons,
the princess strewed celebrations and rejoicings as she passed.[20] On the
fourteenth she arrived in Compiègne, where the king and his grandson
came to meet her. On the sixteenth, the marriage was celebrated in the
chapel at Versailles. After the banquet supper, Louis XV had the couple's
bed blessed by the Archbishop of Reims, the Grand Almoner of the kingdom, and then "gave the nightshirt to the prince" while the Duchess of
Chartres "gave it to the princess."

Midnight sounds while the young married couple take their places in the
same bed. The curtains are drawn, and then "immediately reopened." Just
as it was to be eight years later during Marie-Antoinette's first delivery, the
entire royal family is present. It is a matter of carrying on a tradition: Louis-
Auguste's father, for example, had "publicly consummated" his two marriages in front of the court, just as his ancestors did. In 1770, however, the
wedding night is more discreet. The king formally draws the bed-curtains
on the young couple after having kissed them. The court withdraws. But
Louis-Auguste knows that he is going to be observed very attentively: it is
a Bourbon's duty to be fertile. It is an affair of state.

The "Scrutation" of the Sheets:
A Chronicle of Intimacies in the Royal Bed

Louis XV is the first to come with news of the intimacies of the bed.
Then foreign diplomats make haste, interviewing some close relatives of
the young couple, bribing the servants, intercepting letters. Finally, journalists track down the news and take advantage of leaks, at times carefully
orchestrated, the better to report them to the city. This "intimacy" of the
crown prince's bed is very closely watched over; for instance, the instruc-

tion delivered on 9 August 1773 to the Count d'Aranda, ambassador of the King of Spain to the court of France, devotes a special paragraph to "the matrimonial state of the Dauphin and the Dauphine." [21]

Likewise, the King of Sardinia urges his correspondent, the Count de Scarnafis: "We approve of your exactitude in informing us of all that can confirm you in the idea that no change has intervened in the comportment of the M[ost] C[hristian] King with the Queen." [22] Maria-Theresa, mother of the archduchess, is no less interested, so much that: "The situation is incomprehensible, and I am quite surprised that they are letting things go without dealing with them." [23] Comte de Mercy-Argenteau, the imperial ambassador to Paris, never forgets in his letters to Maria-Theresa to sum up the current situation on "the state of the union." Finally, Frederick II of Prussia, sworn enemy of Austria, expects the Baron de Goltz, his ambassador since 1776, to have the same eagerness to inform him: "As for the interior of the court where you are, word has come to me of scenes that indicate a complete cooling off between the King and Queen. Where does the matter stand?" [24]

Thus, by attentively following the correspondence of diplomats posted in Versailles or Paris, a precise, anatomical state is sketched out of the sexual relations between the princely, and later the royal, couple. It is here, in these descriptions so attentive to the smallest rumors, to the least spot of sperm on the sheets, to the most trivial doctor's report, that we find written the clinical history of the king's weakness, or of his "imbecility," to use that era's customary expression for sexual impotence.

The first of these revelations concerning the prince's private life appears very quickly from the pen of a courtier at the end of May 1770, scarcely more than a week after the dauphin's marriage. The Prince von Starhemberg, who accompanied the archduchess from Vienna, gives a report of the wedding ceremonies in a letter to Maria-Theresa: "The King himself had told me that on the wedding day and on the next day, he [the Dauphin] had seemed barely attentive to her, and that the first nights had passed without any interesting event. It was natural enough to attribute the cause of this coldness only to shyness, timidity, and to some sort of imbecility that this prince belies in his entire countenance." [25]

Even if the contrast is heavy with significance when compared to the odes to Bourbon potency and to the fertility symbolism used during the prince's marriage ceremonies, anxiety is not yet legible on the old king's face. After all, his grandson is only sixteen years of age and has just discovered a younger wife. Mercy duly reports this in his account of 15 June 1770: "He must be let be," Louis XV is supposed to have said.[26] But with the arrival of autumn, when still nothing has come, the monarch makes his first reproaches to his heir: "The King has made some remarks to M. the Dauphin about his state of coldness and questioned him. The young prince answered that he found Mme the Archduchess charming, that he loved her, but that he still needed some time to conquer his timidity." Which Maria-Theresa interprets in her own way: "The Dauphin's indisposition gives one pause, and I fear that he will not live a long time," adding soon after: "I understand nothing in the Dauphin's conduct toward his wife. . . . The more extraordinary the Dauphin's coldness, the more my daughter needs to maintain moderation in her deportment. For the rest Van Swieten [Maria-Theresa's doctor] is of the opinion that if a woman who is young and of the Dauphine's appearance cannot excite the Dauphin, any remedy would be ineffective, and that it would be better to give it up and wait for time to bring a change in such strange conduct."

After the reports come the first explanations. Perhaps the problem lies in an inhibition that is "completely moral, but no less annoying for all that," a "failure of habit and confidence," "a kind of moral frigidity to which the prudish teachings of his education by M. de la Vauguyon have led him." But the consequences of it, as Mercy notes, become "annoying": rumors begin to circulate. The Comte d'Artois, younger brother of Louis-Auguste, becomes a disastrous comparison for the dauphin, since he quickly reveals that he himself is quite prolific.

Another danger threatens both the image of the prince and the fertility of the spouses as well: the "separate beds," a practice, it seems, that becomes more and more common with the princely, later royal, couple. Soon, in face of this desertion of the marriage bed and the ever-deferred announcement of the consummation of the marriage, the diplomats' attempts at explanation drift away from "moral timidity," as they try to glean the opinion of the doctors. The "imbecility" of the king becomes physical. Yet when Louis XV had summoned the physicians in October 1772 to observe his grandson, La Martinière and Lassone, the chief surgeons of the king and dauphin, do not "detect any defect preventing the consummation of the marriage; only the prince's defect of will allows such an unusual situation to occur."[27] But this learned assembly — "Gathering of the Faculty," the lampoonists will say — called to give a ruling on such a delicate subject does not stop the indiscreet looks or the rumors: quite the contrary.

From then on, the physical condition of the young Louis is exposed to all opinions. Maria-Theresa, quite remote geographically but kept abreast of each event and happening in the French court, gives hers on 3 January 1774: "The indifference of the Dauphin, a young twenty-year-old husband, toward a pretty woman is inconceivable to me. Despite all the reassurances of the physicians, my suspicions increase about the physical constitution of this prince."[28]

Most important, the old king Louis XV has just died, eaten away by syphilis. As King of France, Louis-Auguste's duty now more than ever is to be fertile. Attention to him increases, along with reports. Goltz writes to Frederick II on 2 April 1777: "The lack of physical interest that up to now H[is] M[ost] C[hristian] M[ajesty] feels, either for his wife, or for women in general, is undoubtedly the effect of an internal defect, very easy to correct in the doctors' opinion; but this prince has refused treatment, either out of fear of the painful consequences of the operation, or because his temperament does not accept it. As to his constitution, it is very strong; he is filling out, and it is especially to be marked that he bears fatigue on foot and on horse better than anyone."[29]

"Suspicions" with Maria-Theresa, "doubt" for Goltz—rumors travel all the faster since they are founded on nothing but indirect and uncertain echoes. But for one diplomat this problem is even more important. Aranda, the Spanish ambassador, carries meticulousness (and imprudence, for this matter irritates the king) to the point of inspecting the stains of blood and sperm by "scrutation of the sheets." He forms intimate ties with the surgeon Lassone, and he makes Louis XVI's aunts talk. Aranda's letters are most detailed, pitched halfway between bawdiness and case history. Between November 1773 and September 1774, he offers a blunt portrait of the private life of the dauphin turned monarch, a way of recalling to reality a princely body eroded by a mysterious weakness. On 23 November 1773: "One still doubts consummation of the union. We know that in the bed linens of the royal pair there are stains that attest to the act, but most observers attribute them to an external ejaculation of the Dauphin without achieving penetration, which is precluded not by physical impotence but because of an acute pain at the tip of the penis that affects him as soon as he tries to insert it. He has renewed his efforts with all the greater assiduity since he avows a stronger attachment now to the Dauphine. But reflecting on a subject of such importance that, in the opposite case, would have been celebrated with splendor, encourages one to think that the ultimate aim has not been attained."[30] Even more precise details are given on 5 August 1774: "They say that the frenum holds the prepuce so tightly that it does not yield at intromission, and causes intense pain when the foreskin should retract at the time of the thrust customarily given in such a case. It seems that the prepuce is so closed that it cannot stretch sufficiently to free the glans, and thus he cannot accomplish an erection with the requisite elasticity. In former times many young people suffered the same fate, and this impediment is frequent at the time of beginning attempts; but those, generally, must have a more ardent desire than that of His Majesty, tempered as it is by his natural character and his feebleness. With excitement, a little pain, and a good resolve, the frenum becomes completely detached, or at least far enough for its continued use, and then painlessly gives the act free rein. When the young are too timid, the surgeon may be necessary; and with a slight incision, he frees from inconvenience. If the patient waits, it becomes a more painful and serious operation at his age because it demands a kind of circumcision, without which the edge of the prepuce would shrink, rendering the use of the penis impossible."

Finally, on 23 September 1774, Aranda confirms his explanation without any possible error: "The king's personal valets de chambre assert they have seen a perfect and frequent erection, with stains evident on his nightshirt. That was never in doubt . . . But there are no definite signs of good penetration. For the pain, at the instant of intromission, during extreme tightness, becomes unbearable because of the vaginal membrane, so it is altogether likely that the ejaculation took place at the time of His Majesty's withdrawal. Moreover, if the stains are more abundant than would be expected from a few dried drops of sperm, that proves the defect that has been suspected."

The symptoms Aranda describes strongly resemble the condition that, ever since Ambroise Paré's sixteenth-century *Books of Surgery*, has been called "phimosis": "When the glans is covered by the prepuce and cannot be withdrawn from within it and uncovered." To this defect one quality is added: the virginity of the queen. The "vaginal membrane" is intact, to use Aranda's phrase. Louis XVI cannot consummate his marriage because, to put it bluntly, he does not have the force to deflower his wife. The pain from his slight phimosis stops him. For Maria-Theresa, this weakness cannot be allowed to endure: she charges her own son, the Emperor Joseph II, brother to the Queen of France, with a mission during his travels in France in the spring of 1777; he has to wise up Louis. "I no longer count on anything," she writes, "except on the intervention of the Emperor, who, upon his arrival in Versailles, will perhaps find a way to urge this indolent husband to fulfill his duty better." [31]

Once Joseph II has arrived in France, he redoubles his advice to the king, with whom he discusses the matter at length on 14 May 1777, which Mercy confirms a few days later: "The King himself confided to H. I. M. his chagrin at not having a child; he went into the most circumstantial details about his physical state, and he asked for the Emperor's advice." Leaving Versailles at the beginning of the summer of 1777, Joseph II departs with the certainty that the king's impediment is not irrevocable and the hope that the advice of perseverance he'd given to the king and the remonstrances made to the queen should settle the matter. His report, in any case, is similar to Count d'Aranda's; he writes to the archduke Leopold: "In his conjugal bed, he has very satisfactory erections, he introduces the member, remains there without moving for two minutes perhaps, withdraws without ever discharging, still erect, and says good night. This doesn't make sense, since he sometimes has nocturnal pollutions by himself, and without ever getting the job done. He is willing to say quite clearly that he does it only out of duty and that he has no taste for it. Oh, if I could have been there just once, I would have set things straight—he has to be kept erect and pushed, or beaten, to make him discharge his f——, just like donkeys. My sister has not much inclination for that, and they are two maladroit simpletons together." [32]

Even if he was unable to be "there just once," Joseph II's advice bears its fruit. Louis XVI recognizes this and thanks his brother-in-law for it: "I am sure of having done what is necessary, and I hope that this coming year will not go by without giving you a nephew or a niece. It is to you that we owe this success, for, since your trip, things have gotten better and better until a perfect conclusion." [33] The queen herself announces the first news to her mother. On 30 August 1777 comes the victory announcement: "I am the happiest I have ever been in my life. It has already been more than a week since my marriage was perfectly consummated." D'Aranda, that spy of spies, can announce this to the King of Spain even before everyone else: "In my dispatch of 29 August, I wrote to Your Majesty that the Queen had strong chances of being pregnant. This news circulated among the persons closest to the royal couple and must have had a definite basis, for truly there was a delay of a week. Now I can explain with more clarity what I already knew, and what has now become an established fact. Namely that, some days before this delay, the King had finally completely consummated his marriage, which, for seven years, had been very much in doubt. . . . From that time, His Majesty has seemed more content than before, and the Queen appears with deep rings under her eyes that had never before been seen. And it is said that the King often repeats these gallant interactions."[34] The king's smiles and the queen's rings gladden everyone, but, from then on, a pregnancy is anxiously awaited to confirm the news.[35]

In fact, observers remain unconvinced for some time. They all write to their masters. Scarnafis writes to the King of Piedmont-Sardinia: "It seems to me that, if this new manner were as real as they had at first claimed, we should be noticing an eagerness or a demonstrative tenderness between the couple more marked than in the past. Yet it is not possible to detect the least change. Likewise, although the King goes to bed regularly a little after eleven o'clock, the Queen goes, three or four times a week, to play cards in private mansions until two or three o'clock."[36] A marriage seemingly consummated but the couple avoiding each other: this mystery intrigues the diplomats. "I know, by the circumstances in which this prince succeeded with Madame Victory, that he is still new to the business of being a husband with his wife . . . Despite that, there must be some court intrigues that aren't yet clear to me. For, about a week ago, the Queen, pleading some discomfort, spoke of her suspicions of pregnancy," Scarnafis reports to his king on 27 December 1777. The monarch answers: "That seems to me a mystery that only time and circumstance can unveil." So even the "happy circumstance" of the queen's pregnancy, of which Mercy informs Maria-Theresa on 20 April 1778, when "the monthly cycle that should recur on the twenty-fifth or twenty-sixth of March has not appeared at all," cannot restrain these rumors. "Court intrigues," "mystery," the words in the ambassador's correspondence, well express the change in register of the tale of royal impotence: the clinical description of a physical impediment gives way to suspicions, and soon to laughter. It is the season for satire.

The Opposite of a Birth, or The Writing of the Furtive Gaze

The satirists certainly do not fail to comment on the "imbecility" of the king. Changes in court customs encourage their writing. From the marriage and wedding night on, the accent was placed on the private life of the princely couple, a private life that husband and wife tried to preserve from the gaze of the court and to withdraw from monarchic rituals. Marie-Antoinette and Louis-Auguste agreed on this point: little of their intimate life should enjoy the traditional publicity of Versailles protocol. I was able to reconstitute the chronology of Louis XVI's troubles in bed only by dint of rummaging through diplomatic archives that at the time had been state secrets. Marie-Antoinette always conducted herself more as a wife (and then as a mother) than as a traditional queen. Against all the principles of the education of royal children, she went so far as to place her daughter under her own tutelage after the birth of the dauphin in 1781.

In like manner, as much out of fear of gibes as out of personal inhibition on this subject, Louis XVI tried to preserve completely the secrets of his bed. He spoke of it only to very close confidants (his grandfather, his aunt, his brother-in-law), limiting news to the exclusive circle of family allies without ever broadcasting it to any nobles or, even less, to his two brothers, the Comtes de Provence and d'Artois, who were both his potential rivals. The love affairs of the kings had till then been semipublic, vulnerable to scandals and intrigues. The new royal couple tried to keep them private. In fact, one of the sovereign's rare fits of anger fell on Luigi Pio, correspondent of the King of Naples at the court of Versailles, who was guilty, in a report intercepted by the French postal system, of having copied out some ironic couplets sung on Christmas 1781 on the subject of the "imbecility of the King."

This protective attitude, this shrouding of the domestic sphere of the emotional life of the royal couple, is, paradoxically, heavy with dangers for the king, and even more so for the queen. For the logic of the satirists and other journalists is that of the furtive gaze. This involves a perversion of the gaze traditionally directed at the king by the chroniclers of the Versailles court. Among the latter, of whom the Duc de Saint-Simon is the most famous example, the private life of the king (going to bed, getting up, washing, eating, birth, death, but also the procreative act) is offered up to the public gaze, or at least to the gaze of the court, through a highly codified ceremonial. Traditional writing about the court sought above all to be involved with ceremonial protocol so as to understand it better, and thus make fun of it better. But with the lampoonists of scandal at the end of the eighteenth century, the *private* life of the king is stressed. Their writing sets up Marie-Antoinette and Louis as an actual married couple, but only in order to describe their secrets, misunderstandings, and deceptions better. The ritual of the royal bed is no longer a ceremony but a comedy, and the writing is a stolen glimpse of the sexual intimacy that is taking place (or that is not taking place—and there lies the intrigue). A door has been closed on the domestic life of the king. He is no longer, in all areas of his existence, the State Incarnate offered up to the observation of the courtiers, but a particular individual, with his own unique history, endowed with an intimate life, a psychology, a private body. But it is precisely through this door that the satirists want to look. It is this point of view, that of the "keyhole" or of the confessional, and no longer that of the state bedroom of a triumphalist Versailles, that the writers of scandal cultivate.

Thus the echoes of the royal bed are no longer of officially celebrated births; now they are tracked down, often imagined, and always described with the curious and somewhat perverse joy that goes along with the discovery of a secret. It is into this trap of a new kind of writing that the symbolic potency of the royal couple and the virility of the monarch have fallen. The intrigues of the courtiers, however, never change. In 1777 Frederick II causes alarming news to be spread by Goltz about the condition of the couple in order to plant discord between the couple and Joseph II, just as the Comte de Provence attacks Marie-Antoinette almost openly and increases his offensive remarks during the births of the royal children.[37]

Those are the satirists' sources, the keyhole they look through. Their writing takes on the task of giving form to these jealousies and intrigues. "Apocryphal" confessions, courtiers' conversations cleverly "reconstituted," "stolen" correspondence, dossiers found "by accident" are the written signs of these furtive glimpses of the king's private life. The first ones appear in 1771. Théveneau de Morande's *The Cuirassed Gazetteer*, the most famous of all the lampoons of the end of Louis XV's reign, portrays in his "apocryphal news" the guards of the "Deer Park," the supposed place of the king's debauch, in this way: the guards are supposed to have received strict orders from their master to procure some "young virgins" for the Comte de Provence before his marriage. The explanation of this strange behavior involves the "feebleness" of the dauphin, Provence's older brother: "These trials were to prevent here what happened to the Dauphin, who only just consummated on the twenty-sixth March of this year a marriage of May of the preceding year."[38]

This date—flattering as it is—is fanciful, as I have shown elsewhere, but that is the theme that, once launched, was quickly taken up by Boufflers, who indirectly (but very explicitly) addresses some stanzas to the dauphine, that "young lady of the name of Marie who complained at not having any children."[39] It is taken up again in 1773 by another esteemed lampoon-ist, Pidansat de Mairobert, who, in his *English Observer*, "correspondence between Milord all'eye and Milord all'ear," invents a dialogue between a courtier and his observer-spy. The latter remarks innocently: "They say abroad that the Dauphin will never be a man." The former hardly protests: "I never comment on the mysterious discussions of the medical profession on the secrets of nature about which it is often mistaken . . . The Dau-phin has existed some years, even since his marriage, without there being noticed in him those sublime thoughts that characterize a strong soul, one born to command. But even with an excellent heart, one can have wits that are weak, nil, or badly turned."[40] The tone is stripped of violence but not of ingenuity: little by little, very quickly really, a connection between Louis-Auguste's bodily weakness and his lack of moral character is established. In other words, "If Louis governs men the way he governs his wife . . ." Such is the pitiless logic of the satirists, that of the unmasking of politics through the scandalous chronicle of the bed.

In 1774, the violence of the satire and the tone of denunciation increase a notch. The first summer of the now royal couple is spent at Marly. Marie-Antoinette takes some nocturnal walks on the arm of Comte d'Artois, and rumor flies. The young queen, fatigued by her "weak husband," stays out all night and may be finding pleasure elsewhere. Not only is the "sleep-king" an "imbecile," but he finds he is a "royal cuckold," deceived, while the queen is shaken with "uterine furies." The mechanism of scandal is put in gear to prolong the rumor of impotence: weakness of Louis, frustra-tion and exasperation of the queen, cuckolding and deception.[41] Since the king is impotent and cuckolded, he adopts others' children, and does that all the more easily since he's always asleep, sees nothing, and permits his wife anything. Those are the last two elements of the intrigue. The king sees nothing: he drinks and eats; the king adopts: Artois, Coigny, Rohan, Fersen will each in turn benefit from the "rumor of paternity" of differ-ent royal children. Even before the queen's first delivery, celebrated with all the eulogies and symbolism described in the beginning of this study, indeed, even before the consummation of the marriage in August 1777 tracked down by the diplomats of the bedchamber, the counterportrait of the impotent king is sketched out, with its panoply of circumstances and anecdotes. A song in the spring of 1776 amuses the Parisians very much and keeps the royal censors busy:

> Everyone asks himself beneath his breath:
> Can the King do it? or can't he?
> The wretched Queen despairs of it.
> Some say he cannot get it up,
> Others that he cannot get it in,
> That he is a transverse flute.
> But that's not where the problem lies,
> Says Mama Mouchi gravely;
> But only clear water comes out of it.
> Lassone, to whom the prince described
> The sickness that freezes his p———,
> Yesterday told me the mystery:
> The great crowned family
> Is sprinkled with the word flea [*puce*],
> But each has puce in his own way:
> The Queen has puce inherently,[42]
> The King's prepuce sticks to him,
> It's the pre- that spoils the whole affair.[43]

From now on, all the actions of the king in the domestic domain, even the most glorious and the most celebrated, such as royal births, feed the rumors and pens. In fact, if ceremonies and celebrations greet first the birth of a daughter and then of a dauphin, the pamphlets and songs do not fail to turn the official images upside down. Thus in 1779 and 1781 appear two licentious works often reprinted later: *The Love Affairs of Charlot and Toinette* and the first part of the *Historical Essays on the Life of Marie-Antoinette*.

> A young and pert Queen,
> Whose most majestic husband was bad at fucking . . .

Thus begins *The Love Affairs of Charlot and Toinette*, a famous play in its time that many attribute to Beaumarchais. Published originally in 1779, it ridicules the preceding year's birth and ascribes it to a scandalous paternity: "Charlot," otherwise known as the Comte d'Artois. For a time it was the most sought-after pamphlet by the police of the Royal Library. Its destruction cost more than 17,400 livres to Louis XVI's coffers, as attested by the bookseller Boissière's bill, published by Manuel in 1789 in his collection on the police of the ancien régime.[44]

It seems this pamphlet was so sought out because it involves two innova-

tions with respect to licentious songs and previously composed courtly dialogues: a real meanness of tone, along with the first appearance of the word
denoting the sexual act that was not possible ("to fuck," "to be fucked"),
and the beginning of a battle of pictures. Two finely engraved plates attributed to Desrais adorn the two copies that escaped destruction. The first,
"Fraternal Generosity: The Making of a Successor," presents an erotic encounter between Marie-Antoinette and the Comte d'Artois. The second is
even more notable. "The Congress: The Faculty Declares Him Impotent"
is not an image that stresses violence: Louis XVI, clothed and dignified, is
drawn in the midst of doctors. Only the unbuttoned fly calls to mind the
theme of the picture. But it is exactly this theme, illustrated for the first
time, that created scandal.

The *Historical Essays on the Life of Marie-Antoinette of Austria, Queen of
France, to Serve as the Story of This Princess* appeared a few months later, no
doubt during the year 1781, as the last pages of the first part demonstrate
by referring to the recent pregnancy of the queen, delivered of a dauphin
on 22 October 1781. The novelty here lies in the genre chosen by its author (or authors): the biographical essay. Following the princess from her
upbringing to the birth of the dauphin, the essay is a series of scenes of debauchery and vice. The book is thick (eighty pages) and includes no verses
or songs. Here descriptions of facts rely on precise anecdotes, and seem
to be marked with the seal of "historic objectivity." The sexual education
and "initiation" of the archduchess by Rohan, the portrayal of the court
customs of France upon her arrival, the elegant parties in the garden at
Versailles, the unwitting Louis and his cuckolding, the "making" of succes-
sors to the throne by a queen "impregnated in an opera box" by the Duc
de Coigny—all these stages are meticulously described. Some engravings,
of little quality and less obscenity, accompany the text and punctuate the
scenes: "The Queen Marie-Antoinette touches Dilon at the ball," "The first
embrace with the young conscript," "The Decampativos of Vaudreuil,"
and the "Visit of Maurepas." The work ends on a brutal conclusion: "The
king, then, is a null man, of complete nullity, physically as well as morally."

The attacks crossed a threshold in the beginning of the 1780's, an additional rung on the ladder of the representation of impotence. "Fucking"
replaces "f——," pictures appear, and the historical chronicle of scandal
brings about, point by point, an inversion of the glorious tale of the monarchy. In this way, the combination of pornographic attack, licentious prints,
and the rewriting of history go further than the earlier ironies in estab-

lishing the "imbecility" of Louis. The body of the king succumbs to its absolute defeat, the failure of his seminal power.

From the "Flaccid King" to the "Right" of Man

Let us not, however, be misled. When the Revolution is ushered in, if the counterportrait of the monarch is firmly built around his physical and moral "nullity," the dominant image still remains anchored in the majesty and dignity of the official discourse. Louis XVI is not the "imbecile" — on the contrary, he is the "father-king," a reference that is at once political, harking back to the good eras of both Louis XII and Henri IV, and familial. He is the king who is twice a father, "multiplying his image" by means of his own progeny and simultaneously, as if by reflection, through his subjects "loved like his own children." Such a king is welcomed by the works before and at the beginning of the Revolution. Pamphlets linked with the Estates General, bills of grievance, newspapers: that image of the king is everywhere. But the fact remains that, following a chronology whose nuances and inflections must be carefully defined, the portrait of the impotent king, in all its dimensions — imbecile, weak, unaware, deceived — reappears between 1789 and 1791, at first as a side issue, then later brought to the heart of the Revolution itself in the battle for power. From now on, the link between physical and moral "nullity" no longer has to be demonstrated: it is a given, and each camp — Royalists by tradition, Republicans by adoption, and Constitutionalists by temperament — will use the weapon of the king's impotence. This will become, in 1791, a *policy* in the literal sense of the word.

The obscene writings have served their purpose. They were the ones that launched the theme, almost immediately after the "unconsummated" marriage of 1770. They were the ones that in 1789 shaped the counterimage of the monarch of the Revolution. Numerous reprints of once-persecuted ancien régime satires appear. The year 1789 is a great one for licentious literature: reprints are added to new publications not because the new Parisian municipality lets the printers do as they please but because organizing the seizure of "books filled with repugnance" takes some time.[45] In fact, their proliferation is so great that the police commissioners (even those of the Palais Royal, where tight surveillance was still maintained) are often shown to be powerless confronted with the free rein of the written word.

After Marie-Antoinette — certainly the main victim — Louis XVI is not spared by the flood of renewed attacks. *Charlot and Toinette*, for instance, was reissued seven times in just a few months. The revolutionary turning point is experienced, in these repeated or reprinted texts, as an aggravation of the symptoms of impotence. In this sense, reading the many different reprints and forgeries of the *Historical Essays on the Life of Marie-Antoinette* is fascinating. The ancien régime history of this work had stopped at the storming of the Bastille. It is cited among the books destroyed on 19 May 1789 by order of the lieutenant general of police—534 copies of it, which is not negligible.[46] And the Bastille is where its history resumes, once the fortress is taken by assault and its archives revealed. In the beginning of September 1789, then, this foreword appears by way of a preface to a successful reprint: "The anonymous work that we publish was found in the Bastille; perhaps it will fall into the hands of interested persons. . . . Europe will justify the nation that frees itself from such a dangerous influence. Did not an entire people have to be stricken with madness, to let itself be tossed about by the people who will appear on the scene? An entire nation . . . today permits itself the most unrestrained speeches and the most terrible oaths: it must publish the reasons that have led it to this apparent harshness."[47]

We can read here the reasons that led to the surprising success of the *Essays* under the Revolution—sixteen reprints registered for the years 1789–90 alone, followed by six forgeries published between 1791 and 1793. Aside from providing an outlet for a fine commercial enterprise, these reprints "tell about the before," and re-create an ancien régime of scandal that "justifies the nation that frees itself from such a dangerous influence." This rereading is one of the intentions of obscene narrative of the revolutionary era. It has two main protagonists, unsurprisingly: a lubricious queen, "the worst enemy of France," and a king driven toward an impotence that becomes more and more explicit. Sometimes, however, to harmonize with the image of "King of the Revolution," Louis XVI's character is preserved, especially in the initial reprints, while the traits of the queen and the courtiers are changed. But these rewritings quickly turn to the discredit of the king.

In 1791 two forgeries of the *Historical Essays on the Life of Marie-Antoinette* appear that, under various titles, take up the essentials of the episodes while exaggerating them: *The Court of Louis XVI Unmasked* and *The Life of Marie-Antoinette, Queen of France, Wife of Louis XVI, King of the French, from the Loss of Her Maidenhood to the First of May 1791*. A year later the series continues with *The Private, Libertine, and Scandalous Life of*

Marie-Antoinette of Austria, whose success does not falter until 1793, since three republications of it, "with supplements," are offered. The number of pages increases considerably, eventually exceeding the four hundred mark, but the tone and the episodes are as before. Some scenes with La Fayette reveal new material and justify the chronological extension of the licentious tale. The radical novelty, though, lies in the pictorial, or the "twenty-six engravings in copperplate" that "adorn" the volumes. The publisher does not forget to indicate the importance of this in his preface: "We warn the heads of families in advance not to let this work fall into the hands of their children. The unrestrained engravings with which it is accompanied could well produce in them disturbances of which they would repent, and we are at a time when stern morals must guide the education of our youth. One must not, then, place this work in the hands of anyone except grown men." [48]

The commercial cynicism of the statement illustrates a new leap into the violence of representation. For the majority of these graphic works are in fact obscene. Accompanied by captions in couplets, they very directly illustrate the stages of the princess's debauches: the deflowering of Antoinette by a German officer (plate 3), the verification of the "virginity" of the princess by Louis XV (plate 4), the impotence of the dauphin (plate 5), the lubricious poses with courtiers (plates 7 to 10), the "art of fucking" as practiced by the Comte d'Artois (plates 11, 19, 23). The coarsest of these images concern the various moments of "conception" of the royal children: in 1778, "In a box, during a ball given at the opera, the Duc de Coigny hard at work"; and in 1781, "Vaudreuil knows how to make boys; Coigny only made girls." But the most wretched of them always aim at Louis: print 13, when "the king takes the baby in his arms and, to the bewildered eyes of the courtiers and the obstetrician, refutes the accusations of impotence," and especially plate 5, introduced by these words: "Louis XVI was impotent, and, despite all the resources that she used, she could not manage to make him fertile." This is commented on by a couplet:

> Groan, Louis, at how your torpid life
> Outrages your all-too-lusty wife.

It is the first time that Louis is represented in bed, nightcap over his ears and stomach in the air, his sex limp, miserable. The last taboo has been violated: the private life of the king is no longer revealed by words or divulged by confession, but stripped bare by the image. Given the feverish crackdown on obscene pictures carried out by the police of the Palais Royal under strict order of the Paris municipality, we cannot underestimate the import of such a public representation. The "ancient staff" of 1770 has completely withered. What is more, this image is not the only one: in 1791, then in 1792, two others are engraved. The first, included in *The Uterine Furies of Marie-Antoinette*, offers to the compassionate or mocking gaze of the reader a "null king" struggling pathetically in front of an exasperated Marie-Antoinette, a feeble engraving introduced by these rough verses:

> Louis, one evening after dinner
> Drunk with love and full of royal feasting
> Carried his cares to the bed of his better half
> To leave them there, but nothing he did would work.
> Alas! he carried them back. The Sire was so flabby
> That the eyes of Toinette, and all her skillful arts,
> Could not bring the royal jewel to life.[49]

The second print presents a final outrage to the body of the king. It is certainly the best executed and most finely composed: a "slack majesty" illustrating *The Day of Love of Marie-Antoinette*, a "comedy in three acts" dated 20 August 1792.[50] The engraving is of very good quality, and is lewdly subtitled "Ah! fat scoundrel, now you are going limp!" It discloses these royal intimacies by a play of very precise references. The queen, on her sofa, is trying to masturbate a king who is powerless. Apart from his routed virility, the king appears in all the pomp of his past majesty: wearing a wig, royally dressed, with the blue sash of the order of the Holy Spirit. His wife, breast bared, makes one last sign to the reader-spectator: behind her husband's head, she sketches the horns of the cuckold. "Majesty caught in the trap of the bed" could be the title of this obscene engraving. (See Figures 1 to 3.)

Under the Revolution, libertine writers are not satisfied with attacking the body of the king. On the same lewd level, they have constructed a character who is in every respect opposite to the royal weakness. He is the patriot, healthy and vigorous, the "Herculean fucker." He is also the first to "make the king a cuckold," as a print from the end of 1790 indicates. In "Bravo, bravo! The queen is penetrated by the Fatherland," Marie-Antoinette welcomes a fiery member of the summer Federates.[51]

License constantly plays with the fashionable words of politics: former debauches become "National Pleasure," the decrepit Deer Park is transformed into "Patriotic Brothel," the Federate pact of July 1790 itself takes a new name and another appearance, more in keeping with "regenerative" ideals, the "National Cuntfederation [*Con-fédération*]." One could gather from these works enough passages—erotic pastiches of parliamentary meetings, lewd petitions and amendments, delegations of prostitutes, national assemblies of "louts"—to compose a licentious narrative of the Revolution. (See Figures 4 to 7.) But where the court was decadent, in decline, eaten away by venereal diseases or haunted by impotence, this narrative of the Revolution is animated by an energy that is unique to those who believe they are constructing a new man and a new Constitution—what the pamphlets call, not without humor, "fuckative regeneration."

This literature sets in verse, prose, or pictures the transfer of virility from the royal sex to the patriot sex. The power to procreate switches constitutions: Bourbon fertility has been lost, corrupted, and finally eliminated by the sterile pleasures of the court; now, as a last resort, the seminal power of the patriot is alone capable of causing a new body, a new Constitution, to be born. While the portrayal of the patriot "fucker" was developed around the celebration of the Federation, the tale of the transfer of seminal power surrounds the Declaration of the Rights of Man and its adoption, provisionally at first in August 1789 and then definitively in September 1791, at the head of the new Constitution.

Placed before the constitutional bill, the Declaration generates the law: that is the parliamentary interpretation. Playing on the expression "Right of man," the Declaration becomes the expression of a new, powerful ability to fuck and procreate: that is the licentious narrative. It is explored via an entire series of pamphlets improvising on the lewd tone of the Declaration, adopting particular articles such as the "seventeen rights of the patriot fucker"[52] or dedicating the preamble to "that legislative power placed in the hands of the best fuckers of the kingdom."[53] So the declaration of the "Right" of man becomes a kind of erotic talisman, on which the good patriot swears he will be as vigorous and faithful to the Constitution as to his wife. The *Journal des sans-culottes* implies this in September 1791: "Madame, if I had the honor of being your husband, I would never caress your ass except with my right hand placed on the Declaration of the Rights of Man." The talisman is honored and exalted, as an apparently trivial engraving of September 1791 emphasizes: it depicts a woman of the people, the "Democrat," pressing to her heart the Declaration of the Rights of Man rolled up like a manuscript. It would seem a rather mawkish image of constitutionality if it weren't for the fact that the manuscript is rolled up so as to symbolize explicitly a man's erect sex. This democrat does not just cherish the new right of man: she masturbates it, in the expectation of a "political seed" that will no doubt change her condition as citizen. (See Figure 8.)

Even more explicitly—if that were necessary—there is a beautiful engraving from September 1791 that twists to its own purposes the ceremonies that surrounded the act of Louis XVI accepting the Constitution: *The Triumph of the Right of Man*, in which the procession of allegories and of putti, wearing the spoils of the old world (monk's frock, parliamentary gown, nobleman's robes), draws along and surrounds the new idol, the Right of Man turned into an immense erect phallus. (See Figure 10.) It is a brilliantly impressive illustration of the new creative force, a revolutionary force that replaces the traditional fertile symbolism that once glorified the race of Bourbons during the 1770 marriage and the royal births.

Between 1770 and 1791 an immense seminal transfer has been effected around the impotence of the king: the state's power of propagation has been moved from one body to another. Even if the words and images that describe this transition of sovereignty are often more licentious than serious, they exist, and they tell all. We have only to know how to read these works and to be willing to study the engravings that often accompanied them. The intersection of genres, the contamination of text by image, of songs by rumors, of bawdy poems by pornographic attacks, of traditional erotic books by obscene pamphlets—all these connections, perverting the hierarchies and pigeonholes of genres, are shown to be extremely reactive, bringing together the scandalous chronicle of the court, the pitiful narrative of the impotence of the king, and the regenerative glory of the right of the New Man. Revolutionary politics will soon take this into account.

Political Use of the Impotence of the King

Both for defenders of absolute monarchy and for Republican beginners, the symbol of royal impotence resonates with a very political echo: it is a particularly effective weapon, one that can destroy the "father-king" of the Revolution himself. And, logically enough, it is the two extreme camps that use it. For intransigent Royalists, the symbol of the weak monarch is a skillful warning. After October 1789, those days that, for Rivarol as for d'Antraigues or Burke, were the decisive time of the "first regicide," a certain number of nobles begin to remind Louis of his duties, lecturing like a child this "king who wanted to become the father of the Revolution," this political impuissance that endures the insults of the Parisians without reacting to them. In that sense, the first concerted assaults against the king under the Revolution come from his own camp. What is in fact threatened, even before the titles of nobility are abolished in June 1790, is the traditional body of the king, the body that, under the term "Royal Majesty," gathers together the elements of the monarch's visual authority (beauty, fertility, gesture, ostentation), for "Louis must not present himself to his subjects except in an imposing manner, in order to inspire a kind of cult." [54]

For traditionalists, this cult is politically suppressed in October 1789, with insults, physical threats, and "imprisonment" of the king at Paris. Majesty no longer has either the distance or the respect required for such blossoming. And Louis XVI himself has done nothing to preserve it. He has followed the Parisians, has allowed his wife to be insulted without protest; in a word, he is a "null monarch." First he is influenced by his wife and deceived by courtiers, thereafter influenced by revolutionaries and deceived by La Fayette and the Duc d'Orléans. That is the reasoning of the extremists. At its foundation we always find the "imbecile," that figure born in the bed of Versailles: "The look of a sword is terrible. But if one comes to find that its temper is weak, one no longer fears it; it remains null. I think, then, that it is of the essence and of the power of a great King never to let all that he is incapable of be known, in order that it may be believed that he is capable of more." [55]

The Royalist pamphlets try to overwhelm this weak man with sarcasms in order to restore his vigor to him, in a desperate somersault. The attacks are violent because they are the last before the anticipated collapse. The final offspring of a race of kings, Louis is severely confronted with his ancestors. Confession and dialogue are the two privileged forms in this new cycle of attacks on the body of the monarch. Placed in the position of confessing his faults, the king is declared guilty, and must make an act of contrition before he has a chance of recovering himself and regaining his former dignity.

In a short imaginary dialogue, for example, the pope rails against him: "Vain grandeurs! Supreme authority! You have given way to chimerical titles; and of past dignities only the name of a precarious King is preserved, oh unfortunate Louis XVI! If it is possible that from the depths of the tomb your ancestors—who left you as an inheritance the most flourishing empire in the universe, who have transmitted to you a limitless power, an absolute power—if your ancestors, I say, beheld you, if they were aware that from the height of splendor you have become no more than a simple first citizen, stripped of all power, weak, humiliated . . . then, without a doubt, far from pitying you, they would accuse you with reproaches most ignominious and most deserved. Go, unworthy offspring of our blood, and boast no longer of being the grandson of the Bourbons. You have degenerated from our grandeurs and our majesty. You are now nothing more than a phantom of our royal dignity." [56]

A "phantom" confronted with other phantoms: his own ancestors, come back to haunt him in order to teach him a lesson. This is the meeting the Royalist writers imagine. One of the series, the most suggestive, appears in the spring of 1790 at Easter—a favorable time for specters, as everyone knows. Eight short pamphlets are written one after the other, anonymous of course and thus all the more violent. [57] In them, Louis XVI is confronted by the great kings—Louis IX, Henri IV, Louis XIV—and dialogues begin, often political, sometimes bawdy. Following the order of precedence, Saint Louis is the first to visit Louis XVI. In a cleverly engraved frontispiece, he finds him in the process of "forging chains for himself." The saint first exhibits compassion: "Weak and unlucky prince, I come to teach you how to reign." Then, laying down his legendary prudence, Louis IX advises his descendant to "flee to the frontiers to find faithful armies."

In the second pamphlet, Louis XIV intervenes, much more abrasively: "Simpleton! I have known your pranks, your imbecile weakness, and the cruel consequences of your drunkenness. What have you done to your kingdom? Your people have treated you like a child." The recrimination is identical ("What have you done to your kingdom" is the litany of Royalist pamphlets), but the tone, along with the depiction of the king, is humiliating: they are lecturing a drunkard, scolding a child. These two weaknesses are harped on constantly later. Louis XVI is carried away into his frenzies by drink: "I am a poor sovereign / Who no longer has power in hand," he sings after confessing: "This indulgence turned into a habit soon became a need for me. I got drunk almost every day. They took advantage of my moments of drunkenness to lead me astray; they tricked signatures from me; they made children for me; and my revenues were despoiled." He is dressed as a child, "wearing a child's protective bonnet for a crown, carrying a rattle for a scepter, and girt with a toddler's harness for a sash"—and in the antique fashion at that, paying no attention to the commandments of Rousseau, for whom "Emile will have neither safety cap nor harness." This is the king's way of "being soft," constantly falling to the ground, guided by a ghost. Louis XVI does not drink the wine of indignation, he is not a wild child of nature; he drinks "slumber-wine" and is a "baby-king." Here again we find his impotence.

Other dialogues pile up the insults and sarcasms. To list them would take long, but here are the most striking: "ignorant," "weakling," "coward," "poor simpleton of a court card monarch," "poor fool," "senseless dullard," "dolt," "weak soul and body," "play king," "sluggard," "inert," "dull," "vegetable king." Some well thought-out phrases are added: "Open your eyes, stupid, leave the bottles there," "Be firm; if you soften, if you lose potency, you lose your throne," "Your shameful nonchalance joined with a lack of intelligence," "Imbecile schoolboy thanking those who whip you!," "Still in bed! At this hour! Lazy one, to be a king just so you can sleep!" Altogether, this catalogue of insults dismisses the king as impotent, a catalogue to which one final attack must be added:

> Our monarch
> Dumber than a log
> If you notice him
> He's like king fart.
> He doesn't dare say the word:
> He is like a nought.

Then, writes the Royalist pamphleteer with feigned compassion, "the fat Louis XVI burst into tears at these stinging reproaches."

An impotent king, a priori, has nothing to do in a Republican manifesto. There is no room for him, for the bad roles—those of kings who exacerbate Republican hatred—are taken up by tyrants and cruel despots, those "too-powerful" men against whom the Brutuses battle. The image of Louis XVI, at the outset, is not attacked from the radical camp—especially since, as we know, Republicans are rare in the beginning of the Revolution. Not until the spring of 1791 does a rather rich Republican literature come into being with Louis Lavicomterie's series *On People and Kings*, published the year before. However, in the journalism of Desmoulins, Gorsas, or Brissot, royal crimes are still much more bloody, corrupting, or orgiastic than they are instances of monarchic weakness. They reveal more the despotic figure of a Louis XIV or the debauchery of a Louis XV than the impotence of the latest of the Bourbons. Even Lavicomterie, in his popular series *The Crimes of the Kings of France, from Clovis to Louis XVI*, devotes his most horrified descriptions to the subject of tyrant kings and wicked kings. Louis XVI is especially blamed for the power permitted to courtiers' coteries—one of the forms of his weakness—but his reign seems meager compared to the crimes of a Charles IX or even of a Louis XV. Louis XVI could not stand blood and did not like debauches: he is a shabby foil on the heroic stage of the Republican theater whose trestles are put into place in the spring of 1791.

Yet it is the duty of Republican pamphleteers and journalists to include Louis in their attacks. The same goes for the coherence of a political system. But a king who is vilified "just on principle" is not enough: this is not yet a Republic and the trial of the king has not yet begun, nor have the indictments by Saint-Just or Robespierre been published. In this spring of 1791, it is still "Louis the individual" that the Republicans seek to attack. The task is not an easy one. The theme of the weakness of the king will have to be taken up. For if the impotent king is less noxious than the despot, he is still useful to Republican pamphlets precisely because of his "uselessness" and "nullity." The mythic, repugnant figure of the despot-king causes the monarchic principle to be condemned, whereas the uselessness of the "imbecile" Louis XVI, portrayed with ridicule, must cause the humiliation of precisely the reigning individual himself around whom the National Assembly is trying to build a part of its Constitution.

To impose this discourse ridiculing a monarch useless because of his conspicuous weakness, the Republicans seize an opportunity: in March 1791, Louis XVI falls sick. Ten days of fever, intestinal troubles, and stomachaches. The National Assembly, at the suggestion of defenders of the dignity of the king, propose that a medical bulletin should be read daily by the president in plenary session. Here is an opportunity for laughter and Republican protests: a sick king, an Assembly of the orders, and, connecting one with the other, a ceremony of the body. The pamphlets call this the "decline of the royal blood."[58]

This is the first serious illness of the king, if not since the beginning of the Revolution at least since August 1790, and the deputies, worried, wonder what to do. After a brief debate, Abbé Massieu, the Bishop of Beauvais, proposes a motion that the Assembly passes unanimously: "We request that a deputation of six members go every morning to the King until his recovery and report every day on the health of His Majesty at the opening of the session; this will be the way to make it more complete."[59] The Assembly manages this two-headed body that the Constitution establishes without humor, and even with urgency. The Legislative gets news of its Executive.

The next day, 9 March, at the opening of the session at nine in the morning, the delegation makes its report: it went to visit the king, who was sleeping, at six in the morning, and invited Louis XVI's five doctors to join with it. These in turn brought the medical bulletin to the president of the Assembly, who reads: "Fever, a sharp cough, and other symptoms of catarrh continued until four o'clock in the afternoon. During this time, the King three times spat blood. The state of the fever decided us to give a grain of tartar emetic as gastric lavage, which procured copious evacuations by vomiting and stools. These evacuations were bilious, brown and glairy; the urine scant and dark. Aggravation set in at eight o'clock, marked by an increase of hoarseness and of heat in the throat. The night was often interrupted by coughing; the other symptoms have diminished a little." [60]

Whether it is from the pedantry of the description, or disgust when confronted with the illness and its most intimate signs, or the ridiculously pompous presence of those eleven delegates before the president's dais, or the "lively applause" from the benches on the right, or all combined: the Republicans' blood becomes heated and their pens sharpened. Brissot soon flares up in his *Patriote français*: "Is there anything more comical, or rather more heartrending for men keenly sensitive of their dignity as representatives of a free people, than to hear gravely read and enthusiastically applauded a bulletin stuffed with the ridiculous technology of the Diaphoretics that announces that the 'urine is scant and dark' and the 'stools were abundant'? This dirty idolatry might be suitable at the Court of the Grand Lama; but cannot a free people witness its concern for the leader that it has assigned to the executive in some other way than by worrying about his privy? And then journalists copy this rubbish! O adulatores servum pecus!" [61]

Camille Desmoulins, in the tradition of those first Republicans fed on the heroics of Antiquity, is even more sarcastic: "What citizen is not revolted by the baseness of those deputies who applaud thunderously at the speech of a bishop who climbs to the tribune of the National Assembly to make this proclamation, that the stools of a citizen with a cold were copious, and that the fecal matter is no longer so evil-smelling, and is in fact quite praiseworthy. I am surprised that these gentlemen do not ceremonially introduce the urinal and chamber pot of the eldest of the Capets under the nose of the President of the National Assembly, and that the Assembly has not expressly created a patriarch of Gauls to make the proclamation of the quality of stools of the Grand Lama." [62]

The two denunciations resemble each other (though Desmoulins is more wounding), and the same meaning comes through: it is an Assembly of slaves for a sick monarch. The ritual proper to a free nation—the welcomes and applause that the National Assembly should reserve for its heroes— compromised itself by the courtier's art: idolatry of the royal body. The king's weak state here takes on the aspect of a rite of revelation: the "former men," those who have learned nothing, betray themselves at its contact, and again assume the attitude of "slaves."

Brissot immediately tries to reestablish a more equitable balance of priorities: the body of the king must no longer take precedence in the hierarchy of their attentions and ceremonies. An opportunity is soon offered to him: in a message to the Assembly, the king, on the path of recovery, has thanked the deputies for their solicitude for his suffering person, the "head of the nation" temporarily indisposed. And *Le Patriote français* fumes: "No decree authorizes such a title. Head of the executive branch and head of the Nation are two very different things. If by 'head' [*chef*] one understands *caput*, the head, it is the legislative body that is the head of the body politic—that is where the thinking of the nation is formed, the general will, in a word the law. The executive power is only the arm of the body politic. If each of its limbs does not keep to its place, there is only chaos and confusion; order and harmony disappear from the social state." [63] Put back in his "right place," the monarch is explicitly situated in a position of weakness: he is an arm, soon just a hand barely capable of signing vetos. It is an almost exact reversal of one of the organicist representations of the state so widespread before the Revolution, that of the king as head of the body politic.

The ritual continues unabated until the complete cure of the king, whose last medical bulletin comes on the sixteenth of March. The president announces then that "the King can stroll about." Michelon, a Moderate deputy, takes advantage of this to request that "the good citizens of Paris make illuminations." The celebration of the reinstatement of the monarch actually takes place on 20 March: a *Te Deum* is sung at Notre-Dame at which a deputation from the Assembly is present, and the streets are lit up with decorative illuminations. Again the Republicans assail the "grotesque ceremony of the Grand Lama." Brissot writes: "Let us have celebrations, but patriotic celebrations, and not for individuals . . . The purpose alone dignifies celebrations, and the convalescence of one man, whoever he may be, cannot imprint greatness on ideas, or on sensations. Ever mixed with veneration of a man are regrets about his weakness or fears for his strength.

When will we be idolatrous only of virtues, only of the mass and not of the individual?"

Thus the tale of the "royal invalid" finds a Republican moral: idolatry for one particular body is a heresy, an archaic inheritance that must be fought. What would happen, Brissot wonders, if that body had a "debility"? Would one come to "adore the deformations or the malformations of the sovereign"? These words are not written innocently; they recall the sarcasm of Sieyès about peoples who "venerate the natural excrescences" of their masters. Here, however, each reader understands that it is a question of the weakness of the individual king (Louis XVI in this case), of his old difficulty in being a father along with his present feebleness—both medical and political. During this ceremony of the "royal cold," Republican speeches have chosen to use irony (Brissot) or laughter (Desmoulins or Gorsas), at the expense of the weakness of the monarch and the courtly rituals that protect it. For, as *Les Révolutions de Paris* writes (although less vehemently), an independent people chooses its objects of laughter by itself: "We will not be forced to be drunk with joy for ten days, and to show that drunkenness by crowding our windows with lamps for the cure of a momentary weakness of the monarch. And these posted proclamations, these repeated warnings, these importunate drumrolls, these visits to our homes, all these imposing ceremonies constraining us to be happy risk on the contrary making us find the poor invalid quite funny." [64]

By this logic it is no longer recovery that produces joy, but infirmity. For the Republicans, Louis XVI, because of his illness and the ritual that surrounded it, has now become part of political humor, a weapon that up till then had been better mastered by the skillful Royalist satirists of the *Acts of the Apostles*. And this royal entrance into the political carnival, in many respects, is decisive. In fact, three months after the so-controversial *Te Deum* sung for the recovery of the "cold sufferer," the ex-invalid, restored to his top form, is traveling toward Varennes.

The "Gaiety" of Varennes, or The Misadventures of the Pig-King

When, "close to eight o'clock in the morning" [65] on 21 June 1791, the Parisians learn of the departure of the royal family, images of the wicked king and the royal tyrant immediately come to mind. Wicked king because he has betrayed, tyrant king because he wants to rejoin the foreign armies that "are stationed at the frontier." As Brissot avows, "The flight of the King is undoubtedly the signal for war."[66] At nine o'clock the three blasts of the alarm cannon sound, the drums roll, and the tocsin rings. The "disastrous news" brings Parisians into the streets, into the Tuileries, which "innumerable citizens" visit that day, congregating around the National Guard and armed *sections*: "Everything was as if electrified by that first shock."[67] Rumors run through people's minds: "They had reason to fear that robbers, always so numerous in huge capitals, would profit from that moment of confusion and anger to pillage."[68] Parisian newspapers, which I will follow here, become the echo of a kind of urban "Great Fear": "The first impulse was uncertainty, the second stupor; but soon the fire of indignation blazed in every mind."[69] Uncertainty, stupor, indignation: Gorsas here names the sequence that Georges Lefebvre will see at work in massacres—fear, collective mobilization, punishment.

And, in fact, the blood does flow—on the paper of the first broadsides published in the afternoon: "Tremble, citizens, the country is in danger; the storm rumbles over your heads; the King leaves for the Empire to place himself at the head of many thousands of bloodthirsty soldiers who have revolted against your Constitution . . . This King, who a few days before had sworn an immortal and inviolable fidelity to all your decrees, today places himself at the head of a conspiracy in which he thinks blood may well flow."[70]

These "texts of terror," haunted by bloody visions and "horrible spectacles," offer a political drama devoted to a fight to the death. On one side the tyrant, the despotic hydra, an "animal-king with the nature of a maneater," as Desmoulins will write expressively.[71] On the other the "hero-people," martyred and sacrificed: "It is a baptism of blood that sanctifies, as it is a baptism of water that regenerates; to fight as a hero is to die as a saint and a martyr; and to spread one's blood on the altar of the homeland is to expire on the altar of the living God."[72] In this universe of Spartan or Roman Republican rhetoric, we no longer find an impotent king. Alarm spreads in every mind.

Paradoxically, it is the National Assembly that reintroduces the theme of the impotence of the monarch in the course of the debates on the day, and then the night, of 21 and 22 June. In order to protect the constitutional edifice, but also to calm the streets of a capital that he feels is turbulent, La Fayette is the first to initiate the argument of the "kidnapping of the king." Despite the protests of Roederer, Robespierre, and Reubell, and despite the reading on the twenty-first of the *Statement of Case* left by Louis XVI, who personally justifies his voluntary departure, the fiction of the "kidnapping" is accepted without difficulty. This coerced, deceived, and docile king is nothing but a very political variation of the "imbecile king" born in 1770. This fiction excites the humor of the Parisians, who are not duped but just playing the game, and it motivates the writing of the Republican journalists, who are irritated at first and then find in the grotesque allegation of kidnapping the same absurd figure molded during the royal illness of March. Louis XVI does not succeed for long in imposing his tyrannical aspect: whether "kidnapped" or "fugitive," his person remains firmly linked to impotence.

Certainly—as all commentators note—the mood of Paris changes on the evening of 21 June. Great fear in the morning, tranquillity and joy in the evening. Gorsas is the best witness of this in his *Courrier des 83 départements*, sensing perfectly the nuances of that Parisian opinion drawn between two possible narratives of the event—fear of a resolute flight toward foreign armies or ridicule of a kidnapping of the weak king: "The snare-drums are rattling now to beckon citizens to light up the night. Until now there has been no scene of blood, and the unanimous wish is that the sword of law strike the guilty. The town gates are closed, the garrisons are in order. The enemies of the Constitution had thought that the departure of the King would be the signal for a general revolt. The people, however, have never before shown themselves more worthy of freedom. After a few moments of inevitable disturbances, the *sections* of Paris, the Citizen Guard, the administrative bodies, have together seized all the means of ensuring the public peace. . . . All citizens, without exception, as if they had been given the word, have erased the arms of the King and the Queen from above their ensign . . . Not one moment of trouble! The greatest order, the greatest unanimity yesterday evening, even a kind of joy." A pamphlet summarizes this in a monetary play of words at the king's expense: "We call him a counterfeit *louis* in the morning, and a fat penny in the evening." [73]

The next day the news comes out: people learn about how the royal family has escaped, and wait for information about its route. The mood still swings back and forth, between "the Friend and the Orator of the People that cried that blood must be shed" and "this phenomenon of tranquillity, harmony, and gaiety that the aristocracy observed with terror." But it seems that "gaiety" finally carried the day, according to what Gorsas and Desmoulins describe. The former emphasizes, for instance, the improvisation of a burlesque procession around a bust of Marie-Antoinette, "decked out in coif," "paraded in the crossroads, then dragged in the mud and mire, and finally broken to pieces," while the original text of a public notice printed in the morning of 22 June is thus reported by the journalist: "If the King is stopped and brought back, I make the motion that we expose him for three days to public ridicule, a dunce cap on his head, then that we conduct him to the frontier, and having arrived there that we give him a kick in the ass, without allowing any other harm to be done to him," in order to punish "the degeneracy into which he has fallen, the heavy, material stupidity with which we have seen him allow himself to be led here or there, following the caprices of his impotence and the desires of those who surround him, or the winds of circumstance."

"At the time that we are correcting this proof (eleven o'clock in the evening, 22 June) a courier sent by the department of Meuse has just brought to the National Assembly the news of the arrest of Louis XVI. He was recognized in Varennes," writes Gorsas, hastened by the event. By the next day's edition, the journalist can add details to his report and describe Parisian reactions: "Never has Paris presented such touching scenes. The most intimate union reigns among the citizens. Aristocratic papers shrink back in horror, and have not dared to appear. The calmest night was followed by a cloudless day."

Fear has completely fled, and two moods henceforth remain in competition: tranquillity and laughter. On the first side are the majority of the Assembly, the municipality, and all the constitutional newspapers: their victory is built on the argument of the "kidnapping of Louis" and then on the Parisian reception planned for the parade of the royal return, between four and seven-thirty on the evening of 26 June, when five hundred thousand people press around a coach escorted by thirty thousand soldiers: "Not a sign of disapproval, no apparent sign of scorn was emitted by this large crowd. Care was taken not to accord any of the military honors. The royal party was received with weapons lowered. All the citizens kept their hats on their heads as if of one accord."

To this "scornful coldness of the people" corresponds the laughter of that same people. These two sentiments are not contradictory, as Gorsas writes: "One could not prevent the particular expressions with which each person gave vent to his feelings about the monarch, even if no cry, no outrageous word struck the ears of the King or tore him from the regrets with which, no doubt, he is tormented."

These "particular expressions" most often drag the body of the king toward the carnival grotesque. As soon as the details of the arrest are known, on 23 and 24 June, satire and laughter are let loose, a kind of great release reacting to, or rather preparing for, the solemn tranquillity of the return procession. This severe, silent procession, so much celebrated by the Assembly and the Parisian press, evokes its ghostly counterimage in prints and comic tales; we see for instance a "great celebration given by the madams of Paris for their whores on the day of the arrival of the King, the Queen, and their Family, rejoicing in the return of their father and mother."[74] In this imaginary celebration, the prostitutes of Paris come to thank their "cuckold king" for being so kind as to let his "Messaline" deceive him so frequently.

So the flight to Varennes turns into an episode of ridicule that is added to the tale of the sexual drama lived out by Louis XVI in licentious satire: it becomes one more "decampativos." Desmoulins uses this word in his paper on 27 June, speaking of the "general decampativos of the Capetians and the Capets," while a pamphlet offers a tale of the escape arranged around this suggestive vision: *The Reveille of a Grenadier of the Oratory, or the powerful feelings of the national armed forces about the royal Decampativos*. It is not merely a matter of playfully conjugating the shameful verb "to decamp," but of making an explicit reference to royal impotence by alluding to an anecdote that was circulating at the court a dozen years before. This anecdote is reported with a goodly number of details in the *Historical Essays on the Life of Marie-Antoinette*, a pamphlet that was, as we have said before, widely distributed at the beginning of the Revolution.

Vaudreuil, the licentious narrative reports, was the grand master of an erotic game whose only rule consisted of making the king a cuckold: all the art of the Decampativos resided in that. "Some of the groves had been illuminated. In one of them they had set up a throne of ferns, and there they played at being king the way little girls play at being ladies; they elected a king, and he gave his audiences, held his court, meted out justice . . . His Majesty was almost always Vaudreuil; he took it into his head to form alliances: he married the queen to himself most often. He did the same for the other men and women of the society; he had them approach the foot of his throne two-by-two, ordered them to hold hands, and then, with all the respect due to this kind of new sacrament, was heard the sacramental word, which was 'Decampativos.' As this word was pronounced, each man and his mate fled full speed toward one of the groves while the good Louis waited, drinking. Forbidden by the king of ferns was any return before two hours to the throne room guarded by his majesty and his divine bottles. We can be sure that this game mightily pleased the King, who found it quite pleasant to see himself thus dethroned on the grass by Vaudreuil . . . That year they were supposed to order the water cure for the Queen to provoke a second pregnancy, but the doctors all came to the agreement that the 'Decampativos' would produce the same effect even better."

"Decampativos": the "sacramental word" is a sarcastic remark thrown at the body of an impotent king, a drinker, a simpleton, "the slack king" of 1780 (the time of the erotic games) as he is again in 1791 at the time of his flight so ludicrously depicted. Rarely would the connections between the literature of scandal of the ancien régime and the political pamphlets of the Revolution be emphasized in such an explicit manner as by the resurgence of this word about the abortive escape.

But it is above all the image of the "pig-king" or "swine-king" that exposes the body of the monarch to ridicule. This image very quickly fills out until it becomes the particular emblem of the return from Varennes in the radical newspapers, pamphlets, and caricatures. The narrative of the flight is stretched between two aspects of the "animal-king." On one hand, the "man-eater" embodied by the tiger, the hyena, the rapacious eagle, reinforced by the person of Marie-Antoinette, who is presented as the great instigator of the plot. On the other hand, coming after the change of affairs by the "citizens' gaiety," the pig-king, castrated and fatted, a follower tossed about at the whim of events. These images are deceiving — they make a victim of Louis XVI, while in fact the king himself premeditated and prepared his flight for many months — but they are effective. No doubt their complementarity (the castrated pig added to the gluttonous pig join the collection of degrading figures of the king elaborated up till then) and their accessibility (every printmaker knows how to draw a pig, every reader understands its habits) encourage the wide diffusion of this representation. The pig is a successful symbol because it implies the two aspects of royal weakness: the impotent, cuckolded king and the "fat Louis," eater and drinker. In the Paris first alarmed and then amused by the flight of the king, this image of animal degradation appears in a roundabout way in an anecdote reported by *The Chatterbox* [*Le Babillard*] dated 23 June: "A peasant girl says to a grenadier, her manner serious: 'Messieurs, I have six little pigs in my house that I leave every morning in the fields. I watch over them all by myself and not one wanders off. And there are thirty thousand of you who watch over only one pig. You must be silly asses to let him get lost.' Listeners couldn't keep from laughing at the comparison."[75]

Gorsas takes up the anecdote the next day, elaborating on it a little but trying to explain it more deeply: " 'Our boy is enough to watch my twenty pigs, and all Paris didn't know how to keep the only one it had.' This woman alluded to the epithet with which Marie-Antoinette honored her husband. It is well known that in her smart society she calls him 'our pig.' " This may in fact be an affectionate nickname given by the queen, but it strongly revives the image of the impotent, "castrated" animal, incapable of procreating, dedicated to rounding out his own embonpoint. This nickname is also found in licentious pamphlets. In *The Day of Love of Marie-Antoinette*, the queen exclaims, during a "secret" conversation with Lamballe, her favorite: "My pig is a fat mass of flesh who eats, who drinks, but who is limp."[76] Likewise, immediately after Varennes, a satirist has Marie-Antoinette lament to herself, once Fersen has vanished: "Alas! Alas! with whom then will I procure the joys of this world? Not with our pig . . . You have to be Swedish to mean anything to me, or be a great strapping man. Now I am surrounded only by Frenchmen and followed around by a *pauvre sire*. [Literally "poor sire," but idiomatically a shabby lout. Trans.] Alas! Alas! Alas!"[77] Then Hébert, in *Father Duchesne*, canonizes the expression, after completely changing his point of view on the royal couple after Varennes. He imagines the fleeing "pair" in these obscene words: "Mounted astride his knees, holding in one hand a bottle; and with the other, caressing his horned head, she pours streams of wine over him, and licks her filthy swine like a bitch in heat."[78]

But Camille Desmoulins most pertinently describes the figure of this animal-king. Learning of the king's movement to Sainte-Menehould, where Drouet recognized the monarch disguised as a manservant, the journalist invents an anecdote that will indissolubly link the image of the glutton king to the bestial representation of the impotent pig: "What are the causes of great events? In Sainte-Menehould, the town's name reminds our own crowned Sancho Panza of the pigs feet for which it is famous. Let it not be said that he went by relay to Sainte-Menehould without having eaten pigs feet on the spot. He no longer remembers the proverb: *plures occidit gula quam gladius*. ["The gullet kills more people than the sword." Trans.] The time taken to prepare the pigs feet and his all-too-similar face on a banknote were fatal to him."[79]

The anecdote of Louis XVI lost because of a recipe is constantly taken up by pamphlets and political cartoons of the time,[80] especially since, according to the directions given in *Soupers de la Cour* [Court dinners], a famous cookbook of the end of the eighteenth century, "pigs feet à la Sainte-Menehould" demands a preparation time of almost half a day: "Cut each foot in half after cleaning them thoroughly; cook them for about ten hours over a very low flame, with a gill of brandy, a pint of white wine, a pound of salt pork, salt, fine spices, a sprig of parsley, chives, a clove of garlic, three cloves, thyme, bay leaf, basil."

After this, the gourmand pig is the target of all the derisive and ridiculing attacks, the royal pig with his mistress and "swineherd," the queen, disguised under the passport of the Baroness de Korf: "The certificate of the Baroness de Crotz [*sic*] does not fascinate the eyes of upright and patriotic judges; on the contrary, it makes possible a most singular pleasantry [the Baroness of *crotte*, 'manure']. The round form of the new 'manservant' is greatly admired, and everyone thinks that the position of head waiter would better suit this fat pig."[81]

Finally, after having offered this subject for the laughter of patriots, Desmoulins illustrates it one last time in his paper dated 4 July in an account of the king's return. He also would rather imagine a ludicrous procession instead of a grave and silent cortege bringing back to Paris, wedged into the "hearse of the monarchy," a carnival "fat Louis": " 'So I went on a rotten trip,' the king exclaims, 'it was silly, I admit it; oh well! Can't I have my pranks like everyone else? Come on, somebody bring me a chicken.' The animal is brought, and Louis drinks and eats with an appetite that would have done honor to the King of the Land of Plenty, as he had done all along the way. In the carriage that had carried Louis XVI away, those who affixed the seals noticed a large chest; they thought it contained extremely important secrets, or at least the crown diamonds. What was their surprise at seeing, instead of treasure, nothing but big commodes? That's the first time the seals were affixed on a chamber pot! What a fortunate disposition he has! Especially if the foremost qualities for happiness are, as Fontenelle has said, a bad heart and a good stomach! It would be a source of even more happiness for the people if the animal-King, whose species they want to preserve so preciously for us, had purely and simply become a pig."

The scatological allusions to the royal flight are not accidental. If Louis is a pig, he is first impotent, then fattened, and finally reduced to the most degrading animal function. The grotesque cortege that welcomes him into the imagination of patriotic derision could not pass up the dirtiness of the pig-king, just as the carnival aspect of the procession required his gluttony and his impotence. And so develops the "Feast of Saint Blood-Pudding [*Saint-Boudin*]," founded on all the shameful symbols of the pig-king—impotence, gluttony, dirtiness—in which the animal-king is symbolically put to death by laughter.

When the "pig hunt" season is opened in August 1792, this animal symbol linked to Louis XVI reappears with violence. *Le Courrier français* of 4 August 1792 reports, for example, that the hawkers are circulating a large number of pamphlets entitled *Description of the royal zoo of live animals* whose main feature is the description of the "royal Veto" escaped in direct descent from the Varennes cortege, although its appearance has meantime degenerated: "This animal is about five feet five inches tall. It walks on its hind feet, like men. It has fawn-colored skin. It has stupid eyes; a gaping gullet, a red muzzle; large ears; hardly any hair; its cry resembles somewhat the grunt of swine. It has no TAIL. It is naturally voracious. It eats, or rather it grubbily devours, anything that is thrown to it. It is a drunkard and does not stop drinking from the time it rises till when it goes to sleep. . . . It is 34 to 36 years old, was born in a pigsty called Versailles, and it was given the nickname of Louis XVI." [82]

The king, the erstwhile fertile father celebrated by marriage odes and eulogies to royal births, foster father to France, from now on is a castrated pig that is going to be put to death for the Feast of Saint Blood-Pudding: his body has symbolically become a political food. Citizen Romeau will joyously recall this when he describes the "commemorative" culinary ceremony of 21 January 1793: "This feast will above all be characterized by the head or ear of a pig that each pater familias would not fail to place on the table, in memory of the fortunate day when the head of the faithless Louis XVI fell and freed us from his oppressive presence. . . . May all of us equip ourselves with the piece of pork that our fortunes will allow us to eat, and may we imitate the English patriots who on the day of the decapitation of their king Charles II [*sic*] never fail to eat a calf's head." [83]

From one recipe to another, from pigs feet to head, Louis XVI has gone from eater to eaten. This legend born in the days following the flight to Varennes allows all satirical media—licentious, political, ludicrous—attacking the king to unite their sarcasms into one tutelary symbol of the French land of plenty: the carnival pig. This symbol is the outcome of the defeat of the royal body and becomes one of the major symbolical forms of the transition of political sovereignty. The body of an impotent pig, gluttonous and dirty, no longer bears the least scrap of majesty liable to incarnate the monarchical state.

If the figure of an impotent Louis XVI, in all its forms—the "imbecile" of the royal bed, the sleepy cuckold of the bawdy, "King Zero" of the Absolutists, the useless invalid of the Republicans, and the pig of Varennes— met with such favor, it is undoubtedly because it manages to suit the whole range of revolutionaries. The Royalists politically launched the theme in one sense, and the Republicans took it up in another. During the post-Varennes parliamentary debates, the "Constitutionalists" (soon to be the "Feuillants"), who form the majority in the National Assembly, accept it as well. The political keystone of the Monarchist constitution of 1791, which Barnave and his friends save during the first days of July, is in fact a weak sovereign, this weakness being the very condition of his inviolability, as voted on 15 July following a vibrant defense by Barnave. On 25 June 1791, the Assembly, not wishing to hasten its decision, suspends the powers of the king and forms a committee to inquire into the circumstances of the "kidnapping" of the monarch. On 13 July, Muguet de Nanthou presents the report of that committee. He asks a simple question: "Can the king be held responsible for the fact of his flight?" His answer is negative, since the "king is inviolable in his capacity as holder of executive power." The spokesman charges Bouillé and his accomplices, those who undertook the abduction, but Muguet de Nanthou's conclusion is clear: flight does not constitute a constitutional offense. But will this altogether juridical argument be accepted politically? This question launches the debate of mid-July 1791.

Pétion, Vadier, Robespierre, Prieur de La Marne, Grégoire, and Buzot all speak in favor of sentencing the king or for at least the prolonged suspension of his powers. Brissot, in his *Patriote français*, best expresses this point of view: "Either the king is an imbecile, or he is guilty, that's the question. I do not believe that it is enough to declare the king an imbecile, although he has proved little ability and much weakness. Whether he is guilty as a public functionary, that, on the other hand, is what is impossible to dispute."[84] Brissot does not stop at the weakness of the king and demands the trial of this king guilty of treason. He prefers the role of "Louis the faithless" to that of "Louis the imbecile." The Republican reaction reasserts his rights: weak kings remain unsuitable enemies.

The cleverness of the Constitutionalists led by Barnave is to seize upon the "imbecile" and to dress him as a hereditary, inviolable king in order to shelter him from attacks and save his appearance. Better still, the very

weakness of the monarch is the condition of constitutional harmony. This
"feeble king" (neither mad nor despotic, quite simply weak: capable of exercising considerable executive powers *without danger* to the Assembly) is
at the heart of Barnave's argument, which will convince the Assembly to
"halt" right there a Revolution that has turned disturbing. "Gentlemen,"
the orator begins on 15 July 1791, "the French nation has just suffered a
violent shock; but, if we believe all the omens it reveals, this last event, like
all those that have preceded it, will only serve to hasten the end, to ensure
the solidity of the Revolution that we have made. . . . It seems to me that
it would be a great mistake, when founding a hereditary monarchy, and
thus consenting to receive from the hands of birth and chance the one who
will occupy the first place, if you left great importance to the choice and
quality of the man. I believe that, wherever the will of the people gives evidence of ability, wherever responsibility forces the public officer to exercise
his functions, it is necessary that personal qualities act in concert with the
law. But unless you have made a vicious Constitution, the person given to
you by the chance of birth, and whom the law cannot reach, cannot be important by virtue of his personal actions to the health of the government;
he must find in the Constitution the principle of his conduct and the obstacle to his errors. If it were otherwise, Gentlemen, it would not be in the
weakness of the King that I would perceive the greatest danger, but in his
power; I would not mistrust his vices so much as his virtues: for I could
say to those who are now uttering complaints, morally just, albeit childish
politically, those who speak with such fury against the individual who has
sinned; I would say to them: you would be under his feet, then, if you were
satisfied with him!" [85]

The argument suggests that the "king without quality" placed in the
heart of the Constitution of 1791 is the ultimate symbol, well thought out
politically, of the impotence of the king. And what is more, it is precisely
because he is individually impotent, weak, and timorous that the Constitution can entrust him with important executive powers. The "vegetative
body" born in the princely bed of 1770 seems to have found, twenty years
later, its constitutional translation: a corporeally deficient "constitution,"
one could say, playing like the revolutionaries on the two senses of the word.
Examining all the kinds of satire between 1770 and 1791, the defeat of the
royal body runs the gamut, between the spring and summer of 1791, of the
whole range of political options. The "imbecile-king" certainly does not
have the same function with the Absolutists, the Republicans, or the Con-

stitutionalists, and the emblems of his weakness are emphasized differently by them, but they all, at one time or another, agree on using this particular symbol of the body of the king. That is when the image is brought out into the open after having lurked for a long time in clandestine obscene engravings and licentious minds.

I will conclude this chapter with a reading of a pamphlet opportunely titled *The Great Dénouement of the Constitution*.[86] It deals with a "politico-tragi-comic parody" played (explains the cover of the work) on 1 January 1791, just before that rich spring I have mentioned. The writing is visibly of Royalist inspiration, cleverly peppered with those comic effects that the publishers of the *Acts of the Apostles* handle best. The scene takes place in an inn kept by M. Fat Louis, "innkeeper, erstwhile monarch," kept "immobile," "paralytic" in his "armchair." This version of the "zero king" is inspired by anger among those nostalgic for the traditional monarchy. Three drinkers converse in the inn, lecturing Fat Louis. Two are "men with a sad face": Le Rude, whose name indicates his program in political matters, and his comrade Alwine [Touvin], "writer, musician, agent, man of talents, drunkard, and above all initiated into the Club." This second character is not talkative, but his characterizations are enough to show he belongs to the "Rousseaus [gutters, *ruisseaux*] of the Republic." The few words that he does utter are generally insults hurled at the innkeeper whom he refuses to pay. "Swine," "despot," we hear from his lips. Fat Louis has become a superfluous pig there, and the inn could easily do without its weak innkeeper. The last drinker tries to interrupt. He would like to save the monarchical inn and keep the head of Fat Louis, all while earning the trust of the clients. He is Marvelugly [Miralaid] the reconciler, suspected of playing a double game by everyone, but he knows how to speak well. We easily recognize in him a great orator whom Barnave, some months later, would like to succeed, after having been his rival. For Marvelugly, Fat Louis is an "imbecile," but he remains indispensable: "Papa Fat Louis, you are fat and thick like the Constitution of a former monk, and you cut a poor figure of a King. . . . But a jaw for chewing and three fingers for signing, that's all you need today to be a good executive." Here the impotent one becomes of use to the Constitution, the "finger of the executive."

This little narrative of the Revolution, offering the three bodies of one single royal impotence, is a mine. The ore is found at the intersection of different genres of satire, and each kind of politics tries to draw from it a bodily symbol suitable to illustrate its discourse. And that is the end of the body of Louis XVI: the Fat Louis of a fable written by his Royalist "friends," the pig of Republican interpretations, and the weak finger indispensable to the Constitution. From now on, only the tenth of August and the guillotine can change the image of his body—for the Republicans, returning it to the image of the drinker of blood, and for the Royalists, raising it to the mighty efficacy of the martyr. As for the finger of the Constitution, it has gotten broken along the way.

2. Sieyès, Doctor of the Body Politic

The Metaphor of the Great Body of the Citizens

Ever since the works of Ernst Kantorowicz and their (sometimes delayed) distribution, mediaevalist and modernist historians have tried to read the monarchical and absolutist French system through its corporeal representations. Now no "History of France" is complete without a chapter on the body or bodies of the king thought of as metaphors for the former political organization. In the same way, the interpretation of contemporary history does not ignore the political thinking of German Romanticism, teeming as it is with organic imagery. But from this point of view, revolutionary discourse is still uncharted territory. Metaphors of the body are not lacking in the writings of French revolutionaries, but this reading has undoubtedly been made difficult by two sources of interference.

An observer poring over the texts of political commentary from the beginnings of the Revolution will recognize a multitude of metaphors and references. This abundance is generally viewed in an unfavorable light: body words, whether the discourse be medical, religious, philosophical, or at times fantastic or licentious, tend to serve a function apt for pamphleteering, a function more concerned with illustrating or decorating the political account of some event than with a conceptually coherent political way of thinking. Political discourse, then, *abused* words and, almost naturally, carried away by a desire to convince and impress, used metaphors of the organism to give concrete strength to abstract principles, to make projected systems visible. In this sense, the beginning of the Revolution is a

favorable time for the disordered and rather widely repetitive multiplication of bodily metaphors.

The second source of interference is the preexistence of the bodily
scheme characteristic of the monarchical representation of state power.
Thus the French Revolution was considered more as the defeat of the body
of the king than as the elaboration of a fresh corporeal metaphor. Because
no new image of the body had been developed, after 1789 certain revolutionaries consciously avoid using bodily metaphors to designate the political organization to be built. By their lights, the weight of royal symbolism
spoils the register of discourse of the body.

Emmanuel Sieyès, however, seems fully aware of the necessity of establishing his political language on the two registers of corporeal discourse.
On one hand he wants to use "image-words" so as to be better understood;
on the other hand, he tries to effectuate a transfer of sovereignty between
old and new corporeal metaphors of the French political system. In the
winter of 1788–89, Abbé Sieyès is the writer who best marries "imaginative writing" with the political system. At the center of this intersection he
places a representation of the body.

Sieyès knows how to write words that lead to "truth" by metaphor. "My
own role is that of all patriotic writers; it consists of presenting the truth:
that is to say, of striking the ear, so to speak, of the human species, by clothing abstract ideas in an image," he writes in his bill against offenses of the
press in January 1790.[1] The philosopher, he continues — and we know how
he liked to give himself that name — "composes his system on the highest
level" but wants to give "simplified writings" to the reader. The paradox is
stimulating: metaphors — "imaginative discourse" — are the condition for
understanding a complex idea. But Sieyès also knows the trap of image-
words: misuse. He summons a story to recall to his reader those harmful
circumlocutions of political discourse: "I have not forgotten a lesson in animal magnetism on which Messrs. d'Espréménil and Bergasse gave classes
at Mesmer's, not many years before the revolution. There were quite a few
women, and I have too good an opinion of their natural wits to believe that
they could understand anything of all that was said. The professor took
it into his head to use some image that is assuredly quite common; he
compared something or other to the panes of a window. The audience was
inert; but at this word 'window,' I saw everyone turn gently and gravely
toward the window in the room. The mind, empty — though steady — up
to that instant, was suddenly filled, for they were all thinking about their

own windows, and how many connections there are between a window and thousands of ideas! There is no harm in that, certainly. But the fact is that, from that moment on, good-bye silence, good-bye attention. There was not one woman who did not come up with twenty objections, twenty remarks to make, each one of them quite irrelevant to the question at issue, and every one of them applicable only to the panes and windows of her house. That is the danger of images."[2]

The misuse of image leads to interference in the system of comprehension because of multiple and contradictory reappropriations of discourse by the listener or the reader. What Sieyès wants is to strew his political system with controlled metaphors as limits of definition, not as a springboard for unbridled imagination. His metaphors are carefully chosen: they are mirrors bordering the text, allowing the reader to concentrate on nodes of comprehension, not broken windows diffracted into splinters. The most pervasive metaphors are mechanical. They allow us to reach the very heart of the social art of Sieyès, which is "political mechanics" or the "political machine." Sieyès defined this social art—or his ambition as a political writer—in his Views on the executive methods that could be used by the representatives of France in 1789: "Art belongs to us, philosophers. Speculation, synthesis, and experiment also belong to us: yet, of all the arts, undoubtedly the first is the one that deals with ordering men among one another, on a level most favorable to all."[3] He provides the metaphoric key to his comprehension in What Is the Third Estate?: "Never will we understand the social mechanism if we don't resolve to analyze a society like an ordinary machine, contemplate each part separately, and then join them together again in our minds, one after the other, so as to grasp their affinities and understand the general harmony that must result from them."[4]

Many are the metaphors that stem from this "ordinary machine." The clock, of course, is the most common: "Order a clock from a clockmaker." Sieyès humbly compares his Views to the meticulous work of the artisan,[5] to try to escape "metaphysical error," that reproach that is endlessly hurled at him, and to urge on his reader a universe of references that are at once literary and laborious. Another recurrent mesh of metaphors: the philosopher-architect and the construction of his house-politics. "What do you expect?" he demands of the privileged in What Is the Third Estate?. "Your house is held up only by trickery, with the help of a forest of chaotic scaffolding placed without taste and without design, except to prop up the parts wherever they threaten ruin. It must be rebuilt, or else you must decide to live day to day, in the discomfort and with the anxiety of finally being crushed under its debris. In the social order everything is connected. You can't neglect one part of it without risking damage to the others."[6]

There remains the use of organicist metaphor: the political system as vision of a human body. Here my reading begins, but it could not achieve the economy of that "metaphorical placing in context" of the imaginative discourse of the Abbé Sieyès. With the philosopher, a specific situation is reserved for images of the body: the mechanistic metaphor allows us to reach the center of the social art according to Sieyès, while the organic allows us to understand the fracture of 1789. This fracture occurred at the juncture of two impulses: the "antisocial disease" that was eroding the old body and then the cure, the new organization of the political body of the Revolution. At first glance, the most surprising fact is that Sieyès had seen and described this fracture a year before others did: between the summer of 1788, when he wrote *Views on the executive methods that could be used by the representatives of France in 1789*, the fall of 1788, when the *Essay on Privileges* was composed, and the very beginning of the year 1789 and his *What Is the Third Estate?*, Sieyès offers a meticulous description of the rupture that took place in events between May and September 1789. Metaphors of the body are at the heart of this enigma.

Antisocial Disease, or The Body and the Orders

Enigma? Perhaps not. In fact, these same metaphors were used in a number of writings by political commentators. In August 1788, Louis XVI appeals to the opinions and advice of his subjects about the modalities of the convocation of the Estates General. In the answers that start to stream in during the summer of 1788, we find many historical discussions of the relations between the different orders of the kingdom, but almost every time the reader also discovers a "French State," an outcome established without any servile wish to please the king. Thereafter, images of disease, of "degeneration," flow from the writers' pens. Bodily metaphors occupy a central place in them. In this sense, Sieyès is in phase with the political writing of the time. As well as being a prophet, the philosopher-priest is a reader of the works of his time. Just as he draws a number of images and metaphors from the texts of others, he offers his ideas and his systems to his contemporaries, who will reread and plagiarize him: there is nothing more alien to the preoccupations of these "writers for the public good" than an author's copyright of metaphors or principles. Words and ideas circulate, animating a "literary corpus" as alive as the political body built by organicist representations. Sieyès certainly "cuts the Gordian knot" as Cérutti, one of his patriotic friends in philosophy, will write, but he does so in the words of his time: the disease he describes is one among others, fed by others, just like the corporeal metaphor that he offers as a cure. He has, however, the ambition to work "magic" on it quickly. That is his role.

The forms of the "disease of France" described in the course of the winter of 1788 are at once common and diverse. One of these pamphlets suggests that since "political bodies are being compared to human bodies,"[7] there is, "in the trunk that forms the administration of the State," a "deep wound that has long been open, that has imperceptibly gotten larger, and that does not cease enlarging."[8] These comparisons are not new: already on the occasion of the meeting of the Assembly of Notables almost two years before, a wave of pamphlets had sought to denounce "the aggravation of the state of the social body,"[9] the "moral and physical loss of the political body for thirty years now." Then Mirabeau had set the tone in his *Agiotage Denounced to the King and to the Assembly of Notables*. ["Agiotage" is a word Mirabeau himself defines as "the study and the employment of maneuvers . . . to produce unexpected variations in the price of government bonds and obligations, and to turn to one's own profit the spoils of those whom one has deceived." Trans.] "France might be destined to offer Europe for a long time to come the indecent spectacle of these scenes of corruption, disorder, and rapacity," writes the Provençal count while peopling his description with bodily metaphors: a country led toward "degeneration," "denaturation," "converted into an ever more active focus of corruption and disease," in a word: "exhausted." "I pause at, I cry over the state of this poor body, and the reader may find me guilty of having dared to foresee these misfortunes," the pamphleteer writes in conclusion to his opuscule.

Far from dwindling, this metaphoric register amplifies its effects after the announcement of the convocation of the Estates General. Furthermore, the commentators endeavor to formulate a diagnosis. A natural sickness owing to the aging of a country that has endured "fourteen centuries of despotism"—that is the approach of *The bread of the people*: "In the political order of things as in the natural order, everything has a beginning and an end; and the duration of each thing is always in proportion to its ability to sustain its existence without overusing its resources. If the resources of life were not used up, this existence would be eternal. Nothing in the physi-

cal world has such a nature, and infallible experience has proven that the
further one travels from one's birth, the more one approaches the end of
life. . . . In slow revolutions, ever more disastrous, a body wastes away only
by first announcing some inequality in the allocation of the life forces; annihilation finally occurs when these forces have been consumed in the center that is their reservoir. Everything repeats in this cycle submitted to the
contemplation of man. That is why these laws are general, and especially
applicable to the past and present state of France." [10]

Taking the opposite tack, some see in France an organism "still in the
cradle": "The constitution of France is what will always be that of an empire in the cradle, or one that, despite the long succession of centuries,
might not yet be weaned from the smallnesses and regimes inherent to
childhood. [The word *régime* means both governmental system and regimen, diet. Trans.] This age is the time of imperfection." [11]

Playing at being doctors, political commentators are quick to transfer
their reflections on the state of the country to the imagery-laden level of disease: symptoms, crises, wounds, languishing. "France is a body naturally
healthy and vigorous, but weakened by a bad regime," writes Morainville
in the beginning of 1789,[12] seeing the signs of this bad treatment in the
"too-numerous blood-lettings practiced by the leeches of the State" (the
Farmers- and Controllers-General).

This bad regime was also targeted by the author of *Bread of the people*,
who denounces a "lack of food," while another underlines the "sterility"
of the French body.[13] This is what the author of *Finance at the Point of
Death and the Hope for Its Cure* tries to explain when he notes that "the
fat, well-constituted lady" that the kingdom had been has been exhausted
by "maintaining her sixty lovers, sixty!" Similarly, a few days before the
meeting of the Estates, Le Maître complains: "France is now very sick . . .
It is of the greatest importance that we create a good constitution, that we
examine all the wounds of the invalid, that we probe everywhere, and that
we dwell mainly on the most painful places in its great body, particularly
close to that gravest of the crises affecting intestinal difficulties, that over-
abundant evacuation called *deficit*. That's what fills it with melancholy and
depression." [14]

Behind the playful aspect and the word games with medical imagery that
the pamphleteers write, it is the financial crisis that these texts describe
with wit. So much wit, in fact, that defenders of traditional monarchy become mobilized and reply on the same level. The disease is not so much in

the state of the kingdom as it is in the "heads of philosophers": "It is the head-that-spins. Let us beware of it, it is a contagious disease in France," writes one.[15] The author of *What We Have Surely Forgotten* sees a "state of languor," a "state of deficiency" in this "France that reads and discusses": "For a year the country has been inundated with writings, and every brain, more or less exalted, spawns every day new productions that future centuries will review only with astonishment."

It is in the midst of these polemics and these often confused uses of images of the body that the writings of Sieyès appear. In this sense, the Abbé presents himself straightaway as one of the "healers of the social body," a comparison quite common at the time from the pens of pamphleteers and one swiftly extended to the mandate of deputies elected to the Estates General. "How has this body politic, its constitution once vigorous, come to be so weak? It is up to you, gentlemen of this assembly, to return it to its first vigor, even to give it a new strength and to take measures to safeguard it forever from disease and corruption," writes Mossère in March 1789.[16]

Summarizing this problematic and taking up the language characteristic of the debates surrounding the convocation of the Estates General, *La Sentinelle du peuple* reports, at the end of 1788, this edifying story: "Friends and Citizens! Such singular news has been conveyed to me that I cannot keep myself from telling you about it. A lady of high rank, but of a poor constitution, had lived until this day bedridden and infirm. The charlatans who treated her, claiming that she was too weak to walk, and moreover had dizzy spells, did not allow her to get up. During all this time, there was dissipation of every kind in the house: stewards, chaplains, officers, lackeys, stable hands, maids, and companions, all plundered the invalid's income as they chose. The charlatans did not forget themselves . . . It was a public scandal: only the master was unaware of the disorder, and no one could or dared to tell him. A few years ago, however, a foreign doctor introduced himself, it is not clear how, into the house; and having succeeded in approaching the master, warned him that his wife's sickness was not as he had been told. Her great weakness came only from a badly designed regimen, from an overly severe diet, and above all from excessive purgings. In order to be restored to health she had only to develop her strength by exercise and exposure to open air. The husband, who wished only for his wife's best health, entrusted her to this doctor. Sure enough, despite difficult circumstances, he perceptibly improved her condition. But the leeches of the house, fearing reform, schemed so effectively that the master dismissed the doctor. The invalid fell back into the hands of the charlatans, who purged her again, and bled her again, and put her back on the diet so thoroughly, that finally it was evident that she would perish in their hands. Then the leeches of the house, being of the opinion that if the good lady died completely, they themselves would be dispossessed, called back the foreign doctor. From devotion to his profession, he returned without rancor and, although he found the invalid much weaker than before, persisted in his first opinion, and declared that she first had to be gotten up. Her clothes and shoes were sent for, but when the clothes and shoes were brought, nothing was found to fit. Since the period when the invalid had used them last, her limbs had taken other forms . . .

"After much reflection, the three Faculties were sent for, along with the heads of applied arts and crafts. As is usual with doctors, opinions were found to be strongly divided. In brief, there were two opposing sides. One said that it was only a matter of taking the actual size of the body and making new clothes to fit. The other, and these were grave and sedate people, maintained that one must work less radically; and that one cannot, according to the proper rules, clothe the lady without first having made an inventory of her entire wardrobe. All the closets were gone through, and, as the lady is of an ancient family, they found clothes of her mother, grandmother, even great-grandmother; Roman dresses, Greek headdresses, Gothic and Gaulish shoes; all of them had to be tried on her, without omitting her first bonnet and her first slipper. The lady, who was growing impatient, exclaimed that all this was useless. Since her youth, the fashions have changed, and she no longer wants to hear of collars, or of chains, even gold ones, or of steel stays, or whalebone corsets, or of lead weights in the sleeve . . . That's how things stand, and we don't know how they will end." [17]

All during this medical and domestic account of political life before the Estates General, the reader has recognized, in order of appearance, France herself, the bad ministers, the king, Baron Necker, then the representatives of the three orders of the kingdom. Above all, the anecdote poses one of the central questions of the debate on the Estates General: that of the relationship to history. Dive into the archives to find models, or else invent a new "art of society"? Sieyès—and this is where his intervention is shown to be decisive—deliberately opts for invention ("ideal abstraction," say his enemies), and in that choice, in that rejection of the weight of historic reference, his organicist vision of the body politic plays a large role. "That's how things stand, and we don't know how they will end," we read in *La Sentinelle du peuple* in the fall of 1788. It is exactly at that time that "Doctor" Emmanuel Sieyès intervenes.

"Let us imagine a society, one that is the best constituted and the happiest possible," writes the philosopher at the very beginning of his first published text, the *Essay on Privileges*, in November 1788. After this radical call to the imagination, innovation victorious over history, what does Sieyès see? "The great body of the citizens, natural in its movements, certain in its stride, confident in the performance of its actions, always in proportion with the soul of virtuous citizens." The Abbé, to take up the metaphors used in *La Sentinelle du peuple*, places himself resolutely beside the tailors of new clothes and the doctors of the dynamic body that has been put back on its feet, "natural in its movements." Yet what is the body of France in 1788? "Let me say frankly, I find it depraved, and the vice of it seems enormous to me. That is because it tends to debase the great body of citizens. Let us seek members that have deserved well of the body, and mark out the absurd folly of what has demeaned it." Sieyès diagnoses, in the image of the pamphlets of the time, an "antisocial disease" that puts his art to the test while undermining the great body of citizens. It is in the heart of the traditional kingdom, of history, of the "ancient family," that Sieyès locates the disease: privilege.

In this sense, his entire *Essay on Privileges* can be read like a clinical description of the vice introduced by privilege into the body of France: "In the heart of the privileged one is born the need to command, an insatiable desire for domination. This desire, unfortunately all too similar to the human constitution, is a true antisocial malady; and if by its very essence it must always be injurious, consider its ravages when opinion and law come to lend it their powerful support. Penetrate for a moment into the feelings of one of those privileged ones. He thinks of himself as forming with his colleagues a separate order, a chosen nation within the Nation. There no longer exists that body of which he was a member, no longer the people, the people who soon in his language, as in his heart, are nothing but a congeries of worthless persons, a class of men created expressly to serve, while he is made to command and enjoy. Yes, the privileged really come to regard themselves as another species of man. Their appearance becomes a particular characteristic in some races. In the depths of their heart, they reproach Nature for not having arrayed their fellow citizens into inferior species destined only to serve. In this respect, there exists an inveterate superstition that resists reason and even takes offense at doubt. A few savage peoples are pleased by ridiculous deformities, and pay them the homage due natural beauty. Among us, we hyperborean Nations, it is on political excrescences that stupid homages are lavished, excrescences that are more deformed and more injurious, since they erode and destroy the social body. But superstition passes, and the body it degraded reappears in all its strength and natural beauty." [18]

Sieyès uses sarcastic imagistic writing, very close to that of the pamphlets, to trace and describe the disease that takes hold of the body of the nation and divides it. The consequence of this disease is the excrescence, the monstrous deformity born from privilege that he had pointed out with the help of a botanical metaphor in *What Is the Third Estate?*: "It is truly a people apart, but a false people that is unable, for lack of useful organs, to exist by itself and that attaches itself to a real nation, like those parasitic growths that cannot live except on the sap of plants that they exhaust and deplete." The privileged here form, literally, an inchoate entity living at the expense of the body of the nation and degrading it.

With Sieyès, metaphors of the organism call for a goal and a method. The goal: the exclusion of the privileged, which is shown in his political strategy by his wish to exclude the privileged *absolutely* from representation within the Third Estate in the Estates General. His method: the desire to practice the social art in a new domain, against the past, in unknown political territory. The exclusion of the privileged and the practice of this social art are components of the fracture of 1789. For Sieyès, metaphors for the new political organism are constructed over against the old corporeal images. This break, in a body described as eaten away by the antisocial disease, can only be particularized using the vocabulary of therapeutics, but a therapy involving radical remedies. "The body politic is in disarray; it is dead," Sieyès states in his *Views on the executive methods*, the crux of his demonstration. After death must come regeneration, Sieyès writes. This is a violent and sudden radical remedy, accompanying the exclusion of the privileged: it is, most likely, the amputation of the morbid growth, as *What Is the Third Estate?* suggests. It is "excision of the oppressors from the body, a most desirable amputation," or "neutralization," which this same text calls for in its last lines: "It is impossible to say what place the privileged body should occupy in the social order: that is to ask what place we want to assign in the body of an invalid to the malignant humour that eats it away and torments it. It must be neutralized; health and the interplay of all the organs must be reestablished so thoroughly that the body no longer forms these morbific processes that are capable of polluting the most essential principles of vitality." [19]

So the organism regenerates itself. The excess of disease calls for a complete, resounding regeneration. Sieyès says it openly: "We owe our cure to the excess of evil. The excess of evil has done everything." From now on in his discourse images of beginning to walk again express the philosopher's hope dynamically. It is a walk that Sieyès practices in his writing with a forced pace, like a scout: "Everywhere I meet these moderate people who would like the steps toward truth to be taken one by one. I doubt that they know what they are talking about when they speak thus. They confuse the walk of the administrator with that of the philosopher. The former progresses as he can; provided that he does not leave the right path, we have only praises to give him. But that path must have been traversed to its end by the philosopher. He must have arrived at the goal, or else he could not guarantee that it is truly the path that leads there." [20]

Sieyès has given a goal to the path he imagines: "the great body of the citizens." Put back in the context of the winter of 1788–89, it is a matter of thoroughly preparing the Estates General for understanding how the social art of the philosopher can transform three separate bodies brought together under the authority of the king into one single "great body" made up of an infinity of little ones, one single nation made up of free individuals, released from old hierarchies. This path fragments the political writings: many possibilities are offered. Once again, we must locate Sieyès in the context of political commentary; once again, we find the metaphoric images of the body politic. For many writers, a king surrounded by the three orders can only be imagined, let alone described, by adopting or inventing (those are the stakes) organicist metaphors. The body, this "admirable edifice," this natural microcosm, offers its texture and its organization, susceptible to so many interpretations, to the description of the political macrocosm of human government.

The "Admirable Edifice" of Political Incorporation

Bénigne Victor Aimé Noillac, in a pamphlet dated 26 February 1789, *The Strongest of Pamphlets*, offers some of these possible metaphors, usefully gathered together for the "Constitution makers": "What is the foundation of monarchical government? It is neither a headless body, as in Poland, nor a bodiless head, as with the Turks; it is this: in France, the king is the head of the State; the armed forces are the hands; the magistrates form part of the head: they are the mouth, eyes, and ears; they are the organs of the brain, which is the king. The king is also the heart, the stomach; and the magistrates are the vitals. Nobles are the trunk that surrounds them; the people are the arms, the thighs, the legs, and the feet. That is the body of the State. Given that, what ought the functions of the monarch-brain-heart-stomach be? It is certain that the health of the body politic can arise only from the harmony of all the parts; if there is the least obstruction, the least failure in communication, then disorder erupts, fever catches fire, and it can lead the body to its complete dissolution." [21]

In this curious language that mixes reasonably precise anatomical designations with the analogical functioning of the relationships between the organs, Noillac composes a discourse on the harmony, indeed complementarity, of the hierarchy in the orders. His "monarchical government" is based on a just distribution of places and functions, first in society, then in the Estates General. The organicist metaphor seems to him a useful image. He even calls attention to it in the conclusion of this text: "Our descendants will say in 2789: 'It was a thousand years ago that a young king created a constitution for us, became a kind father at the head of a nation, over which he did not wish to reign except in concert with it: he gave back all the authority that had been handed down to him, so as to receive it newly granted.' The nation, moved, enraptured, grateful, hands it over to its father-king, saying to him: 'We place in your sacred hands all our rights; take the fullness of them. You are our Head, we are your Limbs; with you, we have only one heart and one soul.' "

This tale of the refounding of the French monarchy is based on a curious synthesis. It is a praise of the absolute authority of the king (the division into head and limbs) tempered by an intimate fusion, a renewed agreement (the common heart and soul of the monarch and the assembled nation). In fact, it is a reading of the past: Noillac constructs his ideal monarchy on a corporeal syncretism made from ancient and various references. It is what he calls the "monarch-brain-heart-stomach."

The first possible source, this *localist* vision of the French body (to each microcosmic organ there corresponds a bodily function that plays a political role, finding a place in the macrocosm of society), seems inspired by the politico-anatomical discourse of the Spanish physicians of the Golden Century. No direct quotation backs up this correspondence, but the similarity of the metaphors, especially given the distribution in France of writings by Juan Huarte, Montana de Monserrate, Andrés de Laguna, or Cristóbal Pérez de Herrera throughout the sixteenth and seventeenth centuries, tends to support these relationships.

Huarte, in his *Examen de ingenios para las ciencias* [English translation, "The Examination of Mens Wits," London, 1594. Trans.], one of the most famous treatises on the humours in the late sixteenth century, proposes a taxonomy of social groups divided according to the theory of the "wits of the body." The outcome of this corporeal categorization of the world is the prince, who appears as the ideal body: "Blond, well proportioned, of medium build, virtuous, healthy, and of great prudence." In Chapter 14 of his treatise, Huarte defines, with great anatomical and psychological precision, the portrait of the good king in this way: "Here is shown forth what distinctions of ability pertain to the office of King, and what signs he must have who will possess this manner of wit."

The second, Bernardino Montana de Monserrate, a doctor from Valladolid, describes the human body in the Vesalian tradition, as a *fábrica*. But with him, the bodily machine has been made into a fortress, visited floor by floor, room by room, while each humour, characterized and localized, presides over a precise function in the defense of the corporeal building against external aggressions.

A besieged fortress is also how the human body can be envisaged in *Europa, hoc est misere se discrucians, suamque calamitatem deplorans*, the main discourse of Andrés de Laguna, published in 1543. It concerns a Europe threatened simultaneously by the plague and by religious heresy. Images of "political disease" of the body abound in it, while Europe is presented as a woman who is "ravaged and fearful," pale and sad, mutilated by the blows given by the external enemy and undermined by internal listlessness. With Andrés de Laguna, it is a question of forging a medical discourse on the state of the city, comparing war, heresy and diseases, political disorders and harmful humours. He even goes so far as to rate bad ministers and charlatan doctors as equivalent.

The outcome of this incarnation of the social state is proposed by Cristóbal Pérez de Herrera in his *Remedy for the good and health of the body of the Republic*, a small work published at the very beginning of the seventeenth century. He too presents the *fábrica* threatened by all sides, but he is more concerned with describing a possible therapy. As a doctor, drawing out the metaphor to its conclusion, he practices an auscultation on the body of the state, beginning by palpating the liver, "the most sensitive" organ, dispenser of the nutritive elements. He continues by observing the eyes. Here we find the metaphor of the sovereign centered on the head/stomach pairing associated with the double function of command and of the foster father, a metaphor very generally associated with the office of the king. But Herrera goes further in the political localization of the body of the state, imposing the fiction of hierarchical organization and of the complementarity of the "Sovereign" (linked to the two vital organs previously mentioned) and of the four "Captains," associated with the four humours regulating the fluids that travel through the body (phlegm, blood, and the two kinds of bile). Good political, and thus bodily, equilibrium resides in the "agreement of the captains" and the "respect of the sovereign," a just regulation of the entrances and exits leading to the liver, a metaphor of harmony that should preside over the relations between the king and the nobles.

This rich corpus of medico-political writings offers quite a coherent system of explanations of the body (the theory of the humours) and of politics (the sovereign and the agreement of the captains), as well as a source abounding with metaphors (the body besieged by disease, then the intervention of doctors and an eventual cure). It is clear that the political monarchical system between the end of the sixteenth century and the Revolution draws a part of its images from this source to compose its authoritative discourse on corporality, a discourse that has become, with the passage of time, one of the pillars of absolutist legitimacy.

The king-head, for instance, is an ancient image in France, strikingly present from the founding of Bourbon absolutism during the resumption of royal authority under the reign of Henri IV. Ralph Giesey, in his book on royal funeral rituals,[22] quotes many examples of this, particularly Guy Coquille in his *Discours des états de France*. Coquille compares the monarch to the "caput" (in both senses of the word: the chief, the head): "The king is the chief or head and the people of the three orders are the limbs, and all together are the political and mystical body whose connection and union is indivisible and inseparable. One part cannot suffer sickness without the rest feeling it and suffering pain."

This organicist vision of the monarchy as an indivisible body politic under the command of the "caput" very quickly absorbs, during the course of the seventeenth century, the entire civil society into the person of the king. As Robert Descimon and Alain Guéry indicate: "Nothing resisted the royal Leviathan's power of incorporation."[23] Inspired by the work of

Thomas Hobbes, whose *De corpore politico, or, The elements of law moral and politick* was translated by Samuel Sorbière in 1652 under the title *Le Corps politique ou les éléments de la loi morale* [The body politic, or The elements of moral law], this representation introduces and establishes in England and France, concomitantly with the assertion of the absolute power of the Stuarts, then of Louis XIV, the organicist image of the king-head, supreme *Head* of the Church of England, *Caput* of the political organization of the French state. By way of his *Leviathan*, Hobbes fixes the terms of legitimate obeisance of the individual to the sovereign and, in the same way, of any body politic, *corporation*, town, or Parlement assembly. As Pierre Manent writes: "A new corporeal idiom of monarchical legitimacy in the framework of the nation had to be found: Hobbes developed it."[24]

In fact, the English philosopher constructs the "nonresistance" of subjects to royal authority, the hierarchy that constitutes sovereign power, starting from an embodied political representation: just as "each member of the body remains in obeisance to the will of all," the monarch, "who represents the entire body of the State, and who encloses in himself all strength and all virtue," possesses "a sovereign power like the head over each member of the body."

When all is said and done, the representation of this absolutist body is best illustrated in the frontispiece of the French translation of 1652: the head, crowned, and the hands, holding the sword and the scale, are given the king's own physiognomy, his *portrait*, while the body—towering over a town and its surrounding countryside, itself a metaphor for the territorial nation—is made up of a number of animated beings, subjects living with their own life inside the sovereign body, bringing their dynamism to it without exceeding or disturbing its clearly drawn contours. The embodied-nation and the landscape-nation form, in their union, the *range* of royal power: the bodies incorporated by the monarch and the lands attached to his crown. (See Figure 9.) Here, then, is the absolutist conception in all its power as Louis XIV's discourse illustrates it: "As we are to our people, our people are to us. . . . The nation does not make a body in France; it resides entirely in the person of the king."[25]

In this sense, these images of the body of the king represented crucial political stakes. This system of metaphors placing the king in command of the kingdom, attaching to him the Christlike incarnation of the mystical body in which all Christians come to be subsumed, but emphasizing too the interdependence of the organs, fills the ideologically regulating role

with the idea of "constitution." Authority, fame, and especially the continuity of the king's power are organically legitimate to it, just as its goodwill
toward all members of the body is required, and toward its own corporeal
constitution that groups all its subjects together.

This "capital" authority is again recalled by Louis XV in the speech
called the "Flagellation" in the Paris Parlement on 3 March 1766: "The
rights and interests of the nation, of which they dare to make a body separate from the monarch, are necessarily united with mine and rest only in
my hands." The benevolence of the head toward the members allowing the
general good health of the social body is the theme that Louis XVI, father-
king, foster father and physician of his kingdom, very naturally inherits.
This interrelation can be finely rendered by the image of the king-stomach,
the "Gaster" of La Fontaine, resuming a series of metaphors introduced
by Livy, developed by Rabelais, then Shakespeare (in the opening of *Corio-
lanus*), then reaching maturity among the fabulists of the seventeenth century, Baudoin and Audin. It is not surprising that this very metaphor again
finds its place in political discourse during the convocation of the Estates
General in 1789. The longed-for harmony of members of the body politic,
image of the king who nourishes the people in the midst of a grain crisis—
current events give life again to this image. Thus, the author of the *Essai du
patriotisme*, a work of historical compilation addressed and presented to the
deputies in the beginning of May 1789, comments at length on *The Limbs
and the Stomach*, a fable drawn from the third book of *Fables* by La Fontaine:

> That which the limbs think idle and lazy,
> Contributes more than they to the common good.
> The same applies to royal greatness:
> It receives and yet gives as much as it gets;
> Everything labors for it, and just as much
> Everything draws nourishment from it.

Brought up again when the three orders were being discussed, these inherited metaphors are still able to illustrate the hierarchical organization
of places and of the equitable distribution of functions. Naturally enough,
they are used by the supporters of tradition to address the issue of an
"assembled nation": three separate chambers voting by order, the whole
united but organized by "orders" within the body of the Estates General
under the authority of the royal *caput*. At first the Patriots, defenders of

one single assembly where each individual votes, endure these metaphors like just so many lessons come from the past. Noillac, in *The Strongest of Pamphlets*, gives a clear example of this traditional "ordered body": the "Grandees [*les Grands*]" are the trunk and the hands, strength and fist having long been linked to the valiant fighting nobility; the "Magistrates" are the mouth, eyes, and ears of the king, while the people are rooted in the arms, thighs, legs, and feet of the kingdom.

This hierarchical organization and this localization are both taken up again by Laurent-Pierre Bérenger, who, in *The Four Estates of France*, seizes on the image of the king-head-stomach in order to allocate the different orders in the French body: "As the limbs of a vigorous, healthy body are in perfect accord with the wills of the host soul of the head of that body, so does France docilely follow its king like a leader, loves him like a father. . . . Sire, meditate on the old fable of the limbs and the stomach; work equally for all the members of the body politic, since each member works separately and simultaneously, hence commonly, for its royal head. The harmony of the human body represents that of the State, . . . one single limb cannot increase except by the atrophy of its neighbor." Good neighborly terms between the "people-feet-hands," the "nobility-torso," the "magistracy-mouth-eyes-ears," and the "clergy-devotion" (the bodily metaphor does not apply well in the clergy's case, which should be all spirit) are the condition for harmony. Politically, it is translated into the vote by order in the Estates General.

But this hierarchical organization, along with this bodily localization of places and functions and the harmonious relationships that are to result from them, is quite quickly called into question by the defenders of the pre-eminence of the Third Estate. Now it is a "linked body" that the pamphlets set in opposition to the "body as the orders" of the traditional medico-political representation. In this sense, the writers of the Third Estate want to be in step with the medical science of the time, which mainly directs its researches toward the circulation of the blood and vitalist principles, as against the localist anatomy inherited from Latin medicine. These political polemics thus are also reflected in the tensions that now animate medical conceptions of the human body.

On one side, there was a science inherited from the works of the great anatomist of the century, Morgagni, founded on a taxonomy of diseases based on the bodily location of their symptoms and their points of origin, a science whose guiding principle remains "anatomical dispersion."[26] The

just division of the members of the body politic finds its traditional legitimization here.

On the other side of the battle of the doctors is the new "clinical medicine," which will soon find its manifesto in the *Traité des membranes* by
Bichat, a science that tries to detach pathological analysis from the bodily
regionalism of symptoms. The organism becomes a vast system of communication between an infinite multitude of vital principles, a communication
by means of which the human body develops the form of its indivisible
unity. Cabanis, Mirabeau's physician but also a statesman of the Revolution, future deputy at the Council of the Five Hundred, best defines this:
"Through the discoveries of the microscope we have learned that life is
everywhere; consequently, that pleasure and pain are everywhere; and, in
the very organization of our fibers, there can exist innumerable causes for
individual life, whose correspondence and harmony with the entire system,
by means of circulation of the blood and of the nerves, constitutes the 'I.'
Thus, whole, perfect little lives exist only in the totality of one single life
accompanied by all the great organs."[27]

This body of clinical medicine is a political weapon used by the Patriot
writers: in it, the principle of life is neither localized nor organized into
a hierarchy, but is a way releasing each section of the body from the ancient division of the organs, while the blood and the nerves reconstruct one
single, unique body, the indivisible "I," starting from the initial dispersal
of life. This nonhierarchical connection between each member, first principle of life, constituent energy of the "great citizen body" even before the
just paramountcy of the monarchical *caput*, and especially before the effec-
tual localization of privileges, thus meets its most precise correspondence
in the circulation of the blood, or in the vitalist conviction about the pre-
ponderant role of the irrigation of the nervous system.

It is not surprising that these two movements provide sources for the
corporeal metaphors of patriotic pamphlets. The circulation of the blood,
to begin with, is illustrated this way in the *Epistle to all humanity and to this
country in particular on true liberty*: "Our bodies, yours in particular, dear
reader, you must suppose to be a State in need of invigoration and support.
You know that every kingdom has a public Treasury, where the finances of
the State flow in and out. Now our heart is the treasury of our body and the
center of circulation of that precious material that circulates in all its parts
to support and nourish it. All its arteries, all its veins, and that prodigious
and inconceivable quantity of fibers and tiny ramifications that are lost to

the eyes, are like so many hands through which pass the funds of this treasury of the heart, your blood, which carries life and activity proportionate
to the needs and abilities of each of its parts. These same parts then carry
tribute back to the heart in equal measure, to begin again and thus keep the
entire great body living and well constituted. Thus in the body politic each
of the parts cannot refuse its activity without wounding itself, and harm-
fully altering the ensemble of the body, which can pursue a healthy regimen
only by the equal union of each of the parts with the happiness of the whole,
which, without this harmonious circulation, wastes away and languishes."

This metaphor attempts to shed light on the financial problem at the
origin of the convocation of the Estates General. The demand for the participation of all the French, not excepting the privileged, in the common
tax is transferred to the realm of the nervous system by Joseph-Antoine
Cérutti. The writer, in his *Memorandum to the French People* at the end of
1788 (at the same time as *What Is the Third Estate?*), comes to the defense
of the third order. This should no longer be a "dumb idol" or a "truncated
body." On the contrary, Cérutti wishes to return all its vigor to the Third
Estate, which would then impose itself as the true "vital body" to which
all others would be joined, "carried by its mass": "A wild vine with a body
full of vigor and sap until now was not able to produce any fruit, because it
was stifled by its sterile, devouring brothers. These must be removed. The
wine stock must be given the sun, air, and food that belong to it as much as
to the others. Intermediary bodies must in no way be interfering oppressive bodies." Cérutti thus proposes a reversal of corporeal hierarchy, one
he justifies by the vitalist principle endorsed by the people and above all by
him: "The body of the Third Estate must be brought to its full flowering,
or else the life-giving nerve that links together the parts of the State will be
severed."

After that, a path must be found to turn the Third Estate into the single
great body of the nation, even more boldly than Cérutti, Rabaut Saint-
Etienne, and Sieyès. Cérutti takes a first step in his address *To the French
Nation*, which was published in November 1788: "The Third Estate is the
nation, minus the clergy and the nobility," writes the Nîmes pastor simply.
That could pass for a truism if the proposition were not supported by a
more subversive chiasmus: neither the clergy nor the nobility can, in return, claim to be the "nation minus the Third Estate." From this simple
deductive logic, Rabaut draws a principle of incorporation: the Third is the
only body able legitimately to "absorb the whole nation," thus able to rival

the king-head of monarchical tradition: "The distinction of the orders is not in the definition of the monarchy, which is a State made up of a nation and a king. The nation is the body of which the king is the head. There is, thus, from the beginning, and in the nature of things, only one single body that is the nation, and, if the monarch distinguishes some subjects by prerogatives, he does not then intend to make bodies separate from the nation: to give them contradictory interests, or make them enemies, would be to say that the monarch wanted to carry disunity into his kingdom, or that the head wanted to separate the body into contradictory organs. That would entail the ruin of the State; it entails the sickness, then the death, of the body politic." Emmanuel Sieyès pushes this logic of incorporation to its limit: the Third Estate is the whole nation, the single "great body of the citizens."

To this putting back into play of the old political and social "localization" of the social orders in the body of the kingdom are soon added ironical attacks against the harmonious relationships that the upholders of tradition wanted to preserve among the hierarchical and ordered organs. In February 1789 a series of pamphlets appears attributed to the pen of Target, lawyer of the Third Estate, proposing a "rational marriage" between "Monsieur Third-Estate" and "Madame Nobility." The lawyer, in his *Plan for matrimonial alliance between Monsieur Third-Estate and Madame Nobility*, shapes a vision of the union of the orders placed under the uncontested authority of the husband. Here we find images of the body, since this authority is founded on the "prodigious corporeality of the husband, who, unlike the other two organs of the French body, is made up of twenty-three million members, which gives him an incomparable vigor."

This "marriage celebrated in the superb basilica of the Estates General by Monsignor Clergy," then consummated "in the nuptial bed whenever that copulation was deemed suitable by the husband" — a corporeal image of intimate union in one single, unique great body — is soon answered by the hierarchized metaphors of the separation of members. The spring of 1789 is busy with this battle of representations. In other words, for the writers of tradition, Madame Nobility should refuse the bodily humiliation proposed by Monsieur Third-Estate. The description is reversed, then, in the *Declaration of Madame Nobility on the plan for matrimonial alliance between her and Monsieur Third-Estate*: the Third is just a "shapeless mass, a monstrous colossus whose intellectual operations seem to be confused with matter, who can only laboriously and as if by dint of machines, produce the least masterpiece," while the body of the nobility assumes a "delicacy of complexion, suppleness of organs, subtlety of wit, circulating throughout its person from the head to the feet, from the feet to the head, diffusing an innate, infused science."

Another response to Target is even more biting. *The peaceable and good-humoured grievances of Madame Nobility*, despite its title, tears into the Third Estate without any subtlety: "Who are you? Not even half of a State, you are only a third of it." This response relies explicitly on the corporeal division of the kingdom: the clergy is the head, "eye and tongue" of the future assembly; the nobility breathes into it the "spirit of life," heart of the representation that "brings the body politic to life by the activity of an air that is always new"; finally the Third remains, classically, "messenger of all comings and goings, laborer at every machine-work, cook of all the humours," which places it between the legs, the arms, and the "lower belly." A relentless defender of tradition writes in January 1789, in the *Results of the Estates General predicted by Minerva*, these phrases worthy of the language of Louis XIV: "Consult human nature, and it will convince you that there must be only one head, the absolute master, as there must be only one king, one God and one Sun. . . . For if the head has such great precedence over each of the members, even over the ones most indispensable to the good health of the body, that is because its enterprise is the most extensive. It watches over the members, and obliges them to render each other mutual services and duties; it limits desires, commands the imperious passions of the unruly heart, of the greedy, gluttonous mouth, and satisfies the insatiability of the legs and arms, which, without it, would perish."

How Politics Speaks of Recovery: The Constitution of the Sovereign Body of the Nation

Sieyès offers another vision and soon employs another metaphor, that of the "great body of citizens." His essential achievement is to have attached this corporeal metaphor to the political fracture marked by that "magical title," National Assembly. Joseph-Antoine Cérutti very aptly recalls in 1791: "We are indebted to Sieyès for the sudden and salutary change. By substituting the word 'National Assembly' for that of the Third Estate, he has cut the Gordian knot of ancient privilege; he has separated the present epoch from those that preceded it; and in place of the three orders, sometimes divided, sometimes united, but always ready to dissolve, he has presented the indivisible body of the nation, made indissoluble in the perfect union of all individuals, with the aim of controlling everything by its mass. Finally the phrase 'National Assembly' has been one of those that magic uses to change the scene of the world, and cause an invincible colossus to rise out of the earth." [28]

For Sieyès, the constitution of this body, of this colossus, is directed by three conceptual projections, by a triple dynamic: adunation, representation, and regeneration. These words of healing were drawn by the philosopher from theologico-political vocabulary. Mechanical metaphors send Sieyès back to his sources in economics; bodily metaphors are haunted by his religious education.

"Adunation," a very rare word and already an exceedingly pedantic term by the time Sieyès uses it, is the act of uniting, of connecting unassembled fragments into one whole. It was in use until the sixteenth century (its antiquity underlines Sieyès's wish to create a suitable concept by adapting a completely forgotten word) in order to designate the grouping together of the apostles around Christ, or, at another register, the gathering together into the crown of France adjoining or enclosed duchies and principalities. To form one single body from many bodies, all equal, and each perceived in its individual vital integrity—that is the meaning of adunation with Sieyès. In fact, the Abbé absolutely denies the two privileged orders the possibility to "form a body," in the sense of absorbing the sovereignty of the nation. On the other hand, he enjoins the Third Estate and its twenty-five million individuals to embody just such a sovereignty, which would involve—or rather stress—spurning the separation and division into orders. Sovereignty, with Sieyès, is not divisible: it is integral in the nation, and embodied by the Third Estate. Adunation weaves metaphors of bodily unity, recovered from the breakup of the old hierarchies.

"Representation" is described by Sieyès as the only bond capable of uniting the great citizen body and the body of the National Assembly, "just correspondence," "true proportion," between two bodies without which sovereignty "would remain fragmented": "The deputy should think of himself under two aspects: as a member of the body of the Assembly that deliberates, and as member of the body of the Nation for which he legislates." [29] Sieyès is defining here a corporeal doubling that recalls the double sovereign body of the English or French monarchy: symbolic body / physical body of the king. "The many integral parts of one moral body are nothing separately," writes Sieyès. "Power belongs only to the whole. Thus, one should not feel that the Constitution would cease to exist in a country, at the slightest obstacle that arises between its parts represented in the body of the Assembly, since the Nation exists independent of every rule and of every constitutional form."[30] In other words: the nation belongs to the *symbolic body of sovereignty*, a legitimacy that transcends particular and historical constitutional forms. As for the National Assembly, it takes the form of this living, fallible, constitutional embodiment. It is the *real body of sovereignty*, elected by the citizens, alive with opinions and contradictory debates, but subject to "inconveniences," thus capable of being threatened by antisocial disease (that is, by division) and by the shocks of the parts. The members of the real body do not cease renewing themselves, while the symbolic body endures in its fundamental unity. Representation is a homothetic projection of a symbolic body onto a real body, a projection of the eternal, sovereign great citizen body onto the decisive, active assembled body.

"Regeneration" concerns an internal organization for this National Assembly. It is first of all a vitalist principle of animation—Sieyès compares the Assembly to a brain agitated with thoughts and praises its lively discussion, associating the legislative mechanism with the necessary and natural result of the "clash of opinions."[31] Regeneration is above all a means of constantly renewing the body of the Assembly. Sieyès insists many times on this point, summoning metaphors of the organism: the regeneration of the National Assembly must be carried out one-third at a time. The duration of a legislature is fixed by the philosopher at three years, but the body politic is renewable by thirds *every year*: "The oldest *triennat* [three-year appointment] will have been in session for two years; the second *triennat* will have been there for one year, and the new third, scarcely elected, will profit from the experience of its old colleagues, and will be useful in its turn, by making the most recent wishes of the people better known. The regeneration of the assemblies is a law of the greatest importance."[32]

This idea is essential for Sieyès, who returns to it in *all* his organizational plans for the public establishment, from 1788 to Year III. The annual renewing of one-third of the representative Assembly is comparable with him to the circulation of the blood continuously regenerating the organs of the body: "The constitution of a people would be an imperfect work, if it did not cradle in itself, as every organized being does, its principle of conservation and of life; yet should we compare its duration to that of an individual, being born, growing, declining, and dying? I think not. As with any organized body, a constitution must have the art of assimilating the material for its proper development; accordingly, we give it the ability to draw endlessly on its surroundings, in intellect and experience, so that it can always maintain itself at the level of its needs: it is a capacity for indefinite amelioration. That is its true character; it is not at all a principle of periodic, complete replacement. . . . It is not for us to say to our constitution: You yourself will appoint fixed times, and will deploy them with solemnity like so many signals of your approaching destruction. We could amuse ourselves by saying that, like the phoenix, it will be reborn from its ashes, but the rebirth of the phoenix is a chimera, . . . while the permanent regeneration of a Convention is an actual boon." [33]

Sieyès thus is opposed to the periodic renewing of the whole Assembly. The regeneration by thirds that he recommends implies the essential principle of the permanence of the real body of sovereignty. Here we reach the heart of the philosopher's organicist discourse, the core of his political system: as against the convocation—whether occasional or regular matters little—of a legislative organ by the executive power (for instance the Estates General or the English Parliament), and as against the ex nihilo election, even periodical, of a political assembly. On the contrary, Sieyès places right at the center of his plan for the organization of the public administration the permanence of the representative assembly, with this first vital principle: "Since the national delegates represent, in the great body politic, the equivalent of the personal will of each individual, it should be obvious that it is utterly preposterous to ask how often, how far apart the Estates General should be convoked. How prone we are to err, if we try to study any subject whatsoever not according to its nature, but according to old prejudices! Let us forget French chatter, and the alleged profundity of the English: would a sensible man ever imagine that not allowing men the use of their will and their intelligence except at intervals—as if the head and the brain worked only intermittently—could be of profound wisdom? Would anyone be bold enough to say that an individual must do without exercising his moral faculties, despite the most urgent necessity, because someone possessed of a contrary interest does not want to give him permission? The legislative body must be no less permanent than actual living bodies. The legislator is made to give life, movement, and direction to all that is concerned with public affairs. It is up to him to watch ceaselessly over the common needs of the social body. The legislator must be there for them, faithfully, constantly, and completely. . . . By such a simple arrangement, your legislature will in no way present the strange spectacle of a body dying periodically to resuscitate whenever it pleases an interest different from its own to return life to it." [34]

Emmanuel Sieyès thus builds the permanence of the Assembly of the representatives of the nation on the model of royal *continuity*, but in competition with it. For that very reason he now uses metaphors of organism: it is through corporeal continuity that the monarchy has built the representation of its majesty. In fact, of all the constitutional maxims of the French monarchy, none was more popular from the end of the sixteenth century—and during the entire modern era—than the enigmatic expression "The king never dies." The force of this maxim is to defy the physical, corporeal mutability of people, so as to oblige the mind to fix itself on a metaphysical, or shall we say "metaphysiological," reality: there is always a king, royalty is perpetual. Ralph Giesey examined the history of this representation of the royal body in France, noting the first mention of the famous phrase in *The Six Books of the Commonweale* by Jean Bodin in 1576, alluding to the fact that the king of France has effective power immediately upon the death of his predecessor. Bodin writes: "Certain is it that the King never dies, as it is said, for as soon as the one has died, just so soon the closest male in his stock takes hold of the Kingdom, and is already in possession of it before he is crowned." The American historian then traced the expression throughout the entire seventeenth century—and it persists into the eighteenth—via one particular image linked to the moment of permanence of the royal person: the image of the phoenix. Beginning with a commemorative medal struck in 1643 on the death of Louis XIII, Giesey finds this symbol again at each change of reign: "The Phoenix is born and rises up from the Ashes of its father by the Influence transmitted to it from Heaven and the Sun. In the same way the King has been miraculously given to us from above; And from the funeral bed [*lict funebre*] of his father, he rises to his bed of Justice [*lict de Justice*]. [In fact, the new king is first presented to the Parlement.]" [35]

This scene, recycling Christ symbolism, is a recurrent image linked to regeneration, one that is often engraved on the royal coinage of the "invisible interregnum." It recalls the phoenix of fable: it sets fire to its nest, which is also its funeral pyre, and is consumed in the flames; it burns in order to rise from the ashes in a new incarnation. Sieyès explicitly refutes this image of the phoenix, which he calls a "chimera," an "antique superstition," though he does use its regenerative resources. Sieyès is implicitly very aware of the transfer of corporeality that he is in the process of effecting by demanding the permanence of the National Assembly. Only he changes the terms of this permanence: he turns a mystical reincarnation into a permanent elective renewal. His "social art" allows him in some way to secularize a theological term: his regeneration is political, not miraculous. The miracle of the body of the king is transferred to the elective permanence of the body of the represented nation.

Thus, while *adunation* assures the gathering of individuals liberated from the old orders, and the formation of a single, eternal great body of citizens—the nation; while *representation* links organically the real body of the National Assembly to this symbolic body of the nation; *regeneration* breathes perpetuity into the representative assembly. This double corporeal perpetuity, of the nation and of the Assembly, comprises for Sieyès the *national sovereignty* at the same time as the model of *royal sovereignty*. The king had one single perpetual body, his symbolic body, but, thanks to the principle of hereditary succession, he continued his real body into his successor by the continuous circulation of royal blood. In like manner, the nation possesses a redoubled perpetuity: the great body of citizens on the one hand, and the represented body reelected continually by thirds on the other hand, while the circulation of the blood gives life to national sovereignty.

Marcel Gauchet, in *La Révolution des droits de l'homme*, has already insisted on this parallelism between the corporeal metaphors in Sieyès and monarchic representations. In two passages,[36] Gauchet describes this transfer of bodily representations from one sovereign to the other, from the king to the assembled nation: "Representatives [have] become the visible, fallible, mortal body of the invisible, perpetual body of the Nation." It must be acknowledged here that my own work owes much to this simple sentence. Yet it seems to me that Marcel Gauchet establishes this very true idea on the basis of a suggestive but incomplete reading of Sieyès. First of all, he assumes an unconsciousness on the part of the philosopher, saying that he uses royal metaphors of the body "without realizing it, probably," as if it "were not a question of a conscious plan." But Sieyès is aware of his borrowing; he knows that by speaking of the "permanent regeneration" of the body of the Assembly, he places himself in the area of royal representation, the realm of the old "chimera." Fracture is all the more marked since it is "embodied" thanks to the captured weapons of the French Absolutist tradition.

Second, Gauchet connects this transfer of corporeality, as transfer of political power, to the seventeenth of June 1789, when, from the very mouth of Sieyès, the representatives are declared "a National Assembly, one and indivisible." Marcel Gauchet is right on this point: the effects of the principles of adunation and representation, which destroy the separation of the orders so as to unite the individual wills of each into one single body, have presided over the transfer of corporeality. From an ordered and hierarchical division of organs inside the body, Sieyès makes a constituted whole, tied into one organic, indivisible unity. Yet to see nothing but that date of 17 June 1789 is to forget the second part of Sieyès's plan, not adopted, it is true, by the Assembly, but the real culmination of the philosopher's corporeal metaphors: the regeneration by thirds proposed in *Views on the executive methods*, written in 1788. Gauchet comments on what history did indeed decide to preserve: the fallible body of the National Assembly. Yet, in the regenerative plan established by Sieyès, the body of the Assembly must not only be the visible, fallible, and mortal body of the invisible, perpetual body of the nation, but also must earn this perpetuity itself, this durability that places it in direct rivalry with the body of the king: a body that has become perpetually political.

The Diffusion of a Political Philosophy by Metaphor, or Birth of the Giant People

We must plunge again into the language of the pamphlets and brochures of political commentary, when, in the course of the spring and summer of 1789, the writers of the Third Estate inscribe in the minds of their readers the radical ideas of Sieyès by adopting and developing even further the organicist metaphors that the philosopher deliberately used. As a first example of this diffusion by metaphor of political philosophy, the radicality of therapeutic care is an extremely widespread metaphor among the defenders of the Third Estate. The traditionalist pamphlets, even if they often tolerate as remedy some more equitable distribution among the orders, still lead their readers toward harmony through respect for the hierarchies of the inherited body politic. The Patriots trace their path to harmony through processes that are often violent and in any case radical: "The body politic suffers diseases as does the physical body; and the first agitation of it causes great disorder through the whole mechanism. But these violent ·shocks, as soon as they are subdued, procure a state of health more flourishing and firmer than before. The body comes out of it purged, relieved of the weight and vices that hindered its progress."[37]

Surgical images are next to be made use of, taken directly from the language of the *Essay on Privileges* or from *What Is the Third Estate?*. Here, for instance, is the advice that Margot, "the good old lady of 102 years," gives to the deputies of the future Estates: "Cast off all your *esprit de corps*. Open your eyes only on the necessity of simplifying everything that ignorance and avarice have multiplied. See everything, and see it large, Gentlemen of the Estates, spare nothing; *cut to the quick*; let the invalid cry out. When the incision is done, he will thank you. If you leave some gangrenous, putrefied flesh, the invalid will die, and everyone will weep. Restore to proper function twenty-four million arms that have the gout and are paralyzed; slice open the bellies that swallow everything, and digest nothing, with their cakes, their consommés and their sugar; cut away those stomachs that are good for nothing except eating." [38]

This metaphoric language is choked with violent, bloody, morbid images, then images of recovery apt to impress the reader. The historic break, that decisive march of which Sieyès talks endlessly, we hear about in terms of bodily representation: the nobility is a "tumor that, without being an integral part of ourselves, swells and feeds only at the expense of the body." This break is revealed in the French body with a "completely open wound," in the clinical description of the operation of excision of the "tumor," of the "wart," or of the "ulcer" of privilege: "Consider a clever physician, taking in hand an invalid whose limbs are covered with ulcers. This physician does not lose time in applying different balms to each wound: he cares only about destroying the cause of the disease. Where does it reside? In the blood. He bleeds it and purges it; the wounds heal." [39]

The rupture is embodied in this vision of a complete regeneration of the French body, complete because painful: "The people is a polyp that is born again from its very wounds; and that is the time when the nation, after exposing the wretchedness of its injury, will bring into play the means and resources of its regeneration." [40] This schema is quite obviously derived from Christ imagery, which the Patriot writers, annexing biblical narrative to their discourse, are prompt to emphasize. *The Passion, the death, and the resurrection of the people* offers to the Third Estate, as its title indicates, a path of glory in three stages. In every instance, corporeal metaphors—suffering, sickness, death, and then regeneration—are its indispensable embellishments.

Nevertheless, as with Sieyès, after radical remedies comes a new constitution, the moment of fulfillment of the "great citizen body." Just as with the philosophical Abbé, mechanical images are sometimes evoked to designate this new organization: "This burning glass [the Constitution] must be made up of an infinity of little mirrors that, each preserving all the activity of its partial focus, are all united into one common focus to produce the greatest intensity of heat known." [41]

But the organicist metaphors remain the most explicit, and permit the sovereignty of the great citizen body to be expressed. The first possibility, a radical one, is the substitution of the nation for the king as sovereign head of the body politic. The author of the *Principles of government simplified and reduced to seven natural units, conditions for a good Constitution* scarcely treats royal authority tactfully; he takes up the old Absolutist corporeal schema and reverses it to the profit of the people, thereby defining democratic government: "What we call the constitution of the human body is the totality, the intimate union of all the parts; they say that a man is 'well constituted' when he enjoys a healthy, vigorous organization, without deformity; *mens sana in corpore sano*. [A healthy mind in a healthy body. Trans.] It must be the same for a political body. But the human body has only one head to watch over the preservation of all its limbs, and all the nerves or sensitive parts of the body end up at the head as at a common center where the spirits are produced that are then distributed through all the parts of the organism in order to give it life. In the same way, the body politic should have only one head to execute its laws, to watch over prosperity; that head should be the common center of the forces, general movements, and life of the social body. Thus it is the nation, which created the head that it has given itself, that should determine the laws that this head should follow in directing the national interests."

A nation-brain faced with a king, who is ruled by it, and becomes mouth, eyes, ears, or executive arm of the body politic: the traditional bodily images are reversed. But the strangest story, and the most illuminating, is written on 23 April "9871" (1789): the "terrible adventures of Strong-arm the giant." The storyteller (who has unfortunately remained anonymous) imagines that France has just had three children by an unknown father. The first, born at the normal time, "seemed well formed, with the exception of the head, which was monstrous because of its small size. They called it Strong-arm [*Fort-par-les-bras*]." The other two children, "miserable abortions, sons of the darkness that had raped the mother," are called Paladin, for "the one who looked very like chimeras or centaurs," and the Enchanter, for the "Protean monster." In these three children, we recognize the Third Estate, the nobility, and the clergy.

A long tale of adventure follows that ends, as it must, in a fight to the death. In this fight and its consequences we recognize a "social art" worthy

of Sieyès: "O strangest of wonders! the two heads, of Paladin and the Enchanter, coalesced into one. Strong-arm, who was keeping watch with an
attentive eye, had perceived sinister portents: the forehead of the two-
headed monster that plans infamies undeniably frowns and grows ugly by
intervals. This unnatural ugliness is so excessive as to inspire him with indignation. There is nothing surprising, then, in the anger of Strong-arm at
the sight of these two joined heads that fill him with horror. He leaps to his
scythe . . . and with one single blow slices the Enchanter and Paladin in
half, through the middle of the body.

"Those who have seen the first hot-air balloon rise from the gardens
of the Louvre can form some idea of the way those two upper halves of
the bodies proceeded to be lost in the imaginary spaces, with their robes
and their cloaks. The other two halves of the bodies of Paladin and the
Enchanter, which in the centuries of tyranny were called disdainfully the
'lower parts,' and that we others, we anatomist historians, call the noble
parts, remained standing on the earth, and presented to the gaze of Strong-
arm a new spectacle that made him weep with tenderness. These two parts
were composed of a close-knit group of small giants, male and female, all
naked, all thin, all small children, almost powerless and immobile. Little
by little he saw their eyelids open, their hearts beat, their little feet grow
steady; and they stretched their little arms toward him, as if to embrace
him and form with him one single, unique unity.

"Strong-arm stood there all dreaming, in the ecstasy of admiration,
when, all of a sudden, the Genius of the mountain slipped into his brain
through the eyes . . . Scarcely had the Genius entered his brain, than he
fertilized all its immobilized seminal power. Strong-arm's little brain grew
wonderfully like a Montgolfier balloon, but instead of being filled with wind
or gas or smoke, it summoned into existence healthy, burning, luminous,
majestic ideas. It built a hearth of light so ardent that gleams, and even
lightning flashes, often came out of his eyes; and the giant found a singular pleasure in listening to the crowd of little Genii who chatted amicably
with him. From that time on, this multitude would be able to declaim by
way of his mouth. Strong-arm meantime began to take on a truly human
form, and soon his features were ennobled by all the good sentiments from
his brain. He had the deep gaze of a true philosopher, the stern forehead of
a law-giver, and the august and frank demeanor of a good patriot. Strong-
arm tenderly pressed these thousands of little beings to his heart: 'We are
all equal, all brothers, all citizens; may impartial laws unite us forever! The

earth, our common mother, will see to our needs, and liberty, who gives birth to all the virtues, will grant us the delights of heaven.'"[42]

This story, fanciful and unlikely at first reading, discloses an exact meaning in the context of the metaphorical distribution of Abbé Sieyès's political texts. The pamphlets can be tricky—the most unbridled fantasy is often pertinent to the political situation, while the most unlikely turns out to be a coherent discourse. For a reader used to deciphering political parables, the blow of the "scythe" by Strong-arm is a chivalric version of the exclusion of the privileged from the sovereign representation demanded by Sieyès. The crowd of paralyzed "little giants" escaping from their shackles and joining into one single, colossal whole around the heart of Strong-arm is a magnificent image of adunation: the great national body made up by the joining of all the little individual bodies. Strong-arm becomes henceforth the organ of representation and expression for this multitude that surrounds him. Finally, transformed by this intensity, the giant finds a face, a brain, a voice, eyes, and will be able to live "forever": a metaphor just as exact and vivid as the regeneration so dear to Sieyès. Purged of its growths, balanced, adunated, regenerated—here, constituted at last, is the great citizen body imagined by the philosophic Abbé and made clear by the language of the pamphlets.

Dividing the Territory: A "Skeleton" and "Muscles" for a New Nation

This way of "giving a body" to the political hope born from the convocation of the Estates General is not without consequence for the rhetoric and even the thinking of the Revolution. The language forged to tell of the break of 1789—and this constitutes no doubt both its strength of conviction and the originality of its "reading" of the world—mixes apparently contradictory registers of discourse: abstract reflection, political ambition, constitutional will, administrative, juridical, and financial reform, the restoration of public morality, and the metaphoric narrative of renewal. Just as the plans for reform in spring 1789 are charged with organic metaphors, just as Abbé Sieyès's philosophic writing tried to lead minds toward the truth by conceiving the abstract ideal political system in terms of the forms of the regenerated body of national sovereignty, so from now on most of the organizational plans urged on the new France by administrators use these metaphors of the body—a true incarnation of the immense work of reorganization effected over the entire breadth of the kingdom, from the parliamentary rules of the National Assembly to the reorganization of the nation, from the deputies to the Federates.

It is precisely that embodiment that is described in spring 1790 by the author of a work with the evocative title *France compared to the human body*. The author is proposing a reform of the military system: an original scheme for distributing garrisons through the national territory, promotions to be based on merit, increased pay—the classic repertory of proponents of a reformed army, one reform among so many others. But here is what appears as a preface to the work, as prelude and foundation for the reform demanded, a vision of the new France drawn thanks to the Constitution developed week after week by the deputies of the National Assembly, a France ordered by laws, restrained by decrees, balanced by a new division of territories: "It might seem unusual to some people that I take the liberty of comparing France to the human body," our author disingenuously confesses, "but that will not seem surprising when we examine the map of the divisions that has been made according to the *départements*. This division gave me the idea of the skeleton and the muscles that make up our body. The departmental borders outline our musculature, and the mountains are our bones; the major rivers our arteries; the small rivers the veins that fill our interior; the four cardinal parts, North, South, East, West, our limbs; Paris—the ordinary seat of the two sovereign powers—our head, and Versailles the stomach, where an excess of food just missed causing the destruction of the entire body, but that patriots have fortunately put on a diet since October 1789." [43]

This dream vision, "wonderful incarnation," introduces an important debate of the winter of 1789–90: how should the kingdom sensibly be divided? And more important, how should the regeneration won in the political order thanks to the daring ideas of Sieyès and implemented by the decisions of the National Assembly be communicated to the whole territory of the nation? This reorganization of the territory,[44] crowned by a success that still endures, impelled a movement of revolutionary unity during the winter, spring, then summer of 1790: new municipalities, departmental administrations, and national guardsmen take an oath of loyalty to the nation in innumerable "federations" distributed across the entire country. Soon, on 14 July, the anniversary of the taking of the Bastille, a National Federation assembly gathers almost four hundred thousand people on the Champ de Mars.[45]

This time of unity, this spreading of fraternity, of reform having a field day, is fertile of quite suggestive organic metaphors, burgeoning and revealing, of the new *national body*, a way of prolonging the rich debate preparing for the meeting of the Estates General. The abolition of privileges, on the night of 4 August 1789, had made this new order of things necessary and urgent. With the suppression of provincial privileges, a secular organization collapsed, and a more rational dividing up of space was imposed: the establishment of an electoral system based on national representation, complete reorganization of districts and administrative authority. This imperative vitality of reorganization is openly expressed, almost with anguish, by Bureaux de Pusy following the abolition of the old privileges: "The gothic colossus of our old Constitution is finally reversed. The nation applauds its fall; but the first instants of joy were followed by fear and alarm. The laws are without force, the tribunals without authority, the troops mistake disorder for patriotism, and the people mistake license for liberty. It is only by establishing provincial assemblies and municipal assemblies that you can cause order to be reborn, . . . it is only by reestablishing the force of a great national body that you will cure France of its anarchic ills."[46]

Vigilance and a call for regeneration, fear of disorder, and hope reposed in a new territorial organization, old colossus defeated but new giant still held in the hesitations of infancy—the words that Bureaux de Pusy hurls at his colleagues the deputies on 27 August 1789 are soon taken up by the Assembly in its order of the day. "Let a committee be formed to present a *plan of municipalities and provinces*, such that France organized in this way will never cease to form a *whole* uniformly subject to common legislation and administration." That is the motion that the deputies adopt on 7 September 1789, under the impetus of Emmanuel Sieyès. The Abbé will be the soul of this committee, and the division of land is an affair that he personally endorses: "He held to it as if to an exclusive property, and I remember that, when I asked him if he were not the principal author of the division of France into departments, he answered me animatedly: 'The principal! better than that, the only!'" reports Mignet, one of the witnesses of the last years of the philosopher.[47] After having cured the socio-political body of France by the abolition of old divisions of orders and the creation of one unique national sovereignty, after having animated this great body by the triple dynamics of adunation, representation, and regeneration, now Sieyès is attacking another sickness, that of territory in disorder, that of the old provinces. Again, then, organic metaphors take over the reform project of the philosopher Abbé.

Sieyès, however, is not the first to propose a new organization of the territorial body of the kingdom. In 1764, the Marquis d'Argenson had held forth at length on "the art of better distributing force in the national body," suggesting a more rational, less uneven division of France by trying to unify the diverse administrative, ecclesiastical, judiciary, and fiscal jurisdictions.[48] These were divisions and privileges that made the administrators of the end of the ancien régime fear a "despotism of provincial particularisms," the fragmentation of the kingdom into as many "ethnic personalities" as there are defined and divergent regional stereotypes. Le Trosne is aware of this, and, in 1779, still in that project of reform unique to the Age of Enlightenment, wanted to "unite millions of individuals over the surface of the French Empire to make one single body."[49] Another fear, also making the rounds in books of the prerevolutionary years, is the weakening of the local intermediaries of the central government, the harmful overlordship of the provincial magnates, and the consequent loss of effectiveness of the French administrative system. Turgot wants to fight this by means of a more vigorous chain of responsibilities foreshadowing the regeneration of the revolutionary administrative body dear to Sieyès: "In order to banish this spirit of disunion that increases tenfold the work of the servants of Your Majesty, and that necessarily and prodigiously diminishes your power; in order to substitute for it on the contrary an impulse of order and union that would make the strengths and means of your nation concur with the common good, gather them into your hand and make them easy to govern; a plan must be conceived that would connect them by a patent common interest into one single body joined gradually, from the feet to the head of the kingdom, that would join, I say, individuals to their family, families to the village or to the city to which they are attached, cities and villages to the district in which they are included, districts to the provinces of which they are a part, and provinces finally to the State."[50]

Sieyès, then, is not the first to propose this "plan" of which Turgot dreams, nor is he the first to wish to apply metaphors of the body to it. Effective distribution of force, union into one single body, and harmonious relationships of the organs with each other—these are the domains of activity of the organic images of territorial division. Sieyès is the first to foresee this new distribution systematically: he continues to come back to it throughout the summer and fall of 1789.

Between 22 July and 2 October 1789, Emmanuel Sieyès composes four works in which the territorial and administrative division of France occupies an important place: the *Preliminary of the French Constitution*; *Some*

Constitution ideas applicable to the city of Paris; the *Statement of the Abbé Sieyès on the question of the royal veto*; and the *Observations on the report of the Constitution Committee concerning the new organization of France*. The philosopher offers a series of extremely coherent arguments to the constitutional committee entrusted with the project of dividing the kingdom and to Thouret, its most consistent spokesman. In fact, the perception of space synthesizes for the philosopher the two movements of the healing of the social and political body of the nation.

In the social body, healing involved an exclusive incorporation of the Third Estate, thus abandoning to the past the division of society into privileged orders. In the same way, the division of the kingdom is devoted to renouncing provincial privileges. The intention is to promote an identical equalization of conditions, whether this equalization concern the social body or the territorial body. Moreover, Sieyès applies the same dynamic process to geography, having assured the political sovereignty of the nation: "France must not be an assemblage of little nations that are governed separately, just as no class of citizens hopes to keep in its favor a partial, separate, and unequal representation. Such a thing would be a monster either in politics or in geography; it has been destroyed forever. . . . France is a unique *whole*, composed of integral parts; these parts must not have a completely separate existence, since they are not merely joined, but parts forming only one single whole. This difference is vast. . . . It leads from dismemberment into castes and privileges to the great organic whole of the new kingdom, and it is essentially important to us.

"If we let this occasion go by, each class of citizens will eternally guard its particular class values [*esprit de corps*], privileges, pretensions, jealousies. France would never reach that political *adunation* so necessary toward making only *one* great people regenerated by the same laws. All is lost if we allow the municipalities, or the districts, or the provinces that are established to be thought of as so many republics united by links of force or common protection. Instead of a general administration, which, working from a common center, would uniformly affect the remote parts of the Empire; instead of basic principles provided by all the citizens and working together to culminate in a National Assembly, which is charged only with interpreting the general will, we would have, inside the kingdom, bristling with every kind of barrier, nothing but a chaos of customs, rules, and prohibitions peculiar to each locality. Instead of a regenerated ideal, this beautiful country would become odious."[51]

Adunation, representation, and regeneration—this dynamic trinity thus takes charge of the French territory, trying to transform "regional esprit de corps" into one "great organic whole." It is these two corporeal images that we find again and again to designate, in all the discourses, all the sermons, and all the speeches, the two conditions of French geography, its Before and then its After—the "odious monster," then the ideal reorganization. Geography, then, is perceived and then discussed by Sieyès using the same procedures and the same metaphors as society or politics.

The originality of the "geographical" thinking of Sieyès consists of re-grouping the representative system in the territorial division as the French administrative system. The philosopher calls this the "ascending move-ment of representation," a way of delegating legislative power in a series of stages proceeding from the base of simple active citizens to the summit of a permanent National Assembly, and the "descending movement of the Ad-ministration," a delegation of executive power downward from the summit of the "citizen king" to the municipal and cantonal administrations. It is a double movement that animates the kingdom, and Sieyès summarizes it in an illuminating organic metaphor: "The public establishment is a kind of body politic, which, having like the human body a goal and means, must be organized in somewhat the same way. It must be endowed, then, with the faculty of *wanting* and with that of *acting*. The legislative power, the ascending functions of all the assemblies of citizens up to that of the Rep-resentative Body, defines the first; and the executive power, the descend-ing functions of the General Administration toward the agents that receive orders and assure their execution, represents the second of these two facul-ties."[52] Thus, the correct allocation of space, in Sieyès's reasoning, estab-lishes the just balance and effectiveness of government: the pertinence of territorial division, modeled on human anatomy and faculties, assures the functioning of the state.

These principles are immediately furnished with concrete propositions, meticulously detailed and calculated allocations. Upon the submission of the Constitutional plan to the city of Paris at the end of July 1789, the philosopher assumed the role of surveyor and administrator. "Eighty prov-inces or departments," "seven hundred twenty communes or cities," and "six thousand four hundred eighty districts or cantons" make up so many administrative and representative units "into which the kingdom can be di-vided." At each stage of this division, Sieyès places a representative assem-bly and an administrative body, a system of calculated hierarchical intermediaries that—either in the case of legislative delegation (assemblies by canton, then municipal assemblies, then departmental assemblies joined successively to delegate national representation by levels) or in the case of executive organization (central, departmental, municipal, and cantonal administrations)—proposes a *life-giving flow* essential to the healthy functioning of the French body, and creates a space for the mutual carrying out of "wanting" and "acting." "The committee expressly requests two levels between the two extremes: to wit, between the electorate where all the citizens are and the representatives in charge of making the law, between the localities where the lowest administrators are and the center occupied by the ministers and the king. If two levels be thought excessive, consider the extent of France and its population. Reduced to a third of their size, these two bases could easily be content with one single intermediate level. But how could the enormous mass of 26,000,000 souls not need a longer lever to raise it up? In other words, the two intermediate levels are not a matter of choice but of necessity." [53]

Necessity of equilibrium: to suppress the unequal geographic distribution of conditions and privileges while at the same time unifying each division following the same criteria for the entire kingdom, to keep the Administration sufficiently close to those administered, and to restrain the possible excesses of "popular collectives," to vote on laws of national interest but to stay tuned in to local demands. Sieyès's project seeks a kind of optimum: divisions that do not threaten the so to speak organic unity of the country, yet do establish intermediate levels of government capable of satisfying, as well as controlling, each citizen. The organic *indivisibility* of France is thus founded on a just and equal *division*, a paradox that the Constituent Assembly resolves with the help of an often-used formula: "to divide in order to unite." No longer are the divisions of France characterized, as they were in the days of the kings' absolute power, by the maxim "to divide in order to rule." In the words of Mona Ozouf, it is a matter of creating "a division that is not a division," [54] a division that would be capable of "obliterating the chaotic and divergent traces," of "destroying the iron yoke," of "undoing the swaddling clothes" of the old provinces yet not reviving the "fear of a dismemberment of the national body."

Sieyès comments metaphorically on this double obstacle, introducing into the political language of the summer of 1789 images that will continue to haunt the debate over the departments and animate the hope of the federations. On one hand, he wants to forget the old France, a too-rigid division that he compares to a cell block, a prisonlike cloistering: "The old ideas that I fight lead to nothing less than to this species of *political Carthusian hermitage* so mourned by the recluses of privilege."[55] On the other hand, he tries to lead back to reason the oversensitive "provincialists," those men frightened by the possible "dismemberment" of France, by the "parceling out" of different ethnic identities of French regions: "Every new age has its infantile qualities, is easily frightened, unthinking, and alarmed by words; it lets its imagination wander in ways that observers find quite amusing. This is not a fable; I have seen responsible people torturing themselves with the notion of a dismembered, cut-up province. I do not know what was going on in their brains, but I would be tempted to guess that those words produced in them the feeling of horror that one experiences at the sight of a body that has been torn apart, of blood flowing. It is only after some minutes that one can say to them: 'Be assured, the ideal lines that the engineers draw in a province will not knock down any house, will not cut through a mountain, let alone a human body; not one tree will be felled, not a single blade of grass crushed. . . . Again, calm yourselves.' 'But, will I stop being a Breton, or a Provençal?' 'No, you will still be a Breton, still a Provençal, but you will soon congratulate yourselves along with us on acquiring the quality of citizen.' We will all one day bear the name of Frenchmen, and will be able to take pride in that name not just in the theater, because that name will designate a free man belonging to a great sovereign body."[56] [The word *français*, "Frenchman," comes from *franc*, which means both one of the ancient Franks and also "free." Trans.]

The bad and good uses of metaphors of the body intersect in this text by Sieyès tracing the main lines of opposition in the constitutional debate over the division of the kingdom. After furnishing these arguments for the partisans of the Constitutional committee, Sieyès quickly sees his propositions, his images, and his metaphors escape from him: on 29 September 1789, the entire National Assembly seizes the words of his discussion, and the "provincialists" try to occupy that territory, waging a battle inch by inch against the proponents of a system of 80 departments, 720 communes, and 6,480 cantons.

The Debate of the 'Départements': In Search of the Organic Units of the French Body

It was Thouret, a Norman deputy close to Sieyès, who launched the debate on 29 September 1789 by giving a report to the Assembly on "the fundamentals of proportional representation" and "the establishment of administrative assemblies." In this double objective we recognize a distribution allied with the ascending and descending movements of which Sieyès speaks. The report, in fact, is sheltered throughout under the aegis of the philosopher, from the metaphor of the great whole "adunating" the particular movements ("With one common spirit, one single spinal column, all the impulses of the body politic will move"), all the way to the most concrete propositions summarizing the committee's project submitted to the vote of the deputies: "First article. France will be partitioned into divisions of 324 square leagues each, as near as possible, starting from Paris as center, and proceeding in every direction to the borders of the kingdom. These divisions will be called *departments*. Article 2. Each department will be partitioned into nine divisions 36 square leagues in area, as near as possible. These divisions will bear the name of *communes*. Article 3. Each commune will be partitioned into nine divisions four square leagues in area, as near as possible. These divisions will bear the name of *cantons*." [57]

Despite the precautions of all those "as near as possibles" — a means of being less rigid, and sparing the most sensitive deputies the fear of dismembering a body — even so, the mathematical rigor of the project shocks some sensibilities: won't the provincial boundaries be completely ignored, mishandled, broken by an abstract principle? At the end of the ancien régime, maintaining "ethnic personality" is an extremely urgent requirement on the part of the provinces. It draws its discourse from the mixed sources of the physico-psychological characteristics of each "race" making up the kingdom, from the folklore of clime and climate applied to the character of peoples, or from the defense of certain provincial privileges (the exemption from specific taxes, for instance), local ancestral customs, or the right to convene provincial parliaments, those powerful hereditary assemblies in the Dauphiné, Brittany, Languedoc, or Provence, four provinces that, by themselves, pose the main problems and claim most of the particular statutes.

We find in this context, transferred from the socio-political body to the geographical body, the localist legitimization of the organism: the good functioning of a whole depends on the just harmony and on the traditional hierarchy of its members. Not a fusion based on the loosening of the traditional provincial "esprits de corps," but a harmonious juxtaposition of those customary corpulences. The debate that is begun on 14 October at the National Assembly reveals the importance of these resistances to the new division of the kingdom.

The dividing of the kingdom is attacked as an "abstract and useless dismemberment" that some deputies want to avoid by consigning it to the name of some other perception of space. First, there is a "provincialist" perception, illustrated by the speeches of the Abbé Gouttes, Brillat-Savarin, Pellerin (for Brittany), Bouche (for Provence), or Ramel-Nogaret (for Languedoc): to keep the customary divisions broad and vigorous enough so that they constitute living federated autonomies around the central power. According to this logic, the distribution into many departments of an old province is regarded as bodily dismemberment, an "adventurous fragmentation" as the Abbé Gouttes states, or a "political assassination" as Brillat-Savarin denounces it.

Next there is the "municipalist" perception, clarified by the discourses of Aubry du Bochet, Gaultier de Biauzet, or Dupont de Nemours. Here the logic is "cellular" and intends to maintain all the vigor of the national body by regenerating its smallest units, a way of bypassing departmentalization by contracting the smallest unit of life of the kingdom. Gaultier de Biauzet expresses this forcefully: "It would be germane to declare first by a decree that on principle cities have the right to name their heads themselves; this is the only means of propagating the movement of reform throughout the entire organism, which at this time is disordered and without strength. Once this article is decided, your greatest work will have been achieved."[58]

Provincialism and municipalism are not incompatible, harmoniously gathering together little cells of life and autonomous members of the national body, destroying the unity of the departments by the alliance of enlarging and contracting the different constituent lives of the kingdom. Baron de Jessé illustrates this: "The work of the committee seduces at first by an almost geometric precision; but it would be long and difficult to apply, and dangerous as well, for the circumstance is pressing. How can the feeling that attaches the inhabitant of the provinces as much to the name of his soil as to the soil itself be overcome? How can the feeling that links each citizen to his particular city, to his own life, be destroyed? One will say perhaps that these loyalties must be dissolved; but such an attempt over the whole political organism must be attempted only when it has recovered enough health and strength to support this operation. I conclude in favor of the preservation of the division by provinces, and on the provisional organization of municipalities."[59] On 19 October, however, despite these numerous warnings, the majority of the Assembly adopts the "departmental idea" proposed by Thouret "to become the basis of the work connected to the partition of the territory." It is a first victory for Sieyès, but the debate quickly resumes. This time, now that the principle of a new division has been accepted, it is a question of determining the scale of it.

Four plans are submitted for the approval of the deputies: the 80 departments originally proposed by the committee, the 30 departments suggested by Pison du Galand, the 200 by Aubry du Bochet, and the 120 departments advanced by the Comte de Mirabeau. It is not difficult to see in the two proposed extremes the clumsily disguised resurgences of the provincialist and municipalist discourses already rejected by the majority of the Assembly: the 30 divisions of Pison du Galand form the federated body of the old provinces, while the multiplication of departments favored by Aubry du Bochet is a means of confining the territory to the principal cities of the kingdom as fundamental cellular units. Though they are quickly dismissed, these two propositions testify to the persistence of the discourse hostile to the departmentalization of the French body. Whatever the option chosen, this debate on the division of the kingdom relies, in that month of November 1789, on three main arguments, all variations on the metaphoric registers: mechanical images (the department as cogwheel — useful or useless — of a political machine that everyone wants to be the simplest possible), architectural symbols (the departments as keystone of the communal house), and organic representations (the department as limb, muscle, skeleton, or cell of the great national body).

A first group is anxious to preserve absolutely the central coordination of the French organism. In the name of the superior vigor of centralized bodies as opposed to federated bodies, of life distributed from a heart as against life at the periphery, some deputies wonder if reducing Paris to one twenty-fourth of the country will stifle the most essential organ of the kingdom and thus diminish the motive force and its circulation. The Marquis de Gouy-d'Arsy puts the deputies on guard in an explicit way: "A king is only the collection of all the executive powers. A National Assembly is only the union of all the legislative powers. A capital is only the coalition of the interests of all the provinces. And just as one cannot wound the sovereign without outraging each citizen that he protects; just as one cannot detract from the decrees of the Assembly without violating the rights of the people that it represents; just so one could not degrade a capital without degrading the provinces, since that capital exists (as a man's heart reveals at every instant with the sanguinary flux) only to collect and circulate all the productions of the territories of the Republic." [60]

Special provision must be made for the capital: not only will the territorial partitioning take Paris as its central point, but it will have to confer on the capital substantial territories for expansion—a large suburban area is included in the department. Moreover, it has been shown to be indispensable that the descending movement of the administration start from, and the ascending movement of electoral representation culminate in, the heart of the kingdom. This fundamental justification of French centralization will never really be called into question again at the time of the debate.

Duport then introduces a second obstacle to confront the territorial division proposed by the Constitutional committee: the fear of an overload of intermediaries. Do not the four spaces defined by Sieyès—the nation, the department, the commune, the canton, each established on one of the rungs of the representative or administrative ladder reorganizing the kingdom— multiply the assemblies and the number of intermediary authorities? Don't they restrain the movements of the national body, don't they dilute wills and actions? "The kingdom, I repeat," Duport avows with some alarm, "is ready to dissolve and perish by the loosening of all its parts. The multiplication of levels of election and administration will deepen the disease and not cure it. The constitution seems on its way to being completely denatured." [61]

Martin, deputy of Franche-Comté, echoes this: "What need do you have, Gentlemen, of this third cogwheel that is being presented to you under the intermediary title of Commune? The department, the largest of the divisions, and the canton, the most confined, are sufficient to broadcast and accomplish the deeds initiated by the heart of the kingdom. That certainly is all that we need, and all that suffices for us; two levels, and let us stop there. It would seem, Gentlemen, that a people such as the French must not be moved so frequently or manipulated so assiduously." [62]

Finally, the last observation presented during this rich debate, and undoubtedly the most constraining: would not a demographic, rather than geographic, basis produce a fairer departmental distribution? Verdet makes this proposition on 3 November: "Renouncing the partition of France into squares, and having no consideration for the surface area of the divisions, I think France should be divided according to its population, the only sure, equitable basis. Let us divide the kingdom into parts of relatively equal population." [63] This approach takes the living presence of human bodies as a true scale, even if it means injuring the territory by establishing uneven spatial divisions. Thus the Duc de Lévis asserts: "I urge in favor of giving representation to the arms, not to the shields they carry, any more than to miles and acres. Population is the only rule that fixes the division of the kingdom, in homage to the individual to whom we have given back his rights."[64] The speeches of Gaultier de Biauzet, Sinéty, and Barère justify this. A heart or a head left in the kingdom because of a vigorous centralism, movements preserved by a better distribution of intermediaries, a more equitable demographic division—these are the three objections posed to Sieyès's plan, a way of envisaging the proper bodily constitution of French geography under widely different circumstances.

Mirabeau, the rival of Sieyès and Thouret, arms himself with these objections and tries to reformulate them into a plan of 120 departments. This fight about the departments in the autumn of 1789 quickly limits itself to this opposition of numbers—120 departments rather than 80—which is also an opposition of organic metaphors. Pison du Galand announces on 10 November 1789, while withdrawing his own plan for territorial division: "Gentlemen, the two main systems of political organization of the national body have been presented to you; one by your Constitutional committee, the other by M. the Comte de Mirabeau; I propose to discuss them successively and to submit ourselves to the result of a vote." After having struggled victoriously against the old "localist" doctors of the French sociopolitical body, it is Sieyès's duty, supported by Thouret, to fight a bodily representation that competes with national space.

Mirabeau, in two long speeches on 3 and 10 November,[65] proposes a vigorous synthesis of the chief oppositions to the plan of the Constitutional committee: he suggests taking into account the distribution of population, criticizes the useless multiplication of intermediaries, and urges respect for the traditional provincial entities. (The deputy in fact speaks in the name of Provence, the major source of regionalist opposition.) The orator is particularly clever, since his division into 120 departments answers all the questions raised. With more divisions and greater flexibility, his distribution effectively combats the "abstraction" of Sieyès's ideal geometry: "I have taken geographical maps, I have traced out those equal areas of three hundred twenty-four square acres, and what have I seen? Here, an entire surface area was composed only of moors, deserts or hamlets; there, in an area of the same size, many great cities found themselves brought close together; everywhere I found territories of equal size, but nowhere did I find either equal value, or equal population, or equal importance. I vainly tried to redo the divisions in a thousand ways; I put the same surface areas sometimes in triangles, sometimes in squares, sometimes in rectangles, but in vain I exhausted all the geometric figures; the unequal distribution of population, of resources, and of traditions mocked my efforts."

This pragmatism, if it discourages geometry, inspires Mirabeau with another way to divide. First, to maintain the provinces, to respect the traditional regions: "It is not the kingdom that I want to divide up, but the provinces; and just that alone makes most of the difficulties vanish. . . . The result of a similar division is easy to foresee: the departments will be formed in my plan only by the citizens of the same province, who already know it, who already are united by a thousand connections. The same language, the same customs, the same interests will keep them connected with each other. Innovation will be, if I may say so, less radical, and reconciliation will be easier. The dismemberment of the provinces, so imperiously required by a new order of things that abolishes the old privileges, will no longer excite any commotion in the great national body. . . . Here is a division that permits accommodation with prejudices and even with mistakes, which is desired equally by all the provinces and is founded on previously known connections."

Mirabeau, in a way, molds his departmental division onto the old provincial skeleton, using partition into many units smaller than the committee's departments so as to respect regional boundaries. Leave the Bretons to themselves, along with the Provençals or the Dauphinois, by offering them departments shaped to their liking, little cells of life animated by traditional relationships, even if it means modifying them later, while division can cut more at its ease into "deserts," "moors," or less susceptible parts of the French territory. This would mean establishing the division of the kingdom with a keen awareness of the sensitive areas of geography and of national customs, which the orator indicates by recalling the "prejudices" and "mistakes" inherited from the past. Regions have a history.

Sieyès fears history, and endlessly frees himself of the past: the body of which he dreams when he looks at France is new, without engorgements or lesions, one that has just been born to politics. Mirabeau fears history just as much, but only in order to respect it more, to integrate it into his plans of reform. The body politic of which he speaks has already aged when it appears on the revolutionary scene; the deputy takes as his foundation an old organic Constitution to be reformed from within.

This concern for provinces incarnated in 120 territorial divisions endows Mirabeau's plan with other arguments. First, it suppresses an intermediate level in the electoral and administrative distribution, the much-disparaged step that leads from the local to the departmental, the level that Sieyès or Thouret calls the "commune" and that the Assembly will finally adopt under the name of "district." Mirabeau ceaselessly denounces this "rung of rotten wood," this "superfluous and complicated organ": "I regard this intermediate as disastrous. According to my plan, communication would be direct, from towns and villages to the capital of the department, and from each department to the executive power and to the National Assembly. It seems to me that there would then be more unity, more of a whole; that the body would be better connected, and its movements both more regular and more rapid. . . . Having destroyed the aristocracy, it is not suitable to keep departments that are too large, since their administration would be, for that very reason, necessarily concentrated into very few hands, and all our concentrated administration would soon become aristocratic. With 120 departments, on the other hand, one could grant the benefits of being the capital to a greater number of towns, and open the career of public affairs to a greater number of citizens."

An administration closer to those administered, that is what Mirabeau wants, knowing that he makes the most pragmatic deputies happy by add-ing another suggestion that is sometimes evoked, the demographic division of the territory, which the orator justifies in these terms: "I would like a material division, and de facto suitable to the localities, to the inhabi-tants, to the circumstances, and not a mere mathematical division, one that seems almost ideal, but whose execution seems impracticable. . . . It is not through the effect of chance that men are distributed on the earth. Popula-tion supposes subsistence, subsistence designates prices, prices rule taxes. The single given of population, then, disposes many others." Here again Mirabeau takes account of history: the provinces, the bureaucratic aristoc-racies, the unequal distributions of population—all these elements are in-herited from the past, and the geography of the Provençal count demands these imperfections, refutes the ideal. Little cells evolving with the "nature of the Frenchman" (even a periodic redistricting of the departments is fore-seen, following the evolutions of demography, customs, or trade), living cells, pliant, close to each other—that is Mirabeau's perception of geogra-phy, a historicized space in a reformed but inherited body.

Thouret has to respond in a coherent, rigorous, and copious manner if he hopes to convince his colleagues. In three important speeches on 3, 9, and 11 November 1789,[66] he develops the arguments introduced by Sieyès in his works from the summer, and refutes one by one the counterpropositions of Mirabeau. He is abetted, moreover, by the undoubtedly decisive interventions on 3 and 11 November of Rabaut Saint-Etienne and of Target, who had come to support the philosopher Abbé and his ideal Constitutional plans. Thouret wants first to reassure the deputies: the provincial boundaries agree most often with the 80 new departments carved out; no traditional organic unit will be dismembered, nor will the villages be placed under the unfair tyranny of the towns. He then answers Mirabeau, attacking him on three specific points he judges "unrealistic, dangerous, and imprecise": the "variability" in area of departments determined by population, their "evolutionism" in time, and the "absence of communications adequate to the good health of the French body." He firmly reasserts "departmental necessity," proposing through the 80 departments *units of a definite but nonetheless insufficient life*; they are divisions capable of propagating energy toward the local (a "definite life") but *necessarily* (an "insufficient" life) calling for a regathering of the territory into a regenerated great whole, a single and unique organism that is truly alive. Finally, he does not hesitate, in trying to win the agreement of his colleagues, to warn them against the overtimid pragmatism of the preservers of the old provinces; he wants to draw minds and votes toward a greater boldness, the "more ideal geometry" defended by Sieyès and the committee, the will "to make the French body as good as new": "If the prejudices of one, two, or three provinces had to prevail over the general, demonstrable good of the entire kingdom; if the parts did not have to give way reasonably to the whole; or if the nation as a body had no authority over its different members; finally, if those who through their deputies work to make constitutional decrees then refuse to submit to them, we would have no political association, no legislative body, no regeneration to hope for, no constitution to be made. Let us say it clearly: we would not be a National Assembly because we did not want to be, and because after having won the title, content with the word, we did not want to take on the spirit or the daring of the thing, or to fulfill its obligations."

Warned against the "provincialist mind" of Mirabeau, the deputies are reassured, and put in a position to choose between half-measures and the complete regeneration of the country; they are won over to the Constitutional committee's plan, provided some alterations are made. On 11 November 1789, they divide France into "seventy-five to eighty-five" departments and thus, as the author of *France compared to the human body* writes, offer a "skeleton" and "muscles" to the great national body.

The Discourse of the Federations: A Body Joined
Together by the Revolution

The principle of the division of the territory, although subject in its practical applications to consultation with different provinces and all the many municipalities (the "committee of territorial division" of the National Assembly receives ample correspondence [67] in the months that follow 11 November 1789), produces generally enthusiastic press reactions, particularly, of course, from the Patriots. "Recasting the human race" one writes, "a mute giant suddenly become eloquent" writes another, and "marvelous bringing-together" a third.[68] This "molten metal receiving in the mold of the artist all the forms that he means to give to it" is an infinite source of metaphors, which the author of *Short and simple method to learn easily and retain without difficulty the new geography of France* summarizes: "At present, we say: 'We are brothers, we are limbs of the same body politic, we all share the same meal, we join our hands all through the same dance.' " [69]

But in all this proliferation of images, it is undoubtedly Camille Desmoulins who comes up with the rhetoric that is most apt and most imaginative. Sieyès proposed a plan, Thouret convinced the deputies, and Desmoulins undertakes to spread its images and its qualities, and to describe its repercussions; he transforms his newspaper into a chamber of metaphorical echoes. *Les Révolutions de France et de Brabant*, a journal created in mid-November 1789, at the exact moment of the adoption of the division of the territory, punctuates its weekly publications with news of the new departments, and comments, number after number, on the movement as it is sketched out, then gathers momentum, finds its energetic flux, and reaches a civic apotheosis: the desire for federation. Not an American-style "federalism," rejected by all the French administrators as contrary to the proper national centrality, but that dream formulated by Sieyès of a great whole formed from many particular, liberated, fraternal lives, of a united country divided into so many equal and harmonious departments. Camille Desmoulins spreads this dream and, at the same time, perceives its echoes. His journal lives this federative process like an intimate experience, a salutary initiation to the "free, new France."

Desmoulins sets the tone in the opening of the first issue: "Are there still distinctions of provinces? Can we still be divided, or penned in, or cantoned? Are we not one great family, one great body, one same household?

Are there fences, barriers in the field of May? Are we not all under the same tent? Saint Paul, who was eloquent two or three times in his life, writes admirably somewhere: *all you who have been regenerated by baptism, you are no longer Jewish, you are no longer Samaritans, you are no longer Romans, you are no longer Greeks, you are all Christians.* That is how we have just been regenerated by the National Assembly: we are no longer from Chartres or from Montlhéry, we are no longer Picards or Bretons, we are no longer from Aix or from Arras; we are all Frenchmen, all brothers." Placed from the start under the auspices of the regeneration of French space, Desmoulins's pen does not subsequently stop copying out the federative oaths of the various national guards of departments, does not stop disseminating metaphors of the organic unity of the great national body brought together by fraternity.

For example, Desmoulins adorns issues 9, 10, 11, and 12 of his journal, in January and February 1790, with the "Picture of the departmental divisions," and more than thirty times, between November 1789 and June 1790, reprints accounts of provincial federative pacts in Grenoble, Lyon, Nîmes, Pontivy, Strasbourg, Nantes, Carcassonne, Arras, Dijon, Draguignan, Montélimar, Orléans, and Avallon, while the rise in power of the federative process is outlined in the pages of *Les Révolutions de France et de Brabant.* At first an endorsement of the new territorial division of November and December 1789, these pacts take on another dimension following the parliamentary meeting of 4 February 1790. On that day the king himself, received "without ceremony," came to the Assembly to associate himself with the constitutional work of the deputies, who extended this newly acquired harmony by a civic oath, taken by all the representatives: "I swear to be loyal to the nation, to the law and to the king, and to maintain with all my power the constitution decreed by the National Assembly and accepted by the king." From that point on, the provincial federations, hitherto impromptu, formally organize themselves in response to this joint call of the two sovereigns of the nation, the king and the Assembly.

At that instant is born the idea of one great National Federation gathering toward Paris "federates" delegated by each department, the ceremonial embodiment of the "division-union" of the kingdom adopted previously on 11 November. The idea works its way through propositions that Desmoulins reports in detail. Gossin, for instance, spokesman at the Assembly for the committee of territorial division, delivers a lyrical and largely disregarded speech on 12 January 1790: "When Theseus had united in Athens the different tribes of Attica, he instituted, in memory of that event, the great Panathenaic festival. Today, as Frenchmen regenerated by a new fraternity, we find restored to us the power to propose a much more beautiful festival, one destined to recount the union of many provinces into one single people and one single family."

This suggestion, not accepted by the deputies, is however taken up by certain Parisian districts: the Saint-Eustache, for instance, in the beginning of February; then the Cordeliers, in the beginning of March, which suggests starting a national fund to build a "National Capitol" where the Assembly would convene, on the site of the old Bastille, and associating with it, every 14 July, a "commemorative festival" that would receive delegates from 83 departments—a way to "regenerate the great nerve of the Body politic," as the address to all "equal citizens and brothers" points out.[70] Soon private individuals like the Marquis de Villette take up this initiative, imagining a convivial metaphor of new fraternity ("The capital, from one end to the other, will form only one immense family. You will see a million people sitting at the same table"[71]), or the Baron de Cloots, opening wide the unity of the national body to emissaries of the human race: "The Roman conquerors amused themselves by dragging vanquished peoples tied to their chariots, but you Frenchmen, by the most honorable contrast, invite foreigners from all the regions of the earth to raise joyfully the Liberty bonnet as an earnest of the imminent deliverance of their unfortunate fellow citizens."[72]

The provinces themselves finally welcome the plan of the great National Federation, a plan integrated into an organic vision of French regeneration, as this address of the administrative council of the National Guard of Rennes demonstrates, dated April 1790 and printed to be sent to all the National Guards of France: "Let us establish among ourselves the most intimate relationships; that all the forces of the Empire, directed toward the same end, united in the same body, make local insurrections and foreign insults henceforth impossible. The new division of the kingdom makes it easy to carry out the project that we submit to your deliberation. France, divided into departments, will next be subdivided into districts, then into municipalities. Everywhere will be found the civil power that commands, the representative power that delegates, beside the military force that executes. Let a federative pact unite all the militias, and let all these partial federations be immediately joined in one great General Federation. Then, dear fellow countrymen, each national guard will be no more than a division of the great civic army, just as each department is only a member of a great national whole. And if some part of the French organism were attacked by formidable forces, you would see fly to its defense, like blood flowing to a menaced body, detachments sent by all the other departments of the kingdom. Our enemies also, reduced to the fortunate impotence of drowning, will lose their harmful effects, just like the sickness that enfeebled France before its complete regeneration. In order to achieve this general federation, we propose that each department send emissaries, bearers of the wishes of all the groups of citizen, into the capital of the Empire, to the heart of France, so that the federative pact might be formed under the eyes of the legislators of the nation." [73]

As if in echo, many departmental national guards take up those same words in the beginning of the spring of 1790. Mona Ozouf has emphasized the power of this movement, whose current, having issued from the National Assembly at the heart of autumn, begins to flow back dangerously toward its shores a few months later. The Assembly, up till then occupied by its constitutional tasks and no doubt frightened by such a deployment of soldiers and speeches, by an epic that could carry it away, had not passed legislation about any National Federation, and is now put in the position of having to choose. Deputations from the cities of Arras and Orléans present themselves at the Assembly on 12 and 19 May 1790, to demand official recognition of the federative movement by the organization of a festival of national opulence.

Finally, on 5 June, the deputies, not without voicing some anxieties and many conditions, decide to recognize the necessity of a general confederation. A deputation from the commune of Paris, introduced by Bailly in person, carried the decision: "Ten months have scarcely passed since the memorable time when, the walls of the Bastille having been conquered, a sudden cry was raised: *Frenchmen, we are free*. On the same day, a more touching cry made itself heard: *Frenchmen, we are brothers*. Yes, we are brothers, we are free, we have a country. Too long bent under the yoke, we finally resume the proud posture of a people that recognizes its dignity. *We are no longer either Bretons or Angevins*, our brothers from Bretagne and Anjou have said; like them we say: *we are no longer Parisians, we are all Frenchmen*. You have sworn, representatives of the people, to be united by the indissoluble ties of a holy fraternity, to defend, to the last gasp, the constitution of the State. Like you, we have taken this august oath. Let us, it is time, let us fashion from all these individual federations one general confederation. How beautiful the day of the alliance of Frenchmen will be!"[74]

The first commemoration of the Fourteenth of July is thus set beneath the double symbol of the regenerated colossus recovering "the proud posture of a people that recognizes its dignity" (the body righting itself on the ruins of the Bastille) and of the union of citizens into one single national whole (fraternity engendered by the constitutional work of the Assembly). This dual vigor of emancipation and fraternity finds its metaphoric transcription in the images conceived by the Abbé Sieyès, in the giant Strongarm carrying the body of the man liberated from his chains, the man of 14 July 1789. The brothers united by the new territorial division are the members of one single organic whole, one that gathers together when four hundred thousand citizens assemble on the Champ de Mars on 14 July 1790.

Camille Desmoulins tells about this National Federation by way of anecdotes, moral fables, and epigrams, all of which retrace a progressive decompartmentalization leading the French body from atrophy to blossoming. The original, repulsive image of this tale, as also with Sieyès, is a "monster in politics," a "gothic" organization of space: a Carthusian hermitage, with each monk living in a sealed individual cell, refusing all relationships with the world. This is the architectural equivalent of the localist and hierarchical body defended by the partisans of privilege and of the orders. Desmoulins returns to it many times, explaining the federation movement no longer as the blind man recovering sight (an image dear to the philosophers of the Age of Enlightenment) but as the Carthusian monk guided toward his human brothers. The metaphor appears in the fourth issue of the newspaper, in mid-December, when the first provincial federations are discussed by the journalist. The image is repeated in number 13, literally haunting the mid-February issue, when the convents are opened and freedom restored to the regular clergy. Desmoulins's writing is thus in step with the revolutionary history of anticlericalism, which it is easy for the journalist to transfer to another tale, that of a federative movement that swells with multiple oaths and myriad orations.

In the beginning of July 1790, the presence of the released Carthusians finally serves to organize the tale of preparations for the Parisian federation on the Champ de Mars. The parable now culminates as the story of French fraternity: "What can we say of these Carthusians? Some of them had for forty years seen only the silent walls of the great sepulcher of the Rue d'Enfer, and now, led by M. Gerle, they find themselves carried to the center of the great united body of the nation, in the midst of such excitement, amongst a quarter of a million people! I would like to see pictured on those tonsured and unhooded brows all the sensations that those men, whom their law-giver Saint Bruno had left with only their stomachs, and to whom the National Assembly had just returned the use of all their senses by a cataract operation, now experience at this spectacle. They came to pick up their shovels not now to dig their own graves, but to bury the aristocrats; they came not now to learn how to die but how to live in the midst of their brethren. Curiosity surrounds this phenomenon of 1790 with a multitude of women who take a naughty glee in exciting the modest blushes of Bruno's children. They dance around them. Constrained from taking part in the joy and from entering into the round dance, the good Fathers, who have already recovered their eyes and heart, begin to feel again that they have legs and hands. Now they lack only a brain, but I hope that the federative oath will produce its effect there."[75] The forgotten, despised body, held under the yoke of the monastic rule, finds its functions one by one and recovers its senses from contact with the united French brothers (and sisters): regeneration and fraternity meet in a parable of the path of the defrocked Carthusian, one where the body narrates political evolution.

Desmoulins weaves an abundance of such metaphors around the federative movement, associating, for instance, the many patriotic donations offered to the National Assembly by the provincial federations with a rich circulation of blood, just as, some months later, the arrival of the Federates at Paris is described at length by the journalist as an influx of new blood to the heart of the national body, an influx that initiates the recovery of vital energy: "The Federates, on their feet since five in the morning, were dying of hunger. It was an occasion for manifesting sentiments of a fraternity that had been unknown until that day. Everyone hastened to toss loaves of bread out the window, which were caught on bayonets; they handed down cold meats, wine, brandy, liqueurs. Women and girls came out of their houses to carry every kind of food and refreshment to the Federates. Sisters, without fearing incest, received patriotic embraces from their brothers that did not have the tepidity of brotherly kisses."[76]

The great French body is fed, and blood, food, and pleasure circulate thanks to rediscovered fraternity, the *living chain* that Desmoulins, along with so many others, also followed in the preparations for the Champ de

Mars, on the "national construction-site," where was shown "a scene so moving, so animated, so immense; in which all bodies whirl in the ballet of the joining of the orders by the brotherhood of labor; in which the ci-devant marquise, ungloved, holds the hand of a charcoal-burner in her white hand, the coquettish milliner clasps the hand of a Carthusian monk, and the vegetable-seller takes hold of the hand of a dandy. They all are pulling a wagonload of earth, their outstretched arms serving as the shafts, climbing, descending, running, while dragging weighty carts."[77]

The journalist then sees the living chain form again as the national body in the military procession of the Champ de Mars on 14 July, and finds it again in the evening, at the balls and dances: "All the Federates demonstrated the dances of their country, leading the Parisians in lively arabesques in which the province and the capital were intimately intermingled. Cries of elation came from all mouths, and the uncountable dances swept all citizens into an immense movement that looked like a long spinal column, pulsing with intense energy, filling all the senses at once."[78] This sensual bodily chain, animated by the federative movement between the winter and summer of 1790, comes to expression in the common oath of 14 July, taken at noon throughout the kingdom, at two o'clock in Paris: "When the sound of the drum announced the taking of the oath, men, women, children, the elderly, all raised their hand toward the altar with joy, crying out, *Yes, I swear it*. After this oath, it was a touching spectacle to see all the citizens throwing themselves into each other's arms, promising themselves liberty, equality, fraternity."[79]

Indissolubly joined into one organic whole, this national body born from the debate over territorial division, then carried forward by metaphors forged at the time of the federations, can now be brought together with the French colossus that issued from the reading of *What Is the Third Estate?*. This union of a *colossus set upright* and an *organism profoundly linked together*, conceived by the Abbé Sieyès between the prophetic texts of winter 1788 and the organizational plans for the kingdom of summer 1789, illustrated first by images born from the taking of the Bastille, then from the federative movement—this union is the ideal bodily form of revolutionary political sovereignty.

PART II

The Narrative-Body, or History in Fiction

3. Regeneration

The Marvelous Body, or The Body Raised Upright of the New Revolutionary Man

Regeneration is a concept that is charged with a singularly rich meaning at the end of the eighteenth century, so rich that the word could itself handle the tale of the origins of the Revolution: the story of political breakup, the moment when, under the pressure of the event, man would be transformed into someone else.[1] Thus the language of regeneration places the corporeal metaphor, the "narrative-body," at the center of political beliefs and writings. Isn't revolutionary France the very image of a body ready to rediscover its original vitality? Isn't it ready to raise itself up from that torpid sickness that the political writers of the ancien régime described? This politicizing of the concept of regeneration, although obvious in the words of 1789, is recent. In fact, before 1730, regeneration was still used only in religious and medical vocabularies. Explicitly linked in religious discourse to the double return to source—*baptism*, the "re-birth" (re-generation) of man into religion, and *resurrection*, in which the just are raised up into the eternal kingdom—regeneration was also linked to scientific vocabulary since at least the sixteenth century and Ambroise Paré's experiments on the "regenerative faculty" of the flesh after operations on wounds and ulcers. But little by little, during the course of the last years of the ancien régime, regeneration came to designate rebirth in all its aspects—physical, moral, then quite specifically political. I propose to write here about the enigmatic history of a word, a word that by 1789 seems devoted to the metaphoric tale of the Revolution but, a few years earlier, had not yet left theological treaties or

works on medicine. How and when does the creative interference of vocabularies begin to make itself felt by describing the historic rupture in terms of
regeneration? That is the question I wish to follow through the "lexicologi-
cal tools" of the eighteenth century, those voluminous, thick dictionaries
that the sages of the Enlightenment bequeathed to scholarship.

How a Word Enters into Politics: Regeneration of the Faithful, Regeneration of Wounds, Regeneration of the French People

My point of departure, at "the horizon of 1700," can be found in the
Dictionnaire universel by Furetière, in the 1690 edition. The brief definition of "Regeneration" here is very restrictive. The dictionary allows only
the theological meaning and chooses its version: "A theological term used
only in this phrase: 'He has been regenerated in the Holy Font of Baptism,'
to mean, he has been spiritually engendered anew, he has become a child
of the Church." With this as a model, many important dictionaries recognize regeneration only in its religious sense. The *Dictionnaire universel
français et latin* (attributed to Trévoux, 1704 version) uses the same terms
as Furetière, while Prévost's *Manuel-lexique*, still restricted to the religious
sense, gives the two significations of baptism and resurrection. The *Dictionnaire de la langue française* by Richelet also opts, in its 1732 version,
for the theological perspective and does not accept the medical meaning
until 1780, in a revised and enlarged edition. As for the *Dictionnaire de
l'Académie*, it does not accept regeneration until 1740, and then in both
its senses (religious and physiological), but specifies that "To regenerate,
to give new birth, is used only in a religious context." The *Encyclopédie*
crowns this double meaning in a rather long article under a general definition: "It is the act by which one is reborn for a new life." Regeneration /
"religious term" and regeneration / "surgical term" thus have their functions precisely specified.[2]

A first meaning, strictly theological: "By the sin of Adam, we are all
born children of anger. To erase this original sin that makes us children
of the devil, there must be, in the order of grace, a new birth that makes
us children of God. And that is what happens in baptism through the
anointing by the Holy Ghost, of Whom this sacrament is the sign and the
pledge. . . . The second acceptance consecrated by religion concerns a kind
of rebirth for another life, for eternity or immortality. The first regenera-

tion makes us children of God and gives us the right to eternal life; but the second causes us to enter into possession of that inheritance."

A second meaning falls within "surgical terms": "Commonly used in treatises on wounds and ulcers to express the regrowth of lost tissue. There is not, however, any regeneration in the soft parts; the wounds where tissue has been lost close only by means of compression of the open vessels, whose orifices press against each other and are depressed from the circumference toward the center. This occlusion forms the scar. The false doctrine of regeneration in the soft parts [which arose in response to Paré's experiments] has for a long time been disastrous to the progress of the art. . . . It is not thus in the hard parts: there are examples of rather considerable portions of the whole diameter of a bone being removed, and that nature has regenerated; that is to say that in its place a concretion of osseous humours has formed that performed the functions of the lost bone. . . . One thing worthy of remark is that these cures, for which we are very indebted to nature but which we can guide by art, only occurred in young people, in whom the vegetative essence was in all its strength, and who had not yet absorbed too many vices in their growth," writes Dr. Antoine Louis, one of the best surgeons of the century. Thus we cannot trust the slownesses characteristic of dictionaries that admit a meaning more than they initiate it—the word did not, it would appear, enter politics until the end of the 1760's.

The many dictionaries of the very beginning of the nineteenth century, on the other hand, fully welcomed regeneration as an idiom of political language. The evolution of the *Dictionnaire de l'Académie* is, for once, very revealing. The word, absent in 1696, appears in its theological and biological senses in 1740, is passed on identically in the 1762 version, but takes on "political significance" in the reprinted edition of 1798: "To regenerate: used especially in matters of religion. . . . It also symbolically signifies correcting, reforming, extirpating the root of abuses and of vices: 'to regenerate morality,' 'to regenerate an Empire.'"

The "symbolically" meaningful language of the Revolution, then, allowed the integration of the word into the political corpus. This is confirmed by the *Dictionnaire universel de la langue française* by Boiste, who adopts this metaphoric enlarging of the meaning as his own. But it is undoubtedly Reinhardt's work, *Le Néologiste français, ou vocabulaire portatif des mots les plus nouveaux* (The French neologist, or the portable vocabulary of the newest words), that, in 1796, most clearly emphasizes this extension. Classifying regeneration among "the words already in common use but now employed in a new and wider meaning," the author gives the following definition: "A term of theology and chemistry. Recently, it has been given a wider scope. Today it signifies the improved, perfected reproduction of a physical, moral, or political object." Reinhardt then illustrates his argument with a few examples drawn from the political language of the beginnings of the Revolution: "We owed to Louis XIV the advantage of being the most civilized Nation in Europe; perhaps we will owe to Louis XVI the benefit of a regeneration that will be enjoyed by our descendants," or again, "A Nation that works seriously at regeneration must necessarily purify itself of its vices and immorality." The author concludes by disclaiming the word: "The term has been harped on to satiety," which he hastens to illustrate with numerous variations drawn from revolutionary political discourse: "The Jacobins claimed to be the *regenerators* of the human race," "A *regenerative* law," "The first dewdrops of *regenerative* philosophy, destined to change the face of our societies," "A *regenerative* Republic of the Universe." Through these examples and this phrase "harped on," the political meaning of regeneration and the variations it can be subjected to are sketched out.

Between 1765, when the most erudite definitions of the *Encyclopédie* are written, and 1789, when the distorted uses of the word by revolutionary language begin, regeneration has besieged the sphere of government. The employment of the word in a political context is officially attested to in 1788 by the use that the monarchical power makes of it. The Estates General, according to the royal decrees of the summer of 1788, must "work toward the regeneration of the public good."[3] The very first appearance of the word in its political acceptation seems to date from *Voyage en Italie* by Charles Duclos, written in 1766, in which the author, having described the decadent state of the city of Rome, as much from the point of view of morality as from that of the political system and of culture, offers valuable advice: "Rome seems in great need of regeneration."[4]

With these two dates, 1766 and 1788, we undoubtedly have the true chronological limits of the appearance of political regeneration. In the course of those twenty years, regeneration meets its antonym, "degeneration," in the sphere of political vocabulary, for the negative concept of the "loss of natural qualities" had been charged with a moral and political meaning for several decades. First Bossuet, then especially Voltaire in his *Histoire de Louis XIV*, had made great use of this item of the historical vocabulary that was linked with the fall of empires. At the end of the eighteenth century, when writers were denouncing at length the decline of the "French Empire," it was precisely degeneration that occupied people's minds. These descriptions were not neutral. By rhetorical effects, they induced an emotional response to a fundamentally pessimistic discourse, a hope in which restitution became the central figure. The "regeneration of the kingdom" is a concept whose emergence was thus prepared by the massive use of a preestablished pessimistic discourse, typically characterizing the morals of the French court and the end of the reign of Louis XV. One might say that degeneration implies regeneration and its images, just as the description of the court of Louis XV by implication praises the "severe morality" of his successor. It is at the turning point of the two reigns that regeneration enters into politics.

The texture of the political language of the mid-1770's explains the swift success of the word. In fact, regeneration seems to come naturally to complete the spectrum of expressions that designate the hope for a better humanity. "Perfectibility" or "perfectioning" would be an exemplary name for this verbal continuum. Integration works here not by contradiction (degeneration versus regeneration), but by parallel induction of meaning (perfectibility/regeneration). Finally, the burgeoning intertextuality of the political and social vocabulary in the second half of the eighteenth century also encouraged the change in register of regeneration. Language working for the "public good," language of the philosophers, those "doctors" of customs and social morality, language of public commentary, of treatises and plans of enlightened public opinion—such language welcomes many a word from domains previously more strictly specialized, such as the natural sciences, medicine, or theology. The abuse of words did not have to wait for the ebullition of revolutionary discourse. In the beginning of the 1760's, the censors of the French language already reproach the Marquis de Mirabeau for his "gibberish,"[5] Cérutti for his "mixed and vain eloquence,"[6] Diderot for his "exaggeration,"[7] then Rivarol for his "physiognomical language."[8]

These crossings and borrowings favored the annexation of regeneration by politics, a transfer that is accompanied by increasingly numerous metaphors comparing human body with social body. In this sense, the fate of regeneration in the language of the prerevolutionary years is revelatory of the power of public opinion. Regeneration is not only a fashionable word, but it is also a manifestation of this fashion, a word whose meaning is quickly broadened to respond to the growing need to hold forth on politics in a discourse that welcomes an abundance of metaphors capable of captivating the public, of feeding the writers of "political and philosophical" works, or of inspiring the rhetors of the academies. Metaphors of the body, such as regeneration, by proposing a synthetic and imagistic explanation of the world, by offering a model to describe history (decadence/renaissance), by joining meaning with knowledge, the traditional vocabulary of theology and the scientism of medical language, metaphors thus appear as one of the favorite registers of idiomatic innovation.

On the eve of the Revolution, the Abbé Grégoire most precisely defines the new uses of regeneration. His *Essay on the physical, moral, and political regeneration of the Jews*, a work awarded a prize in 1788 by the academicians of Metz, poses very clearly, even in its title, the terms of any global undertaking of regeneration. It is a matter of the "possibility of reforming the Jews," that is to say of "improving them" and thus allowing their full integration into French society. Here the meaning of regeneration is found under several entries: (1) religious—"To reform the Jews in keeping with the intentions of Christianity"; (2) social—regenerating the Jews comes down to "integrating them into our society"; and (3) political—"A regeneration reconciled with the political and civil laws of nations." Grégoire's essay, taking into account the debates, innovations, and transfers of meaning of the preceding decade, in a way offers a regeneration that has come to signify maturity in the political language of the Revolution: "We will first have Jews of two kinds: some forever vowed to ignorance, and stagnating in the mire of prejudice; others raising themselves to the height of their century, and transcending their mistakes: those hasten with us to put their shoulders to the wheel, either for humanity, in order to extend the benefits of the law to all their brothers, or out of self-love, to make the obstacles that they have conquered more salient, and to enlarge in our eyes the distance that separated them from a degraded horde. The Jew is born with the same dispositions as we; we muzzle his usury, we restrain his commerce, we direct him almost necessarily toward other aims, we enlarge his soul, we raise up his heart, we fight prejudices, we provide him with the most powerful motives to cause him to be enlightened; he has at his disposal our education, our legislation, and all our discoveries that he will share. The ensemble of all these means will produce a universal impulse that will shake the entire Jewish nation, and carry along even the reluctant; for when someone who wishes to keep absurd opinions and heterogeneous habits has to struggle constantly against instruction, evidence, authority, pleasure, example, ridicule, and necessity, it is surely impossible for reason not to recover its rights, for character not to take on new imprints, and customs assume better forms."[9] Regeneration tries from then on to imprint itself on the "human clay," an imprint that is deeply marked in the characters and morality whose object constitutes the entire formative project of Grégoire as adopted by revolutionary ambition: to rectify man physically, morally, and politically.

Imagining the Revolutionary 'Homo Novus'

"Can that which is not a man create a man? . . . There he is, quite definitely: a man. Might his nature have changed?"[10] In 1789, the body drastically transformed by politics is straightaway established as a two-sided variety: the "before" and the "after." This enigma exists wholly at the point of temporal upheaval, the historic rupture. The discourse about this break occupies an essential place in the political imagination of the French Revolution. This ideal renewal of human nature by a political event is best illustrated by the call for the regeneration of man. The symbols of the collapsing "feudal barbarism" are answered by those of the "new world": "The epoch of a new revolution is moving on the wings of time. . . . The earth opens up: entire regions disappear; the sea takes their place; the universe seems to reach its dissolution. But no, on the contrary, another world has arisen from the waters, under which it has been fertilized and made fruitful, in order to feed thousands of generations, who will disappear one day along with it, when the need for a renewal has returned. The course of events is the same on the surface of the earth. All that exists, all that crawls on the earth, disappears only to provoke a new procreation. Thus everything is destroyed and re-created alternately: everything masters and yields in its turn. This variation stems from nature. It makes itself felt morally, physically, politically, on the whole and in the details."[11]

If this being—this new man produced by palingenesis and placed in the cyclical transition of two worlds, surrounded by his symbols—appears often and regularly, that does not mean that the tale of the Revolution did not subject him to rules. On the contrary, it is essential to emphasize how—at what times, in connection with what events, in what system of representation, and following what development—the regenerated Frenchman is put into place in the course of 1789, how an enduring symbol of the revolutionary mystique, of its epiphany, was integrated into the political imagination.

The "before" side literally obsesses the text in the early days of the

Revolution, a time when the political upheaval of the mid-1770's and of the transition from the reign of Louis XV to that of Louis XVI is played again. Louis XVI did not succeed for long in linking his image (or his body) to the words of regeneration that entered into politics at his accession. The convocation of the Estates General alone restores currency to that discourse about the king-father, the king-restorer of the French nation. Between 1788 and 1789, then, the degeneration/regeneration pair imprints its interpretive grid again on political commentary.

The discourse of "exhausted France" finds its most suggestive outcome in the famous "Notice" of the *Révolutions de Paris* dated 12 July 1789 that proposes to describe precisely the "before," the "despotic monster." The history of the monarchy is rewritten as the "enslavement of the slaves of the kingdom of France," a government that "could be based only on the destruction of morality." Loustallot offers to his many readers a tale of "the kingdom's increasingly monstrous vices," a tale whose true precursor is Richelieu ("Degrading servitude succeeds the honesty of the reign of Henri IV"), whose great arranger is Louis XIV ("Ambition, splendor, and the courtier mentality have dug the abyss that has swallowed France"), and whose principal "beneficiary" is Louis XV: "The mire of debauchery infects public morals. Dissolution passes from the court into society; luxury and licentiousness pass from bishops and high benefactors down to the Levites. In a word, corruption overflows from the ranks that surround the throne to the nearest neighbor, from the capital to the entire empire. The people are little by little possessed by languor; they have become the slave of the government, of the privileged, as well as of their own pleasures and great sufferings." Just as in 1774, this discourse of "degeneration" produces a rhetorical effect that is not without hope: a new world can succeed this exhausted one, a world regenerated by respect for laws, by virtue. The slave people of former times stands up again: that is the image that the words about degeneration summon. The "expiring colossus" that personifies that "France abandoned to itself, using its own hands to tear apart its entrails"[12] is answered, in a tale that wants to cover the whole metaphoric range, by the rediscovered hero stopping the collapse of the empire: "O my Nation! To what degree of abasement have you fallen! Your name, once so respected in Europe, has fallen into scorn . . . Your glory has disappeared, your laurels have faded. But an invisible hand has stopped you at the edge of the precipice. Century eighteen! return to France all its energy; return

to it all its virtues . . . Hero! Join me; do not hereafter step down from the
chariot except to climb up to the Capitol."[13]

The hope of regeneration entertained by the convocation of the Estates
General is embodied in that ideal character who would rise up and save
France. The representation of the new man is merged suddenly in a crucible that is defined both by a political morality and a biological setting
aright, a renewed human nature whose most suggestive example appears
in a beautiful text by Pétion dated February 1789: "The free man does not
walk with his head bent; nor is his gaze haughty or disdainful, but rather
assured; his walk is proud; none of his movements proclaims fear; full of
confidence in his own strength, he sees no one around him of whom he
need be afraid and before whom he might have to abase himself. His joy is
pure, it is honest, his affections are gentle and good; these sentiments of the
soul give his body the most perfect development, the most beautiful proportions . . . How much do constraint, how much do depressing and irritating ideas attack our temperament, disturb our health, ravage our external
form: the cheeks cave in, the complexion becomes livid, the eye dims, our
limbs shrivel, we are without strength and courage. The least moral revolution occasions a physical upheaval. Take a child painfully constrained in an
uncomfortable posture, forced to fix his looks on a book that he would tear
into shreds if he could, and compare him with one of the same age who is
playing, amusing himself in complete freedom, comes and goes as he likes,
drinks and eats when he likes, and you will see that the latter will be infinitely more agile and robust. This difference between two children applies
just as much between two peoples. I imagine these two peoples in the same
climate, one free and the other slaves; the men of the free nation will be
physically larger, more handsome, more courageous; morally, they will be
more virtuous and better . . . Make man free if you desire his happiness,
if you wish to see him handsome, strong, and virtuous. The deeper we go
into this truth, the more we follow it in its developments, the more striking it will seem."[14] It is through this graft of physiological, psychological,
and moral elements onto a political rhetoric that the universe of the regenerated Frenchman is sketched out in 1789, thus leading the intertextuality
of the two prerevolutionary decades to its end.

During the year 1789 conditions are favorable to the development of this
"new man." I have distinguished two of them, each determining different
modes of appearance and treatment of the same figure: the propositions

that accompany the meeting of the Estates General, then the celebration
of the taking of the Bastille. Regeneration first plays the role of dream: it
is a matter of imagining the Frenchman of tomorrow, the Frenchman of
the "after" time. This is a hope expressed by the whole series of pamphlets
that discuss the convocation of the Estates General. Many plans describing
what is to be done and foreseeing the "restoration of France" are, starting
in 1788, thrown into the intense debate of ideas.

This utopian tendency, designing a future described as a space of perfection, is pursued and amplified during the first half of 1789. Until the
beginning of June, while the Estates settle their procedural quarrel, Constitutional plans and financial reforms occupy the political imagination. A
vision of the "new man" is attached specifically to these plans of an ideal
city. The time of rupture is strongly marked here: with the coming together
of the Estates, the Frenchman enters into an almost instant future. "The
king, developing the intensity of his thought, imperiously affixing to it the
seal of perfect justice, will ordain, will command, that at the instant peace
is born, Man be regenerated and life burst forth; immediately, heaven joining its supreme Will with that of the monarch, and aiding his manly efforts,
he will reign over a fully happy people," [15] exclaims the author of the *Memorandum on the regeneration of the public order*. The time to come, almost
already there, is thus the condition of regeneration. However, as its name
indicates, the "new birth" is placed, in an instant future, in ideal osmosis
with a mythified past: the image of rupture integrates in a complementary
way the belief in immediate perfectibility of the human race with the return of the Golden Age. The Frenchman will find again the vigor of his
ancestor—that is the customary expression. The future can be explained
only by explicit reference to the past, a past that can be expressed through
a few symbols, of which "chicken in the pot" is one of the most striking:
"One does not have to be a sorcerer to predict that if all the articles [of
the planned Constitution] pass, there will be no kingdom more flourishing than France . . . Regaining the gaiety and vigor of our fathers, we will
dance, sing, and rejoice in the shade of those ancient oaks under which they
used to gather to eat chicken in the pot." [16]

The Frenchman, heir of fortunate fathers, is placed at the source of a
celebrated lineage: he speaks and acts for eternity. Thanks to the regenerated body of 1789, this radical upheaval of time sets in harmony the ancestor and his descendant, the Golden Age and the good fortune of latter
times. Some pamphlets are decidedly futuristic and project readers toward

that mythic time, such as *The Estates General of the year 1999* that proposes a dialogue between a "Frenchman of the twentieth century" and the regenerated man of 1789. The descendant claims of course to take his inspiration from the lineage born in 1789 and then describes his perfect country, the "most flourishing empire in the universe." [17] The first figure of the "new man," sketched by works saluting the opening of the Estates General, is a peaceful character, with calm habits, reviving a golden age of tranquil well-being, evolving as it were in a purified space, in the perfect geometry shaped by utopian discourse.

Apparently remote from this serenity, the "new man" illustrated by numerous descriptions of the taking of the Bastille is a being full of strength, vigor, even of violence, who symbolizes the regeneration of a "chain-breaking" people.[18] The literature that comments on and celebrates the fall of the Bastille constitutes, in fact, the second major phase in the regenerative set of themes of 1789. Already before July, however, numerous texts were promising rectification and the revolt of the Third Estate.

Previously, I described by way of example the giant Strong-arm acting as "formidable" embodiment of the Third Estate, who suddenly finds his brain illuminated and his body emancipated on 23 April 1789, the eve of the day initially foreseen for the meeting of the Estates General. Following a similar vision of triumph in *A Free France*, a pamphlet republished several times during 1789 (especially in its third edition, immediately after the taking of the Bastille, with added notes celebrating "the finest days of our history"), Desmoulins presents his description of the regenerated man. The Frenchman who has now become invincible is henceforth ready for every sacrifice: "Fiat! Fiat! yes, all this good will go into effect; yes, this regeneration will be accomplished; no power on earth is able to prevent it . . . We have become invincible. I myself, frankly, I used to be timid, and now I feel another man. In the example of Othryades the Spartan, he remains alone on the battlefield, mortally wounded, gets up, and, his hands shaking, erects a trophy, and writes with his blood: 'Sparta has conquered'; I feel that I would die with joy for such a fine cause, and, pierced with wounds, I too would write with my blood: 'France is free.' "

Such textual effects occur abundantly in certain works written just after the events of mid-July. Alongside brief or factual accounts of the taking of the Bastille, there are numerous texts inhabited by images of the "triumph of the French People." [19] These images of discourse all carry the energy of a rediscovered vigor: the "new man" no longer evolves in the space of an ideal geometry but is raised up by fighting the "despotic hydra," in a landscape of violence and intrigue. A pamphlet from July entitled *The tomb of ministerial despotism, or the dawn of happiness* claims to recognize the strength of the "sturdy Gauls" in the Frenchman as conqueror of the Bastille. Others, in a myth that is especially common in the eighteenth century, focus an "energetic firmness" on the time of the first Franks.[20] Gauls or Franks, beyond the polemics on the racial origins of the French, the regeneration of July 1789 wants above all to be the virile, or least sturdy, bearer of an incorruptible energy: "Frenchman, you have reconquered your liberty, that liberty of which the first Franks, your ancestors, were jealous; you will again become like them, strong and healthy, like them you will let your beard grow, and you will wear the long hair that they favored. Goodbye hairdressers, beauticians and merchants of fashion, now you will cover yourselves with cotton or homespun. From now on you will scorn all the ornaments of luxury, and you will make use of all your physical and intellectual faculties." [21]

Giant, colossus, Spartan, Gaul or Frank, the regenerated man born from the taking of the Bastille is a renewed body, which the "fuckative regeneration" of the pornographic tale of the Revolution does not shrink from dramatizing: "Married at the flower of her age, beautiful and virgin, what a celebration was the first wedding night for the young cunt of Mme Cuntlicked, who is anxious to immolate her scarcely blossomed virginity on the altars of the most lovable and grateful god! This memorable night, this delicious night was the one that followed the great day of the French Revolutionaries, on 14 July 1789. By uniting herself with a Frenchman on that day, one had to presume that she would marry a hero; and the night that followed that hymen, she had, for the same reason, to put in her queynt the burning, victorious tarse of a Hercules. . . . That at least is the ticklish idea that she conceived of a man who would enter her bed fresh from conquering the Bastille, and take her after having routed despotism; it is quite certain that regenerated men are hard-cocked demigods, and consequently more than ordinary men." [22]

By the play on words colored with a sometimes ironic lyricism, thanks to that intertextuality traditionally linked to regeneration, it is the awakening of the Frenchman that revolutionary language follows up through all the possible narratives of the political event, a mediation that can metaphorically disseminate the universe of regeneration while at the same time being constantly threatened by the perversion and interference of the meaning of the concept itself. This sudden awakening makes of the "new man," whatever the tale may be that takes charge of him, an energy-carrying model of the body. The rapid evolution of the "French race" in political imagination seems striking, almost miraculous, and *The trumpet of judgment* describes, under "the benevolent gaze of Hercules" that brings forth in its author "the boiling heat of the pen," that change of the Frenchman's nature: "When I look back, [it would seem] that the journals from the beginning of the year were made by children, and under the influence of arbitrary power, turning all heads, compressing all thoughts; since then we have become men, we have reconquered our country, weapons in our hands." [23]

This admiring, or complacent, backward gaze is illustrated by another semiapologetic pamphlet, *French Citizens, or the triumph of the Revolution*: "Nothing is more wonderful than the revolution of France. In less than a year, it presents what one might seek in vain in all the centuries; an immense people grown old in despotism, suddenly making burst forth at the very instant of its political resurrection that energy and heroism that all free peoples display. Already accustomed to the most extraordinary things, electrified by the same sentiments, all Frenchmen make the noblest sacrifices, without counting them, to honor the freedom they love. We must offer this scene for the emulation of peoples who will want to profit from our example, and for the emulation of our own posterity, who will have to walk in our tracks to conserve the most glorious conquest: our regeneration." [24]

A pamphlet from December 1789, *The Inauguration of the Year 1789*, presents this coming of the "new man," offered for the "emulation of peoples" and for that of "posterity," expressively. Liberty introduces before Jupiter the glorious months of 1789, and causes them to climb up Olympus. The procession begins with these words: "Man has returned to all the rights that justice had given him," then continues: "One saw the Year 1789 appear. Its walk was noble, its air inspiring at once fear, veneration and respect; all the months had gathered around it, but one could make out especially June, July, August, September, and October. On the foreheads of each of these months, time had already engraved the most remarkable epoch of its course . . . On one noble countenance could be distinguished the month of July; her hand was leaning on a menacing lion. The terrible animal, bristling its superb mane, seemed to be preparing itself for new combats; that month was still decorated with shining armor, its helmet was covered over with the colors of liberty; engraved on its forehead could be read its exploits: 'The taking of the Bastille,' 'Adoption of the national cockade.' " For the tale of the Revolution, political rupture is also a physical mutation: the glorious months wear engraved on their bodies the imprints of their regeneration.

This double personality of the "new man"—dwelling in utopia or storming the Bastille—is nevertheless the result of one and the same rupture. It is a product of the identical interrogation about the power of historic time as it affects the Frenchman. How can a being grown old under the ancien régime radically transform himself? Doubt, though it might take hold of more than one revolutionary, has no place in the imagination of the wonderful regeneration revealed by the pamphlets of spring and summer 1789. It is as if doubt had to be driven away by massive recourse to a burgeoning symbolism. This serves as an absolute value: it alone gives to discourse, by embodying it, the power to form a narrative of the history of the restoration of the Frenchman. In the revolutionary language of 1789, there is a veritable fund of shared imagery from which Patriot authors draw the metaphors, figures, and symbols capable of embodying this "paper being," the regenerated man.

Faith in the wonderful mutation of man passes through these textual phases: we are present at the birth of a literary type that is currently widely adopted by political discourse, a general plan for a reform of morality that the inventive mind of Restif de La Bretonne had outlined even before the Revolution. His great series, begun in 1769 with *The Pornographist, or Prostitution reformed*, continued regularly until 1789; one by one, *The Mimographer, or The theater reformed*, *The Gynographers, or Women reformed*, *The Andrographer, or Morality reformed*, *The Thesmographer, or Laws reformed*, and *The New Emile* located the foundations of the dream of total regeneration of society, its morals, and thus of the subtlest components of society, in a utopian space common to plans of the era. Restif, who planned to conclude his Summa with a *Glossographer*, wanted to "reform" more than just language. The imagination of the Revolution generously welcomes this general plan for reform of the country, and each of the subjects treated by Restif finds its metaphors and tropes—figures of speech, for instance, like that multitude of dynamic metaphors. The temporal break is transcribed in these mythic figures of dwarves becoming tall, bent-over slaves that rise up, sleepers who awaken.

These representations are important not because they are original—on the contrary, they rely on the commonplaces of oratory—but because they are the witnesses of an endlessly reaffirmed belief in "the dawn of happiness"[25]: tottering trees gaining support from the new stake (liberty), dried-up plants restored to fruitfulness by renewed sap. The old rhetoric, most often amorous (which is paradoxical when we think of the prudish morality that animates most of the journals), is integrated by the Revolution into its own political imagination. The images of awakening and rebirth, also quite numerous, take part in this same vein. The Frenchman is reborn to political life, he "awakens from a long doze, breaks his chains and, through noble energy, raises himself to the level of the man of Antiquity, above all those who exist."[26]

An image from 1789 celebrating the fall of the Bastille gives a striking illustration of this vision. In *The Awakening of the Third Estate* we see the Frenchman in revolt coming out of sleep and breaking his chains, while two of the privileged (the noble and the prelate) take fright and make as if to flee. The caption, in falsely popular style, is explicit: "My faith, it was time for me to wake up, for the oppression of my chains was giving me too many nightmares." The "new man" is a man on the move, he hastens toward his happy fate: "The time of servitude is past, the happy reign of liberty has replaced it . . . All the ways are made smooth. Let us run, O my fellow citizens! Let us hasten to enter into the course! Let us go with the victor's palm! Let us hurry, ah! My Brothers."[27]

But the regenerative myth with which the writers play most remains the millennial prophecy. Drawing from religious sources of regeneration, the pamphlets do not hesitate to celebrate in the "new man" the "miracle of a new birth." Taking God as witness, the citizen emerges glorious from the breakup of 1789, which is thus compared with the Last Judgment. *The Veni creator of the citizen, The Dies irae, or the three orders at the Last Judgment, The Passion, the death, and the resurrection of the people* — all these pamphlets work on the same theme. Adapting mystical language to the political universe, they promise a revolutionary Second Coming: "Here then is the day of wrath, of justice and of vengeance . . . When the king, empowered by his people, proud and grateful for the love of his people, ascends the throne of Truth, to examine everything, to deepen everything, to establish everything, to reform everything, to regenerate everything! The cry of the convocation [of the Estates General], like the crack of a revenging thunder, will call from the obscurity of the Provinces the guilty and the innocent; all will gather on the steps of his throne . . . Then the mighty book of truth will be opened; all is inscribed there; all is indelible. On one side will be seen the vileness and rapacity of the nobles; the hypocrisy and greed of the

priests . . . On the other page, reason will discover how a loyal people, sub-
missive and confident, have wiped away humiliation, vexation, injustice . . .
O memorable and terrible day! Day when man will raise himself up victorious from the prejudices of the nobility and from religious ignorance . . .
Day when the wicked will be under the feet of the good, when the fancy
will be crushed by the simple, the haughty by the humble."[28]

The rupture here is close to *miracle*, the marvelous suddenly introduced
into the domain of the political imagination. A "new man" is then sketched
out, born from the single instant of rupture, a sudden and complete regeneration that causes the destiny of man to converge, in a lightning flash, on
the time of perfection. The value of time is essential here: at a single stroke
the "new man" is born, fully formed and ideal, according to this radical and
optimistic discourse, this discourse animated by miraculous regeneration.

Regeneration, or The "Alphabet for Children"

A much more skeptical, but no less voluntaristic, approach develops to
the regeneration of the French after 1789, to stay within the chronological limits of this study. This second discourse insists more on the bur-
dens that still, even after the decisive break, oppress the Frenchman of the
dawning Revolution — "centuries of corruption," "habits of frivolity." The
citizen, "grown old under the despotism whose maxims he has lapped up
with his milk," as Marat incessantly recalls, will be able to be changed
only at the end of a long and difficult evolution. The imagery of this discourse is inhabited by two complementary political procedures: the surveil-
lance/denunciation/punishment of adversaries and, in counterpoint, man
refashioned by revolutionary precepts.

Two visions of the "new man" thus seem to be sketched out in the beginning of the Revolution. On one hand, there is the instantaneity of the
regenerative rupture as it unfurls in the plans for general reform and in
the pamphlets celebrating the fall of the Bastille. On the other hand, there
is an integration of the New Man into the community through strict education, a virtuous counterpart of the rigorous exclusion of the Old Man
judged incapable of reform. Through this duality, the very conception of
the Revolution is questioned after 1789: two philosophies are outlined, two
conceptions of man, two corporeal metaphors (restoration and awakening
versus the mold and the chrysalis). These contrasting attitudes are pre-
ludes to long-lasting political oppositions.

During 1789 a privileged moment develops this questioning: a debate that best illuminates these two antagonistic figures of regeneration. It is the parliamentary discussion of August 1789 on the Declaration of the Rights of Man and of the Citizen.[29] Though most of the deputies agree in recognizing the importance of the upheavals and the sudden and irremediable nature of the break with the ancien régime, many, if they do not actually mourn it, do at least remain aware of the weight of the past, thus introducing the note of skepticism that is so lacking in the eloquence of the patriotic pamphlets on sudden regeneration. Mirabeau, defending his declaration plan on 17 August before the Assembly, expresses this stricture at the root of his thinking: "Gentlemen, the declaration of the rights of man in society is undoubtedly nothing but an exposition of a few general principles applicable to all forms of government. From this point of view, one would expect a work of this nature to be quite simple and hardly susceptible to disputes and doubts. But the committee that you have named to take charge of it soon perceived that such an account, when it is intended for an old, and almost obsolete, body politic, is necessarily subordinated to many circumstances, and can never attain to anything but a relative perfection. In this respect, a declaration of rights is a difficult work."

This difficulty is marked by a striking contrast: a simple text will declare man free, will put into effect the regenerative rupture of the Frenchman, while at the same time he is designated as "ignorant," "old," "obsolete," even "unconstituted." In the context of August 1789, this contrast soon becomes harrowing. The Terror and local revolts cause the specter of anarchy to rise. To declare man "free and equal in right" at that precise moment seems to offer to the people both freedom and its abuse: "license" and disorder. Faced with that regeneration proposed by the Declaration of Rights, the Assembly must take a stand. The debate lasts from the first to the fourth of August, categorizing the possible forms in which mankind renewed by politics can appear.

The defenders of traditional monarchy mobilize themselves to denounce the "declarative danger." The Duc de Lévis, and then La Luzerne, Bishop of Langres, expostulate on 1 August: "A declaration of the rights of man must be a succession of simple truths, drawn from nature: it must, as its name indicates, *declare and never order*. That's reason enough for the uselessness of a declaration, one capable of becoming dangerous, because ignorance could abuse it,"[30] cries the former, while the latter adds: "There are many people who are in no state to hear the maxims that you present to them. My opinion is not that we should keep the people in ignorance, but I want them to be enlightened by books, not by laws or by declarations, a much too sudden step. Let us not place anything useless in their hands; let us avoid the dangers of abuse, and let us make good books. I propose, then, that there be no declaration of rights put into the Constitution." [31]

The Declaration is not only useless but dangerous, establishing regeneration by forced marches, as absolute principle, while the people have remained on the other side of the temporal breakup, in the ignorance of former times: "Before we use the bridle of the law to impose the principles of this declaration on the people, they must first be submitted to the feeble intellect of a population that does not understand them, and that will not understand them, because long oppression has plunged them into profound ignorance, while public unrest leads their intellectual faculties astray, surrounded as they always are by watchful enemies who know well how to poison the sources of their safety." [32] Thus the key phrase of the Duc de Lévis, "The declaration must declare and never order," is taken advantage of by the adversaries of the plan: declarative rupture, without order, is the way to catastrophe, to chaos.

The Patriot camp must answer this very coherent argument. It wants to believe in the regenerative strength of the declarative text. The first possible reply lies in the miraculous and dynamic power of the rupture itself. A few pamphlets, taking part in the radical imagination of the *homo novus*, present the Declaration as the signal necessary and sufficient for the recovery of the French; they associate the text with the peaceful society that it will cause to be born, connecting the "seventeen principles of our regeneration" with happiness. "Finally, the time has come when a great revolution in ideas will, so to speak, transport us from the mire of slavery to the lands of liberty. The time has come when everything is changing around us, when our customs, our laws, our government, we ourselves, will become new. We have finally broached the great question of the Declaration. We will establish that happiness our fathers lacked," exclaims Le Hodey in his paper,[33] while one of his regenerative fellow citizens presents the declarative plan in these triumphant terms: "The declaration will establish everything in a state of clarity, there will no longer be the least question, the smallest problem to resolve. Everyone will have the proper mind; no one will be under any misapprehension." [34] These texts dream of a veritable code of happiness, a way of forcing the fate of a nation by writing words that symbolically mark the breakup: a declaration that must in an instant succeed in making a new country out of a kingdom grown old.

This language of political miracle carries little weight within the Assembly at the beginning of August, however. It quickly collapses before the alarming news coming in from the provinces in turmoil left in anarchy. Barère openly expresses this doubt when faced with the language of miraculous regeneration, and directs his friends toward more prudent reflection: "It was natural to examine if the declaration of rights, that product of the *new world*, could be naturalized in the *old*, and if the ideas of emerging republics were suitable for old empires."[35]

The allusion to the American declaration is not accidental, for it is in the name of this example that certain skeptics refuted the French Declaration. Malouet developed this point of view in quite a brilliant way on 1 August: "I know that the Americans have converted the rights of man and of the citizen into legislative act, but they have taken man in the bosom of nature, and present him to the universe in his primitive sovereignty. For American society, newly formed, is made up entirely of landowners already accustomed to equality, foreign to luxury and to indigence both, hardly knowing the yoke of the taxes, or of the prejudices, that dominate us. Such men were undoubtedly prepared to receive freedom in all its energy: for their tastes, their customs, their position called them to democracy. But we, Gentlemen, we have as fellow citizens an immense multitude of men without property, who expect to win their subsistence from assured employment, from conscientious government, from continuous protection—a population that is sometimes irritated, and not without just cause, at the spectacle of luxury and opulence. . . . It is absolutely necessary to confront the Declaration of the Rights, and make it harmonious with the necessitous state in which the man for whom it is made finds himself." Malouet, stressing the "primitivism" of the American people, absolutely refuses the image of the "regenerated Frenchman," and, in the priorities to be established, places order before the Declaration. That is why, at the conclusion of his long address, he proposes to resubmit the question of the Declaration "to one last examination," and to dedicate himself to the discussion of the "principles of the French government." The Patriot deputies find themselves placed before a double front of rejection: on one side, we have the resolute opponents of any text of rupture, who see in it the birth of abuses and disorder, and on the other side, the partisans of postponing the Declaration until after establishing the new constitutional order, who would prefer to limit the claims of the Frenchman before offering him rights.

The discussion of 1 August allows the Patriot deputies who support the necessity of a Declaration of Rights as a preliminary to the work on the Constitution to construct a refutation of traditionalist and monarchist arguments. To do this, they are inclined to favor a text that would be simultaneously declarative *and* productive of order. What their opponents think of in separate, definitively irreconcilable terms, they want to be one and indivisible. Therein lies the great strength of the French Declaration of Rights elaborated in the agitated context of the Terror: it symbolizes rupture, declares the new world, but also ordains the nature of the man to come, offering itself as a rigorous educational precept. The regenerated man finds here a double dimension: he rises up, energized by the words of the Declaration, and then molds himself by means of the education that that same text induces, as it comes to be known. The Frenchman is reborn to the world as a free man, breaking the slave's chains; the Frenchman then perfects his nature, casting off the superstitions of the ignorant.

Directly answering the Duc de Lévis and the Bishop of Langres, Barnave understands this double will to regeneration most quickly and synthesizes it most accurately: "They said the declaration was unnecessary, because it is already written in all hearts; dangerous, because the people will abuse its rights as soon as it knows them. But experience and history answer, and victoriously refute these two observations. This declaration has two practical uses: the first is to establish [*fixer*] the mind of legislation; the second is to guide the mind toward the object of that legislation. I think that it is indispensable to place at the beginning of the constitution a declaration of the rights that man must enjoy. It must be simple, within the grasp of every mind, and it must become the national catechism." [36]

Thanks to this final formula, Barnave presents the Declaration in its two acceptations: it "establishes" the time of rupture and "guides" the Frenchman toward the prescribed apprenticeship of freedom. For the "catechism" is above all of educational import: the condition of the actual regeneration of the new man who, once this condition is declared, sees his mind ordered little by little. Delandine, just after Barnave's address, explicitly asserts this: "Without a doubt, man must know that he is free, but we must do more than just declare it to him, we must order him." This same Delandine uses a superb metaphor to designate those two regenerative moments: "By

 ᵊediately breaking a dike kept intact for centuries, we must shelter ourselves from the flood whose waves could carry us away, by digging a wide, deep bed into which it will flow, well-behaved and tranquil." The regenerated man summons two images, the broken dike and the deep channel: the miracle of his sudden surge and the crucible of an education that will make him "well-behaved and tranquil."

From then on, it is easy for the Patriots to line up metaphors and arguments. Target talks about a body where Delandine had dealt with geography: "The people do not always sleep. They wake up and gather their strength to shake off a yoke of which they have wearied. It is then up to us to direct and guide their efforts and wisdom, with prudence."[37] After having presented himself as one who makes a declaration, Virieu now wishes to institute it: "There must be a declaration. Two dangers require it: the ignorance of the people that can abuse its strength, and the ignorance of the people that can defend its liberty. The necessity to raise them up, and then to enlighten them on their true rights, is thus imperative."[38] Durand de Maillane wants to be just as effective a propagandist: "I demand a declaration of the rights of man that will serve as a basis for the constitution and as a guide for this Assembly and its officers. This declaration, which should be posted in the towns, in the tribunals, in the very churches, would be the first door by which one could enter into the edifice of the national constitution. A people that has lost its rights, and that demands them, must know the principles of its regeneration, learn them and publish them."[39] The "door" evoked by Durand leads to a reading room that is also a classroom. This "edifice" of regeneration allies a threshold and a pedagogy, a declaration of entry into the new house and a rigorous inner ordering. That is where the regenerated man is born and takes shape.

This care to impose order on rupture stimulated Patriot imaginations: metaphors, especially those of bodily training, took the new man into their charge. This is also the time when the problematic of the "duties of man" intervenes in the debate, introduced by Grandin on 1 August and supported by Camus, Dupont de Bigorre, Sillery, and Grégoire on the fourth. These obligations, concomitant with the rights, are the most precise illustration of that alliance of rupture and order peculiar to regeneration. Obligations remain in the Patriot camp. Certainly, all of the clergy, low and high, rally quickly to the Declaration of "rights and duties," but its most vehement defenders are all heralds of the revolutionary party. The arguments in favor of duties follow, moreover, from the national catechism dear to Barnave. It is a question of providing a guide to the Declaration, of making an edifying morality lesson from the text of rupture: "It is not prudent to set forth the rights without establishing the duties. A declaration of rights is like a treaty on morality; it might not be understood by all classes of citizens, and might be abused."[40]

Abbé Grégoire, in his imagistic language, knows how to offer to the man "reborn to liberty" the mold of duty in which he can form his mind and body: "In general, man is more inclined to use his rights than to fulfill his duties. In the first instance, it is enough to give in to the current, while in the second, one must laboriously swim against it. In a time of insurrection when the people, for a long time harassed, tormented by tyranny, recovers its expropriated rights and is reborn to liberty, it easily travels through all extremes, and it is more difficult to bend it to the yoke of duty; it is a compressed spring that rebounds with force. Present the citizen with the safeguard of a power he would be tempted to believe unlimited. On the coiled spring of rights, impose the counterweight of duties. Let the Frenchman know not only what he wants, but also what he must; show him not only the circle that he can travel round, but also the barrier that he cannot cross."[41]

All Grégoire's metaphors—the river's current, the spring, rebirth, the circle—are immediately led, guided toward constraint: the current is made into a canal, the spring restrained, rebirth placed under the yoke of morality, and the circle closed. Rarely before had such care been taken to associate dynamic regeneration with formative regeneration with such strength of imagination. Yet, another pedagogue of the debate of the Declaration of Rights illustrates the double movement of regeneration with the same precision and an identical virtuosity—Rabaut Saint-Etienne, who on 18 August uses all the conviction of a pastor before his possibly wandering flock: "We want to regenerate ourselves; the declaration of rights is thus essentially necessary. . . . Moreover, I would wish for clarity, truth, and precision in the principles and the consequences, so that everyone might grasp them and learn them; I want them to become an alphabet for children, and to be taught in the schools. With such a patriotic education a strong and vigorous race of men can be born, and know well how to defend the liberty that we have won for them; always armed with reason, they will know how to resist despotism."[42]

Between the Declaration and achieving "strong and vigorous men," Rabaut locates the mold of the new education, that "alphabet for children" the regenerative enterprises of the Revolution will steadfastly main- out the miraculous. In the general plans for reform saluting the

Estates General and in the pamphlets celebrating the taking of the Bastille, force and vigor instantly graft themselves onto the body of the *homo novus*; for Rabaut or Grégoire, the physical quality, promised at the rupture, is imprinted on the body only by dint of a severe apprenticeship. Adopting the declarative principle by a vote of 570 to 433 on 4 August 1789, the majority of the Assembly endorses this educational impulse.

Chased off by the "awakening" of the new man, beaten on the legislative terrain of the National Assembly, the defenders of the monarchical tradition do not for all that abandon the fight against regeneration, that narrative-body about rupture, and then about revolutionary action. The Old Man, in fact, will find ways of taking vengeance by language. The story of the Revolution, forging its "magic words," [43] does not stop recounting its own fears (the monster of conspiracies) and its own successes: regeneration is one of its symbols. Soon, in the fall of 1789, satirical language — typically counterrevolutionary — takes advantage of the diffusion and even of the triumph of the term, and devotes itself to the game of rerouting its meaning. Since Patriot language wants to regenerate, satire offers to regenerate *everything*; since that language has created for itself a proliferating imaginative foundation, satire introduces *all* possible symbols into it. By this process of "linguistic agitation," Royalist writing defends itself against words that have, in the course of the summer, shaken, then overthrown, its ancient power.

Between December 1789 and January 1790, a series of texts coming under the traditional genre of "literary Christmas presents [*Etrennes*]" amuses itself by portraying the new Frenchman, embodiment of the first year of the Revolution. The assessment seems contradictory, since one can read in it the reversal of the figure of the "new man" by counterrevolutionary discourse. When he is attacked head-on, the regenerated man becomes a symbol of excess, of the arrogance of a Revolution that, through word and idea, wants to rival unique creative divine power. This pride is of course the forewarning of an imminent fall: "Accursed be that creature that is pleased with itself; it takes the blame for nothing, it is the source of every fault. It will soon be the unfortunate victim of its sin of pride," [44] prophesies a Royalist pamphlet dated 1 January 1790.

Another lampoon, a countercheck to the Olympian reception of the glorious months of 1789, presents the "descent into Hell of the Frenchman of 1789," "death by starvation for having lived solely on hope." [45] The "new man" is a figure of excess and blindness, a false prophet in the biblical tradition, a nefarious hero defying the gods of ancient mythology. He is a character found often in discourse hostile to the Revolution, first with Burke, where revolutionary regeneration is really a regression to the barbarous games of a bawling infancy, then later with Maistre, describing, in his *Considérations sur la France*, that "inexpiable delirium, that blind impetuosity, that scandalous scorn of all that is respectable among men: an atrocity of a new kind, that made light of its infamies; above all an impudent prostitution of reason, and of all words made to express the measure of ideas of justice and virtue."

But the privileged mode of satiric counterattack lies in the domain of the "misuse of words." Thus, denouncing those "sumptuous expressions that they stun us with every day," the author of *The Misuse of Words*, a dictionary that comments severely on the new revolutionary language, introduces "regeneration" in these words: "A series of catastrophes (financial, economic, commercial, moral) that, since 1789, has perverted our country."[46] The new man, son of this "catastrophe," a being of the ridiculous voluntarism of a "kingdom to be regenerated by enlisting,"[47] becomes a figure widely used by discourse hostile to the Revolution. In this sarcastic writing, regeneration is distorted by the procedure of excess/dearth of meaning, a play on political language of which *Sleep in peace, good people* offers a comic example: "We should chase all the court anthropophagi with basset hounds that would tear up their backsides; we should make all the bishops of France and all the fanatic non-juring priests march in procession, their heads covered with ass's hoods, and let loose on them all the ladies of La Halle; we should, instead of conserving this old royalty, previously an object of veneration for our stupid ancestors, give ourselves the president of the National Assembly for a king. That is the regeneration that is so desired. Then there would be no more intrigues, there would be no more court, there would be no more seductive women holding out lures to the sovereign. The worthiest of the new Frenchmen would be called to maintain the balance of powers, and his hands would always be pure, and the Golden Age would be reborn, or rather would be realized, on earth; and all the girls that we marry would be maidens like the Eleven Thousand Virgins, and all our wives would be faithful, for there would no longer be either perfumed abbots, or marquesses, or colonels, or impudent businessmen, or arrogant ministers. Finally, we would all be happy. Above all, we would have given a great example to the Earth; and who knows if, thanks to well-directed airships, we would not at last succeed in having the inexpressible charms of our absolute regeneration tasted by the inhabitants of

other planets? The true wise man, the true patriot, puts no limit on his ambition when it is a question of working for the regeneration of the species;
he is a conqueror who carries happiness everywhere."[48]

Exhibiting the full range of emblems and hopes of the regeneration of
1789, from the restoration of morality to universal ambition, the satiric
text of the counterrevolution leaves only a ghost of the ridiculed temporal
fracture, a specter suitable for seducing the naive pretensions of the "regenerators" of the French people. The new man here is no more than a
"fine word," vain, useless, even dangerous, susceptible to malfunctioning.
Regeneration does not come out of this corrosive reading unscathed. It has
changed from a "fine word" to a "coarse word": "I will not at all hide from
you the fact that with this fine, charming word of regeneration, I hoped
we wanted a little to return to the natural order of things. But I am afraid
that this coarse word has announced to us the mouse from the mountain,"
"Monsieur Nothing" complains in a pamphlet from the end of 1789.[49] [The
Latin quotation "The mountains are in labor, and bring forth a laughable
little mouse," stands behind this reference. La Fontaine abridges it as *de
grande dessein une souris*, or "from great plans, a mouse." Trans.]

But this misuse must not, in return, mislead us: the regeneration that
satire dismantles is that of miracle. This miracle, born from the hope of
the convocation of the Estates General, formed on the ruins of the Bastille,
does not resist the passing of revolutionary time. In fact, its imagination
is built, suddenly and richly, on historic fracture. Once this is past (May–
July 1789), the figures of marvelous regeneration wear out, undone little
by little under the very weight of the enthusiasm that caused them to be
born. During that time, the Frenchman remains "ignorant," and the administrators and politicians complain of "disorders." The miraculous language connected with the sudden awakening of the New Man seems actually charged with "coarse words" when taxes and the high price of grain
recall the inertia of a kingdom in decline. Into this breach, necessarily gaping, hollowed out between the rupture of miraculous regeneration and the
dead weight of an "old, decrepit world," the discourse of the misuse of the
word, along with that of ordered and guided regeneration, collapses. The
former plays on the imagination of the historic rupture to ridicule it: in it,
the Frenchman becomes too handsome, the age too golden, young women
too virginal, and the universal pretenses of revolutionaries end up reaching the moon. Regeneration, from then on, present in all mouths, no longer
raises bodies and no longer frightens anyone.

Yet the career of this regeneration is not finished; far from it. For pedagogues seize it. It is time to recall the double definition of regeneration offered by Dr. Louis in the *Encyclopédie*, even before the word had entered into politics. The scholar saw in regeneration, classically, a theological term: baptism and resurrection. The Frenchman, born from rupture, come back from among slaves and sleepers, has been transported by this miraculous regeneration thanks to the imaginative world of the little pamphlets. Dr. Louis also discerned in it, more professionally, a surgical term. The regeneration of bones, of "hard parts," can produce, especially in young subjects, impressive effects when it is carefully directed. Antoine Louis even speaks of an eleven-year-old boy who is said to have recovered the use of an atrophied tibia after serious injury. On the other hand, the "soft parts" of the flesh are no longer amenable to the regeneration of wounds. To see here a parable of the "national catechism" according to Barnave, of the "strength" and "vigor" procured by the "alphabet for children" with Rabaut Saint-Etienne, does not seem to me to force the interpretation. It is in medical terms that revolutionary regeneration works, once the miracle has passed (but it did play its role, since it alone launched the process): it is a question of guiding the increase of strength by political art, of placing splints on the legs of Frenchmen and of ordering their sensibilities, while little by little exclusion is striking the unreformable, those "soft, old" parts of the social body.

4. The Monsters of a Fantastic Aristocracy, or How the Revolution Embodies Its Horrors

In agitated minds, early July 1789, at Versailles where (as Sieyès writes) the deputies defend the "body of their National Assembly" that is emerging, and in Paris where they comment with anxiety on the movements of the royal troops surrounding the city, a strange being is born. A few days later, once the dangers are provisionally averted, once people can laugh at the "terrifying" plot that has been thwarted, this strange being appears in engravings and takes shape in some texts: the "giant Iscariot, aristocrat." This engraving,[1] unsigned and undated, is distributed in the summer of 1789, then later reprinted whenever needed to adorn the chronicle of the aristocratic "great beast"—September 1789 and the debate on the royal veto, October 1789 and the court's "Austrian conspiracy," November–December 1789 and the formation of the main counterrevolutionary newspapers and clubs, June 1790 and the abolition of titles of nobility, July 1790 and the fear of a conspiracy fomented against the celebration of the Federation. This engraving needs first of all to be *seen* (Figure 11).

Its colors are impressively vivid: the monstrous body made of green scales partly covered by a "Chainmail sleeve" and a "Cuisse" of iron, a head of hair mixing green snakes and their mouths of red blood, of the same red as the tip of the dagger or the spots of "redness" that trouble the pale pink face, gold facings on the corselet, gold again on the "crown of barbs," on the sword and the claws. The revolutionary political cartoon plays endlessly on these striking colors that it flaunts all the more readily since they can both mask printing imperfections and also draw the eye of strollers passing by the windows of print shops.

This engraving can also be *understood*. A Bastille in the background; the symbols of tyranny in the creature's hand, on his head, and at his side. Here is the "monster of despotism," lurking about the fortress that he wants to defend, "spotted" by the engravers, journalists, and pamphleteers at the turning point of mid-July. All of whom lost no time in elaborating the historical, literary, biblical, naturalist, and medical references borrowed from the teratological universe in order better to "embody" the adversary. This phenomenon is denounced by one of the victims of this ostracism by turning the monstrous figure against its parents: "Propaganda has raised itself up in the midst of all the peoples of the Earth . . . and its flanks have been opened up over France, and thousands of hideous serpents have been transformed into lampoonists. This new family brought with it the morals, the character, and the spirit of the monster that had conceived it."[2] Iscariot, then, is just a close cousin to the "Hydra," to the "Great Beast," and a more distant but nonetheless allied relative of the Austrian "Hyena" or "Harpy," then of the "Royal Veto"—so many imaginary creatures with monstrous bodies that people the representations of the aristocratic conspiracy; these are the monsters that the Herculeses, the giants of the people, the "giant Strong-arms" or the regenerated goddesses will soon come to fight.

This engraving must also be *read*. In fact, like most revolutionary political cartoons, this image does not "function" in an isolated way. It belongs to a network of interwoven, heterogeneous, contextualized representations. This monstrous body is accompanied with commentaries, texts, plays on words, anecdotes, even competing images and edifying morals. Iscariot is one of the "body-stories" of the fantastic history of the Revolution. It is first commented on by the engraving itself in a succinct but important explanatory caption: "This monster represents the Figure of a Furious Child, having hair made of Serpents surmounted by a Crown of Barbs. It holds a dagger ready to strike those who are opposed to tyranny. It is clothed in a Chainmail sleeve and Cuisse of Iron. Its feet and hands are Armed with the Tiger's Claws."

Iscariot also appears in a pamphlet quoted many times by the press in the summer of 1789, *The last cry of the monster*, "an Indian story."[3] The author, beginning by referring to La Fontaine, sets his fable in an imaginary kingdom, "Gallia," which is nevertheless rather close to the France of mid-July. The Gallians—governed by a sultan who is, however, beyond reproach, "Civis-King"—are divided: some are proud, "growing inordinately," others are coarse gluttons whose "stomachs become bloated and taut like a drum," and the final group, too fearful, "remain knotted and rickety," new examples of those "ideas made into bodies" introduced by the political writers of the beginning of the Revolution to fashion a metaphoric language capable of capturing the readers' attention. The sultan calls "Kernec" (Necker) to solve his problems. Kernec finds the source of the evil: a "tree of bronze" that casts a shadow over the kingdom, an evil tree protected by a fearsome monster, "Iscariot," and inhabited by magicians: the fairy "Cangilop" (Polignac), the enchanter "Umaïr" (Maury), and the sorcerer "Vadul" (Duval d'Eprémenil). An expedition is mounted, led by Kernec and "Sanelor" (the Duc d'Orléans), the purpose of which is to chase these beings from the shadow and uproot the tree of bronze, in order to allow "1,200 builders" to construct a new temple on the site of the evil tree.

It is a chivalrous tale, mixing genres—the biblical (allusion to the Tower of Babel), the mythical (Medusa's head, Hercules and Antaeus), the fantastic, the epic. The climax of the tale occurs in the struggle between the knight Sanelor and the monster Iscariot: "The prince hurls himself on the monster who, for his part, defends his life and his refuge with a furor equal to the vigor of the attack. . . . Three times, the hero gathers his strength to strike a decisive blow, and three times the scales that envelop that monster repel the terrible steel. Finally he forces him to leave his dark lair. Then, throwing his weapons away, he seizes him and strangles him as Hercules strangled Antaeus. The dying monster let out a horrible cry, and the breath of his demonic spirit escaped from its fundament, becoming a black vulture going to rejoin its comrades in Lucifer's den. The tree of bronze, falling on its own, made echoes of the sound of its fall ring out. The impure horde of fairies, enchanters, and magicians ran to hide the shame of its defeat in the shadow; and the great Civis-King, the valorous Sanelor, and the wise Kernec, along with some good architects, hastened to raise the first stones of the temple of public felicity." The central figure in this Manichean imagination of puppet show and fairy tale, Iscariot, finds a role that is made to measure: he is the "terrifying" but servile (thus reassuring) embodiment of the despotism that Patriots and their heroes bring down. But nothing is quite as simple as that. This monster conceals a few mysteries.

Iscariot: The Story of a "Narrative-Body"

Iscariot's success, it will undoubtedly have been observed, stems from a play on words, in fact on letters: "Iscariot" is an anagram, although slightly incomplete, of "aristocrat." This linguistic variation is sufficiently amusing to be quickly taken up by a press and pamphlets that are as greedy for "political entertainment" (to use the title of a column in Gorsas's *Courrier*) as they are for projects for legislation or for parliamentary proceedings.

First comes an entire pamphlet, dated 3 October 1789, another period of aristocratic plotting, that plays on the monster's name and presents a detailed portrayal of it: *The Iscariot of France, or the Austrian deputy*. Then, a few weeks later, Jean-Louis Carra, in the widest read and distributed Patriot journal in Paris at the time, the *Annales patriotiques et littéraires*, published with the help of Louis-Sébastien Mercier, makes the play on letters rebound by presenting it to his readers on 15 January 1790. It is immediately taken up by *L'Observateur* of 16 January and by the *Chronique de Paris* of 17 January. Soon after, close to 20 June 1790, when a vigorous and final debate is set in motion between the nobles and the Patriots about the Assembly's abolition of titles of nobility, a new version of the engraving of the previous summer appears, repeated without variation except for the background, from which the Bastille has disappeared.[4] In a year, the monster has won all the supports of representation (engraving, pamphlet, newspapers), has crossed numerous genres (cartoon captions, stories, entertainments, denunciations), and, above all, has perpetuated its body: little by little, it has been detached from the strict context of mid-July 1789 to become the largest image of aristocratic conspiracy. Made up of vivid colors, multiple references, and subtle letters, it does not exit from the political scene of conspiracy. Its career is a success, almost as stunning as the vogue for "magic words" of the beginning of the Revolution—"Liberty," "Regeneration," or "Aristocracy."

This success is due to the way this figure itself is understood, to its essential ambivalence. It is a simple representation, offered to the common gaze by its vivid colors and its crude appearance. Then it is a monster of the tale, animating the Manichean imagination of fantastic plots with its presence. Finally it is a play body, playing on its own name to elicit another. Already, in a few months, Iscariot, leaving behind this pretended initial simplicity, offers itself to three different interpretative gazes. But this interlocking is not finished: the more one strips this body of its successive appearances, the more complex it becomes, or at least the more it establishes its understanding on multiple registers. Readings of this image are thus set into an almost disconcerting game of reflections. For, in the minds of revolutionaries, the Iscariot, as much as a monster, as much as an anagram, is a biblical reference: it is Judas Iscariot,[5] called by the name of his native district, son of Simon Iscariot. Judas the traitor, last of the apostles. Carra places the monster explicitly on this register: "Iscariot is the anagram of Aristocrat; we know that it was the surname of the traitor Judas, who handed over Jesus Christ to the Jews because Iscariot was his peer (Matthew 10:4)."[6]

But the cartoon had already clothed the body of the monster in symbols for "Giudecca," as Dante designates that part of his *Inferno* where traitors are engulfed. The colors of the engraving speak as subtly of the Bible as they speak openly to the eyes. The tips of the hair, russet, or red more precisely, are in direct reference to the color of the traitor, still designated at that time in German-speaking countries under the label of "Judas, Ist gar Rot,"[7] "Judas the very red." Yellow is the other color of Judas's treason, that of his cloak when he comes to kiss Jesus in the Garden of Olives to point him out to the soldiers, and that of the gold that he receives from the High Priest for that deed, the same gold that is found on the corselet of the giant Iscariot, aristocrat of 1789. Another characteristic of Giudecca: the death of the traitor, which Dante surrounds with the deepest terrors and the cruelest punishments. Judas hangs himself in the Potter's Field, crying out his despair while his stomach literally explodes, eviscerated, under the weight of his soul, so heavy with remorse and sins, which escapes through his anus in the form of a black bird. We recognize here the burlesque, or at least scatological, outcome of the story of *The last cry of the monster*, borrowed directly from the figures on the capitals of the cathedrals at Vézelay and Autun. To the "terrible cry" of the suffocated monster answers, as a grotesque echo, the "black vulture" flying away from its "fundament." Iscariot experiences a degrading death, he "dies of a fart," suffocated, suffering. It is certain that biblical erudition, the symbolism of colors, and this death suspended between terror and laughter all contributed to the success of the monstrous figure of Iscariot.

But it is the monster's derivation from the tutelary figure of Marie-Antoinette that wins its "legitimacy." The October 1789 pamphlet *The Iscariot of France, or the Austrian deputy* is completely explicit on this subject. Iscariot is a "female monster" of Austrian origin: "The Austrian deputy, governor and tyrant of France, fruit of one of the most licentious cohabitations, is the composite of heterogeneous substances, made of several races, in part Lorraine, German, Austrian, Bohemian, etc., etc. She wears the fearsome hairstyle of the fourteenth apostle, of the same nature as Judas. Like him, she put her hand in the dish to steal and squander the treasures of France: her hard eyes, traitorous and inflamed, breathe only fire and carnage to achieve her unjust revenge; her nose and cheeks are spotted and empurpled by a corrupt blood that is exuded between her flesh and her already livid hide; and her fetid and foul mouth harbors a cruel tongue, which cries out that it thirsts for French blood! Now, all the more fearsome since she is at the age of ambition and of the greatest sensual excitement for pleasure, her extreme pride aspires to reign over hearts and over the Empire at the same time. Lately returned from her fainting, occasioned by her accesses of rage that move her with violence to strike, break, and trample on everything, as if possessed by the infernal spirit and falling from a high evil, she now finds herself disturbed by a convulsive torment by her bitter regrets at the removal of a turncoat and of a tribade [the Comte d'Artois and the Duchesse de Polignac], odious objects of her unspeakable pleasures."

The imaginary monster is here enriched with a precise figure, the portrayal of the "Austrian," endlessly repeated,[8] playing on invariable corporeal elements, but also with a genesis: perverted procreation, "unspeakable pleasures." The monster always resembles the queen and is born from hybrid pairing; this portrayal and this genesis are continually used by cartoonists and satirists. By "Iscariot" in the first place: the image of the summer of 1789, through the tresses of snakes, evokes the "Antoinette-Medusa,"[9] and through the red of this same hair, connotes the "Royal Redhead."[10] The same contrast of colors on the body of the monster, the red of the stains on the face and the green of the scales, and the same superimposition on the body of the queen: the "nose and cheeks are spotted and empurpled by blood" while "the flesh and hide" are already "livid." All that remain are the "tiger's claws" of the Iscariot, fitting symbolism for the one whom the lampoonists nickname the "Archtigress of Austria." But what is striking, in the image as in the written portrayal, is the disease with which this body is overcome. The "pimples," the "corrupted blood," the "faintings," the "accesses of rage," the very deformity, are the symptoms of a bodily defect of shameful genesis. For the monster is a monster from its very conception. The theme readily adheres to the person of Marie-Antoinette: her relationships, as much with the Comte d'Artois as with the Duchesse de

Polignac, and more precisely because they are double, adding lesbianism to debauchery, are quite systematically placed at the origins of the gang of monsters that peoples the terrible conspiracies. Thus the monster is a mutant figure, an issue of the "uterine furies" of the queen and the "venereal sickness" of the Comte d'Artois, symbolic defects that, according to the lampoonists, infect the courtiers at Versailles. Monstrous pathology is only a variant of the bodily degeneracy striking the leading people of the kingdom in the imagination of the antinobility discourse at the beginning of the Revolution.

Iscariot himself does not escape this peril: his monstrosity is congenital. The ultimate interpretation of this body, suggested by the interweaving of narratives, commentaries, and wordplays surrounding the engraving, is this truly monstrous idea: Iscariot might be the degenerate product of the union of the queen and the Comte d'Artois (himself an anagram of "aristo"), as the pamphlet from October 1789 suggests and as the engraving's caption implies. The "furious child" bears moreover the physical signs of his mother (redness, spots on the face, tiger's claws) and of his father (the green of the livery of the Comte d'Artois and the snake encircling the waist, a reference, but without its positive aspect since here the animal no longer bites its tail in a sign of eternity, to the arms of the prince). At the origin of this monstrous birth, we find rumors about the birth of the dauphin circulating in 1781: the count might be the real father. The queen, if one follows the scandalous chronicle constructed by the satirists, may have ended up by poisoning this bastard dauphin, dead on 4 June 1789, so that he could escape the patriotic education the new times wanted to lavish on him. Having gone through Hell, like Dante's Judas, where he finishes outfitting himself with the instruments of his monstrosity, the red-haired son, "furious child," returns to earth under the influence of his mother to haunt the Bastille and defy the dawning Revolution. It is in the course of this conflict between two geneses, the fantastic and the terrible, and between two tales of origins, revolutionary regeneration and monstrous birth, that Iscariot is born, the giant aristocrat.

However, once this tale and this genealogy are reconstructed, once the monster has emerged from the shadows and been brought to light by multiple commentaries that have sketched his traits, Iscariot keeps a part of his mysterious "aura." If the complexity of this imaginary being is not completely reduced, if this representation resists interpretation, it is because the effort of interpretation itself (of the contemporary reader and of the researcher of today) engenders the monstrous. Iscariot, in fact, exists only thanks to the infinite crossings of the genres, narratives, and references that constitute him: beyond his own appearance, his representation *itself* is monstrous. Just as this aristocrat is born from the heterogeneous crossing of many bodies, so also the engraving and later the narratives are born from the crossing of disparate inspirations and often contradictory references, whence comes the confusion of signs, reference points, and values. Terror crosses laughter, biblical reference takes over from pagan mythology, colors bleed into each other. Iscariot is born from Patriot propaganda, but he owes his success to the mélanges of genres, to the confusion of commentaries, to the ambivalences of readings: to the spectacular monstrosity of his body as the essential vector of his meaning, the product of the hybridization of bodies *and* discourses.

Iscariot embodies, or at least exemplifies, a larger movement of diffusion, perversion, destruction of the meaning of the words and images of political language.[11] The author of *The Misuse of Words*,[12] a dictionary already cited for its suggestive definition of revolutionary regeneration, confers an exorbitant power on the designation "aristocrat": "No expression has been more in fashion from the beginning of our revolution," so exorbitant that, leaving the shores of its etymology, the expression is threatened with going astray: "This word has been vastly successful in our time, everyone applies it to what he does not like at all."[13] This diffusion of the word goes beyond its initial usage — "The name of aristocrat has produced more effects than one expected"[14] — and thus escapes its initiators by the same token. The hundreds of pamphlets of 1789 that include the word "aristocracy" in their title[15] place the word, and thus the class that it is supposed to designate, between oversignificance and insignificance. The journalist Elisée Loustallot perfectly defines the stakes of this quarrel in his *Révolutions de Paris* in November 1789, when the vocabulary of the Revolution is laid out: "The word 'aristocrat' has not contributed less to the Revolution than the cockade. Its signification today is very broad: it applies to all those who live on abuses, who lament lost abuses, or who want to create new abuses. Aristocrats have sought to persuade us that this word had become insignificant. We have not fallen into the trap."[16]

Did the Patriots really avoid the trap? Iscariot, monstrous figure of the aristocrat, can help shed light on this question, since he is emblematic of the threat brandished toward the other while threatened by that very adversary. In fact, the monster corresponds initially with a wish to stretch the meaning of the word well beyond its etymology ("Aristocracy: government by the best," is how the word is defined in numerous works from spring 1789), and thus impose on a political group a body that guarantees an immediate and massive revulsion on the part of the public. But the representation is "led astray" by political language and images. It ends up being sidetracked, trapped, by the very ones it was supposed to frighten. Monarchists accept this challenge of representation and answer without fear. They take up the game, gibing at the "fine Patriot minds that waste their time finding the anagram for aristocrat." [17] They offer their own solution: "If these anagrams, which are mere amusements, were to enter into a serious dissertation, it should be noted that in the word 'aristocrat' are found both Aristotle [*aristote*] and Socrates [*socrate*] . . . One also finds in this word 'aristocracy [*aristocratie*],' *sire, roi*. In this so-called monster, there is nothing but honor for aristocrats." [18]

So the monster finds a respectability that definitively contradicts its meaning; it risks being integrated into the Royalist counterimagination, which absorbs the offensive representations presented to it and reverses them, challenges them by "positiving" them. The Patriots themselves do the same, devouring without much hesitation the monster that counterrevolutionary satirists offer them: these "democrats," these "Sans-Culottes," or, in a more naive register, these "Mariannes," at first glance harmful but very quickly recaptured as marks of respect. From then on, even before it can be taken in hand by the challenge of the Royalist counterimagination, Iscariot completes his career. As if they had felt the danger, the Patriot engravings and pamphlets abandon the "furious child." The symbol has lost its success and sinks back into the underworld, to public indifference. The trap of the perversion of the image has just barely been avoided. Iscariot did not have the time to become a compliment, even if it was no longer an insult. This political animal thus had only an ephemeral life, but a burgeoning and feverish one, a monster's life, due as much to its birth and appearance as to the very numerous and heterogeneous registers on which the revolutionaries wanted to establish its presence. What killed it is a bulimia of signs. It died of a surfeit of significations. Its body, though, resuscitated for the occasion, symbolic of the "terrible" tales of the Revolution, was able to serve as a guide in this strange spectacle: from now on, with these monsters, we must be on our guard. In general, they are much more complex than one glance at their primary body would make us think.

Imagining the Aristocratic Conspiracy: Spaces and
Images of Teratological Intertextuality

"The male has the head of a buzzard, the belly of an elephant, and the talons of a vulture. This monster is so enormous that it can cover all of France with its body. It has as a companion an equally monstrous female, who has four feet, four hands, and as many eyes. These two monsters gobble the subsistence of a kingdom. Fortunately they are sterile. They plunder, suck up and devour; but nothing fattens them enough or stays with them, so it is thought that they will be forced to perish wretchedly on the soil that they have ravaged . . . These animals have three throats that join in the same mouth, and form a frightful voice. To make them shout, it is enough to utter two or three words that are so discordant with their constitution that their limbs tremble from hearing them. These animals roar when they hear the gentle name 'liberty.' Then their nostrils flare out, their eyes glitter, their bellowing redoubles, and all other animals fall silent." [19]

This "monstrous beast found in Paris," described by two newspapers in 1790, resembles a species related to Iscariot. It is, however, an interesting generalization, as if the monster, from a growing menagerie guarded by a strictly political cage of interpretation, had managed to escape and walk among all the "citizen-everybodies" of the city. Thus, the monster becomes the symbol of a widely shared imagination, bears on its body the echoes of the century's press and pamphlets, and foregrounds fantastic writing, a genre with a long literary tradition. The effects of this imagination, press, and literature are reinforced by the political conjuncture unique to 1789: this description of the terrible body supports one of the major narratives of the Revolution, the fantastic universe of the conspiracy.

The resurgence of these paper monsters is already evident at the end of the eighteenth century. In the 1760's, newspapers and engravings are filled with these "discoveries of monsters in the cellars of the capital," of articles announcing the discovery of a "wild child" or a "man-tiger," of tales of expeditions that describe terrifying exotic men, animals, and fish, along with a famous chronicle of a "hunt for the great beast." For it is really the engravers and writers who spread those images and tales about the beast of the Gévaudan that made the monster a main topic in current events.[20] These representations and newspaper articles, quite numerous, following from nearby or afar the apparitions and ravages of the beast, provided the

framework of a description in which the "terrible" language and its corporeal imagination are embedded. Quite often, revolutionary monsters are
only a politicization of this narrative framework. The beast of the Gévaudan
arises from very diverse genres: from natural history, from chronicles of
current events, from hunting tales (first individual, then collective, finally
royal), from criminal investigation, and, obviously, from fantastic fiction.
The great red wolf, the wild dog, the domesticated dog of the Estaing
family—we no longer know which one (or ones) terrorized the countrysides
of the Gévaudan and tricked hunters, scientists, journalists, and shepherds.
All those sightings, extending from 1764 to 1767, place the animal at the
intersection of the most everyday reality with the most fantastic imagination. A synthesis of this monstrous turmoil, a "pseudo-scientific" language,
emerges from it in which precise description is blended with physiological
and psychological analogies on animal behavior, a language that is always
indulgent toward the spectacle and narrative of the terrible body. Then,
as in the case of the monster of 1790 described by Parisian journals, the
detailed description (four feet, four hands, as many eyes, three throats)
melts into a mingling of species and a vision of wonders to compose a hybrid being, deriving as much from perverted anatomical science as from a
"body of terror" rooted in myths and tales. The appearances of the beast of
Gévaudan in fact quickly favored the grafting of visions of fantastic wolves
onto the traditional folkloric background of tales told round the fire. There
even existed, at the end of the 1760's, among the narratives and images in
circulation—especially in the South of France—a "Faramine," a mysterious monster, half-bear half-dragon, sometimes even resembling a werewolf;
it specifically attacked humans.

The Parisian engraver Jean-Louis Desprez, one of the best in the business, offered, between 1774 and 1776, a series of several "Chimeras,"[21]
variations on the monstrous representation directly inspired by the mis-
deeds of the beast of the Gévaudan but nonetheless accommodating a
clearly political shading. These chimeras, in fact, are adopted, copied trait
for trait, from the German Protestant bestiary that demonizes the "Papist
monster." Startling (or titillating), they meet distinct success with the public, so well do they succeed at blending the precision of features in the
drawing of the monster with the almost clinical detail of corpses being devoured, a vision of terror worthy of a Bosch or a Brueghel.

In 1784 the political universe, taking advantage of this vogue for fantastic animals, firmly takes hold of this inspiration. This appropriation takes

place in a pamphlet presenting the *Historical description of a symbolic monster captured alive on the shores of Lake Fagua near Santa Fe, through the efforts of Francisco Xaviero de Meunrios, Count of Barcelona,* a pamphlet of twenty or so pages accompanied by an engraving of a harpy. This monster coarsely resembles Marie-Antoinette, satirized under the title "Madame Laspict"; the pseudonym "Meunrios" hides under a transparent mask, "Monsieur," the Count of Provence, brother of the king [*frère du roi*], of which it is the simple anagram. The factions of the court thus seize hold of a fashionable genre, the teratological fantasy, and the factional rivalry finds polemical expression in battles of fantastic and allegorical animals. Here — in the pastiche reemployment of a fashionable motif, in the offensive allusions and satiric barbs, in the blending of image and text, in the more or less learned references to allegorical culture — we have the typical illustration of the waves of pamphlets that shook the French court more and more frequently toward the end of the ancien régime. However, at this end of the 1780's, thanks to the burgeoning imagination grown up around the beast of the Gévaudan, the pamphlets permeate more widely than the courtiers' milieus alone, since "Madame Laspict" is not an isolated print circulating in the closed world of Versailles or Paris: almost a dozen republications and counterfeits of the pamphlet financed by Monsieur, and especially the engraving of Marie-Antoinette represented as a harpy, are circulating in Paris,[22] kept track of by the police, noted by the bookseller Hardy, and presented in a variety of forms as the different "descriptions of monsters" proliferate.

The different representations of the fantastic monster thus gather around the image of the queen. If one is to believe the chronicles in the newspapers and lampoons, Marie-Antoinette was the only body terrible enough to succeed the beast of the Gévaudan. Between 21 September 1765, when Antoine de Beauterne kills, in the name of the king, an imposing red wolf near the so-called Les Chazes, and the end of the 1780's, when the "Harpy" terrorizes the "carrying baskets" of the picture-peddlers of Paris, the monster tale developed two species worthy of becoming typologies in the fantastic imagination. Two forms emerge: the half-natural, half-fantastical devouring animal and the degenerate political being, half-human, half-beast. The Revolution welcomes these two stereotypes without forgetting to mate them, making of the two only one single monster, but all the more terrible. The animal found in Paris in 1790 is a good illustration of it: it unarguably belongs to the bestial category, lends itself to the play of scientific description, and understands political language very well, especially the "gentle name of 'liberty' " that infuriates it. The conjuncture from which the revolutionary monster arose belongs to an entirely political grafting of the "Gévaudan" type of body onto the type of the "royal female."

This chronology of hybridization can be meticulously documented. The Revolution first adopts from court satire the bestial image of Marie-Antoinette, who is swiftly caricaturized by Villeneuve as a harpy holding between her talons a Constitution that she means to tear to pieces. During the summer of 1789, this figure extends its appearances and generalizes its effects by successive moltings from the degenerate characterization of the queen to the symbolic form of the aristocrat beast. As we can follow from reading a description in the *Petit journal du Palais-Royal*, the pieces of the queen's body, monstrously assembled, end up by recomposing the aristocratic "statue" in its entire morphology: "A magnificent bronze statue excites the liveliest admiration from its singular composition. It has the head of a woman, the body of a harpy, the pudenda of a cat, the talons of an eagle, and the tail of a pig; it has been noted that the features of its face had much in common with those of Marie-Antoinette, Queen of France."[23]

The journals and engravings open the monstrous political representation born from Marie-Antoinette onto a wide range of possibilities. These political monsters from the queen's lair begin by attaching themselves to very definite people, drawn from the first émigrés of July 1789: the Comte d'Artois, the Duchesse de Polignac, the Prince de Lambesc, Condé. *The hunt for the stinking and ferocious beasts that, after having overswarmed the Court and the Capital, have now spread out through the forests and the plains* thus presents Marie-Antoinette as a "panther escaped from the Court of Germany" that has, after her stay in Versailles, resumed "all her Germanic rage," surrounded by Artois, who becomes a "tiger escaped from the Versailles zoo," and by Polignac, compared to a "She-wolf from Barbary that, by a monstrous freak of nature, having coupled with the above-mentioned panther and Tiger, as well as with a prodigious quantity of animals of different species, has become suddenly enraged."

Very quickly, however, these monsters become more than simple continuations of a satiric court tradition. Having moved beyond an individual figure, and because of the gathering together and *collective* flight of "émigré monsters" (imagined by the pamphlets since we know that those nobles had actually *scattered* into Belgium, England, Italy, or Germany), these

monsters turn into the degenerate political allegory of the general body of
the nascent counterrevolution. In the course of the summer, their field of
intervention enlarges even more. They leave the single attacks ad hominem,
without completely abandoning them, to assume the stance of patriots attacking "despotism" and "aristocracy." Despotism: they are the "Bastille
monsters," Iscariot for example, or the "Hydra" so often denounced, that
"furious beast that has at least a hundred heads, a hundred arms, and that
wants to devour everything," [24] a beast that one finds depicted again in *Hydra of despotism laid low, or The patriotic hunt of the great beast.*

There are more specifically "aristocratic" monsters, multiple but repe-
titious, to which some descriptions from the autumn of 1789 can testify, when the intense controversy over the constitutional place of the
king and over the nationalization of the property of the clergy agitates
minds and imaginations. Then those creatures arisen from the half-natural,
half-political couplings (Gévaudan + Antoinette) appear in full daylight:
"An individual has just found in his wine cellar a kind of monster lying
crouched in a barrel, which had fallen there no doubt through the barred
window. The top of its head is that of a monkey; it has the eyes of a screech-
owl, while its face is like the snout of a pig; it has the ears of a donkey,
a short, hairless neck, a large stomach covered with bristling hairs, a very
short tail, and claw-like feet. Its cry is frightful, like that of the white-tailed
eagle, its walk tottering, like that of the satyr: it is opinionated, insensitive,
and dances only when given wine. Owners of extraordinary animals are informed that M. l'abbé Maury will give them more detailed information." [25]

To this description we must immediately add that of a beast found about
the same time by the journalists of the Palais Royal: "A ferocious, extremely
dangerous animal has been discovered in the environs of the Louvre. The
naturalists that were consulted assure us with all their science that it is
the same that the ancients called Minister. It has a seductive voice, a devi-
ous gait, and its face, although in the same proportion as a cat's, inspires
fear. It seems to have a predominant taste for new fruits, especially for
those from a tree that has been transplanted from New England and that
is called 'regenerative.' They say, however, that a very old lady, dressed in
the old style, bristling with daggers, has come to lavish caresses on its red
coat and to receive the same from it. Her name is Aristocracy. They even
publish that the decrepit old woman has found an elixir for long life in the
monster's venom." [26]

This, the "monster Privilege" in two versions, the clerical and the aristocrat, succeeds at peopling the imagination of the counterrevolutionary plot: from Marie-Antoinette, the attack on the metaphoric body has reached first those close to her (émigré princes and princesses), then the symbolic seat of their political system (the Bastille of despotism), and finally the political order that must support them, the aristocracy. Following the same pattern of attacks, the corporeal forms extended their range of activity, from deformed human body to monstrous animalization. We observe here, in this bulimic tale devouring more and more metaphors, characters, and symbols, how the frightening conception of aristocratic conspiracy is gradually consolidated.

In reading these descriptions, we readily recognize a certain number of classic attributes of the terrible body. Going by frequency of appearance, references to the tiger (seven occurrences) come first, among the seventy or so monstrous figures counted in the pamphlets, engravings, and journals of 1789. The colossus-giant (6), the hydra (5), the monkey, wolf, and falcon, as well as the panther and leopard, must be added; together they represent the animal most frequently attached to negative individuals. Between the exotic monster (tiger, leopard, panther), the ogre of fairy tales, the hydra of classical allegory, and the wolf of the French countrysides, these political animals make up a balanced imaginary menagerie.

Nevertheless, beside this unsurprising bestiary, other characteristics take on meaning under the pen of Patriot writers: first of all, the malfunctioning of procreation. The aristocratic monster stems in fact from mutation, the creature degenerating from man (or woman) to beast, and from animal to political. Descriptions here are telling: the three chief high-born monsters—in the order of frequency, Marie-Antoinette, la Polignac, and the Comte d'Artois—are the products of the "corrupt air of the Court," an atmosphere that is favorable to bodily illnesses but also to endogamous couplings. The "court family" has in fact no options, in the imagination of antinoble discourse,[27] except to choose between two eventualities: endogamous degeneracy in the clan or degradation and bastardization. In both cases, noble blood is equally corrupted: "The blood of the Comte d'Artois is completely destroyed from over-violent exertions, and exhausted of all vital principles from an excessive dissipation of his means . . . Violent poisons and principles of caste pass through his veins. This blood, if the doctor is to be believed, has changed into such a subtle and contagious virus, that if it were spread on the ground, it would infallibly impregnate it, and would breed aristocratic serpents."[28]

This monstrous portrayal is directly inspired by the scandal of the degeneration of the nobility, a scandal circulated widely by satirists since the end of the reign of Louis XV. Debasement is the first threat, as Théveneau de Morande pointed out to the nobles in 1774 in his *Historical glance at the genealogy of the principal modern peers of France,* in which the author of the *Cuirassed Gazetteer* tries to spot the false worthies and the real bastards among *les Grands.* From his brilliant pen, the monsters of perverted genealogy emerge: "The nobility of France, once so fastidious on the point of honor, has lost this precious asset with the times. Luxury, softness, subservience have corrupted everything. Cupidity has made misalliance so common that there is not a Noble Family in the court that could enter the Knights of Malta without a dispensation. [Pure blood and legitimacy were required for this much esteemed Roman Catholic chivalric order. Trans.] Titled Lords call that [marrying rich commoners — Trans.] 'taking dung to fertilize their lands.' But the proverb says that 'it is not the sow that ennobles the boar, but the boar that ennobles the sow' . . . Yet that is nothing compared to much more shameful marriages that princes do not blush to conclude and whose offspring can resemble nothing but terrible forms."

"Terrible forms": most of these monstrous visions of the body of nobility describe a "rotten carcass," an organic degradation that hurries a race toward its exhaustion or its "dehumanization," toward its progressive mutation into a degenerate beast. It is by corruption of noble lineage, the successive depraved passages from body to body, from generation to generation, that the monstrous is constructed, producing a congenital defect in the nobility. It is also a way for vulgar satire to put to good use that fear of debasement so present in the treatises on nobility of the period.

The first terror, at once the cause and effect of monstrous procreations of the nobility, remains venereal disease. The noble is in fact precisely placed in the center of these insults and these suspicions, by a transference of the moral deprivation attributed to the privileged caste to the realm of corporeal pathology. Smug descriptions of maladies succeed each other in satires to sketch roughly the diseased figure of the decadent, ailments that "end up burning, consuming the body, drying out the muscles, impoverishing the blood, weakening the resources, to the point that the machine, once dismantled, burnt to a cinder and destroyed, offers nothing but the sad spectacle of a hideous skeleton. It is in this way that almost all the potentates and opulent princes of the Earth perish. To acquire a just and precise notion of these sad extremities, can only be accomplished by contemplating the monsters of our emigrated aristocracy."[29]

It is a vision of the Last Judgment: libertine nobles destined to decom-position, exhaustion of a body deprived of substance: "To die on the bed of horror, to see oneself eaten away down to the bone, to feel one's limbs fall away from putrefaction one after the other." [30] The nobles can only mask their worn-out, monstrous bodies, hide them from view: hypocrisy, pre-tense, then conspiracy are the scenes in which they play this role of decom-position: "Proteus could take all imaginable forms." [31] But it is precisely in the mask itself that monstrosity lies, for revolutionaries always defined themselves as the "unveilers," the "removers of the mask." Once the veil has fallen, the true body leaps to the eye. That is the "monster unveiled," a schema used again and again for the discovery of conspiracy.

This disease of the body is also, and especially, a political disease. The terrible body embodies monstrous thinking. This reaches the point where, through a superior form of mutation, political symbols come to be grafted onto the body, to become living members or organisms: "I see the aristoc-racy in the form of a hideous monster, having ears in the form of crosiers, eight white feathers on top of its head, a horn in the form of a sword in the middle of its forehead, and nostrils in the shape of pistol barrels." [32]

The distinctive marks of the clergy and of the nobility enter clearly, car-nally, into the attributes of the monster. By forging the aristocratic monster on the body corrupted by social and political function, the patriotic dis-course of the Revolution builds its victory on noble blood, upon theories of undefiled blue blood. Monstrous representation is a bodily response di-rectly addressed to noble ideology: it claims for itself the myth of corporeal privilege that had been peculiar to noble "racism," that ideal body elabo-rated between the end of the sixteenth century and the beginning of the eighteenth century, when it produced its greatest theoretician in the per-son of Boulainvilliers.

Boulainvilliers's thinking can be divided into two main propositions: (1) the origin of the French nobility goes back to the Germanic conquest, since nobles are the direct descendants of the Franks, who subjugated the Gallo-Roman ancestors of the members of the Third Estate; and (2) this German blood gives the right to privileges; it is the guarantee of the bodily superiority of the "noble race" with pure blood.

If the first proposition, concerning the origin of the nobility and of the French monarchy, remains present in the ideological debate of the end of the eighteenth century, the second, or the nobility's racism of blue blood, quickly fell, if not into oblivion, then at least into the realm of derision. Fought effectively by the ideology of merit, it now, even with many nobles, has only antiquarian value. We can count very few works by the nobility at the end of the eighteenth century that endorse this racism of pure blood. Even the theoreticians of counterrevolution prefer the ideology of merit to justify the social hierarchy that they advocate: virtue no longer goes directly with blood, it is rather blood that must back up merit. But Patriot pamphleteers and journalists soon make a hobby-horse of this racist, outmoded theory. They understood all the irony and perceived all the attacks that could be mounted by turning this corporeal definition against the "red heels," the last supporters of the argument of particularism and of the privilege of the "noble race." Generally, Patriot newspapers place the speeches of Father Ménestrier or of La Rocque—noble writers of the end of the seventeenth century—or of Boulainvilliers in the mouth of their noble "characters." This is why we can speak of "political imagination," the entry of the figure of the nobleman into the space of fantastic mythology: the noble speaks, in revolutionary literature, using a language dating back more than a century, or close to sixty years in any case if one takes as a final point of reference the publication date of Boulainvilliers's *Essais sur la noblesse de France.*

To illustrate this statement, examples are not hard to find of this turning of noble racism into something engendering the monstrous body. The fable of bodily haughtiness is overturned, and pamphlets and newspapers have a field day. Thus Sieyès, Gallophile of course, vigorously attacks those Frankish and Germanic races that Boulainvilliers claimed descent from: "The Third Estate must not fear to go back to times past. Let it turn back to the year that preceded the conquest; since today it is strong enough not to let itself be conquered, its resistance will undoubtedly be more effective. Why should it not send back into the forests of Franconia all those families that cling to the foolish boast of having come from the race of conquerors and having succeeded to their rights? The purified nation will then be able to console itself, I deem, for being reduced to believing itself composed of only the descendants of the Gauls and Romans. In truth, if one insists on distinguishing birth from birth, can't we reveal to our poor fellow citizens that the blood of the Gauls and Romans is worth at least as much as what might come from the Sicambrians, southrons and other savages from the woods and swamps of ancient Germania? . . . Nobility of birth has been passed down on the side of the conquerors. Well then! We must make it pass down on the other side, and the Third Estate will once again become noble by becoming conquerors in its turn."[33]

This theme abounds in the Patriot journals: the physical defects of the nobility imply ignominious genealogy. Brissot waxes ironic in his *Patriote français*: "Is nobility then a natural quality inherent in the blood, engraved by the hand of divinity on the body of a few individuals? Such a system is too absurd to merit debate. I will believe in nobility only when I see it born with spurs, and their subjects with a saddle on their back." [34]

Awaiting this scarcely probable metamorphosis, Patriot discourse offers the noble another body, born from allegedly superior blood now ironically diverted toward degeneracy: the "forests of Franconia" no longer engender heroes but "savage beasts." The language of 1789 thus brings its personal touch to the definition of the monster. The terrible body, in teratological tradition, is first of all deviant because of its appearance of being *contra naturam*: "When nature seems to forget its own laws," noted Ambroise Paré, in his seminal text of 1573, *On Monsters and Marvels*. But revolutionary politics implicates this "counternature" by introducing it into the sphere of conspiracy: the aristocrat, having become a deviant monster, is relegated to the shadows of history. His blue blood is transformed, by a physiologico-political mutation, into an "impure blood" that engenders monsters and resentments, an impure blood with which the revolutionaries want to drench themselves. [An allusion to the ending of the *Marseillaise*, "may their impure blood drench our furrows." Trans.]

The Paper Monster: The Fictional Body of Political Event

How can the fortunes of monsters in the Patriot universe of 1789 be explained? The political imagination as it thinks about conspiracy is, from this point of view, of a remarkable productivity; it consumes vast numbers of monsters. In the development of this burgeoning bestiary, the role of revolutionary language itself must be emphasized, a language open to multiple reappropriations and to the most audacious neologisms. Political writing devours references and preconstituted genres, and fantastic narrative does not escape this process of recycling—far from it. The language used in 1789 is one of the most appropriate for both inheriting and generating monsters. It is undoubtedly that which makes it such a living organism, a privileged receptacle of fashionable genres. The hybrid writing of the journals or the revolutionary pamphlet is based on the referential complicity of the writer and the reader. There too lies the essence of the pamphlet about current events: it is itself a monster, able to join together in a few pages extremely diverse genres elected by the act of reading. The many-layered pastiche, multiplying the intersections of literary genres and linguistic games from various fashionable styles, confers its own hybridity on it. In 1789, this cultural complicity comes to be fused in the crucible of political language. The body of the monster is fertile soil, on which come together writings of a "philosophical" century that has never hesitated to blend rational reasoning with terrible emotionality.

The first of the teratological traditions finds its origin in scientific discourse. Species taxonomy, vitalist experiments, phrenological method, anatomical dissections performed on monstrous bodies to try to uncover their mysteries, researches exactly contemporary with the Revolution,[35] all seem to indicate that scholars had ardently investigated this problem that resisted their skill. This experiment of the body gone awry, and the discourse that tried to put it in order, is found again in the work, in the state of pastiche, in political writing from the beginning of the Revolution, as in this anticlerical lampoon of February 1790 using the style of Buffon to itemize the different monstrous categories of monks: *A natural history of monks, written following the method of M. de Buffon; adorned with illustrations.*

The different "political menageries" published between 1789 and 1791 also parody scientific style with ease, endlessly classing and reclassing the "political animals," attempting cross-breedings and experiments, from dissection to surgical operations, under the supervision of "Patriot doctors." These, popularized at the time, quickly appear as the consecration of this writing: the Revolution creates monsters, but only in order to take care of them better. "I am as old as Methuselah, as sage as Cagliostro, and as infallible as the *Almanach de Liège*"—that is how the "Patriot operator-dentist-doctor" presents himself to his readers. "I have gone round the world 22 times; I have treated a quantity of emperors for the contagion of vices; I have exterminated gangrene from the tyranny that was beginning to reach the heart of the Kings of France; many times I have saved secretaries of State from ministerial rage; I have cut more than a thousand heads from the hydra of despotism and tended to the gall of the dogs of aristocracy; and I have just recently successfully pulled the monstrous teeth of the clergy of France, leaving it with nothing but stumps to grind the elements that have been granted it by divine mercy and by the wisdom of the representatives of the nation."[36]

Another genre parodied by "monster texts" is diabolic initiation—visits to hells haunted by Dantesque and Bosch-like creatures, pastorals of fear turned to derision by the many "descents" that nobles and ecclesiastics undertake to Lucifer's realm. The mixture of genres is again needed, since monsters of the apocalyptic tradition and creatures of pagan mythology cross with ease under the pen of pamphleteers. Thus the pope, when he is symbolically put to death in May 1791, passes, by the single logic of pastiche writing, from the "gates of Paradise" where he is denied by Saint Peter down to Lucifer's abyss by voyaging in "Charon's skiff." [37]

Another significant borrowing is the allegorical register. The most common types are the Fury, the Hydra, and the Colossus, well represented in the monstrous bestiary of the pamphlets. Reviving the classical opposition between kindly, gentle, and reassuring allegories and mean-spirited, obvious, thin, caustic — indeed, polycephalic — allegories, pamphlets like to tell of the allegorical dreams of their characters. Thus, a pamphlet of 1789, *The curtain lifted, or things as they are*, portrays a Frenchman led by "a woman of the most majestic size," "naked and magnificent." This "goddess Truth" leads the free man toward the "France of tomorrow," while, suddenly opposing them, barring them from the path of the future, a monster, this one negative, "Munici" (from "Municipality," a body intended to symbolize the Parisian municipality against which this radical satire is written), rears up: "A genie of an enormity out of all proportion, and growing before our eyes. The name 'Munici' is written on its forehead. It has one hundred arms, any one of which would suffice to strike us down." A fight is begun between the goddess and the monster, worthy of those grandiose struggles between light and dark that allegorical representation makes a specialty of: "Truth opposed the blows of this terrible monster, of this immense colossus, only by confronting it with a book from which sparks flew that seemed to strike it down and reduce it to ashes. I read, on the first page of this divine book, Decrees of the National Assembly."

Even more than scientific, biblical, or allegorical inspiration, the monster of pamphlet writing is constructed from two dominant registers inherited from the fantastic writing of the seventeenth and eighteenth centuries. The first genre is that of the "body of terror," illustrated by the literature of the fairy tale, made up of devouring ogres and famished wolves, a literature whose "primitive violence" Robert Darnton emphasized,[38] a violence that later versions of these tales and an overallusive reading have caused us to forget for a long time. The monster of *Contes de ma mère l'oye* (Tales of Mother Goose) is still, as Darnton says, a "boorish" ogre. A similar primitivism is found in the revolutionary pamphlet, passages in which the "aristocratic monster," far from being laughable, recovers the essence of its frightful nature, and again becomes utterly the devouring monster: "How ugly is the true face of the aristocrat! This monster presented itself to me in the form of all its vices: its eyes were red, inflamed, its pupils glinting, its forehead wide and flat, its eyebrows black, thick, each forming a half-circle, its nose eaten away so that I saw only the two holes through which it breathed, its mouth open because of two frightful tusks that came out, as if to show the ferocity of the animal. The more I stared at it, the larger its head grew to my eyes; I was dying of fear; in vain did I hide my face—I saw it always ready to devour me." [39]

"I was dying of fear": here we find the chief function of the "aristocratic monster" in Patriot writing. Its frightful body, embodiment of ideas thought of as terrible, does terrorize. It is inscribed in the panic-filled fear of the aristocratic plot, essential source of this revolutionary siege mentality present in its coarse state in a good number of pamphlets of denunciation, texts that belong to a *writing of nightmare*. "I lived a nightmare with the appearance of a terrifying phantom," confesses the author of *Dream of an inhabitant of Scioto*, describing the "dragon of the apocalypse" that threatens revolutionary Paris, that "monster whose clawed feet crushed the city, whose claw-like hands trapped the people and whose fanged mouth devoured men."

The second characteristic of the aristocratic monster portrayed by revolutionary writing is drawn from another genre: ironic subversion. This time, it belongs in the domain of laughter. Here again, political writing is only an adventitious adaptation of a successful genre of the eighteenth century, the ironic bestiary. The fairy tale keeps its primitive ferocity, the ogre embodies its central figure, and devouring is its constant theme; as for fantastic satire, it prefers to play with the terrible. In this respect, the article "Vampires" from the *Dictionnaire philosophique* by Voltaire, the great master of the genre, is exemplary: "Businessmen who sucked the blood of the people in the nascent dawn . . . These real suckers of blood did not live in cemeteries, but in splendid palaces." Irony imprints the political motif on the monstrous body, but the vampire is no longer "terrifying." Voltaire's vampire is not a nightmare being, as it would have been in the fairy tales, or even of the "cemetery" as it will become again with Nodier; rather, it haunts the palaces of *les Grands* politically. This deviation from the meaning carries with it the power of laughter.

Revolutionary satires, very Voltairean in this sense, will not forget this trail of political laughter leading to the monstrous body. Iscariot died of a fart, and many terrible political animals that the various Herculeses of the people fight have that weakness too. It is through the anus that their life is drawn from them, but it is also through there that they defend themselves, rather ridiculously. That is how the author of *The Club of Les Halles* describes it: "The hidra [*sic*] countered the attacks, hurling red ball-and-chains on all sides. To the surprise of the valorous Patriots, it must have launched some by the backside."[40]

The monster is a hesitant body, a hesitation that, according to Tzvetan Todorov, is precisely the characteristic of the fantastic narrative,[41] a body endlessly vacillating between fear and laughter, a body led toward its ambiguity by a writing that is itself amphibolous. Bodies of terror, these paper monsters are the terrifying embodiment of a danger presented as incessant and formidable by the denouncers of plots; beasts of irony, they are too closely bound with the political situation of the moment and with sabotaging the adversary's values to be anything but amusing. They do indeed talk about a terrifying body, but in general they are only a "reference to this terror," not the terror itself, which remains within the unsayable and unrepresentable. Terrifying bodies, maintained in mediation, elements of the "paper war," always do nothing but precede or accompany the real war. They are not that war. This hesitation between laughter and fear is, more generally, emblematic of the writing of the beginning of the Revolution; it certainly makes its success. "Anxious laughter," Mikhail Bakhtin's phrase, characteristic according to him of Romantic laughter,[42] is in fact one of the conditions of the career of the monsters. This body plays on two extremes: a pole of anguish and a pole of mockery. The course of its diffusion into minds follows the ambivalent contours that the crossing of anxiety with laughter sketches out. One is afraid of that which one mocks, one makes fun of that which one fears: the terrible body is at the center of this play of writings and expressions.

By this incessant turning of laughter to fear, and its borrowings from the most heterogeneous genres, fantastic writing amounts to a genuine narrative of the Revolution. That is the final characteristic of the genre. Functioning in the fictional mode, the terrible body tells a tale; it makes a story of the Revolution in progress. This body is in fact carried by the wave of pamphlets of fairy tales, fables, dreams (or nightmares), and voyages that greet the beginning of the Revolution. *The Dream of a Parisian; Letters from an ambassador of Tippoo Sahib where much is spoken about the affairs of the*

kingdom of Gogo; *The Adventures of Gigy, prince of the blood*; *Dreams of a
solitary philosopher*; *Chronicle of the Grand Turk*; *Arabian Tales* or *Tales from
India*; *The Fable of the flown away birds*; or *The Correspondence of Babouc*—
all these works with evocative titles tell in their way of the convocation of
the Estates General, the conflicts between the king and the Assembly, conspiracies, events in Paris. Reviving the exotic narrations of Montesquieu or
Voltaire, perpetuating the tradition of Rabelais, and above all pursuing the
series of *Chronicles of Persia under Mangogul*, "a dissertation on the cause
of the decadence of the Empire" that had met with a fine success in the beginning of Louis XVI's reign, these texts "fictionalize" politics. Through
the use of devices by turns linguistic (anagrams or deformations of names),
literary (the use of fantastic genres), geographical (change of country), or
historical (moving backward or forward in time), they transfer the events of
1789 toward the words, space, or time of a fiction with political references.

Here, in these words, these countries, these times out of joint, characters meet political monsters or fairies. The monster is born in shadow, of
a baleful race, appears suddenly to everyone's view at the time of a plot,
battles, then withdraws, pursued by the Patriot—that is the basic structure of this "History of France" falsely delocalized and detemporized, of
this historic fantasy. The success of the fantastic genre comes from this
too, that the writing manages to detach itself from concepts in order to
make of History a story, and from ideas, bodies. The monster, then, an
idea embodied in a degenerate body, is the principal actor in this tale in
the role of evil—"Iscariot," "Gigy," "Mazur-Ten-Brick," "Banian Griffaël,"
"Super-bogigas," or, more classically, "Hydra," "Hyena," "Tiger"—while
the Patriot takes the flattering role of "monster-hunter," "Sanelor," "Suri-
nastin," "Tunder-Ten-Trunch," "Strong-arm." It is a question, after all,
only of the anticipation of a genre more connected with contemporary civilization: cartoons, for example, in which superheroes and "wonderwomen,"
in the name of the values of Good, fight against the forces of Evil inspired
by the other world, be it fantastic, mafioso, communist, or diabolical. The
Revolution is readily narrated as a struggle of the marvelous against the
terrible, a mode that is favorable to the pedagogical and imaginative dissemination of its values. In those multiple pamphlets of the fantastic genre
(close to a hundred in 1789), the Revolution, experienced through this
mode of narrative, as Lynn Hunt notes, is related in tone to the English
"romance" or the French *conte*.[43] The monster is the key element of this
narrative, the guardian of the kingdom of shadow, the fictional but dis-

tinctly political being that is combatted by the adventurers of the "temple of public felicity," in mock-pathetic style to be sure. Comparing revolutionary politicians to these adventurers and their enemies to aristocratic monsters, the pamphlet—itself a "literary monster"—defined an imagination in which Manicheanism, as politically reductive as it is fertile of imagery, very quickly structures the framework of political thought. From then on Patriots will be heroes, and aristocrats, degenerate monsters.

No writer better defined this language of the fantastic narrative of the Revolution than Joseph-Antoine Cérutti. A former Jesuit adept at the "rhetoric of depiction," a talented speechifier on the academic proofs of the end of the ancien régime, Cérutti knew the art of persuasion in its finest details.[44] In January 1790, he tries to define, well before La Harpe, the new language forged by the writers of the Revolution. His *Portable Dictionary of Exaggerations* [*Dictionnaire portatif de l'idiome exagérateur*] is a model of analysis that directs its stern gaze on the rhetoric of 1789. "I thought to compose for the use of the world a portable, reasonable dictionary of all the terms and all the phrases that form the language of exaggeration," he writes, "which comes back to the same thing, the *language of effect*. Whoever wants to produce gems, or even magic, has only to study an article or two from my vocabulary. It will communicate flames to the coldest wits, wings to the most limited wits. Its greatest usefulness is for eloquence, which at present holds, so to speak, the scepter of opinion and the helm of affairs. Everyone wants to be eloquent; everyone will be able to be so by meditating on my work. It teaches the various ways of troubling, of agitating the calmest heads.

"I believe that this vast conception could not have hatched in a more favorable, or more solemn, circumstance. We are in a time when, gradually, everything increases and grows larger. Actors have exaggerated their roles, writers their style, artists their forms, heroes their courage and ideas their embodiments; even women have accentuated their manners. . . . Delicacy has turned into energy and, today, every sublime physiognomy is an eloquent preface. The heat of enthusiasm has become our natural heat, and inspiration is now as common as respiration. It was time to teach a language in proportion to this steady increase, or rather to the sudden swelling of our ideas. When a science is perfected, its idiom should be fixed. Today, exaggeration dominates French thinking."[45] Cérutti distinguishes nine possible figures of speech in exaggerated style, and offers his reader keys to comprehension of common political discourse, of the "formulaic propaganda" [*langue de bois*] of the revolutionaries, and analyzes all its appearances and functions.

Synthesizing his knowledge, the writer ends by dividing the exaggerative idiom into two great currents, each one engendering its own narrative and its particular bodies: "Exaggeration, like unto those two barrels of the Fable that poured the river of good and the torrent of evil on the Earth, is divided into two dialects, of which one expresses all that is marvelous, and the other, all that is terrible. The marvelous and the terrible, which are the two extremes of nature, are for that very reason the two extremes of our sensations." The two methods of revolutionary narrative can be recognized in this distinction. Regeneration animating the New Man, raising Patriots, awakening slumbering slaves: the marvelous takes hold of their appearances and changes them, at will, into Herculeses, colossi, goddesses—in every case, into miraculous beauty. Degeneracy deforms enemies and bad citizens: the terrible decomposes harmony and transforms body, at will, into a bloody, diseased, or impotent monster, an aristocratic hydra with many heads, by turns ridiculous and terrifying. Revolutionary writing is carried along by its own corporeal metaphors toward marvelous remedies (regeneration) or terrible impulses (the monstrous). Thus, words of regeneration and those of the monstrous belong to the same language of persuasion. This language, peopled with corporeal metaphors the better to consume readers' minds, seems indispensable to writers of the Revolution. It alone can engender the narrative of the event, animate heroic figures, fill with terror or disperse by laughter the enemies of the Patriots; it alone succeeds at undoing ancient images, freeing them from their traditional "make-believe." This two-faced imagination, inscribed in fictional bodies of the narrative of political event, although constantly threatened by perversion and loss of meaning, continued to make its Manichean effects felt through the course of the revolutionary decade.

gémis, Louis, ta vigueur inactive
outrage ici ta femme trop lascive .

I

2

ah! gros coquin voila que tu debandes

3

4

1. *The Private, Libertine, Scandalous Life of Marie-Antoinette of Austria,* Bibliothèque Nationale, Reserve Collection.

2. *The Uterine Frenzies of Marie-Antoinette,* Bibliothèque Nationale, Reserve Collection.

3. *Marie-Antoinette's Day of Love,* Bibliothèque Nationale, Reserve Collection.

4. *The National Cuntfederation,* Bibliothèque Nationale, Reserve Collection.

5

6

7

8. *The Democrat,* Bibliothèque Nationale, Collection of Engravings.

9. Frontispiece from the 1652 translation of Thomas Hobbes, *The Body Politic, or The Elements of Moral and Civil Law,* rights reserved.

5. *The National Pastime,* Bibliothèque Nationale, Reserve Collection.

6. *A Rough Draft of the Constitution* (in *The Labors of Hercules,* n.p., 1790), Bibliothèque Nationale, Reserve Collection.

7. *The Golden Age,* Bibliothèque Nationale, Reserve Collection.

10. *The Triumph of the Right of Man,* Paris, private collection, rights reserved.

11. *Iscariot the Giant, Aristocrat,* Bibliothèque Nationale, Collection of Engravings.

12. *The Tennis Court Oath,* drawing by J.-L. David, Versailles, Musée National du Château, photo Réunion des Musées Nationaux photo service.

10

11

8 bis

13. *Study for the Figure of Barnave,* drawing by J.-L. David, Orléans, Musée des Beaux-Arts.

14. *Hunting the Great Beast,* Paris, Musée Carnavalet, photo Agence Bulloz.

15. *The Papal Brief of 1791,* Bibliothèque Nationale, Collection of Engravings.

16. *The Exhibition of the Body and the Civic Coronation of Michel Lepeletier* (in *Les Révolutions de Paris,* no. 185), Bibliothèque Nationale, Collection of Engravings.

13

14

15

16

17. *Bitter Forms,* engraving by C. Normand, after L. Lafitte, from an idea of
L.-E. Poirier, Bibliothèque Nationale, Collection of Engravings.

5. David, or The Struggle of Bodies

When Jacques-Louis David, at the age of thirty-two, returned to Paris at the end of September 1780 after his long stay in Rome, he recovered, from shipments made to the Royal Academy of Painting, three paintings of roughly identical size he had painted in the course of the two preceding years capitalizing on his Italian discoveries.[1] Two "Academies of Man," the first representing "Hector dead at the foot of Achilles' chariot," the second a "dying warrior" seen from behind, generally referred to by the name *Patroclus*. And one *Saint Jerome*. Three canvases, three bodies, one dead, one dying, and one ecstatic: a certain coherence animates this corpus of his Roman apprenticeship, although its developmental stages still remain evident. Those who saw them, including the Royal Academy, while quite attentive, accorded little importance to these works, deeming them promising, certainly, but rather trivial, riddled with defects. Having seen *Hector* in Rome, exhibited in the Mancini palace in September 1778, Bouquier, an aesthete and traveler, certainly appreciates the "refined softness" and the "vigorous chiaroscuros," but pronounces a condescending judgment: "Although very mediocre, [this academy] allows talent to penetrate its mediocrity."[2] Criticism focuses on the poor contrast between skin and drapery, as much in the shading as in the rendering of substances. David, moreover, went through a profound moral crisis at that time, recorded in the correspondence with his master Vien. As for the work that he finishes, the *Funeral of Patroclus*, he is not satisfied with it, reproaching himself for his "too-French manners,"[3] which, in the parlance of the time, signifies an exaggerated attachment to preciosity and frivolity of language, and thus, here, of bodies. The young painter decides to travel. He arranges a long stay in Naples in the company of the sculptor Suzanne, on Vien's recommendation.

The return to Rome is described by David himself as a revelation, the world lit up by a new dawn: "It seemed to me upon my return that I had just been operated on for cataract, and I at once made, with an entirely new inspiration, a monumental figure seen from behind that won me great honor among my friends from the *pension* in Rome."[4] Beyond the cliché (the painter's inspiration) and the confusion of a memory reported well after the fact (returning from Naples, David first painted *Saint Jerome* before producing the "monumental figure from behind," the dying warrior), David's revelation is real. One after the other, between the last days of 1779 and the first of 1780, David paints two bodies that please him, unlike *Hector*, which had, wrongly no doubt, depressed him. The break in his aesthetic itinerary, undoubtedly forced by the narrative of the painter himself, is revealed through two developments: of facial expression and of the contours of the body. His *Hector*, even if he was the best defender of Troy, had none of the qualities of an overdeveloped athlete. His is the "Greek beauty,"[5] which David breathed into this gracious, almost mannered, recumbent statue, its face calm, smooth, almost expressionless, arms resting on the ground, a being superbly relieved of its warrior's body.

This image stems directly from the "indeterminate" (*Unbezeichnung*) that Winckelmann, the theoretician of the ideal beauty of the classical revival at the end of the eighteenth century, made the essence of the beautiful in art, that will of the artist to eliminate all accidents of form, too-lively movement, overemphasized characteristics, too-intense colors, bodies too marked with elaborate musculature. "From unity results a quality of elevated beauty, which is its indeterminacy: that is, its forms cannot be described by other points or other lines except those that alone form beauty; there results a form that is not peculiar to one determinate person, and that expresses neither a distinct state of the soul nor the feeling of a passion, that would mingle with beauty traits that are foreign to it and would break its unity. According to this concept, beauty must be like the purest water that is drawn from the heart of a spring and that is judged all the more healthy since it has less taste, for it is purified, then, of all foreign bodies."[6]

On the other side of David's revelation, *Saint Jerome* and *Patroclus* are telling faces supported by robust bodies. The contrast is striking with *Hector*, even more so with the actual models that inspired David: Ribera's *Saint Jerome*, seen and studied in Naples, and the *Dying Gaul*, an ancient statue he had seen at the Capitol.[7] The inspiration is clear: the same posture, the same drapery, identical arm gestures, and an equally ecstatic gaze in the two *Jeromes*; the same positioning of the body of the two warriors, that strange seated body, seen from behind with David, dying. Yet the corporeal options are opposite. Ribera represented an inspired ascetic, David an athlete of God; the Gaulish gladiator, fragile, fallen, is at the threshold of a graceful death, while Patroclus remains a body filled with life whose death throes are almost an oxymoron. It seems that David was more concerned with the body than with the subject illustrated. His Saint Jerome is too well fed, and his dying man, quite energetic.

It is in these "filled" bodies, in these "energetic contours," that the painter finds his style: the contour of muscle rather than grace, the body energetic to the point of a vital sensuality that prevents Saint Jerome from suffering and Patroclus from dying. The expressions on the faces welcome this abundance of vitality. Saint Jerome's features abandon the dolorous expression of Catholic tradition to express another ecstasy, difficult to describe, made of gentleness and sensuality, anxious certainly, even tormented, but one pierced by the certainty of being chosen. As for the face of the dying warrior, David has, even more simply, held back his brush. The act is deliberate. One can walk around the body of the original sculpture, one can observe the face of the Gaul; with David, the dying man effaces his expression. As if the painter had wished to avoid posing to his art, and to his judges, the problem of facial expression, threatened, faced with certain death, by the "grimace," that insolent perversion of neoclassical physiognomy.[8]

The back of *Patroclus*, however, from the loins to the shoulders, equally massive and muscular, with finely worked contours, the flesh caught in an almost blinding light, the curves emphasized by the shadings and the drapery, is *another* face, the real face of the warrior. It tells of David's confidence in the expressiveness of the body, even if it meant, quite often, turning the rules of verisimilitude and of propriety upside down. David, in 1780, is a very poor, or rather restless, reader of Winckelmann.[9] He certainly departs from those bodies admired by that German enthusiast for antiquity, the Hector for example, but after his revelation, he inflates them and treats them in his own manner. He endlessly threatens the classical revival theorized by the master and his praise of the serene beauty inherited from the Greeks. The young French painter tries to draw this beauty toward a "different majesty," the one attained thanks to the vigor of the soul and the heroic posturing of the bodies.

Ten years later, after having won an exceptional notoriety essentially thanks to the expressiveness of his bodies, David finds himself faced with the revolutionary event. Quickly rapt with enthusiasm, but still a novice in politics, he makes the decision, in spring 1790, to paint *The Tennis Court Oath*, the event that the already mythical narrative of the Revolution tends to identify as its starting point. David had already attracted the interest of the "Patriots," even before 1789: his vigorous opposition to rococo style and to "courtly" subjects, along with his "aura" of Antiquity and the whiff of scandal that surrounded several of his depictions of ancient history (the *Two Horatii*, the *Death of Socrates*, and, especially, the *Brutus* exhibited in the Salon of 1789) could convey to some that "The genius of this painter anticipated the most recent upheavals."[10] Yet David, in 1789, is in no way involved in a political career. He is quite simply at the cutting edge of the antiacademic spirit of revolt that is sketched out in the fall. It is only later, in October 1790 and then in September 1791, that the Jacobins first, then the National Assembly itself, will look into the painter's project, at the prompting of Dubois-Crancé, Mirabeau, and Barère, with an eye to finance it. For the first time, David meets a contemporary subject that he deems worthy of his "expressive bodies." These, in the mind of the painter, will be able to express themselves in an "admirable scene," comprising, according to his avowed plan, the most ambitious painting of the Revolution, and why not the greatest painting in the world?

But to paint a contemporary, political, and revolutionary subject, as David wanted to do, came down to placing the bodies he drew in often dangerous contradiction to the canons of propriety and the codes of beauty of the norm, that of the classical revival. Danger lies above all in expression: the faces, the gestures, sometimes escape the grace and the beautiful serenity of ideal beauty. The enthusiasm born from political rupture and the assertion of the sovereignty of the Assembly undoubtedly led David to overstep the bounds and pervert, or even forget, the rules of the new classicism. David transferred a concept from the realm of art: the imagined being, the ideal being that David constructs is no longer merely beautiful, it is political; it is no longer merely beautiful, it is regenerated; the figure is no longer merely beautiful, it also becomes terrible. It is this disruption of a canon of the body by the intrusion of history that I would like to follow here: how, from an ordered body, with a beauty that is assured, justified, and made legitimate by an extremely solid aesthetic theory, an actual corporeal, culturally dominant code, the painter makes another body, with a beauty that sometimes seems too little or too great, in ever-threatened equilibrium. Instead of being an illustration of the "art of the concept"[11] that is the new classicism, this body violates it and the norms it comprises and the attitudes it seeks to maintain, and thereby itself becomes a problematic narrative of the revolutionary event. From an aesthetic ideal that is calm and serene, David, while placing it at the very foundation of his inspiration, tried to make a narrative of history, a metaphor for revolutionary fracture. (See Figure 12.)

Under the Clothes, Bodies Laid Bare: The Line of Ideal Beauty

At the starting point of his project, David placed naked bodies. The preparatory sketches, along with the few figures painted to scale, confirm this unambiguously. The characters in the foreground of the painting, veritable allegories, offer an unsurprising illustration of the principal forms of neoclassical bodily appearance. The nudity is essential, since it allows the painter an exhaustive analysis of gestures and anatomy by a procedure that is standard with him, the confrontation of bodies in contact. It is also a useful nudity, since it gives the painter the possibility, at least in the preparatory phase of the painting, to bypass the "trap" of contemporary dress. The tradition adopted by the new classicism in fact absolutely repudiates modern dress, and deems it undignified (it lacks nobility) and encumbering (it constrains the natural body). Régis Michel recalls that we must wait for Hegel and his criticism of the "ideal system" before we are able legitimately to admit the validity of contemporary dress in great painting.[12]

In this sense, David, by this choice of preliminary nudity, of this fundamental nudity, constructs not only a procedure of design, a technique of painting, but also a compromise with the rules of the traditional neoclassical body. Even more, the bodily grace of Barnave, undoubtedly the person most labored over by David, a poised and serene ephebe, his body evident and harmonious, appears as an aesthetic symbol, a corporeal manifesto of neoclassicism, a declaration of Winckelmann's theory (see Figure 13). Barnave's is the ideal nudity, the *nec plus ultra* of classicism.[13] Not carried away

by the enthusiasm of the oath beyond propriety, equilibrium, and fundamental "indeterminacy," but more aptly posed in his gesture like an "Idea
of Oath," marrying in his own body the male virtue and grace of his forms
and a "fulness of flesh" exactly delineating the hermaphrodite beauty of
Antiquity reread by Winckelmann. It is not an equivocal beauty but one in
search of primitive purity, that of the Apollo Belvedere: "The artist used
just the material that was necessary to express and make visible his intention. An eternal Spring, like that which reigns in the Elysian Fields, endows
his ravishing masculinity, in the maturity of age, with an adorable youth-
fulness, and plays with tender caresses on the proud structure of his limbs.
Neither vein nor tendon warms or animates his body, but a divine spirit,
that irrigates it with the gentleness of its flux, circumscribes its entire outline with its fulness. His fine hair, like the tender, fluid tendrils of a noble
vine, plays, animated by a light breeze, around his divine head. His calm
muscles, like molten glass, blown into barely perceptible undulations, reveal themselves more to reflection than to sight."[14]

Beyond the particular, emblematic case of Barnave, the corporeal modeling of the principal figures of the painting, of this primitive corporeal
frieze, stems from an aesthetic philosophy that, from many points of view,
must be attached to the principles of classical revival. Thus, the modeling of the bodies of *The Tennis Court Oath* offers a gestural code organized
around three summits: face, hand, and torso, three corporeal poles oriented according to a directing principle, elevation. The triangle uniting
hand, face, and torso is in fact not settled flatly, but appears resolutely directed upward, following the diagonal of the arm and the gaze. Outside of
the actual subject of the drawing, the oath, this elevation must be related
to the corporeal schema of the ideal beauty of the new classicism: an elevation that is revealed, for example, in the valorization of torsos (the "sacred
torso" of Winckelmann, without any doubt the corporeal sign to which that
theoretician was the most attentive); in the general orientation of the foreheads, that face with the "elevated beauty"; and in the calm modeling of
the musculature of the shoulders and arms whose harmony seemed essential to the German critic, an equilibrium to be found between "gentle firmness" and "primitive vigor" — the *ataraxia* of the Olympian gods.

"How can the movements of the soul show themselves externally by the
harmonious action of the muscles?" That is the academic problem posed to
painters and sculptors with renewed eagerness by the anatomist doctors of
the time, in this case Jean-Joseph Sue in his *Elements of Anatomy Designed*

for the Use of Painters and Sculptors and Connoisseurs [Eléments d'anatomie
à l'usage des peintres et sculpteurs et des amateurs], published in 1789. A
direct link between heart, sentiment, and musculature seems to be at work
in the neoclassical man: "He who does the most, feels the most, and as a result becomes more resolute than others who seem more cowardly," Goiffon
and Vincent recall in another manual on anatomy "for the faithful representation of humans and animals both in painting and in sculpture." In the
body of the new classicism, everything proceeds from the torso (seat of the
heart) and rises toward the face (especially the eyes, seat of the mind) while
irrigating the muscles (particularly the arms and hands in the present case
of the oath), vectors of heroic action. A confirmation of this general principle of elevation can be seen in the reproach formulated against David in
1791: "The legs are a little heavy," emphasizes *The Crutch of Voltaire* in its
commentaries on the Salon du Louvre, "but in compensation," adds this
pamphlet, "all the heads are eloquent."

"The heads are eloquent," a compensation, if the critic is to be believed,
for the extremely attentive work brought to the modeling of the upper
body, this elevated triangle joining hand, face, and torso. Thus, the privileged bodily mirror of the soul — corresponding to the painting of feelings,
that torso that is seat of the heart — is the face, an expressive face poised
upon the nobility of the body. We know that the study of passions reflected
in the face is one of the great projects of classicism, a project taken up
by the theoreticians and practitioners of the classical revival of the eighteenth century, made particularly pointed and precise under the impetus
of physiognomy. "The human face itself becomes an animated painting in
which each movement of the soul is expressed by a feature," writes Monnet
in *Knowledge of the Human Body Explained for People Who Teach Drawing*,
an extreme readability of the body, manifest in the painting of eyes and
mouths, which is at the core of David's enterprise when he draws the faces
in *The Tennis Court Oath*.

This attention devoted to the elevation of the body is confirmed by
another indicator that intersects with the specifically pictorial study, the
poem by André Chénier, dedicated to David: *The Tennis Court* [Le Jeu de
Paume], an ode that is intended as the literary version of the painting. The
analysis of the corporeal vocabulary of this poetic piece is quite revealing
about the anatomical points stressed in the *Oath*. With Chénier, the body
and face of the man taking the oath are equally elevated: the face is centered
on the forehead and eyes, and the body is completely oriented toward the

torso and the arm swearing the oath. The body of the man taking the oath is also turned, in the image of the neoclassical body, toward an action marked with serenity: tragic action (dying, crying) as well as dynamic action (walking, leading, advancing), actions contrasting with futile gestures (laughing), with precipitate acts (fleeing, hurrying), or uncertain ones (being blinded, trembling). This body thus leaves to the enemy laughter, cold sweats, and flight, to concentrate on its own sure, decisive movement, one that leads it straight toward the sought-after eternity. (A continual coexistence of the verbs "to die" and "to be born" presents the cycle of life as a perpetual renaissance within heroic action.) The man of the oath, with David as well as with Chénier, thus centers his calm expressiveness, following the neoclassical code, on the noblest corporeal elements (eye, forehead, torso, muscular contour) and the most heroic actions (dying, leading, swearing, being born, and so on).

To this fundamental equivalence a fascination more directly tied to the political conjuncture is added: David inscribes on his canvas the passion that the men of the Revolution had for the body that speaks loudly, with a voice that carries. This idealization is embodied in the favorable treatment he reserves for Mirabeau and Barnave, the two great orators of the Constituent Assembly. The tension that animates the body of the ideal deputy follows more exactly a diagonal that leads from the eyes to the arms: the buccal orifice is never the passage for the lies, laughter, or expulsion connected with the anal orifice as in the drawing of the grotesque body, but majestically the mouth becomes the gateway of eloquent speech, linked to Patriotic enthusiasm. Representation magnifies the body of an "eloquent hero": it manages to give him a mouth—that rather problematic orifice, it must be said, for classical art—when the new word comes for him to speak.

This movement of the body is shown in the neoclassical painting through brushstroke, line, and contour. The body of the new classicism is the perfect body of the drawing.[15] This line plays a determining role: it assures the corporeal truth of the drawing by rigorously conforming to the rules of anatomical precision, but it also causes the body to enter into the sphere of the ideal. The ideal (bodily perfection) becomes truth (anatomical modeling). The drawing must transcribe this bold equivalence. Neoclassical art fashions a body that is at the same time real and ideal. With David, for instance, Mirabeau is "idealized in a realist way": he loses his smallpox scars, has his contours strengthened, but keeps the massive, almost bestial appearance that makes him recognizable to the public and that shows as his own political truth. *Marat Slain in His Bath* will also conserve a tragic corporeal realism (the open, bleeding wound, sign of the martyr) but, in David's representation, will in part lose the more morbid evidence of the skin disease that disfigured Marat's appearance.

The Davidian body finds its strength in a perfect polish, and in doing so it inscribes itself fully in the aesthetic of classic renewal. Rigorously finished, it has eliminated anything that could permit belief in its imperfection—anything, for instance, connected with growth, excrescence, protuberance, or physical decrepitude—all the while preserving the elements that constitute its verisimilitude. There is for instance a carefully studied pyramid of ages, from the young men appearing at the windows (the painter's actual children) down to the old man carried by vigorous Patriots, or, above all, David's essential attachment to the expression of faces and gestures. Led by its gestural elevation and heroic certainty, held between the perfection of its beauty and the truth of its anatomy, the body of the new classicism is thus capable of an immediate integration into the political sphere. It establishes a direct connection not only between physical beauty and moral goodness (the figure of the hero) but also between beauty and natural truth (anatomical contour). It follows that both the good and truth can, at any instant, become "political." It is a fascinating correspondence: beauty, by the rendering of musculature, the painting of energetic expressions and corporeal elevation, will be used to portray men of a new political scene. It is a correspondence between ideal beauty and politics that also seems, for David, to be the chance to paint "something else" besides the classic Winckelmann body.

From Ideal Beauty to Ideal Politics: Regeneration of a Concept

To paint *something else*: if the bodies in their first state are naked, David never concealed—it would have been ridiculous to do so—that he would eventually have to clothe them. Clothing, that affront thrown at the beauty of the body, that stumbling block placed before the nudity of ideal anatomy, is the essential sign of the painter's own engagement. For one of the first times ever, David agrees to represent on canvas the ignoble, the ignoble that, in 1789, bears with it a hope that rejects the rules and conventions of classical painting: the political event. *Clothing is politics*, and from then on, David's bodies are charged with the emotions of an immediate narrative that carries them well beyond ideal beauty. To paint a "body politic," that is David's ambition in embodying the National Assembly caught in the instant of its foundation, the oath. What is more, the artist found a political text that guided his brush toward bodies, he found a text to serve as prime support for his expressive bodies: the "word of the oath" uttered by the rash and menaced deputies of the National Assembly on 20 June 1789 in the tennis court at Versailles. Immediately, he wants to place bodies above political words, according to a technique that he will use again in a number of his revolutionary painting projects: a portrait of the king leaning on the tablets of the Constitution; the sword of despotism piercing the bill of indictment drawn up by Lepeletier against Louis XVI; Marat holding his pen in one hand and in the other the note from Charlotte Corday; the statue of the French people with its body engraved with value words.

David's body politic is, literally, a declarative body, a slogan-body. The text of the Tennis Court Oath lends itself to that. Let us reread it: "The National Assembly, having been summoned to determine the constitution of the kingdom, to bring about the regeneration of the public order, and to maintain the true principles of the monarchy, and considering that it can in no way be prevented from continuing its deliberations in whatever place it is compelled to establish, and that in fine wherever its members are assembled, the National Assembly is there — 'Decrees that all its members take immediately a solemn oath never to separate, and to re-assemble wherever circumstances demand, until the constitution of the kingdom is established and made firm on solid foundations; and that said oath being taken, all the members and each one of them in particular, will confirm by their signature this unwavering resolution.' "

The very dynamics of this political oath, its constant metaphor, is corporeal. The *members* are, by their union, a *body* that must establish a *constitution* whose purpose is the *regeneration* of the country. Certainly, there is one element that escapes this corporeal metaphor of the National Assembly — the "true principles of the monarchy" — but we know that David, like Sieyès before him in his definition of the "great body of citizens," will forget those principles in the course of the execution of his project. David will be openly reproached for this by a Monarchist critic, who had read the oath carefully and saw the version that David gave of it at the Salon of 1791. David represented the Tennis Court Oath literally. He drew the corporeal projection of a political text itself constructed around organicist metaphor: here is a body politic made precisely from human bodies.

This great body possesses a head: Bailly, the man who, in the name of others, reads, speaks the oath, and then listens to his brothers take it. Bailly is the face of the Assembly, "magnifying all the feelings of the common soul," and is situated moreover in the center of the painter's composition. The national body also possesses a heart, the group of the three religious men: Dom Gerle, Grégoire, and Rabaut Saint-Etienne, the regular priest, the secular priest, and the minister. This group, shifted slightly forward in comparison with the central axis of the drawing, is united by a specific movement: the three men clasp and embrace each other. The contour of their arms joined together clearly outlines the very shape of the heart that beats for the whole of the body politic. Another anthropomorphic principle is that all the individual bodies drawn join together to form parallel series of "corporeal lines." This is quite visible in the composition of the painting: series of faces and hands linked sketch out human rows. These are the painting's lines of convergence. Philippe Bordes has emphasized this general arrangement of groups working from an overall sketch of the composition kept at the Fogg Art Museum: the link between each of these groups, the "corporeal lines" of the drawing, which amount to the skeleton of this great body, is essential to the structure of the work. The composition of the *Oath* is clearly established according to two axes linked by a certain number of lines of convergence, sometimes broken:

1. A frieze of people in the foreground that represents the *expression* of the body of the Assembly.

2. The vertical axis drawn from the group of the three religious men and extending up to the head of President Bailly: the *heart and face* of the body.

3. Finally, the lines of convergence bearing the series of multiple heads and hands: the *skeleton* of the body.

Jacques-Louis David drew, enclosed in a room, a body that was infinitely multiple but profoundly one. Here is a body in which each deputy, each "member" possesses an individual "in-tension," unique actions and feelings, but remains absolutely integrated like part of a coherent whole. This experience of corporeal fusion stems very precisely from a description worthy of Sieyès. For here is a body formed by *adunation*, a regrouping of scattered individuals into one organic whole, and by *representation*: the expressive appearance of individuals (the ones given emphasis in the frieze in the first row) is possible only because these men carry onto the apron of the stage the feelings of the mass of deputies, a reiteration of the delegation in the very heart of national representation. Similarly, David inscribes on his drawing Sieyès's third movement of the process of political incarnation: *regeneration*. *The Tennis Court Oath* is a visualization of the regenerated body politic.

This concept figures at the heart of David's ambition. To begin with, it literally engenders the text of the oath read by Bailly. The regeneration of the country is the aim of the Constitution that the assembled deputies defend, and thus the goal of the painter's work. David himself recognizes this and, in a letter introducing his project with the purpose of securing a grant that would allow the completion of the canvas, in October 1790, he writes: "Let us begin, then, by erasing so many centuries of error from our chronology, let us confuse them with that chaos that preceded the flood; let us forget oppressive tyrants and victims. Regenerated France dates from 20 June 1789."[16] By designating historic rupture, and then metaphorically placing it within biblical history (the Flood), David explicitly emphasizes the two essential aspects of regeneration: its identity indissociable from temporal fracture on the one hand and its religious aspect on the other hand. The regeneration of the *Oath* bears as much the mark of historic event (1789 succeeding the chaos of "centuries of slavery") as that of an almost mystical renewing of the human species (the Flood and the birth of modern times). David painted a body agitated by history and by events, turning upside down the serene beauty that takes its source in an idealized derivation from Antiquity. But he also painted a body animated by the eschatological expectation of the new world, of the new city, a way of pushing the aesthetics of regeneration to its limit: bodies that would refuse to be "reasonably" planned by divine intelligence, denying Winckelmann's definition of spiritual beauty,[17] but on the contrary thrown toward that feverish moment of the "immediate expectation of the divine," the time when the ark of the Flood touches the sacred goal. Sudden temporal and millenarian fracture, the raising up and resurrection of the body—those are the two forms of the regenerated vision of *The Tennis Court Oath*. This conjunction is essential, for it is what gives strength to the regeneration represented by the painter, and also produces the impression of burgeoning in David's *Oath*. The work claims to embody the total Figure, the only burgeoning capable of suggesting the importance of the event, an actual revolutionary *form*, a painting at once political, moral, and religious, a painting that belongs to an aesthetic manifesto while at the same time celebrating the political and sacred birth of the Assembly of 1789.

The painting is thus the representation of a rupture; it takes place in the decisive instant. In his sketch, David fixes men at the very instant when political enthusiasm, because of the oath, turns into initiatic rite: bodies pass into the world. They have just been born to politics. Mirabeau confirms this in an address to the Jacobins on 6 November 1790, detailing his instructions to the painter: the tennis court hall is "the first temple where liberty took birth."[18] The association established by the orator, joining the temple and birth, is called the "political baptism" of the Assembly. Mirabeau uses the framework of religious interpretation offered by regeneration, a new birth associated as much with baptism as with the resurrection of the Just. David complies without hesitating: the deputies in his drawing raise themselves up from among the dead. David wanted to paint men waking up from a nightmare, the nightmare of the "centuries of error," as he says.

In the same address, Mirabeau continues his instructions and insists on going carefully into the meteorological conditions surrounding the scene of the oath: storm, flood, lightning. The orator specifies a landscape of the end of the world. Further on, he hints that the room could have been "the tomb" of the deputies. David again follows the recommendations of the Jacobins to the letter. His scene takes place in a dramatic environment, with gusting winds, billowing curtains, clothes soaked, lightning beating down on top of the royal chapel. All this is to indicate the time of the "Flood," to place the oath at the heart of an apocalypse. But this dramatic storm seems to be the very condition of birth, of the rebirth of the deputies to the world, a way, with David, of choosing the Just at the time of the Last Judgment. This state of resurrection is very explicitly attached to certain figures: the ecstatic Robespierre, as if raised from the tomb, and Father Gérard in prayer before this miracle of revolutionary regeneration. There is certainly no doubt that David wanted at once to celebrate men raised from among the dead and to baptize a new political class. There is even a miracle in this drawing, represented by the painter in the group of Maupetit de la Mayenne, that sick, dying old man who has had himself carried into the room and manages to hold up a feeble hand to take the decisive oath.

David sees in this "wonderful regeneration" the result of the process of incarnation of the body politic of the new National Assembly. In anatomical terms, this figure takes form in a great organism made up of a multitude of little corporeal fragments; in political terms, David offers us a vision of the embodiment of the nation according to Sieyès; in aesthetic terms, critiques of the Salon of 1791 make clear the value but also the risks of the project: "The eye drawn by a swarm of beauties of detail cannot however detach itself from the ensemble." [19] It is the Hobbesian figure of the *Leviathan*,[20] a corporeal triplicity—natural body, political body, mystical body—brought to the unity of a great sovereign organism, a political figure at once monstrous and miraculous that soars over the room of the tennis court.

The revolutionary event, then, led David to perturb and place in jeopardy the "elevated grandeur" of ideal beauty according to Winckelmann. The mark of this disturbance is imprinted on numerous bodies in the *Oath*. Certain figures, such as Barnave, Bailly, and the religious group, bear signs of the calm beauty of the norm; others, Robespierre especially but also the group of Martin d'Auch, or Prieur de la Marne, along with the general enthusiasm, the "swell" of the painting, compose a landscape in upheaval in which the agitation of the senses, of bodies, and of expressions is far from the grace of the "charming Barnave," and seems to deconstruct the concept of ideal beauty. It is certainly a question here of an intention that is not new to David; starting with his *Patroclus* of 1780, as I have shown, he seemed to want to inflate the body. What is new is the multiplication of these enthusiastic bodies, "cramming" the drawing, making the concept of ideal beauty almost implode. We must not forget that aside from the *Funeral of Patroclus*, a painting of 1778 more or less rejected by the painter, David had until now insisted on concentrating his work on small groups. With the *Oath*, he poses as principle of representation the multiplication of bodies made enthusiastic by politics.

Yet these bodies, for many, explicitly for some, adopt the very attitudes and "exaggerated" gestures that, according to Winckelmann, are "taboo in noble art, and a bloating of contour." They are like the "grimace of the body." The dignity of the being, the moral value corresponding to ideal beauty, comes from the rectitude of the bodies according to the academic canons, a key idea of classics since the Greeks. Winckelmann, for instance, could see just in the "crossing of limbs" a physical expression capable of breaking the beauty, of distorting the calm grandeur.[21] Yet the composition of the *Oath* is precisely constructed on the crossing of limbs, not only in the case of "negative" bodies (Martin d'Auch, his arms crossed over his chest), but also by the collective superimposition of arms and embraces. Elation, enthusiasm, "electrification," in the Mesmeric sense of the word, here corrupt neoclassical taste. The bombast introduced by the political event strews movement everywhere in the bodies of the Assembly. The "gri-mace" is a visualization of this fusion between the event and the bodies, judged impossible by many theoreticians, this fusion between the Event and the Idea. Through the drawing of bodies, David effects an adaptation of ideal beauty to the disrupted form of political "truth," or the revolu-tionary event: the appearance of bodies in the *Oath* is a troubling crossover attempted between ideal beauty and political truth. David has drawn an imaginary body, a mental political creature.

The classic metaphor of ideal beauty according to Winckelmann should be recalled here.[22] Before painting Helen, the woman of perfect beauty, the great Greek artist Zeuxis chose five young women: only the union of differ-ent beauties could make the image of perfection apparent. Unable to find all the graces that he had to represent united in one real body, the painter invents an ideal body. He thus joins anatomical imitation (each one of the scattered beauties is faithfully rendered) to the idea: the regrouping of imi-tations makes beauty, an epochal meeting of the ideal with the real.

For David, the construction of the body of the Assembly proceeds ac-cording to the same logic, but transferred from the domain of beauty to that of politics. How, in fact, does David propose to demonstrate the strength of his subject? He combines the bodies of the deputies into one single body and composes an Ideal Assembly by joining the "ecstasy" of Robespierre, the "enthusiasm" of Prieur, the "confidence" of Barnave, the "strength" of Dubois-Crancé, the "speech" of Mirabeau, the "wisdom" of Sieyès, the "fraternity" of the clerics, and the "calm determination" of Bailly, qualities that the painter combines in the great body of national sovereignty represented by hundreds of hands and faces running along the length of the drawing's lines of convergence. David groups together these political qualities that often contradict or annihilate each other in the real Constituent Assembly into one imaginary creature, the better to fashion a *conceptual body*: ideal politics. David composed his body following Sieyès's political model (adunation, representation, regeneration) and according to the metaphoric example of Zeuxis. Revolutionary politics, the great citizen body, is his Helen. Ideal beauty was thus overturned by the enthusiasm of the event, but bequeathed to David the conceptual framework that allowed him to compose a different body, a body politic.

From 'Ataraxia' to 'Parenthyrsis':
Bodies Consumed by Low Pathos

In two instances, the painter has pushed bodies toward the "grimace," toward what is "taboo in noble art": by the representation of the political event, symbolized by the novel and provocative choice of contemporary dress, and by the representation of a miraculous regeneration, which disturbed ideal beauty by its feverish enthusiasm. Political body, regenerated body: David's project is distanced from ideal beauty, all the more so since it includes a third defiance—the danger of the "terrible." These bodies that should have remained on the calm, serene shores of Winckelmann's sea— "that natural state of the waves whose immobility mirrors the harmony of the Ancients"[23]—hasten on the contrary toward the breaking waves of revolutionary history. The drawing, while resolutely and massively integrating regenerated figures, does not evade the issue of the difficulty of passage, or the dangers that this fracture causes the revolutionary man to run. It is a reflection on history and its hazards. David did not forget to put the bodies taking the oath in danger. The general atmosphere that surrounds the scene, as I have said, plays on the drama of the act of emancipation. The work of the painter graphically displays the effects of the storm and the wind that reveal the external danger surrounding the tennis court, threatened as it is by the king's troops. Moreover, some of the figures, few but expressive, bear the weight of slavery, of the Frenchman grown old under the ancien régime, who has stayed on the other bank of the revolutionary river. Martin d'Auch, the single opponent of the oath, and the man that David designates in his sketches by the class label "the aristocrat" are figures who refuse political regeneration; they are inert members confronting the miracle of bodies.

But this danger that weighs on the Assembly, more suggested than overtly demonstrated, this threatening atmosphere that Mirabeau so "required" in his note to the painter ("Expiring despotism still threatens," he writes in his address planning the future painting), David, by a brilliant inspiration, integrated into the very interior of the body of the Assembly. This body, "miraculously" regenerated, in the words of Joseph-Antoine Cérutti, is also a "terrible" body, stretched between these two phrases of "exaggerated language." In the heart of the regenerated body, David painted a "terrible" thing, capable by itself of representing the passion that animated it.

He made the exact counterpart of this body of deputies, the inverted image of the hydra, the monster that recurrently symbolized the former despotism. That is the strength of the representation: this assembly of deputies — even aside from the dramatic elements in the periphery (wind, lightning, people agitated) — integrates the classical image of the enemy into its own figuration. This great body made of a multitude of heads is also, *a contrario*, an image of the Other, of despotism, of the aristocratic monster, of the "great beast," as the cartoonists of July 1789 called the counterrevolutionary plot under the guise of the hydra roaming between Versailles and the Bastille.

The most famous representation of this monster, widely distributed in mid-July, is *Hydra of despotism laid low, or The patriotic hunt of the great beast.* (See Figure 14.) The caption is explicit: "On 12 July 1789, around four o'clock in the evening, a ferocious beast with a horribly monstrous form was sighted on the route from Versailles to Paris. Experts maintained that it was of an aristocratic species and that it was ready to come ravage the capital. Immediately the cry 'To arms, to arms' rang out. All citizens ran up with rifles and halberds, and looked in vain for this devastating monster. Finally, on the fourteenth following, they learned that it had retreated into a lair called the Bastille, near the Porte Saint-Antoine; they ran to besiege it, and after forcing it into this last entrenchment, it came down to who could cut the most heads off of it, for the monster had many, and like those of the Hydra, all of them had to be cut down to prevent them from being born again."

The heads in this cartoon, certainly more laughable than terrible, represent the principal conspirators of the Royalist coup of mid-July, born exactly in reaction to the oath illustrated by David. From Marie-Antoinette to Lambesc, we pass a few ministers and advisers to the king. The "great beast" of July bears only about twenty heads, but pamphleteers are prone to speak of "a hydra with a thousand heads"; Marat will go up to forty thousand in 1790. One must imagine, then, such an animal adorned with several hundred of the faces appearing often in the political imagination surrounding a conspiracy. Cartoonists, with their rather crude pen point, never succeeded in representing it, but David offers a superb inversion of it. The heads of his *Oath*, however, are not to be cut off, but celebrated. The hydra of despotism defended the Bastille; David's ideal monster defends the tennis court. On this matter I leave the last word to Pithou, an art critic who, in his commentary on the drawing exhibited at the Salon of 1791, very justly felt this transfer from a monster of political evil to the universe of ideal politics. Inverting a metaphor, itself monstrous, generally designating, in his word, "the tyrannicide *furor*," he writes: "This painting will produce the opposite effect of Medusa's head." The malefic monster horrifies and petrifies; the monster of the political ideal fills with enthusiasm and rapture. In both cases, the represented body produces a full range of effects.

We know today, thanks to the study of the painter's notebooks of sketches and drawings,[24] that David, in the years 1789–90, had monstrous allegories of despotism very present in his mind and did not hesitate to reproduce them in his notes. He had even thought of proposing, for a plan of a painting ordered by the city of Nantes, *Exhausted France Saved by the Breton Patriots* [La France épuisée sauvée par les patriotes bretons],[25] in 1789–90. A composition based on the Manicheanism of the revolutionary political imagination, it is an edifying painting separated into two parts, one designating the old world by means of a monstrous bestiary, and the other representing a dynamic new world in the guise of Breton Patriots coming, under the leadership of the mayor of Nantes, "to protect exhausted and expiring France and to save her from the claws of the despotic monster."

David revealed a few details of this allegorical composition in a letter: "You must imagine France as it used to be, torn apart by all the predators, the abuses that tear it into rags, the false dignity that triumphs and the true merit in shadow that they do not deign to care about, business languishing, the farmer lying on sheaves of wheat and dying of hunger, the clergy and the nobility arguing among themselves about the price of his successes." Political and temporal Manicheanism, France "torn into rags by abuses," the predatory nobility and clergy—one finds here the tone and style of pamphlets presenting the despotic monster and integrating it into the narrative of the nascent Revolution as a symbol of absolute evil. David explicitly confirms this obsessive presence of political evil in his mind, and, still on the subject of the Nantes project, notes down in his sketchbook, among other negative figures to imagine, "the hydra of despotism."[26]

The monster comes directly under his pencil without our having to push an interpretative reading of his work beyond what is reasonable. David himself, having plunged into the cultural and political context of the revolutionary moment, had in mind this Manicheanism of lampoonists and journalists that opposed two imaginary creatures embodying the most opposite political values: the great citizen body represented by the National Assembly, the Federate soldier, or the popular colossus, faced with the hydra of despotism, its neck bristling with the multiple heads of privilege and aristocratic conspiracy. It is very important to emphasize here that David, far from thinking up his composition in the shelter of his studio, is an artist plunged into cultural and political context. His work is impregnated with this contact, and it is not at all unimaginable (contrary to what certain art historians tranquil in their erudite certainties claim) that the painter consulted the political cartoons of his time, wandered about in the streets, or, even worse, that he read the newspapers, sometimes even the lampoons. The commentary on a drawing of 1790–91 destroys the isolation of the "great painting" and calls for mingling sources and references in several disciplines. This necessarily heterogeneous, or in any case "nonspecialized," study would like to insist on emphasizing that. Ideal beauty and the despotic hydra can coexist in the same work, as can the marvelous and the terrible, just like regeneration allegories and political reasoning in Sieyès.

Where, though, can this Manicheanism be found at work in the drawing of the *Oath*? Aside from a few very minor figures, the very unanimity inclines the bodies toward beauty and raises them up toward regenerative grace. This is the usual take in classical commentaries on this drawing, and it is certainly fair to say that David renounced representing political evil on his canvas. Vampires, abuses, the hydra itself, all these monsters have disappeared. In fact, these monsters have been more absorbed by the regenerated bodies than chased from the canvas. The immense body made of heads of deputies is itself, as I have said, an inverted image of the hydra, and the movement of this body, majestic and calm in places, but convulsive, disordered, electrified, "mesmerized" in others, suggests an integration of evil within the body of the Assembly. A strict defender of ideal beauty could not refute me: some of his bodies are so exalted that they seem bewitched by evil.

To take a famous comparison from that corpus of great neoclassical expressions, the Laocoön[27] (another body grappling with the monstrous—the two serpents of Apollo) suffers but does not cry out; he masters his passions, the marvelous and the terrible, like that dying aesthete, the gladiator of the Capitol. As Régis Michel has pointed out, his mouth, whose opening is too weak to emit a cry, proves this. The evil that stifles him, the monster that clasps the suffering hero, cannot penetrate into his smooth body, closed to terrible expressions. Inversely, and dangerously, the number of open or half-open mouths in the *Oath* is impressive, emphasizing the political ecstasy and passion that usually speak openly, and cry out, for themselves.

It is in this agitation, through this fever, that the body of the Other, the multiple heads of the hydra, is present, and pervades. The Assembly has laid low the monster that threatened it. In this victory, it has found a dynamism, but also a danger: it risks *devouring* the monster. For the Assembly, under David's pencil, tends to absorb *everything*—thus the painter represents deputies who were absent at the time of the oath, and yields to the temptation to fill ever more of his drawing. David's Assembly tends to live by the tensions that pervade it, tends to summon those rifts that, once the creative event is past, will never stop threatening it. In 1793, the question is posed by David: does he have to preserve the figures of Mounier and the other Monarchists? Does he have to let Mirabeau, Barnave, and Bailly remain in place, even though they were afterward recognized as traitors? The body of the Assembly, at every instant, is thus threatened with becoming a "political monster": an aggregate of contradictory divisions and interests. David allows a glimpse of the tumults of a parliamentary life that the revolutionaries never quite knew how to manage. Similarly, the painting is constantly on the verge of Winckelmann's *parenthyrsis*, the "low pathos" that he so despised, bodies haunted by pomposity, mouths ready to open too wide to proclaim passions or give voice to the first factions.

The painter even inscribed in his painting a short fable that tells of this danger and questions this exaggerated language that he was not able, did not want, to resist. The scene takes place in the group surrounding Martin d'Auch. A deputy, on the right of the composition, clearly indicates to an overexcited comrade that he must respect the opponent, that is, maintain silence and keep his mouth closed, remain closed to the enemy. True Republicans are impassive. No doubt this deputy understood the threat that weighs on an assembly riddled with the swell of political enthusiasm. To contain one's passions, to contain one's body, is precisely to close oneself to the hydra of despotism, never to risk incorporating it into oneself. From this measure of the body, from this moderation without expression, David made at once—and this contradiction brings to the work its exceptional interest—a rule and a prohibition, a measure and moderation that he profoundly desired (thus the figure of Barnave, thus the calm nudity of the first sketches) and that he profoundly rejected. These multiple tensions—between the contained body and the enthusiastic body, between disordered gestures, interwoven limbs (whether fingers or legs), and the calm beauty of certain deputies, the majestic diagonals of arms forming circular arcs, between the open and closed mouth—animate the drawing by elevating bodies without forgetting to put them in danger. David thus narrated Revolution through bodies. These bodies, like the Revolution, by endlessly absorbing the evil that threatens them, have constructed their own dynamism. A movement stretched between the marvelous and the terrible, founded on an exceptional strength of absorption—what Sieyès calls "adunation," and David represents in this immense body—which is also a will to devour. Such a movement cannot be complete except when it has nothing more to feed on. Only then does an appeased body take its place. But in 1791, when David tries to finish his sketch of the *Oath*, there is still much to devour, too much no doubt for a painter who has always called himself sensitive: Mirabeau is dead but suspected of treason, the Jacobins and Feuillants have begun to tear each other apart, and the king has tried to escape. Bodies are offered up steadily to the drawing, but appetites grow still keener.

Thus at the starting point of David's project we find the ideal body of tradition rediscovered by the classical revival, theorized in exemplary detail by Winckelmann, an ideal body that the painter wants to offer to the representation of politics. But then this taking in charge of ideal beauty by the political event turns out to be delicate. Clothing, faithfulness to the text of the oath, and historic fracture all pose infinite problems and threaten continually to corrupt the ideal body, like so many inflections toward the bodily "grimace" that the representation of regeneration entails, an almost prophetic upheaval of attitudes. Revolutionary millenarianism, that "marvelous" language of bodies, tends to chase ideal beauty from the painting. This beauty, finally, is devoured from within by the "terrible," third, decisive moment. The body that David has left in his drawing, following these three metamorphoses—political, marvelous, and terrible—seems like a cruel provocation thrown at fundamental beauty. No doubt it is the awareness of this intolerable contrast that will make the completion of the project impossible. David, caught between ideal bodies and incorporation of the terrible, will prefer to forget his attempt, overwhelmed by that "low pathos" that ended up, as he will confess, "freezing his brushes."

The documents collected by Philippe Bordes[28] prove that David becomes determinedly involved in a political career during the summer of 1792, though the painter was still, on the preceding 5 February, speaking of the "great painting that he had to finish." In March and April, he "was extraordinarily busy with drawings of a popular celebration," preparing for the festival of 15 April 1792 organized by the Jacobins in honor of the Swiss of Châteauvieux. Then in the course of the summer, he is completely taken up with his participation among the Jacobins and with the preparation for his election to the Convention. The painting of the *Oath* is abandoned. The painting is buried, relegated back of political involvement: when he drafts an autobiographical sketch in April 1793, David "does not immediately recall" his composition of 1790–91. Similarly, on 14 November 1793, before the Convention, David, evoking the first years of the Revolution, speaks of a "moment of trouble and uncertainty," "when our tyrants, when error still led opinion astray," to explain the pantheonization of the traitor Mirabeau, who figures prominently in his sketch of the *Oath*. David's great project is, literally, erased from his memory like history.

A few years later, though, in 1798, David seriously contemplates resuming his project. But the words that he writes then, in the rough draft of a letter most likely never sent to the minister François Neufchâteau, emphasize how painful the completion of the *Oath* is: "Revolutionary chance disrupted all my ideas. Public opinion, which remained in flux for a few years, my own misfortunes, and many other circumstances froze my brushes. Today, finally, when minds are calmer, when healthy ideas are recognized and not confused, either with revolutionary extravagances or with the treacherous reactions that followed; today, I say, when the public mind is quite settled, people vie with each other to tell me to take up my brushes again, and all these voices repeat in unison: Finish your painting of the Tennis Court, never has a finer subject been found in the history of peoples that we have put forward. All these repeated words have warmed my genius anew, and if on top of it all you were to come to my aid, citizen minister, one word from you would inflame it. . . . You must know in advance that it is the greatest work that ever a painter has dared to undertake. The painting represents roughly a thousand or twelve hundred personages, in the most energetic attitudes. A man would have to be devoured with love for liberty, as I was and still am, to have dared to conceive of such an undertaking. The canvas measures thirty-two feet by twenty-two. No less than a church is necessary to finish this immense painting.

"P.S.: Now that I no longer have before my eyes the people who composed the legislative body of the time, and since most of them are quite insignificant for posterity, between ourselves, my intention is to substitute for them all those who have since won renown, and who for that reason interest our descendants much more. It is an anachronism, that is true, but it would certainly be to my liking. Such anachronism famous painters have already employed, casting aside unities, either of place, or of time; that re-proach will at least not be made of me. Observe that this will be the last work of such importance that will issue from my hand." [29]

The project is ambitious, but the postscript is even more telling: the painter proposes to substitute for the event, for the historic fracture of 1789, a gallery of portraits of great men after the Revolution. Thus, Jacques-Louis David loses the greatest representative project of the *revolutionary instant* from his memory, renounces representing the great body of the Revolution caught at the instant of its marvelous regeneration and its terrible frenzy, a body bearing good *and* evil, embodying the saved *and* the damned, animated by the general will *and* its opposite. The synthesis of the two possible narratives of the Revolution—the marvelous of regenera-tion and the terrible of the monstrous enemy, of the aristocratic hydra— that David had undertaken to paint together on his canvas caused the ideal beauty specified by tradition to implode, as if under the blows of History. But this project of a total painting of revolutionary emotions, of a cosmic oeuvre, of a representation of the foundational event of the Revolution, has disintegrated in its turn when confronted with this History that, after having believed too much in rupture, in political regeneration, has redis-covered divisions, factions, eliminations while at the same time wanting to deny them and forget them by successive rewritings.

Thus ideal beauty has, in a way, taken its revenge on the History that David had the ambition to incarnate through these bodies that are beau-tiful but also political, beautiful and regenerated, beautiful and terrible. Now that history has proved to be impossible to represent, "freezing the brushes" by its own contradictions, the artist turns back to his first inspi-ration, the body of ideal beauty that from then on, after the Revolution, he will devote himself to representing: the calm, serene, almost weighty look of all the paintings of the imperial epoch, the preciosity even of certain bodies of the period of exile in Brussels. The body, once transfigured by political event, was now tempered by the rediscovered rules of ideal beauty, as if drawn up by David to respond to the fear of that excess of signification that the multiple "emotional posturings" [*grimaces*] of *The Tennis Court Oath* could provoke.

PART III

The Body as Spectacle:
The Flesh of Political Ceremony

6. The Great Spectacle of Transparency

Public Denunciation and the Classification of Appearances

At the beginning of the first chapter of Book IV of *Origins of Contemporary France*, Hippolyte Taine stresses the importance of classifying appearances in the eyes of the revolutionaries. "Plump, well-fattened" fops fated for the guillotine and half-starved sansculottes here make up the two faces of the same nightmare: Taine constructs the image of a Revolution in which bodies determine political motivations. The historian compares revolutionary politics to a will to observe everything, an immense cataloguing of bodies and humours. The Jacobin, himself an embodiment of this surveying gaze, lives only for the unmasking and destruction of his enemies: "Above all, for the Jacobin, it is a question of surveying, then annihilating, his adversaries, stated or presumed, probable or possible."[1] The precondition for this "annihilation" is the classification of appearances. Taine describes it with incomparable literary verve: "Fundamental rule: according to the Jacobin maxims, any superiority of condition, any public or private advantage that a citizen enjoys and that other citizens do not enjoy, is illegitimate. On the nineteenth Ventôse Year II, Henriot, Commandant General, having surrounded the Palais Royal and carried out a roundup of suspects, gave this account of his expedition: 'One hundred and thirty fops were arrested . . . They are not Sans-Culottes; they are *plump and well-fattened*.' Henriot was right: to eat well is to be a bad citizen." As soon as a revolutionary portrayed by Taine sees a "plump" man, he "makes him disgorge his ill-gotten gains" and "chastises" him. Aristocrat: "one who has fine clothes." Aristocrat: "one who has two good shoes." The culture of his difference has become the first mark of suspicion. Even more than a hallucinated nightmare, this vision of revolutionary politics is, for Hippolyte Taine, the necessary condition for an act of writing. His literary art is a *narrative of portraits,* and his "evaluation of society" a description of the different bodies of which it is comprised. Similarly, revolutionary struggles become a rivalry of figures, a universe in which appearances oppose each other, in which the thin diminish the fat, just as, writes the historian using another metaphoric register that is dear to him, that of tree imagery, the "Jacobin woodcutters trim the forest of privilege and pluck the exquisite blossom of the easy life."

The animation of these portraits, like their opposites, makes up what Taine calls "History." This rests on a "scientific" documentation: the historian has gone to the archives and has drawn from them thousands of "little significant facts" that prepare the portraits, organize the classification and the struggle of appearances. Taine explains himself in *On Intelligence,* his methodological confession: "All the little well-chosen facts, important, significant, circumstantially detailed and minutely noted—that today is the substance of every science. Each of them is an instructive specimen, a terminus, a salient example, a distinct type to which the whole procession of analogues can be reduced."[2] The "scientific" historian places his portraits, his "types," in "columns" of little facts, and the narrative brilliantly unfolds, proposing the most expressive gallery of characters ever described concerning the Revolution, "types" and "columns" carefully annotated, linked to the archives that fed Taine's ripening genius. That is the transparency of political space doubly justified: it was not only the very condition of revolutionary denunciation (the Jacobin developing by way of enemy bodies surveyed and punished); it is also the substance of how history is written. Taine's narrative is transparency turned into style, linking together these typologized bodies, born from little facts, emerged from the womb of the archives.

As a good positivist (without laying claim to the title), Alphonse Aulard, professor, after 1886, of the "course on the history of the French Revolution" at the Sorbonne, and, after 1891, holder of the "chair" of the same subject,[3] tenaciously tries to deprive Taine's work, *Origins of Contemporary France,* of its literary "aura" and of its scientific prestige. For two entire school years, between 1905 and 1907, Aulard's teaching at the Sorbonne addresses this deconstruction. At the end of 1907 the result of his researches and verifications appears: *Taine, historien de la Révolution française.* The academician Taine has been dead for almost fifteen years, the last volume of his history published in 1884: the time has come to destroy the idol. Intelligently, Aulard attacked only the area of science, leaving Taine his "admirable writing." But the Sorbonne professor conscientiously set out to verify all the sources, all the references adduced by his elder. A singular opacity arises: Taine's history is no longer a transparency referring the bodies of the Revolution to the archives, but a particular imagination created largely from whole cloth. Taine believed too much in his sources; his credulity was without limits with regard to accounts that brought him the "chosen portraits" and "little significant facts" that turned little by little into his tendentious interpretation. The portraits came from his pen all the more readily since they were exemplary, and the examples all the more salient since they were chosen by Taine, sometimes wholly fabricated. Aulard, knowing this, permits himself to be severe: "One can say, after careful verification, and without prejudice, that in this book an exact reference, an exact transcription, an exact assertion, is the exception . . . Even if all these little significant facts, even if all these portraits that he has collected and produced, were true, the narratives or the scenes that he forms from them would be false because of the abuse of generalization. . . . It is a literary conception of history. His ingenious and always ardent verve inspires him with brilliant, admirable pieces. These are only antitheses, surprises, figures of speech. It is a literary pyrotechnics. Historic truth turns out to be sacrificed, in every instance, to the necessities of art."[4]

What Aulard calls into question, the "literary conception," is first of all the way of writing, but it is also the foundation of Taine's "science," that so-called transparency of history to the bodies that animate it, bodies of history found issuing from the archives as these "types," these "portraits," and these "columns of significant facts," a transparency that the Sorbonne professor sternly attributes only to the detailed, prolific, and rather reactionary imagination of Taine himself. If Taine wanted to write history through horrifying portraits of revolutionaries, it is in fact his own corporeal fantasies that he makes show through. Aulard reacts against Taine's "physiognomic" conception of history. No, the body does not lead without detour directly to the political soul—that is the brunt of the professor's refutation. On the contrary, Aulard bases his "science of history," that of the Sorbonne, not on an erudition that is physiognomic, but that is instead *psychological:* what reveals the politician is his "character," not his appearance; what animates history is the "opposition of minds," not the struggle of bodies. From texts of the revolutionary era, of which he read and published many, Aulard draws "opinions," "sentiments" (for instance the "republican sentiment," the "democratic sentiment"), that he links together by "principles" or "institutions."[5]

Bodies and little facts have given way in this history to characters and political institutions. Aulard illustrates this dissociation of the body and the mind endlessly. His hero, Danton, is the symbol of it: "horrible face" set upon a "sublime character." Similarly, the opposition between the Girondins and the Montagnards remains an enigma for the Sorbonne professor: their characters are equal, both groups are Republicans, while only their means contrast them. This rivalry of bodies does not justify, for Aulard, the final drama of these "enemy brothers": the professor never understood the confrontation, always deplored it, just as he denounced the "physiognomic wanderings" of Mme Roland, who "judged people first on their appearance, unable to endure ugly men."[6] Aulard endlessly tries to "psychologize" the relationships of bodies, the very relationships that he dreads and that Taine excelled at portraying.

Another historian, a new hero: Albert Mathiez, the rival of Aulard, chose Robespierre. This choice only introduces into historiography, it is often thought, a social dimension, a belated aspect, moreover, in the career of the Jacobin historian. This choice, in fact, summons a classification of appearances. Mathiez often adopts Taine's images, but reverses them. Between the two corporeal visions of history, almost decadent with Taine, almost mystical with Mathiez, Aulard, good, solid professor, is the only one to preserve the science of characters. With Mathiez, oppositions are radicalized. If one must love Robespierre instead of Danton, it is because everything sets them against each other: political choices, class alliances, but above all morality, and bodies. Where Aulard spoke of "sentiment" and "opinion," Mathiez describes a morality whose precepts, once again, are visible under exterior appearances. Danton's orgies make him monstrous, just as they killed Mirabeau, another corrupt man, another degenerate body. The virtue of Robespierre makes him chaste. Danton gives of himself generously, too lively, too sensual, sweating immoralism from every pore of his skin, agitated in all his limbs; Robespierre preserves his morality, scarcely sociable but sincere, scarcely interested, incorruptible. He remains cold, corporeally reserved, but "women felt him different from other men, for they knew instinctually that Robespierre would give himself *completely*, when the day came that he gave himself."[7]

In like manner, the opposition between Girondins and Montagnards, for Albert Mathiez, is particularly significant, corporeally telling. Mathiez wants to destroy both the hypothesis of Quinet, who wrote about that struggle, "You tear yourselves apart, and you make only one," and that of Aulard, whom the Jacobin violently addresses: "He refuses to admit that between those enemy brothers there was something else besides the deplorable misunderstandings of characters, besides hurt feelings or rivalries of ambition." Aulard thought of Girondins and Montagnards as two characters of the same Republican spirit; Mathiez makes of them two moralities and two antagonistic bodies.

What obsesses Mathiez (to the point that he makes it the subject of the opening lesson of his course in history at the University of Besançon in 1912) is the opposition between virtue and corruption, between resistance to temptation and abandonment to the senses, between bodies restrained by morality and bodies yielding to pleasure, since "money and women, in any latitude, under any government, in any era, are the two great means of seduction, the two sovereign traps where morality and bodies are caught."[8] This 1912 lesson, *La Corruption parlementaire sous la Terreur*, is thoroughly suggestive. Taine made of social transparency (which is a necessary condition for reading the body) a "political tribunal" where he summoned his numerous portraits. Mathiez, however, raises political denunciation, ruled by virtue, to the level of a "tribunal of morals." Just as much as it is a long praise of Robespierre, this code of morals in action invites his listeners at the University of Besançon to discover another character: Mathiez tells the story of the "venerable Raffron du Trouillet," Montagnard deputy of Paris, who, when the Convention was discussing the Constitution of 1793, "proposed instituting above the National Assembly a sort of tribunal of morals, a national censor that would supervise the deputies and revoke them at the first suspicion of debauchery or corruption."

One senses how quick Mathiez would have been to drag Danton before such an authority. Yet siding with Robespierre's opinion, the historian confesses fearing above all the power of corruption, that poison that made the plan of the old Montagnard itself unrealistic, since "the tribunal of morals would need, in its turn, to be supervised, and so on infinitely." Mathiez follows this institutional idea with precision, dwelling on Raffron's second proposition, in November 1793: a "censorial tribunal" animated by an interlocking of honest precautions, 83 citizens elected by the 83 departments, among whom the legislative body would choose 21 "Spartans," of whom only 15 would sit on the jury after a drawing of lots, a tribunal that "would judge the denounced deputy openly in public session" and "would limit itself to declaring whether the person charged has kept or lost public morality. In the latter case, the man condemned by the censure would be immediately stripped of his functions and exposed to the supreme punishment."

The following spring, the "terrible Vadier," continues Mathiez, proposed that each deputy "give an account to the people of his political and private life, and present the state of his morals and his fortune." Couthon supports Vadier: "Yes, citizens, let us all give a moral account of our political and private conduct; let us make known to the people what we were before the Revolution and what we have become, what was our employment, what was our wealth, if we have increased it and by what means, or if we have become richer only in virtues; let each one of us have this moral account printed and let each say: it is the truth that I present to you; if I deceive you in only one syllable, I call the national sword to strike down my corrupt body."

The Assembly, raised to its feet with applause, votes for the proposition of Vadier and Couthon by acclamation. The vote is called back into question a few days later through an intervention by Robespierre, who points out with what Mathiez calls "his cold good sense": "Knaves are more likely than honest people to know how to present to the public the moral account that was demanded of them." The plan is put one last time into place on 4 Vendémiaire Year IV, when Garrau, supported by Lebreton, cries out: "To prove to the People that we have not robbed them, I demand that each of us make a declaration, written and signed, of the wealth that he had before the Revolution and the one he now possesses." Again (but it is a long story) the proposition, first adopted with enthusiasm, is repudiated after a few days of reflection.

From this tale, Mathiez draws a lesson: corruption insinuates itself by ways ever more ingenious and by loopholes ever less visible, which a tribunal could never see. The Incorruptible, rejecting the plans for the censorial jury, understood it first: "Robespierre, Ladies and Gentlemen, was right. One does not cultivate virtue, one does not cause it to be born artificially. It is quite difficult to stop corruption by preventive means. Cunning knows how to hide vice, and appearances know how to disguise what the senses feel." Mathiez appropriates the discourse of the conspiracy, that of Robespierre: the body goes forth masked. Only the supreme order, the Terror, will be able to make the guilty tremble: "They will live in continual, obsessive fear, lest their mischief be unveiled, and some will tremble so much that their eyes, their hands, their mouth finally will betray them, for they will be able to calm their fright only by denouncing their accomplices and by denouncing themselves at the same time." The Terror, with Mathiez, reveals moral truth, since it alone knows how to tear off the mask and the "disguise" that hide the tremblings of the body. When the Terror falls, and Robespierre with it, the mask reappears, and the body covers itself.

Taine wanted to see all bodies; this transparency printed its mark both on the "historical physiognomy" of the historian—a society is judged by the portraits it offers—and on his embodied writing. Aulard feared to look at bodies, considering them and the anomalies they conceal as an obstacle to the just understanding of the characters of the men of the Revolution. Mathiez denounces bodies: he perceives in them a mask, contrived features that try to hide moral and political contradictions. The Jacobin historian would almost come to thank Danton for having such a loathsome skin. Between the "cold good sense" of his hero and the "fat, thundering, rotten" Danton, capable "of buying the youth of his wife," the struggle is unequivocal, in body as in soul. Most of the time, however, the "rotten ones," "crippled by debts and scolding actresses" (Fabre d'Eglantine), "lover of a ci-devant countess" (Julien de Toulouse), "Capuchin stripped of morals" (Chabot), "Jew of a most scarlet Jacobinism recently settled in Paris" (Frey), "lover of a scheming pensioner" (Basire), "suspected of friendship with very old duchesses" (Courtois), "handsome old protégé of the queen" (Hérault de Séchelles), know how to dissimulate their moral perversions by pretenses of the body. Mathiez is continually drawn between the dream of transparency and the obsession with conspiracy. It is he, when all is said and done, who remains the closest companion to the revolutionary mentality. Identified as he is with Robespierre, and even with Marat, Mathiez is like them even in his writing.

Thus, in the last phase of the nineteenth century, between 1880 and 1914, when Aulard's university history is formed, along with Mathiez's Robespierrism, and when Taine's literary history is being completed, metaphors of the organism are the stakes in their polemics, rereadings, and rewritings. Historians were not alone, then, in wanting to "read the body": this terrain is occupied as well by Darwinism, Bergsonism, the "energetic

souls" of Gobineau, not to speak of Gustave Le Bon's crowd psychology, of
Alphonse Bertillon's criminal anthropometry, or naturalism, or decadent-
ism. All these sciences or pseudosciences in turmoil pose the classification
of appearances as a condition of their existence: they position themselves
in the great spectacle of transparency.

Beyond these rich debates at the end of the nineteenth century—which
I was anxious to present, albeit briefly, to situate my research in an area
that was more active then than it seems to be today—the idea that the
political gaze directed at appearances has played an important role in revolutionary culture and praxis seems rich with meaning. Lynn Hunt, for instance, has foregrounded the place of Republican dress, leagues away from
a simple disguise, in the ceremonies of the new government.[9] Others have
worked on the politicization of bodily figures.[10] All these studies insist on
one central point: the obsession with transparency that, mixed with the
fear of the "conspiracy of appearances," exercised the revolutionaries. They
had to read the new society through bodies so as to denounce those corrupting mediations, masks. Such are the conditions and aim of the rituals
instituted for celebrations, assemblies, oaths, processions—all the gatherings of the political community. Out of fear of being suspected, everyone
must submit to these rituals. The carnival and its masks are forbidden in
1790—newspapers and pamphlets become accusers, and various projects
for "regeneration" of political morality succeed each other: all the veils
are to be stripped away so we can read the body straight, in every possible
way. Transparency wins in all the political arenas: everything is public—assemblies, lectures, deaths, opinions, property, writing, or, sometimes, the
education of children. Thus revolutionary political space clashes with that
long-lasting development that privileged the autonomy of the private. The
Revolution accordingly tends to accentuate the equality between the members of this community of transparency. In the most radical texts and proposals for ceremonies, from 1789 on, the autonomy of the private is absolutely rejected, while equality is demanded. Transparency of the political
gaze ought to extend, as in the plans commented on by Mathiez, all the way
to the "moral accounting" that exposes public *and* private life to the gaze
of all. I would like to come to understand through this study how, from the
beginning of the Revolution on, this space of transparency is constituted,
and how the scaffolding for this spectacle of the body offered to the sight of
all citizens is erected.

Space Made Transparent: The Parisian
Press of Denunciation

Taine does not just describe the spectacle of transparency; he tries to discover its mechanisms and causes. With his revolutionaries, transparency is necessary for the "pleasure of suspicion," then for the "joy of annihilation." This association forms the essential part of the first five chapters of Book IV of *Origins*. It is a question, for Taine, of showing how the Revolution, through the systematic practice of public denunciation, could become the vessel for all the harshness and frustrations accumulated by mediocre, resentful men of letters like the little clerks of the royal administration during the last years of the ancien régime. This thesis, which first appeared in satiric literature hostile to the social and political upheavals of 1789, is taken up again by Taine, who makes it the chief motivation of men of the Revolution. It ends up as a simplistic explanation of political denunciation: a moment of great release, a moment of revenge when, in a political space made violent by transparency itself, they finally accuse the former privileged one of all the evils in order the better to take his place.[11] The explanation no doubt contains a bit of truth: the works of Robert Darnton[12] have shown, with so many more nuances than Taine, how much the frustrations of certain literati kept at the bottom of the social ladder in the last years of the ancien régime could pour out in licentious and lewd lampoons on the privileged classes of the court and the town, writings that were particularly abundant at the very beginning of the Revolution. But the association between frustration and denunciation casts discredit on the latter, frequent though it was, and justified as both civic and positive by the revolutionaries themselves.

Public denunciation was thus brought under discussion in the beginning of 1789 by Patriot pamphlets and press. These texts marked out the space of political transparency, and tried (to use a distinction established by Roger Chartier) to constitute a new scene of words on the political matter wider than the "public sphere" of the ancien régime, and to establish a process of judgment more radical than the "tribunal of enlightened opinion."[13] The "sphere" and the "tribunal" are directly inherited from the practices of the debate of the Age of Enlightenment, removed politically from the ascendancy of the monarchic state, sociologically distinct both from the court and from the people.[14] Revolutionary political transparency

is certainly founded on this debate, but has the ambition of enlarging the
competence of political decision to include the appeal to the people, and
means to focus the radicality of its gaze on power itself. The "denunciatory texts" of the beginning of the Revolution thus not only fixed the rules
that must make this space of transparency legitimate—how can one distinguish good denunciation from base calumny?—but also themselves pur-
veyed many public denunciations, accusing authority and political enemy.
The space of political transparency is then "theorized," "historicized" by
the Patriot pamphlets and press, but also "put into practice." It is, moreover, this very simultaneity that marks its originality.

The researcher quickly meets this multiplicity of denunciatory signs in
the writing of political commentary at the beginning of the Revolution. A
number of titles of newspapers or pamphlets obviously express the intentions of the authors: observation, then denunciation, go together here. In
the titles of Parisian newspapers of 1789–91, the "senses" of the observer
are constantly increased, the political taking its cue from the literary gaze
traditionally directed at the people of big cities, such as *The Spectator* of
Addison or Restif de la Bretonne's "owl" watching over the alleys of the
Nights of Paris. Ten titles from 1789 are centered on the eyes: *The Observer,
The French Observer, The Spectator, The Club of Observers*—all insist on the
"supervisory function" attributed to the writer, a function again made explicit by "auditory" titles such as *The Listener at Doors.* Almost forty newspapers in three years emphasize in their title the functions of observation
and then of denunciation.

Pamphlets are not to be outdone. Seizing on one of the principal text-
book cases of the century, the "problem of Molyneux," the blind man suddenly returned to sight by a cataract operation, the writers of the Revolution spin out the metaphor by politicizing it. We can establish its narrative
through the titles of a few works that appeared between 1789 and 1791: *The
sighted blind man, or truth recognized* seems to be cured, for he has found
the *Secret for returning sight to the blind.* No doubt it is the *Eyeglasses of
the zealous citizen* that allowed this clarification of the gaze, or else, even
more surely, the lantern that holds its *Speech to the Parisians,* that *National
magic lantern* that projects the transparency of the political space onto a
cloth. Then *One can see clearly at midnight,* and *The National Assembly unveiled* appears naked to spectators happy to see the *Portrait of deputies at
the Estates General as they reveal themselves there* as well as the *Particulars
of aristocrats unveiled.* One is of course sometimes taken in by these prom-

ising titles. *The Surveyor [Le Surveillant]*, for instance, whose masthead—
"The title alone of this newspaper announces well enough what its object
is and what its principles will be"—nevertheless exhibits a denunciatory
bent, quickly becomes just a common newspaper. Whatever it may be, this
generalization of "titles of supervision" is symptomatic of the beginnings
of the revolutionary press.

By following the career of a small, specialized journal of 1789, *The
National Denouncer*, we quickly understand on what registers these numerous writings play. First, the absolute dramatization of the event: conspiracy
is everywhere, politicians are corrupted one by one, only the honest writer
can save his fellow citizens by denouncing vices, by stripping off the mask.
The National Denouncer, beginning its career at the start of August 1789, a
prolific time following the July conspiracy, starts with denunciations of all
kinds and promises to be uncompromising in the epigraph of its first issue:
"I undertake to tell all the truth and to unveil all physiognomies." Then,
from publication to publication (almost ten issues in two months), it takes
up, in a dry and repetitive style ("I denounce today"), the list of the chief
enemies of the Patriots: Maury, Despréménil, the "feminine committee
of the opposition," the "pullulating remains of the expiring aristocracy,"
always ending its issue with a warning to readers: "I exhort all my fellow
citizens to keep an eye open on one and all." One can find a similar construction in a number of these ephemeral newspapers of the beginning of
the Revolution: *The Listener at Doors* or *The Patriot Spy in Paris*, or again
The Patriot Confidant, finally the *Revelations as useful as they are interesting
of all that happens in the mystery of the court, in the National Assembly, in the
city hall, and in all the countries where the enemies of French liberty live*. All
these texts center their writing and their appeal to the reader on this mode
of the "secret unveiled."

Was acting as informant thus a "journalistic invention," contrived to
justify those writings that play on the absolute dramatization of the event?
Far from being a marginal genre, public denunciation constitutes one of
the successes of the press from 1789 on. Reading Marat's *The Friend of the
People [L'Ami du peuple]* reveals this clearly; it debuts, in September 1789,
as a "journal of commentary on the debates of the Assembly and on the
Affairs of the Time," then quickly, at the beginning of 1790, veers toward
a constant dialogue with "correspondents" who, most often, arrange for
letters of denunciation to reach the editor. Marat then uses these letters,
written moreover in part by him, to censure traitors' way of life and to an-

nounce the great conspiracies.[15] This practice plays an important role in his attempt to secure the loyalty of the readership: requests for information on such-or-such an individual, denunciations, calls to vigilance, summonings to mobilization all weave the narrative framework of Marat's writing and attach his readers to him.

The denunciatory genre is first a "stylistic bait," a writing of spectacle unveiled. That is quite visible in the "teasers" that figure often at the top of the page, which news vendors cry: "Revelation of all that happens in the mystery of the court," "List of all the sisters and pious ladies, with their names, that of their parish, and full details of all their adventures with the curates, vicars, and habitués of said parishes," "You will learn by turns the causes, the private lives, and the moral conduct never revealed till this day," "I will give you an exact account of their clandestine operations," "Here are the names, titles, and addresses of the main fugitives," "Citizens, lend an attentive ear to a great and horrible denunciation." [16]

Another sign of the success of the denunciatory genre: the counterrevolutionary satiric press very quickly seizes the model to offer, in a pastiched form, an ironic response to it. "False denunciations" circulate among the Parisian pamphlets: *The great and horrible conspiracy* thus imagines the "conspiracy of the girls of the Palais Royal" who, by their libertine art and their knowledge of poison, would corrupt the blood of all the Patriot deputies. Others construct fantastic conspiracies with coups d'état coming from "dirigible balloons," "Mongolian invasions," or "clerical poisons." Denunciation here is turned back on itself by laughter: the business of parody and of political pastiche, so flourishing in the press of the beginnings of the Revolution, clearly makes use of it; the "misuse of its words" proves the success of a genre.

Very quickly, journalists and pamphleteers portray themselves as observers and denouncers. Declarations of intention are particularly suggestive. The writer does not care to wait for information and render it in a neutral style but, on the contrary, carries out the investigation himself, scrutinizes the "masks and grimaces to find what is false in them, and discover a deformed appearance beneath them," [17] and then mobilizes opinion. Some call this the first "investigative political journalism." Classically, Brissot nicknames himself the "Patriot Sentinel" in the first issue of *The French Patriot*, just as the editor of *Rougyff*, in the tradition of Marat, wants to be the "Sentinel Citizen" and describes himself as being animated completely by "the electricity of denunciation": "I have a thousand eyes, a thousand far-seeing lenses, a telescope aimed at Paris; a million electrical wires surround me and, all at once, they will make me sound the alarm, jump to the rifle, to the sabres . . . nay, to the cannon."

Others are even more precise. Not content with eliciting denunciations from the readers—"I receive all the denunciations that the sentinels of liberty address to me"[18]—they present themselves as actual investigators tracking down the truth of bodies, mixed in the crowd, "disguised as a priest covering all the streets of Paris and Versailles to have the latest news"[19] or "posted at the court, as a false confidant and consequently an informed observer of those surroundings where the remnants of aristocratic fury still breathe."[20] Journalists are lying in wait: "I have searched, going back to the shadowy source of horrible treason . . . and I have discovered unspeakable plots," writes the editor of the *Hanover Butterfly*, while the *Second Opinion for Good Patriots* finishes drawing up the portrait of the new investigative journalism, using two more traditional metaphors: "I announce that I will unveil the intrigues of the factions, that I will follow their tracks just as the faithful bloodhound follows those of the deer or the buck, and that, lamp in hand, I will pursue them through the tortuous and tenebrous ways where they suppose they can hide their criminal designs."

Creating a role for himself and meeting success with it, the Patriot journalist must still legitimize his denunciatory practice. Desmoulins, as always, is the first to dress his ideas in ancient clothing, endowing denunciation with historic underpinnings. Cicero and Cato become the masters of Patriot denouncers, calling on a "Declaration of the Rights of the Accuser" translated by Desmoulins as a preface to his pamphlet of the end of 1789, *The distinguished millers of Corbeil*. Cicero's speech *Pro Roscio Ameriae* [One of Cicero's earliest speeches, "For Roscius of Ameria"—Trans.] ("It is good that there are many accusers in a state. It is up to you, Gentlemen denouncers, to enter into agreement about which ones are good for nothing and which ones are dissimulating; you can do nothing more pleasing for the Nation. If there is evidence, or half-proofs, against someone, you can still rush at them; for at night faithful dogs must be allowed to bark at passersby, because of thieves") is the political sibling of the "famous decree of the Roman Senate, the *Caveant Consules ne respublica quid detrimentum capiat* [Let the consuls beware lest any harm come to the republic], or the greatest latitude in public denunciations" adduced by Mirabeau to justify the violence of his accusations against the Comte de Saint-Priest in his *Letter to the investigative committee*.

After Cicero, the second ancient reference is Cato, brought "more than seventy times" before the Roman courts but always emerging triumphant from the tribunal, a figure of severe and upright politics who defied on the altar of truth any calumny that tried to overwhelm him, the "warmest partisan of denunciation, who his entire life performed the function of accuser, even when he was being plagued with attacks."[21] Desmoulins develops this example with a certain whimsy, adding his own dialogue with his political adversaries: " 'But,' a priest cries out, 'will you let yourself mouth poison?' 'Don't you see, Father, that what you call poison, and what you blacklist, others call the remedy of the soul?' . . . 'Then,' cries Abbé Maury, 'I will be slandered; they will even say that I have committed a desecration.' 'And I,' cries Despréménil, 'they will say that I am a cuckold.' 'Gentlemen, you know that Cato was maligned and brought to court seventy times; is he not still the wise Cato? That should console the honest people about whom something bad is said. Be Catos, and you will have no fear of the freedom of the press.' "[22]

These historic references supporting public denunciation—reinforced by the English example quoted by Mirabeau, for whom "denunciation in the legislative body is regarded as a duty"[23]—are not fortuitous. Denunciation appears as the touchstone of the defense of the *total* freedom of the press. In fact, Patriot journalists try to integrate "public denunciation by way of the press" into the "fundamental rights of the citizen." The debate of 24 August 1789 at the National Assembly, when the deputies argue about Article 11 of the Declaration of the Rights of Man, illustrates this strategy. The parliamentary intervention led jointly by Rabaut Saint-Etienne, Barère, and Robespierre tries to remove the limits that encroach on the total freedom of the press, while the clergy would like, on the contrary, "to conserve the morals and integrity of the faith" by proposing an arsenal of measures, including the reestablishment of preliminary censorship, to battle against licentiousness. The adopted bill, a compromise drawn up by the Duc de La Rochefoucauld,[24] is liberal, since it praises freedom of the press ("one of the most precious rights of man"), but places writers and printers in a position of having to "answer for abuses of this freedom" as a way of establishing a limit to denunciatory initiative.

That is precisely what the most radical journalists feared who, even before this debate, tried to mobilize their readers. The pressure doesn't let up with the adoption of Article 11 of the Declaration of the Rights, and the demands for total freedom of the press make themselves heard during the whole summer of 1789. Marie-Joseph Chénier proposes, from this point of view, the most virulent and the best-argued work. His *Denunciation of the Inquisitors of Thought*, written in July and appearing in September, makes denunciation out to be one of the "natural rights" that preserve the harmony of the community. "A fairy had endowed a prince with a fortunate quality: the ability to hear and to see, from the greatest distance, the voices and bodies of his people. Without leaving his throne, he was able to inform himself about everyone's way of thinking, and to recognize in their constitution the destitution or opulence of his subjects. Freedom of the press now will take the place of this fairy. For words must be able, like shafts toward their targets, to reveal injustice and reach the heart of bad citizens, concealers of plots against the nation": the first argument of Patriot writers is clearly asserted in this little tale invented by Chénier. Only freedom of the press is able to establish a direct, immediate connection between the power of looking (like the prince in the story, while the journalist often presents himself as the "king of opinion") and the duty to be honest and virtuous, or, even better, between the power of looking and the *right to be looked at*, everyone thus participating in the community of seeing.

This immediacy of denunciation is a constraining power, imputing guilt to the enemies of the public good, but it is also a power of revelation, disclosing the misfortunes of each citizen to everyone. It is in this open space that all the traditional intermediary bodies are drowned: hierarchies, corporations, academies, so many solidarities that protected the social or cultural groups of the ancien régime and founded precisely the "public opinion" of old, but that must from now on give way to the "citizen gaze." As an instrument of Patriot journalists, the watchmen and guides of a people once ignorant, denunciation is now raised to the rank of instrument of education and bond of the national community thanks to the appeal to the people, the only recourse capable of judging the truth of accusations. By this claim of discourse (denunciation associated with truth) and by this evolution of the intended public (denunciation involves the people itself by "appealing" to its good judgment), the space of political transparency is enlarged. The defense of denunciation becomes the occasion for a general praise of the "revolutionary journalist," who is the true successor, according to Chénier, of the philosophes earlier in the century. In this praise, one glimpses the ties of the "brotherhood" of journalists, which Loustallot, on 12 June 1790, in issue 49 of *Révolutions de Paris*, proposes designating under the name of "Federative pact of Patriot writers," joined by Desmoulins, Marat, Fréron, Gorsas, Carra, Audoin, and Chénier, all swearing, in the manner of Antiquity, to "defend freedom to the death."

Indignant opponents, demanding preliminary controls and censorship aimed specifically at individual denouncements, respond to this pact and this praise of public denunciation by way of the press. A number of pamphlets announce their "disgust" and their "incredulity"[25] before the flood of "slandering lampoons" that "invade Paris": "I want to banish back to the void the abject lampoonist who hides the bitter gall of the blackest calumnies under the roses of a pompous style: such, I think, my fellow citizens, are the duties dearest to the man of letters who preserves his honors with probity."[26] "Men of letters" against "abject lampoonists"—the struggle is constant in the beginning of the Revolution, embodying the rivalry of two forms of political authority: the "public opinion" inherited from the ancien régime, ruled over by academic and literary sociability, as against the "public transparency" of the Revolution, pervaded with the lively and numerous "tracts" of journalists appealing to the people (their readers). "Men of letters" rail against the "mad freedom" that "corrupts France even more unarguably than it instructs it . . . and propagates the denunciatory venom from race to race down to the most remote descendants."[27]

Two main arguments are advanced by the opponents of denunciation in the press who want to maintain barriers against the omnipotent gaze of journalists. First is the classic argument later taken up by the counterrevolutionary tradition: denunciation is nothing but the melting pot of frustrations and animosities on the part of lampoonists who were once destitute and jealous and who now hold, thanks to public speech, the dangerous power of observing and speaking freely. This practice can engender nothing but anarchy, with the worst citizens hastening to denounce the best, earning the favor of public opinion and of the idle "credulous people" thanks to a clever pen.

The second argument is that denunciation raised to the status of journalism will soon make all public offices undesirable, since no one would risk accepting a position as a public figure if put to the constant test of transparency: "If one is perpetually exposed to criticism, if one is endlessly exposed to the sarcasm of the wicked, who would want to be an administrator!"[28] Thus the "daylight test" that the Patriot journalists so clamor for with their demands, exalting the civic virtues of public denunciation, is experienced by traditionalist writers as essentially destabilizing, weakening, or, in a word, fueling anarchy. *The denouncers denounced*, a pamphlet

from the end of 1790, summarized all these arguments by reviling the "denunciatory craze" that has seized political pamphlets, seeing in them the
source of all the violent images engendered by "the imagination of lampoonists," and criticizing the conspiracy theories that often haunt Patriot
journalists: "The old free peoples did not try to find enemies and crimes
everywhere. To believe in some evil, they had to witness it, not simply hear
it denounced."

Clear-sightedness, Rite of an Absolute Democracy

In this battle of the press, the "denouncers" do not start without weapons; without them, they would quickly succumb to the "denouncers denounced" counterattack. Patriot writers also seem to find it necessary to
"make rules" for the practice of public informing. Marat, a great user of the
genre, while encouraging his readers to denounce traitors to him, stipulates
strict conditions: "Any denunciation that is unfounded, yet made through
love of the Country, will not expose its author to any punishment—since
man is not infallible, one mistake does not make him a criminal. Any
man unjustly denounced will be honorably acquitted, and any denouncer
in good faith will be required only to offer him the hand of an equal. But a
slanderous denouncer will be branded by public opinion, and the virtuous
man falsely denounced will win a mark of honor. There will be exhibited in
a Court of Justice two placards, one of which will contain the names of officials who have engaged in misconduct, the other the names of slanderous
denouncers. Above all, every denunciation must be signed. This practice
does not tolerate anonymity." [29] The journalist makes denunciation into a
test, an ordeal, an initiation rite capable of proving the worth of the new
political class. And as Desmoulins adds, in *Révolutions de France et de Brabant*: "I take it upon myself to rehabilitate this word 'informing' . . . In
the present circumstances, the word 'informing' must be treated as honorable." [30]

These "present circumstances" offer political denunciation two principal ways toward transparency. I will set aside here the venal motives that are
not negligible in the establishment of this "dramatic tale" of the Revolution
with indubitable success. First, the *surveillance of conspiracy* is a veritable
genre in itself in the beginning of the Revolution. The writer unties the
tangled threads of conspiracies and hands over his discoveries to the public:
"We must unveil to the eyes of the Nation, of Europe, of the entire Universe

the shadowy injustices, the bloody conspiracies, the network of assassins of which we were to have been the victims. We must loudly publish and publicly denounce the names of the perfidious conspirators . . . so that those guilty ones be handed over to horror, to general and universal execration." [31]

These denunciatory pamphlets work in a series: one pamphlet flushes out the conspiracy, a second confirms it, a third invalidates it. Thus one can count almost fifty pamphlets concerning the single affair of the supposed conspiracy of the Duc d'Orléans against the king in October 1789. Denunciations and answers swell to the point of constituting a dramatic universe in which the Revolution itself is nothing but a giant conspiracy.

The role of denouncer is presented as eminently cathartic. By revealing the conspiracy, by denouncing the conspirators, he purges political life and allows ideal transparency to be found again, at rapid intervals: "It is a great thing to know the details of the dangers that one has run when one has escaped them; the man who, after having for a long time been the plaything of the floods in the midst of a stormy tempest, and reaches the harbor without incident, gazes with a sort of pleasure on the fury of the waves in which he has trembled at each minute at being swallowed up . . . With what inexpressible satisfaction will we not see in our hands the details and the proofs of all sorts of those destructive conspiracies that have caused us, night and day, such cruel alarms. It is you that I address, citizens of all classes whose days have been so horribly threatened. Reflect on these perpetual fears . . . and say if there is a better way of compensating for them, of consoling yourselves, of bringing back calm and security than by unveiling to you steadily the bloody plans that you have escaped, the names of the conspirators, their methods and their hopes." [32] The denouncing journalist makes his own the panic of his readers, welcomes them, and then reveals them with his pen to purge the public space, to "bring back calm and security."

The second great type of denunciation by way of the press explicitly involves an *apprenticeship in the democratic process*. It is a matter of lists, published generally before each electoral term, of candidates whom the pamphlet writers judge, evaluate their just worth, and often denounce. Thus in response to large detailed lists preceding the Parisian elections to the Estates General, there appear *Whom should we elect? or, Advice to the people on the choice of its deputies to the Estates General*; *Three words to Parisians on the necessity of publishing the names of their candidates*; or, even more explicit, *The candidates of Paris judged, or antidote addressed to the electors of Paris*. The genre is followed by a whole series of denunciations aimed at the candidates for the elections of September 1789 in the districts of Paris (*The circular of districts, denunciation of the apostles of despotism*), and then by the constant warnings of Marat, Desmoulins, Gorsas, and Brissot. These lists have one point in common: they take into account the small experience the Parisians have with voting, and, fearing the hesitations of an "ignorant" people easily "seduced by beautiful words," comment on the careers and "private life" of each candidate. It is a question here of deliberately *setting up the people as a public*, giving it the "weapons of judgment" of which it had previously been deprived, the only way of enlarging the tribunal that the Patriot journalists wish to address. In a way, through these lists, writers fashion for themselves a people-qua-public just as they make traitors and enemies. It is a double construction whose fragility and sometimes illusory nature we will see repeatedly throughout this study. It is however in this jump from "public opinion" to "people-qua-public" that the main fracture of the revolutionary press resides.

Denunciation, urging a political transparency despite, or rather because of, the ignorance of the readers, is at the heart of this development. "To recognize the most capable men," that is the refrain of these lists, a didactic calling of the journalist who chooses a candidate and urges him on his readers: "We must clarify the choice of Parisians, by driving out abuses, mistakes, false views, ignorance, hypocrisy . . . Those who have chosen the provincial deputies are ignoramuses who did not understand the word 'Constitution' . . . It is on the vote of these ignorant laborers that the fate of France will depend!"[33] To remedy this "deficiency in patriotic instruction,"[34] the journalist proposes lists of sure men and, above all, denounces the corrupt. *The candidates of Paris judged*, a pamphlet from the spring of 1789 attributed to Mirabeau, specifies almost 35 names, "removing the mask" from them:

BEAUM[ARCHAIS]. Traitor, cringing body, satirical and flatterer.

L'ABBE LE COQ——. Cunning, gourmand, imbecile acrobat.

TARGET. Has made some reputation for himself by his works, but has gone on to dishonor himself by supporting Beaum[archais] and by cringing lower than him.

D'AMB——. His flatterers, at dinner, call him Fat Cicero.

MOREAU. Government pensioner, he has very earnestly mutilated the history of France.

PANCKOUCKE. He must be distracted from the pleasure he takes in stretching out his heavy encyclopedic mass.

"We believe we render a service to the public by unmasking the inept, vicious, criminal men who have dared to put themselves on the ballot to represent the city of Paris," the author goes on, to justify his list. The use of the vote is here as much a trap as enfranchisement: only the writer can guide the hesitant or ignorant elector.

The "brotherhood of Patriot journalists" tries to play this role of clear-sighted intermediary in June 1791, when the lists of electors in the various Parisian districts are established in view of the elections for the Legislative Assembly.[35] Then a number of very complete and very detailed series of "bad individuals to be crossed from the electoral rolls" appear. Marat, between 17 and 21 June, in the course of three issues of his *Ami du peuple*, looks into the lists of three districts (Notre-Dame, Théatre-Français, and Quinze-Vingt) and points out 102 "blackguards" whom "Parisians should mistrust." Marat wants his fellow citizens to "resist them on all sides" and to "continually keep an eye on these rotten members of their own body."[36] His description constantly mixes moral vices and physical defects: it presents, from the two sides of the "mask of composition," the portrait of the baleful man of politics laid bare by the gaze of transparency.

There are few innovations in the features of a bad citizen, but a psycho-pathological language appears that, by its very repetition, develops a certain effectiveness, catalogues of morality founded on scandalous anecdote: "Since most of these aristocrats are arrant rogues, I would urgently wish that my correspondents had shameful anecdotes passed on to me on their account. That is the touchstone for the public." The "dinner parties," the "chow-downs," the "orgies" form a first group, for "the meals are suitable for seduction and useful to the intriguers who wish to make a name." The observer denounces this seduction, citing those "drunkards who open up only when they are a little warm with wine" and those "dissolutes who spend all their time at the table of two old strumpets on government pension who fête them night and day."

Debauchery is the second vice laid bare: "impudent libertines," "inept good-for-nothings who pass as lovers of their own sex," "drunkards living with public women," and "chasers of public women no longer able to seduce respectable ones" make up a gallery of "exhausted syphilitics" that the good citizen should recognize without difficulty.

Another type of body earmarked for condemnation: the courtiers, "cringing dogs, bowing and scraping to everyone," the "arch-rogue gossiping comfortably and full of insolence," "Messieurs the Dukes, egoists, dull,

full of themselves," "the inept man who puts all his merit into the management of his coiffure." Wining and dining, sex, and manners—the observation and writing of Marat have no difficulty in offering to the Parisians these
easily recognized stereotypes. The vicious spirit, by the performative magic
of the word, literally becomes a body, a "model with broad physiognomy"
that can be read progressively from its first step of comprehension, the easi-
est, that of the "sinister cut-throat figure," up to the "art of unmasking the
cunning corrupt ones," a more elevated science derived from the courtier's
skill celebrated by Gracian, of deciphering the minutest corporeal signs.

Marat, good teacher of public denunciation, lavishes some advice. In
L'Ami du peuple we find the most suggestive expressions and the most
characteristic descriptions of these political bodies gone wrong, "men
dressed up as women,"[37] "pretty sirs well curled and prim little misses
well coifed,"[38] a reading of bodies sometimes revealed by more discreet
but nonetheless recognizable signs. Marat for instance tells the "guards
placed at the tollgates who survey all entries into Paris" the best way of
recognizing a suspect: "It is to look at his hands; the fineness of the skin
will be enough to announce a traitor disguised,"[39] advice that, far from
being a simple figure of speech, Marat warrants as "very patriotic and most
civic"—Marat, who was able, he says, to verify these characteristics *de visu*,
by being present at the interrogations of aristocrats: "They were interro-
gated by the committee of surveillance and general safety; and as I myself
am the observer, I was present at all the interrogations. . . . It was a curious
spectacle to see these old courtiers with fresh complexions and soft, white,
plump hands . . . We should, to recognize them, adopt a few foreign customs. When pirates make captures, the first thing they do is to thrust their
hands into those of the prisoners, and to judge from the whiteness and the
softness of the skin, if he is a common man or someone high."[40]

This political denunciation based on knowledge of the enemy's "physical defects," a journalist's universe for which Marat procures his most
brilliant but also his most frightening portraits, is justified, at the same
moment, by Brissot as the foundation of the new democratic life. *Le Patriote français* of 11 June 1791 is clear about its anxieties as to the preparation
of future legislative elections: "The mass of electors will be good and honest, because the mass of the French people is good and honest; but it can
still be ignorant of the character of the men it has to charge with its interests: so it must be enlightened. But how?" Beyond the method he proposes
(a screening ballot of a short-list of candidates, allowing the virtues of the

men present to be evaluated), Brissot answers this question with a long text, published in three installments in *Le Patriote français* between 12 and 15 June, intended to serve "the public discussion made in the heart of every society on the merit of all the candidates." *Whom should we elect?* is the title and subject of this text. Brissot first defines the space into which he introduces his reflections, the revolutionary community compared to a bodily machine animated by a just and balanced movement: "In this general body, the genius of freedom awakens, the Declaration of Rights is dictated, the French form a society. But the formation of the new government has not placed us above all the difficulties that oppose our progress and our stability. The machine is built—now it must be kept going by carefully regulated movements." Brissot sees this great body attacked by "unspeakable diseases": intriguers and hypocrites. These men whom he "keeps an eye on most vigorously" the Patriot denounces to "the man of good who is not forewarned," grafting in a way an antibody onto this "easily abused gaze": the power of transparency carried by the power of vision of the journalist. "Let us carefully lead the people away from their weakness: their tastes or their prejudices could set them in opposition to rigorous duties and earnest principles. Friends of luxury and pleasure, lovers of the senses and made-up faces, those whom their professions have familiarized with the aim of making money and the means to acquire it, would not know how to adopt the austere conduct that must characterize the supervisors, the organizers of public fortune."

From then on, Brissot begins a litany of "Bewares" and "Take cares." On 14 June a first series starts out with falsely naive questioning: "Whom should we elect? Everyone says: the most capable man, the most virtuous one. But by what signs can he be recognized?" Where Marat draws up lists of particular faces and bodies depraved by bad morality, Brissot generalizes the practice of public denunciation: he sketches concepts, abstract figures that still wear a body. Marat individualizes this great supervised body that Brissot conceptualizes: to both of them, the journalists of Republican radicality trace the wide field of transparency. Thus we read: "The hypocrites have more than one trick, and we must guess which one they use today."

To do this, Brissot distinguishes two categories of pretenders to the public's favor: the friend of the people and the man of the people. Launching a pointed remark at his comrade (although Brissot is anxious to withhold any direct reference to Marat's newspaper by spelling the bad word "friend" in lower case), he denounces the first and promotes the second.

The "friend" is a mask and the "man" a sincere body. "The friend of the people is almost always a man whose mouth is full of this phrase but whose soul is full of mockery; who, at the club, shakes the craftsman's hand, but at home behaves like a Count; who borrows only the name of the 'people,' like a tinkling bell, to lure its attention," writes the Patriot. Whereas the "man," although of comfortable background ("a citizen whom leisurely fortune, joined with the moderation of his desires, places above temptations, the surest guarantee of incorruptibility"), appears without any perverse separation between the face and the soul, transparent to the point of fusion with the national body: "The man of the people blends with the people; he does not need to cry out, to get attention, that he is the friend of the people; he does not endlessly boast of the sovereignty of the people, he believes in it. The man of the people is in the highest place, at the heart of opulence, simple, good, communicative, and is so without effort, without feigned affability. Exclude from your choice those friends of the people, pompous and all smiles; elevate only men simple in their ways, and the others will correct themselves or disappear." Brissot bases this portrayal on a social redistribution of citizenship [*civisme*], advising that the elected ones be chosen from among the "class of Patriot writers," or from the doctors, then from men of the law, but withholding votes from the "incorrigible race," ci-devant princes and ci-devant nobles.

Equipped with Marat's portraits and Brissot's advice, the Parisian constituent is instructed even more by Desmoulins, who, at the same time, goes further in the pages of *Révolutions de France et de Brabant* and in some pamphlets. The "class of Patriot writers" enters into the electoral campaign, and denunciation shapes the space where it will develop. Desmoulins thus reprints some extensive extracts from Brissot's *Whom should we elect?* in his own journal, dated 18 June, and dreams of a "battle of truth" led against the corrupt man—"to attack him in broad daylight, to call him out into the plain, to leave him the advantage of the place, the wind, and the sun, and to confront him with a battle that he cannot scorn."[41] Desmoulins then imagines a strange building consecrated to "the interrogation of candidates," what amounts to an architectural metaphor of political transparency: "A vast amphitheater, in the middle of which rise up the benches for the judges, and then for the candidates, and then the rostrum of the accuser and defender, and, all around, an immense gallery for the philanthropic protectors of our laws but also of our innocence: our public."[42] By means of the newspaper or the pamphlet, here the ideal spectacle of an

absolute democracy is offered to "our readers," each politician being placed
under the eyes of the public, able to be summoned at any moment by the
supervising writer, the "Patriot sentinel," before the "people-reader," the
final authority of judgment.

   To denunciation as a test of transparency the journalists assign a central
place in the apprenticeship of democracy, that political system that philosophers before then had declared impossible to put into practice in any
large country, and that they reserved for the Swiss cantons. The Patriot
press makes this claim: to enlarge the *agora* of the ancient city or the canton
to the scale of national political space by means of the pressure and surveillance offered by the revolutionary *medium*. Denunciation, then, assumes
a very coherent place in the functioning of the political system: developing steadily under the journalists' gaze, politicians are *forced to perfection*.
Bonneville describes this perfection quite precisely in *The Iron Mouth* in
April 1791, when he fashions the "Portrait of a man who loves good and who
strongly wants it," or, in other words, an "extraordinary politician": "The
man who must resuscitate lethargic nations is always prepared by nature
in a profound silence, like beneficial rainstorms. A very fine sensibility, an
ardent imagination, and an honest heart—that is all his inheritance. He
gives no hint of what use he will make of it: always simple, frank, always
open, like nature, everything he is seems to be an invitation to those about
him to subjugate him, to chain his heart, to strip from him the esteem of
honest people, the benevolence of his friends, even his own confidence, his
gentlest hopes. Nature seems to have destined him, from his first years,
to be deceived in everything, as if to force him to examine everything for
himself. His endlessly active soul always keeps watch, even fights ghosts,
like shadows of danger. New ordeals ever rise up, which make him stronger,
more clear-sighted, but also harder, more inflexible. . . . Despite all the obstacles, he will create a force for truth, which he will make a naked and
all-powerful truth, no matter how he does it. Do not expect him to be the
pliant and ingratiating companion, a walking doll; on the contrary, he iden-
tifies only with those who have suffered, who have fought for the good cause.
Soon the self-proclaimed wise men and the so-called friends of mankind
will perceive that his penetrating eye goes right through masks and reads
their hearts. They will close the door against him; but he can see through
the door into the crevices of their soul. His gaze, despite all obstacles,
will teach them that an account will be demanded of their false virtues." [43]
This portrait of the ideal politician combines the dreams of Brissot, Marat,

and Desmoulins. This exceptional being fashions around him the space of "clear-sightedness" dear to Patriot journalists by acquiring little by little, by successive ordeals and vigilant zeal, a "penetrating eye."

Reading the Body

This transparency of the political space expresses the new confidence that animates the reader of the body at the end of the eighteenth century. Denunciation by unmasking is not a mere rejection of deceptive appearance; on the contrary, it is rather the wish to understand it better. The aristocrat, the corrupt man, the debauchee try to compose a face for themselves—but the observer [surveillant], however, sees the reality of their features, brings the ugly grimaces back into view so as to make the true portrait appear.

This confidence is illustrated by the success of two pseudosciences in France at the end of the ancien régime and the beginning of the Revolution: physiognomy and physiognotracy. The works of Lavater won an exceptional popularity; they were published in a long series between 1775 and 1778 in Zurich, then translated into French in 1781.[44] They were applied by Gall to the "phrenological" science that "allows a comprehension of individual dispositions through the study of bumps on the skull," which was discussed, severely, by Kant in the Critique of Judgment. Physiognomy, according to the definition of Lavater himself, is "the science of the relationship that connects the internal to the external, the visible surface to the invisible part it covers,"[45] a science that has for its aim the knowledge of "the perceptible signs of our forces and our natural dispositions." Lavater tries to discover the significance of the forms of the face, guided by his confidence in a universal harmony and a just hierarchy of bodies: "Nature looks the same everywhere. It never acts arbitrarily, without law: the same wisdom, the same force shapes everything, fashions everything, creates all the varieties according to one single law, one single will. Everything is subject to order and law, or nothing is."

Choosing order, and therefore submission to the Creator who placed revealing physiognomies everywhere, the scholar wants to read this "divine alphabet."[46] This is a rather paradoxical meeting: divine creation with "scientific" scrutiny. Scientific apparatus is essential to understanding the success of Lavater's formulas. Lavater relies on a very precise mapping of the pattern of facial features, calculating and plotting on paper the angles that

unite and link the different elements, recomposing on the sheet the proportions of the human face. Lavater constructs an ordered geometry of the
dimensions of the face established in proportion to the height of the head,
which is taken as one unit, and is itself equivalent to one-tenth of the total
height of the body.

Sides of the nostrils	1/13
Height of nose	1/4
Height of eyelids	1/12
Height eyelid–eyebrow	1/24
Angle from one eye to the other	1/6
Outer corner of eye–edge of face	1/6
Width of nose	1/6
Width of mouth	1/4
Height ear	1/3
Width ear	1/6

This plan for the "scientific" reproduction of human proportions finds
its consecration in the mechanization of the drawing, of the portrait, which
appeared in France at the same time as the diffusion of Lavater's theories.
Sectioning the natural size of the profile of a face can then be modulated
in reduction. The invention dates from 1786 and is presented by a scholarly journal, *The Physico-Economical Library*: "M. Chrétien, musician at
the King's chapel, has just conceived an instrument by the help of which
one can make a profile or three-quarter portrait in three or four minutes, without knowing how to draw. The price of this machine does not
exceed 24 livres."[47] The ingenious system allows one to project geometri-
cally a motionless face, so that the final tracing, reduced in proportion to
one-fourth, is dependent exclusively on the apparatus, the executor con-
tenting himself with following the curves of the real profile. Starting in
late 1788, Edme Queneday des Riceys distributed this invention, profiting
from the vogue for portraiture, which, at the beginning of the Revolution,
was to immortalize the new political personnel. Under the name "portrait from physiognotracy,"[48] he produced almost 2,800 representations
between 1788 and 1790: politicians and curious onlookers passed through
his studio near the Luxembourg.

The two projects, Lavater's and Queneday's, form part of the same absolute: the transparency of the body. One reads in the features and proportions of the face all the virtues or defects that the Creator placed there,

the other effaces the hand of the artist, that sometimes clumsy, sometimes clever, but in any case opaque intermediary between the body and the drawing, to replace it with the neutrality of the simple mechanical reproduction.

But Lavater goes further. Like any religious approach to science, his establishes an ideal, and then establishes each case in accordance with its relationship to the norm. Here is the ideal face: "A forehead that rests on a horizontal base, straight, dense eyebrows strongly pronounced; clear hazel eyes that seem black at a little distance, and whose eyelids cover only a fourth or a fifth of the pupil; a mouth of horizontal cut whose upper lip gently dips toward the center and whose lower lip is no thicker; a round but slightly projecting chin; a straight, rather wide nose and short hair, dark brown, with curly locks. A face above all where conformity of length between the three parts is perfectly preserved."

This strict code for reading the face, reinforced by respect for harmonious proportions, rejects any abnormality of physical and moral deviation: "Perform experiments then, and you will find that the forehead is that of a fool, if it is one whose fundamental line is two-thirds shorter than its height. The more markedly the radii of a protractor whose right angle is applied to the frontal angle form acute angles in an abrupt and harmful way, in unbalanced proportions, the more the individual is a fool." Or again: "Any face whose lower part, counting from the nose, is divided into two equal parts by the central line of the mouth, any face is stupid whose lower part is longer than one of the two upper parts. The more the profile of the eye forms an obtuse angle with the profile of the mouth, the more it indicates a weak and narrow-minded man." [49] From this correlation of the deviant with the corporeal ideal Lavater's approach gains its whole meaning, placing itself deliberately in the sphere of judgment of taste (Kant speaks of a "knowledge without concept"), thus in a hierarchy of appearances all of whose deviations, including the satiric (cartoons use the same "scientific" tables as Lavater, but apply distorting angles to them), are possible, though not desirable.

It is on just that ground that the reading of the body peculiar to Lavater was immediately contested. Starting in the 1770's, *L'Encyclopédie*, for example, can be ironic, in the article entitled "Physiognomy," about "that pretended art that teaches how to recognize the humour, temperament, and character of men by the features of their faces." Between the "science" of Lavater and the "pretended art" that the *Encyclopédie* sees it as, a multitude of opinions intervene that, by the very debate that they sustain, extend the influence of the physiognomic code of the Zurich sage while at the same time perverting it. Recently translated, his presence is felt, his work carried on by certain experiments with the "Mesmer tub" [50] at the beginning of the Revolution. The Marquis de Luchet was inspired by him, as his *Gallery of the Estates General* of 1789 shows, a work matched by Dubois-Crancé with some descriptions in his *Supplement to the Gallery of the National Assembly* as well as his *True Portrait of Our Legislators, or Gallery of the Pictures Exhibited for Public Viewing from 5 May 1789 to 1 October 1791*. Rivarol provided a more satirical perspective and an even more physiognomist writing in *The Great Men of the Day*.

Desmoulins too, who loves to draw up the portraits of his principal adversaries or friends, does not hesitate to use the resources of this fashionable pseudoscience. In issue 16 of *Révolutions de France et de Brabant*, the journalist "expatiates upon physiognomy applied to great politicians": "It is an infinitely curious and original piece, the report inserted into the *Journal de Genève* that detailed Lavater's meeting in Basel, his spectacles glued on M. Necker's face, admiring in the complexion of a pale yellow the beautiful ideal of a great statesman, and tracing with a sure hand the character of the hero according to the analysis of his nose and his chin." Desmoulins contrasts this portrait with his own, countering Necker with Sieyès, who shows the true countenance of rupture with the era of the courtiers: "The first time I saw the Abbé Sieyès, I was very pleased with his head . . . I fancied I perceived in it the character of the forehead and that paleness that frightened Caesar in Cassius and Cimber: I was overjoyed to see in him the traits of a conspirator, and I took him for a Roman." Similarly, prolonging this reading of the body with laughter, Desmoulins descends to the "aristocrats and pensioners," and, going from the forehead to the more significant extremities, finds their "nails very long, undoubtedly the better to snatch coins."

Desmoulins understands here the resources of a political reading of the body. Of course, he is not stupid: his project does not lay claim to any Lavaterian scientific objectivity. It is only a deviation of it, playing with the "physiognomic" fashion or the "physiognotracic" vogue. The "physio" is a successful genre in the beginning of the Revolution. Journalists are not unaware of this: the reading of the body becomes a political weapon under their pens. *The Deaf Man of Palais Royal*, who "sees events from the physiognomy of people" before writing them down, could illustrate this art of deviation. He opts for Lavater's point of view, the precise gaze focused on the body, but transfers its effects toward the political arena, recognizing "events" and "conspirators" rather than a hierarchy of souls. "I will judge revolutionaries from the candor of their gestures," states *The Deaf Man of Palais Royal* in his first issue.

This laying bare is one of the weapons of revolutionary writing: it transforms a "scientific" method by offering it a political subject, its communications giving birth to a flourishing network of images, to an *imagination*. The figures of this imagination of reading the body are all grouped around the theme of unmasking. First, the instruments of clear sight: spectacles, lorgnettes, lanterns, rays of light, all symbolic of the scrutinizing eye, all derived, often thanks to laughter, from the great jumble of scientific experiments of the time.

An ephemeral newspaper of 1790, *The Enchanter Merlin's Lorgnette Found Under the Ruins of the Bastille*, thus presents the eyeglass "that has the virtue of showing men as they are." Faced with such a discovery, "all the Court was in consternation; everyone trembled for his face and his ears." The journalist undertakes to "communicate to the public all that the lorgnette offers to his newly opened eyes." The first vision corresponds, in the second issue of the newspaper, to "a mass of mud and blood," which is the truth of the statue of Louis XV when focused on by the revealing lorgnette.

In a pamphlet of the same genre dated April 1789, *The eyeglasses of the zealous citizen*, the Patriot, thanks to that instrument, "unmasks the clergy, the nobility, and the magistracy, and forces them into their last retrenchments," before "making all of it public." He can see and describe two kinds of bodies: that of the privileged, "their mouths twisted by calumnies, their ears torn apart by listening too hard, the hair on their heads standing up from the fever of conspiracies," and the body of the Frenchman before 1789, "pale and barely covered as a sign of his exhaustion."

To these lorgnettes and eyeglasses, the "marvelous rings" or the "magic lanterns" must be added. The author of *The first attack of the claw* proudly boasts he is able to slip onto any politician the "ring" that causes "men to say and write not what they want others to hear and read, but what they really think."[51] The keeper of the *National magic lantern* announces a novel spectacle that is close to the dreamt-of transparency: "You are going to see what you have never seen, what the dawn of freedom alone could produce." This blinding and beneficial light allows the writer to project several scenes in which are sketched out the "traits of despotism and of aristocracy," terrifying faces and deformed bodies, after which appear the "images of the Nation," colorful and festive.

But the privileged symbol of the laying bare of the hypocrite and the traitor remains the simple lantern. [*Lanterne* is both lantern and lamppost, the latter often a handy gibbet. Trans.] This is not just an image of punishment, a support on which one hangs the enemies of the people; its first value is a denunciatory light. Many are the characters who pass before the "tribunal of the lantern" in 1789, a tribunal instituted by Desmoulins himself in his *Speech of the lantern to the Parisians* in which he tries to unveil the "naked truth" of the conspiracies of mid-July. Associated with this lantern is Diogenes, who was experiencing remarkable popularity at the time,[52] making a great comeback in the role of informer. Carrying his lantern from the Estates General to the Hôtel de Ville while passing through the streets of Paris, Diogenes sees clearly. He unmasks and denounces traitors, and in April and May 1789 mounts to the rank of "hero of the Third Estate"[53] before becoming the hero of the Patriot party. Desmoulins readily tries to embody his qualities: "Diogenes will not remain idle; through my efforts he will roll his barrel through the city of Paris. I will denounce all the abuses, I will pursue all the bad citizens, all, until they have torn the life from me and blown out my lantern."[54]

The philosopher [Diogenes], whom they represent as conversing at will with the enemies of the Patriots in order to unmask them—revelatory maieutics[55]—becomes, in the writings of the radical pamphleteers, the only figure worthy of "recounting the liberation of the Parisians": "I found myself at Paris during the memorable week when the revolution that has just been carried out began and when freedom emitted the last cry of childbirth . . . I saw with pleasure your games and your interrupted spectacles. I had finally met men, and I broke my lantern. Since then, I have perceived my error . . . Pride, ambition, jealousy, corruption have been reintroduced into hearts. Ah! I cried out: Diogenes, where is your lantern, where are your men? Can it be that the same citizens who, a short time before, showed so much modesty, zeal, and disinterestedness, today strive only after the right to command and secure a position? Many of you, Parisians, have been impressed by the charm of their diction and the strength of their eloquence: they have taken the mask of the public good and have seemed to be zealous courtiers of Patriotism and liberty, in order to blind you."[56] And the philosopher reincarnated as a Patriot proceeds to give a list—from the most famous men (La Fayette and Bailly) to the smallest "sneaks of the municipality"—of those "snakes hidden beneath the flowers." Diogenes, hero of denunciation, takes on the appearance of the people itself. With the journalists of 1789 he becomes the equal of the Hercules portrayed by the artists of the Terror: a "summons" to follow revolutionary action. Embodying his denunciatory function, never content with truth or unmasking, he is a figure of excess: his gaze will never be clear enough, space will never be transparent enough, aristocrats will always find better and better masks. The Revolution will never be finished.

Armed with a method of reading the body along with an imagination of clear-sightedness, revolutionaries place the figure of the aristocrat in the center of the space of transparency. From then on, a typical portrait is elaborated. Emerged from Lavater's propositions and from his "science" of reading bodies, the fantasy of the enemy revealed by the very deformations of his appearance develops by successive derivations of meaning. The body of the aristocrat achieves a recognizability yearned for by the Patriot imagination, thus finally undoing the eternal dangers of the mask. It is an appearance in which the negative past, the faults of the privileged, and the conspiracies to come can all be read, a body that is profoundly unadapted and unadaptable, that is the image of the noble, then of the aristocrat, an image that can be grasped as well through the press as by skimming through the substantial corpus of political cartoons treating this inexhaustible subject.

One can try to group these negative appearances into three imposing families: first the bent and grimacing ones, physical defects attributed to the malformations of courtiers; then the effeminate, overly *soigné* ones, covered with ribbons and powder, the periwigged fops we find in English cartoons; finally, the big and the fat, potbellied and paunchy, who animate the "Rabelaisian quarter of an hour" of the counterrevolution, to cite a jovial expression used by a Patriot newspaper to designate the "Red Book" of pensioners of the court.[57] Each time, the political and moral defect is made concrete in the physical metaphor of the character: hypocrisy finds its political corporeal form in curvature, disdain in a haughty look, pedantry becomes feminine languor, and all the vast property the privileged have acquired shows up as monstrous fatness.

Camille Desmoulins makes a specialty of these physical descriptions that mix irony with political denunciation. He draws up the portrait of the courtier this way: "It is a singular profession to give your hand to a princess, your hat to a prince, your reverences to a king. How can one have such a calling? There is expressed on your physiognomy a particular curvature in which (and that is quite amusing) one sufficiently recognizes the court aristocrat."[58] Or again, addressing his character with indignation: "Your body has been utterly deformed by prostrating three times before an imbecilic sultan. You are unworthy of having that forehead raised toward the sky, and those two straight feet, made to hold upright the proudest of animals. Go walk on four paws to Constantinople or stay hidden in the antechambers of the Tuileries."[59]

Deformed body, face made just as ugly by the grimaces and the mimicking attributed to that character inherited from literature portraying the court: "This madness [the nobility] is of the most extraordinary order. It seems first, from the little one can observe, that it is vanity that turned the head of the poor man: his eyes and his manner of staring haughtily, his forehead and his manner of creasing it in a frown of insolence, his mouth with its disdainful lips, everything proclaims, even before he speaks, the character of excess."[60]

The second characteristic of the aristocratic body is its effeminacy. Gone are the strength and vigor of the conquering Franks; the privileged are now nothing but "idol of the boudoir" or "charmer behind the scenes," to use the phrases of the newspaper *The Spartan*, whose masculine title stresses the Patriot character. The portrait of the dainty, of the overrefined and timid man with a fragile, powdered beauty, is then sketched out: a noble whom the Patriot writers cause to rise up as a kind of stock figure when they need a deformed mannequin to contrast with the neoclassical athlete with whom the Hercules or the giant of the populace is to be identified.

However, the appearance most generally attributed to the privileged remains that of the "too fat." The aristocrat is "the man who has fattened himself by starving the people," as Marat presents him in one of the first issues of *L'Ami du peuple*.[61] One of Marat's most frequent descriptions outlines the caricature of a society of the elite corrupted by eating well and drinking well, the people who are "grateful only for a full belly": "Our vampires live in palaces, drink the most delicate wines, binge on banquets, sleep on eiderdown, and forget our misfortunes in their abundance and pleasure."[62] This ridiculing portrayal, which we have already come across at the core of the denunciatory system of the lists of "rotten ones" from *L'Ami du peuple*, is propagated in a spectacular way as much by political cartoons as by newspapers. With Desmoulins, for example, the "fat man" is embodied to the point of obsession by the omnipresent character of the Vicomte de Mirabeau, younger brother of the Patriot orator, also called

"Mirabeau the barrel" or "Riquetti the ton," who sings, along with his aristocrat friends of the Assembly — those "vile little titled fat men with their drunken faces" — a few drinking songs, like this one:

> Rest assured! down to the kitchen I run
> To see if that lamb is getting done.
> Courage, my children! Try to serve me,
> Not as a bourgeois with a face so flat,
> But as a gentleman, a bold aristocrat.
> I'll have you sent six flagons of Bordeaux.
> Set right down here the meat pie with fricandeau,
> Garnish this spot with the matelote . . .
> Let us take off fancy clothing and the plumed felt hat,
> Give me the apron and the white cotton cap:
> Lo and behold! the kitchen boy, greasy and fat! [63]

The gold accumulated by the nobles turns into fat; this equation is revealed, in the logic of the grotesque portrait, as an inexhaustible source of inspiration. Politics and physiognomy ceaselessly intersect to fashion this portrait: "There is a very heavy, very weighty individual. If, in imitation of all the Great Ones, he ate a part of the State's revenues, his embonpoint at least does honor to the many succulent meals won for him by the enormous paunch that he carries with much fatigue; and the public papers, that announced that this pig ate for four, and drank accordingly, would have had to add that France was in no way fertilizing a barren land in him, and that he was putting our taxes to very good use," [64] one of the numerous "antifat" [65] lampoons ironically says about Monsieur the brother of the king, who has become for the occasion the prototype of the noble parasite and bloodsucker.

Patriot discourse offers an ironic and virulent spectacle of bodies so that the aristocracy, rife with defects, ends up by becoming a veritable pathology. A body of distinction is no longer a virtue, a merit, or a privilege; it has been transformed into a simple political disease. This disease, which is followed attentively by, for instance, Camille Desmoulins, "causes havoc in the great private mansions": "It is above all the race of the privileged that is attacked with this plague, from which all the diseased expire from extraordinary suffocation, as if by a restored aristocracy. Others lie fainting in languors and consumption. This *aristocratic spleen* eats away alike at the septuagenarian duchess and the toothless field marshal and the young viscountess who flatters herself, when she no longer has her fresh convent colors, at still being far away from the order of uglies with the privilege of rouge. . . . I advise you, then, ladies and gentlemen: the vinegar of Maille and all the salts are useless against these faintings, heart attacks, migraines, and crises of nerves that the decree of 19 June and the suppression of all the titles of the nobility causes you. Therefore I urge you to search out the true remedy in a little pamphlet entitled, *The True Mirror of the French Nobility*. The historic part especially should radically cure you. Take and read." [66]

This extract emphasizes the force of this radical reading of the degenerate body: antiaristocratic rhetoric gives no respite to its enemy and decks it out with all the vices, twisting for its own use all the discourses of physiological description, from medicine to physiognomy. The discourse of the nobility, even when it recovers some of its power in the beginning of the nineteenth century, can only ineffectively combat this defeat of the body. In French political culture, the noble, "fat debauchee" or "sickly précieux," will often remain a character expressing an outworn, decadent image.

From physiognomy to pathology, the reading of the body develops its references and creates its imagination, elaborating the spectrum of all the possible appearances of negative figures, ranging from the absolutely realist portrait of a precise individual to the caricature isolating and generalizing some trait to make it the phantastical symbol of a disease of the social and political body taken as a whole. The imagination in its reading of the body allows this transition from the denounced individual to its archetype, this perversion of the physiognotracic portrait into its caricature. Denunciation is favorable to this sudden jump from the everyday world to the world of political imagination. In other words, the reading of appearances, despite its vaunted objectivity, offers procedures of categorization/decategorization, of symbolic types, which are at the very heart of the process of political mobilization. This vision of the world leads most often, in fact, to an absolute Manicheanism. Denounced, stylized individuals are grouped together around an omnipresent referential framework: the "Patriot" denounces the "Aristocrat." The pamphlet is composed without nuance around this fundamental pair.

The paths of this imagination are particularly suggestive. The first version of the reading of the body, simple, physiognomical, and descriptive, is the list of bad citizens. In the form of pamphlets, several lists exist indicating the name, function (especially under the ancien régime), address, and sometimes, indicated by a word, the psychologico-physical character of the persons considered suspect. *The list of aristocrats of all shades making up the monarchical club*, which appeared in June 1790, is a good example. After a brief foreword that of course represents the list as a lucky find made by chance at a meeting, almost four hundred names of "aristocrats" file by, grouped into two issues of eight pages each.

This procedure is often used again by the press, with some journalists specializing in these lists of informing. *The Enemy of Aristocrats*, in six issues in 1791, offers numerous portraits that allow the recognition of particular individuals, portraits from which we can extract the "traitor Dusochoi": "About 5 feet 1 inch tall, age 26, hair and eyebrows dark chestnut, hollow cheeks, knock-kneed, hair short like a priest, eyes haggard, naturally fearful, and the head always covered with a round hat."[67] What strikes one immediately in these descriptions of denounced individuals is their precision. Always—and many examples could be given, particularly beginning with *L'Ami du peuple* in which appears, early in 1791, the most precise gallery possible of "sneaks" and other "sell-outs" of the municipality—the appearance itself is offered to readers as a vector of mobilization. On this model circulate lists of academicians, members of parliament, nobles, ecclesiastics, and the like.

To this first meager reading in the faithful description of real bodies, a vision deformed by polemics comes to be added. From the first, the subjection to abuse deprives the denounced individuals of their realistic physiognomy. Several lists are specifically "lampoons of insult." Through words of polemics, a current genre in that period of tension, the caricature of the traitor, of the "blackguard," "horrible monster tearing apart the spoils of citizens," "barbarian," "cut-throat," "feudal despot," "perverse and disgusting intriguer" is sketched out.

The other traditional register of corporeal deformation is the "scandal list." Revolutionary denunciation gathers here the heritage of those numerous lampoons that, in the form of lists of degenerate nobles and courtiers, had, at the end of the ancien régime, succeeded in drawing up a stern picture of libertine morals of the high people of the world. Revolutionary pamphlets pursue this tradition in two forms. On one hand, there is the vein of "private lives" that, from Louis XV to Marie-Antoinette, had made the success of court lampoonists, and gives, from Maury to Charles d'Artois, from Chapelier to Mirabeau, the occasion to denouncers from all sides to draw up scandalous portraits of the new political class. On the other hand, collective lists—libertine ecclesiastics, extravagant nobles, clients of real or imaginary bordellos—also contribute to drawing the image of the degenerate. The character is no longer just a simple body whose apparent characteristics are noted; he becomes a monster who is insulted and a degenerate who is tracked down. However, quite often, it is a question of the same individuals. They pass thus from one space to the other by the simple deformation of reading the body.

More precisely, if one follows in the newspapers the description of a symbolic person, for instance "Maître Estienne" suspected by Marat and his friends of being a hireling of the municipality of Paris, one can grasp the double register on which the journalists' denunciations essentially play. *The Enemy of Aristocrats*, at the end of 1790, gives a first description of Estienne: "5 feet 2 inches tall, 28 years old, hair, eyebrows, beard and eyes black, rubicund face." [68] In the same newspaper there follows, a few days later, another description: "Formerly completely naked, now well clothed, clothes of all sorts of colors, round hat to hide his muzzle." [69] In the second draft of the portrait, three new elements appear: careerism, coquetry, and the mask, all three an integral part of another universe, that of aristocratic fantasy (corrupting ambition, the mania of finery and hypocrisy).

Marat, in *L'Ami du peuple*, also welcomes Estienne: "Dressed in the bourgeois style, 5 feet 2 inches tall, face full and rubicund: eyes, beard, and hair black, accent Gascon, 28 years old; he insinuates himself into all circles under a hundred different disguises." [70] The first characteristic of the aristocrat, hypocrisy turning to conspiracy—the mask and the disguise—is confirmed here, but the description of the body retains an almost clinical precision and sobriety. A few weeks later, Marat resumes his denunciation of the same person, now qualifying Estienne as "head of La Fayette's merchants" and describing his function: "Has occupied in person a few positions as Court valet. Raised by the Jesuits. He has the epaulettes of an aide-de-camp or head of a division, his place setting at the table of the general, and 10,000 livres a year in salary. At the end of ten years of service, the virtuous Bailly has engaged to grant him in retirement the position of inspector of prostitutes." [71]

This very complete portrait definitively swings Estienne into the domain of physical and moral stereotype: he is no longer himself, but a model archetype of the "aristocratic category," and has become, in a way, a caricature of his own body by way of his perverse education, his care for appearance (the epaulettes), his gluttony (the place setting at the table of La Fayette), and, to complete the sociopolitical embodiment, his shameless loose living ("inspector of prostitutes"). Denunciation follows this path: it leads from the individual man to the type, it gives a body to the "concept" of the enemy, imposes manners, gestures, corpulence, a physiognomy on the "aristocracy." This transformation constructs a political imagination for reading the body.

Counting the debauchees, scornfully eyeing the "walking dolls," weighing up the "chow-downs," suspecting the overzealous friends of the people, reading, even through the masks and obstacles, the vices on the appearances of political men, the denouncers try to base the democratic culture of the Revolution on a novel functioning of gazes traversing public space. This wish to say everything, even sometimes the most absurd (the "shadows of danger"), imposes in fact upon all the characters on the political scene an ordeal whose rules, in part fixed, are of course accepted: everyone is aware that his own existence can be attacked from all sides.

This "democratic ordeal" that the press inflicts on politicians after 1789 is certainly nothing but an enlarging of the rumors put into circulation by the lampoons of the ancien régime, reputations that could make the rounds of public opinion and, even more, the court. However, from this court life in which everything was known, we pass on to a political space offered to the elector in which everything becomes public, including suspicions of debauchery and corruption. In this sense, the discourse of denunciation is integrated into a phenomenon of "laying bare" the political scene. Making politicians grow inside a "cage of glass" (of which many variations can be found: assembly amphitheaters, the Champ de Mars of the "federative pact," or the panoptic political system imagined by Desmoulins), keeping them always under their observant eyes, journalists fulfill a "mission" (to enlighten the people, or to transform the people into a public) that they describe as exemplary even if it is not without danger. This boundary of the private domain, of the secret intimacy that the observers want to bring to light, is exactly what allows people to resist so well the omnipotence of the political as well as the drift of necessary vigilance toward the obsessional fantasy about conspiracy. It is by endlessly pushing back this boundary that the Revolution will find the guilty, more and more numerous and varied, more and more monstrous and hateful, and will offer them up to punishment. All the "conspirators" eliminated will be so in the name of this absolute transparency: guided by the observations and warnings of a few watchmen [surveillants], the community sees the personal defects of all its "enemies" written large in their public actions.

Emmanuel Sieyès will lucidly analyze this blurring of the border between public and private after the traumatizing experience of the Terror, pointing out the two states of the revolutionary society: the *re-public* facing the "bad plans" of the *re-total*. The philosopher then chooses the first— even if the sovereignty of the people is limited in it—over the exorbitant sacrifices of the second, "a ruinous monastic conception of public matters as private matters." [72] No doubt the journalists of 1789 were not sufficiently aware of the terrifying powers of the "re-total" that they tried, with acts of denunciation and appeal to the people, to construct to satisfy the people-public that they claimed to address. For the words in circulation in 1789, seeking absolute transparency in the spectacle of bodies, and recklessly associating private life with appearance of public action, and vice versa, ended up inventing a system of inspection that was extremely demanding, too demanding: the ceremony of political transparency could now be nothing but sacrificial, and come to resemble an altar where observers would make the bodies of their enemies pay for the least suspicion of degeneracy. And everyone knows that these suspicions are born from a trifle—useful for clans who want to fight with each other, convenient for factions who want to tear each other apart.

7. The Bodies of the Political Carnival

The revolutionary festival is now likely to see "more artifice than fire in its *feux d'artifice* [fireworks]."[1] Mona Ozouf has described this evolution of attitudes to festivals: confronted with the spectacle of festivity, revolutionaries, worthy imitators of the philosophers, prefer the low-keyed emotions of the ceremonies of simple presence, spectacles stripped of the spectacular. The *Encyclopédistes* denounced the "abuses" of traditional festivals, those occasions of drunkenness, debauchery, and unrestrained impulses. Jocose parties, carnivals, masquerades, pantomimes, plays, drinking bouts, jousts, and fireworks are all condemned by the enlightened century as hollow, equivocal, superstitious, and useless practices. Mona Ozouf has commented on this disdain for the festival of laughter, a "senseless din," and for the body that it carts into "crowds obstructing the streets," this body caught between the "veiled threat of masks," the "disgusting spectacle of people fighting over loaves of bread or sausages," and the "bursts of grotesque laughter, loud and obscene." In short, this body of the traditional festival wields an "excitement that disconcerted . . . reason." It seems very natural that the Revolution welcomes, as an inheritance from the Enlightenment, this wish to promote a festival almost without spectacle, a festival in which the participation of beings alone would be enough to ensure the emotion favorable to the formation of the pedagogical message, cementing the community by the dramatic enactment of reconciliation, the festival of a body taking an oath, for instance, a body symbolic of the new regime, dynamic enough to draw energies into a fraternal community, calm and serene enough to preserve its gravity and reassure onlookers. The revolutionary festival seems to have a hatred of scandal. Laughter, too loud, too uncontrolled, agitating the bodies in the crowd, is nothing but scandal.

This revolutionary festival sometimes has great difficulty in presenting the face it aspires to, however. Thus the Federation of 14 July 1790, touted as an example of the peaceful, rational festival, is in fact followed by four days of laughter and organized spectacles. In like manner, the year 1791 (often forgotten by the historiography of revolutionary festivals passing swiftly from the Federation of 1790 to the funeral celebrations of 1792) is only, apart from the tears poured on the very real corpses of Mirabeau and Voltaire, an accumulation of outbursts of laughter, even if anxious laughter: a burlesque procession celebrating the abolition of entry tolls in Paris, the "burning" of the pope in effigy at the Palais Royal, the ludicrous distortion of the body of the king, a week of festivities and spectacles on the occasion of the final adoption of the Constitution. Parisians then reveal a neglected aspect of their festive practices, and thereby a privileged spectacle of the body: laughter that deforms, that disguises, or that intoxicates. It is as if municipal government, by authorizing — certainly most often with caution and against its will — burlesque processions alongside parades of the National Guard, had had to make a concession to the "nature of the French," the natural disposition that most political commentators still recognize (despite the call to regeneration launched on the occasion of the fracture of 1789) as frivolous, gay, attracted to their customary festivities. But this practice of "laughter," if it seems contrary to the calm, imposing festive ideal of the Age of Enlightenment, remains no less eminently political. By drinking and dancing at the barriers on 1 May 1791, Parisians bury the Farmers General, hated symbols of the old days. By laughing at the spectacle of an effigy devoured by flames at the Palais Royal on 4 May of the same year, the onlookers burn the pope. The practices of a carnival denounced by the Revolution reinvest bodies — sometimes explicitly — with political ceremonial. In the course of revolutionary festivals, they laugh more than we would expect, but this lively emotion is charged with a very politically cogent meaning: the laughter of the Revolution turns into political sensibility.

The Festival of Laughter, or The Need for Artifice

Parisians are never indifferent to the spectacle of laughter. It answers a real "need for artifice" that the organizers of civic festivals had to take into account. This double history of the political festival, both festival of reason and festival of laughter, sometimes competitive but often complementary, begins with the start of the Revolution. In July 1790, to commemorate the taking of the Bastille, the National Assembly arranges the "festival of the federative oath" at the Champ de Mars. Joined together in an immense arena, provincial Federates, soldiers of the National Guard, and Parisians band together, a simple naked image of community reconciliation. This vision struck people's minds and remains, for many witnesses as well as for historians, the "happiest day of the Revolution." This Champ de Mars ceremony, setting spectacle and its "theater of illusions" aside, aims only at reuniting harmoniously, side by side, in an immense amphitheater, a crowd of almost four hundred thousand people.

Mistrust with regard to the contrivances of the festival, confirmed by numerous projects and accounts, reinforces the event as the ritual dreamed of by the philosophes: a reunited people, without need of sausages, or games, or revels, or pyrotechnics. The Federation would be at once the revelation and the illustration of a political and philosophical way of putting on a festival. Linguet, in a pamphlet of July with a very revealing title, *Address to the French people concerning what should be done and what should not be done to celebrate the memorable and national festival of 14 July 1790*, recalls thus to Parisians the bad examples given by the festival of the ancien régime, the "festivals of despotism," in which "drunkenness," "gluttony," "distribution of money," and "spectacles of actors" distorted the ceremony, making it "noisy and gratuitous."

The text cites a famous example to illustrate the dangers of this festival of spectacle: the fireworks of 1770 at the time of the dauphin's wedding, where the crush and hysteria had left almost two hundred suffocated bodies on the ground. "This mania for connecting the loud and joyful drunkenness of the people with public exhilaration is disastrous," Linguet concludes, seeing in the participants of the old festivals a "pack of blind, starving dogs." Finally, he offers his vision of the ideal festival to his readers: the "fraternal embrace" is the sole requirement, "simply joining together the largest possible number of spectators, because then, every spectator will become an actor in the most august scene."[2] Contemplation, silence, and propriety are the three essential values of the reunited community: it is here, in these phrases, that the "political education is formed" and that the body is educated.

This symbolic stance is inscribed in the clear directions for the festival. Yet under the patronage of the municipality of Paris, the days following the oath of 14 July are completely given over to street festivals, to demonstrations of public joy. The other side of the revolutionary festival, diversion, in a way completes the bodies of the philosophical oath that took their places on the Champ de Mars. *The great Kindness of the National Assembly*, a pamphlet reporting the detail of the events of mid-July, compares this joyful week to the "Roman Saturnalias," that "public exhilaration that lasted several days." Another text is even more explicit: "All the distinctions of rank ceased then in Rome; slaves could with impunity tell their masters whatever they wanted. Does not the festival of the Country that we have been celebrating since the Fourteenth present us the same image? Doesn't that spirit of freedom that mixes all ranks reign everywhere? Do we not see Parisians from all sides hastening to receive the deputies from the provinces at their tables? Everywhere they make libations on the altar of the homeland and of liberty; they sing, they dance as in Rome in all the public places."[3] Then he praises, in turn, drink, laughter and jokes, dances and balls— "virtues" far removed from the values habitually extolled by the *Encyclopédistes*.

Consult the other programs announcing the "jubilations" planned between 14 and 18 July 1790, as well as the government archives, and we perceive the real presence of practices of festive laughter. A first banquet is served in the afternoon of 14 July near the Bois de Boulogne, a banquet of elected bodies to which a few Federates are admitted, a meal that is certainly "simple and frugal," but where "hilarity excited fraternal love and the purest patriotism," where "*bons mots*, songs, charming coquetries" made the rounds of the tables.[4] Behind the words ("hilarity," "charming coquetries"), a festive pedagogy reigns, where laughter finds its place again, a pedagogy prolonged a few hours later by the spectacle of a "general illumination of all the streets."

"It is through games and spectacles that we can inspire in men the love of morality and the courage of virtue," continues the author of the *Faithful description of all that preceded, accompanied, and followed the ceremony of the National Confederation*, who even launches into a comparison of the "week of joy" with the festivals of the Middle Ages, a comparison that is revealed to be hardly "enlightening," in the sense that the Age of Enlightenment of the eighteenth century tended to despise that "gothic period." The chronicler thus places parallel to each other the revolutionary festival and the tournament of chivalry: "If we have inherited some of their [the knights'] sensibilities, we must direct them toward a noble end; we must love freedom as they loved their mistresses, and we must laugh at aristocrats as they envenomed the rhymes of the bitter verses they aimed at their enemies. May the fanciful honor of the courtier paladins of tournaments be replaced by the joy and virtue of Republican souls." Between "hilarity," "coquetries," and the chivalrous jousts, the *Faithful description* tries to turn toward politics the emotions stimulated by comic spectacle.

The festivities are prolonged. Every evening of the week, the statue of Henri IV on the Pont Neuf, cleverly decorated, is surrounded with dancers. On Sunday afternoon, 18 July, great jousts take place on the Seine in front of the Louvre. Three hundred "athletes," the chronicle says,[5] including "boatmen dressed as Venetians," a "Jeannot," a "harlequin," and "another burlesque character from our southern *départements*" parade in Paris from the Porte Saint-Antoine to the Tuileries, stopping at the Palais Royal, where they are "presented to the crowd," before competing on the water between the Pont Neuf and the Pont Royal in front of tens of thousands of Parisians. The "joyful procession," preceded by the National Guards and military music, seems to have drawn a good deal of attention. After the jousts, won by the "blue" team over the "red" team, the winners were "fêted, embraced, carried in triumph." The spectacle follows the Seine, the axis of Parisian festivities, from the Pont Neuf to the Champ de Mars, passing by the Palais Royal, then down to the place of the Federation.

Occupied on 14 July by four hundred thousand people proud of their simple presence, the Champ de Mars is invaded at the end of that afternoon of 18 July by the "spectacle of the aerostatic festival."[6] Carrying on the fashion for launching hot-air balloons, the municipality, following the numerous printed proposals brought to its attention, organized the flight of a "tricolor aircraft" whose departure would salute the "knowledgeable maneuvers of the citizens of the National Guard." "Two or three brave Patriot aeronauts will climb into the nacelle and will undertake the voyage of the skies; they will see if the peoples who live on the moon are free, and if they are not, they will leave with them the Declaration of the Rights of Man that makes Tyrants turn pale"—thus, dreaming and lyrical, a new Patriot

Cyrano declares, taking on the defense of these "bold navigators who sacrifice themselves for the developments of the sciences."

Sacrifice is indeed the word, for the reality of the matter, on that 18 July, was hardly glorious: the hot-air balloon caught fire, crashed to the ground, and seriously injured six of the soldiers of the National Guard maneuvering on the field. The revolutionary festival, seeking spectacle, finds the dangers denounced by the philosophers. However, the "character" of the Frenchman seems, in the eyes of commentators, to outweigh those possible dangers, and calls for periodic reunion with the spectacular and laughter. "French gaiety" demands such productions, a gaiety that even the tragic collapse of the balloon seems not to have tamed: "A fat balloon that falls back down when it wants to rise up looks rather like something that's not hard to guess . . . eliciting those *bons mots* that the occasion always inspires in French gaiety."[7]

Does gaiety contradict patriotism? That is the debate constantly posed by the organization of these spectacles, a debate that has for a long time been neglected, leading the bursts of laughter of revolutionary festivals back to the mere "spontaneity" of a public of big children. The idea of a role left to the spontaneity of actors still insufficiently masters of their emotions (explaining the lapses into laughter—masquerades, drinking bouts, ludicrous processions—that kept slipping into the reasoned festivals of the Revolution) is not, however, supported by an attentive reading of accounts of festivities. It is a question, on the contrary, of elaborate productions, carefully prepared by the Parisian municipality (we even find receipts for payments made for the purchase of barrels of wine[8]), an outline of a pedagogy of joyful celebration. Through these ceremonies, constantly directed, even in their attractions, toward a political meaning, the organizers undoubtedly wish to enlarge the community of emotions even more. Grouping people together is not enough: the senses must be impressed forcefully by the presentation of a spectacle, of a diversion bearing a political message. That tricolor hot-air balloon rising up into the skies four days after the solemn oath on 14 July 1790 imposes itself as the spectacular, "artificial" version of the profession of Patriot faith. The revolutionary festival does not seem to want to renounce the spectacle, that spectacle condemned by the philosophers. It relegates it to the margins of great demonstrations, but assigns it a complementary mission: to complete the pedagogical message by producing an attractive version of it. The Revolution does not renounce fireworks, but gives them a few dominant colors. The pyrotechnicians of blue-white-red have not abandoned the festive spaces.

On Sunday 18 July 1790, to return to the Pont Neuf, it is precisely a fireworks display that opens the last night of the "week of joy." Fireworks remain one of the great attractions of the time, followed by various "illuminations," for instance on the façade of the Hôtel de Ville where the oath of the Federation is reproduced in letters of fire. All insist on the spectacular aspect of demonstrations and on the power of diversion, emotions that are prolonged all night during banquets. The week had already been fertile in festival meals, organized on multiple scales—National Guard, District Assembly, municipality, National Assembly—and scattered around the Champs-Elysées, the Champ de Mars, or the Place de la Bastille.

"It is useless to describe the joy that will reign at these wedding parties of freedom. Tosts [sic] will not be spared; the good Silenus will preside over the festival. Countless tables will be placed here and there along the paths that surround the field of liberty and in the Champs-Elysées," predicts one of the chroniclers of these festivals,[9] adding, to give a political meaning to these rejoicings: "We must chase away the exhalations of despotism with our songs, our dances and our laughter."

In fact, at the conclusion of the day on 18 July, great balls are given in various places in Paris. First at the Bastille, a ball set in a rural décor reproducing, with the help of ingeniously placed shrubs and greenery, the towers of the old fortress, a very symbolic décor: "What a night, entirely spent in pleasures, for the men who had spent so many long and painful nights in this same place, and who danced in the same place where for such a long time, their grave had been dug."[10]

Equally important for the number of Parisians that they brought together were the ball of the Rotunda of La Halle (sixty thousand people), the ball of the Hôtel de Ville, and the ball of the Champs-Elysées where, around the greased pole, "loud bursts of laughter and Patriot slogans" are heard and also organized. The Revolution finds its festive transcription in these "bursts of laughter," in this "delicious mixture of familiarity, union, and liberty," the "fond prattle, tender joyful effusions, and male virtues," emotions that could certainly recall the so castigated excesses of the festivals of the ancien régime, when contests and balls marked the time of a coronation or a royal wedding for Parisians, but now have become chiefly the avenues for "Patriot emotions."[11]

The Revolution does not seem to put an end to the frivolous festivals that regularly emphasized monarchic rituals; changing their message, the Revolution strives to maintain them, alongside the huge mass assemblies. The week of the Parisian Federation is very enlightening in this respect. Concentrating only on the simple, majestic ceremony of 14 July 1790 at the Champ de Mars would miss the sideshows of spectacle and laughter; to take into account only those displays of lively emotions would amount to neglecting the evidence of a new, regenerated ceremony. The revolutionary festival, in its diversity, in its spaces and its contradictory festal rhythms, comprises a whole, playing on social transparency as on an instrument: "All these festivals, infinitely varied, made up really one single festival," recalls a commentator.[12] The Parisian public loves this diversity. The municipality cannot neglect it and does not try to impose too brutal a rupture on the habits of merrymaking. The two aspects of the revolutionary festival, laughter and reason, will continue to coexist.

The Three Forms of Political Laughter: "The Wars of Epigrams," Grotesque Travesties, Blasphemous Outbursts

How can people's attention be seduced and captured? It is this necessity that justifies the festive use of laughter, leading to the organization of the "laughing and laughable" battle of bodies, when the two political camps, Royalist and Patriot, rival each other by inventing characters and situations to attract readers and listeners. This struggle of persuasion, taking advantage of laughter's power of conviction, is an ancient inheritance. The virtue of *eutrapelia* extolled by Saint Francis de Sales in his *Introduction to the Devout Life*, then by his disciples, according to the principle of "civil devotion," furnishes a system of reflection on the resources of laughter and the use of "decent joyousness," very close to what will be, much later, the practices of revolutionary laughter. In the former, it was a question of inscribing the spiritual into the world by capturing the attention of the faithful by an oratorical seduction, one of whose weapons was laughter; in the latter, the public must be convinced of the worth of a just political cause. In the tradition of Saint Francis de Sales, we find that Jean-Pierre Camus, Bishop of Belley, one of the most important preachers of the first half of the seventeenth century,[13] is able in 1630 to praise the "fertility of wit joined with a graceful joyousness that the Greeks call Eutrapelia,"[14] and justifies its use of laughter in these words: "It is this embellishment that can mix joyousness and modesty with so just a temperament that raillery by no means descends to buffoonery, to sordid and fruitless behavior. I do not know how in fairness you can blame qualities that cause man to exercise one of the functions that distinguish him most from the irrational animals: laughter. And who does not know that the one who laughed at everything [Democritus] had a sect no less populous, or less esteemed, than that weeper who poured tears on all subjects of which he became aware? How many preachers whose chief praise, in the opinion of Saint Jerome, ought to stem from drawing tears from their listeners, in fact say such pleasant things that laughter in their audience often and usefully takes the place of tears."[15]

Camus introduces two fundamental controversies by giving the force of the seduction of laughter to his eulogies: the definition of "good laughter" on the one hand, decent, colorful without being "burlesque or licentious"; the struggle of "laughter" and "tears" on the other hand, the opposition between two languages and two ways of soliciting meaning. This debate comes back to the fore at the end of the seventeenth century, when Bossuet, poet of the "spirituality of tears," becomes involved in a controversy with the Jesuit Father Caffaro, defender of "decent joyousness" and of the devotional use of comedy. La Bruyère, in his *Characters*, also takes sides. He seems to refute directly the praise of the Salesian and Jesuit laughter by condemning Christian "spectacle." In *De la chaire* (From the pulpit), the writer is particularly severe toward laughers and amusers: "Christian discourse has become a spectacle. The gospel sadness that is in the soul is no longer noticed there: it is supplanted by the allurements of mime, by the inflections of the voice, by the regulation of the gesture, by the choice of words, and by long enumerations. We no longer listen seriously to the Holy Word: it is one kind of amusement among a thousand others; it is a game in which there is competition and betting."

This same "game of amusement" capable of seducing the audience is at the heart of the polemics agitating the milieu of revolutionary writers. One finds in it the debate between the persuasion of laughter and the persuasion of tears, that "serious, cold language of reason" defining the good revolutionary according to Lequinio.[16] One also notices in it a violent "battle of laughter." What kind of laughter? How can it be used? Patriots and Royalists endlessly oppose each other over these questions between 1789 and 1791. Even though the disputes are rough, I think that I can disengage three principal forms of laughter animating the polemics and debates.

Joseph-Antoine Cérutti, to introduce the first of the three, discusses the "advantages and origins of French gaiety."[17] The ex-Jesuit tries to put the virtue of *eutrapelia* at the service of Patriot language, in a way appropriating the persuasive ambition of preaching so as to transfer it to the "eloquence for the public good." Cérutti defines the French character by its "vivacity" and its "cordiality": "You have," he writes to the Frenchman, "a fund of gaiety that can inspire others, and reconcile your most obstinate enemies to you. I assure you that I could distinguish one of your compatriots just by the way he listens to me speak. A friendly, perhaps cunning, smile would be his first response; a pleasantry would come an instant later to animate his conversation; and even if we had begun with the most serious subject, I have no doubt that we would end with the most delightful banter." The writer then undertakes a mission, to insinuate himself into the "banter" in order to convince: "Nothing seems more likeable to me than your gaiety, and also nothing seems more useful: it is an adornment and a resource."

An adornment of the spirit, a resource for the discourse of persuasion; Cérutti unwaveringly joins the rhetoric of the "decent joyousness" of religious preaching. He does, however, introduce politics into it, for Cérutti tries to define the use of laughter politically. He thus draws up the precise picture of political morals reported with a more or less pronounced taste for gaiety. Laughter and "despotism" do not go together well here: "Gaiety is not found in a despotic state. Gaiety cannot exist in a despot who is too revered not to be hated, too surrounded by grandeur not to be encumbered by it, and taking too much pleasure to have any. Nor is gaiety communicated to the unfortunate subjects of the despot. The reason for that is very simple: the flocks caper in the field, in the heart of freedom; entering the stable they become sad; they bellow with horror when they enter the slaughterhouse."

Yet laughter and "republic" are not associated either: "It will scarcely be in a Republican State that one will find a certain gaiety. Happiness is there, but not playfulness. The idea of amusement and banter does not go very well with the grave ideas of the republic; a song would little gladden people occupied with a system, and the silly jokes of one individual mean little to the one who endlessly contemplates the needs of the public." Between the "horror" of despotism and the severe "happiness" of the republic, only "temperate monarchy" can favorably welcome French laughter: "Your climate prepares you for gaiety, your government connects you to it. There is only one monarchic state, monarchic the way yours is, where gaiety can show itself with success, and reign without constraint. Enough liberty, not enough independence; powerful and friendly masters who govern through love; subjects obeying through honor. That leaves the field open to the lively, playful wit. Do we need to be perfectly convinced of the difference there is on this point between a republic, a despotic state, and a temperate monarchy? Let us consider a family: the father governs, the slaves languish, the children play. The father represents the republicans; the slaves, those unfortunate victims of a despot; and the children, those gay subjects of a monarch like the king of France."

This prerevolutionary text very clearly poses gaiety as a given of the temperate monarchic regime: the French are the "children" of the king and of laughter. The Revolution does not take place on a new terrain, but must welcome these children. Certain revolutionaries will wish to reform them by the principles of the Republic: to make them arrive at "happiness." Condemnations of "frivolity," "light character," and "banter" follow each other in this case to counter that "Frenchman of long ago" with the "new man," body and mind raised up by the Revolution. On the other hand, in Cérutti, the strength of conviction favors childishness itself: politics, respecting the mode of government peculiar to the gay French character ("constitutional monarchy," a new form of the "temperate monarchy" of the past), insinuates itself by banter and laughter into the "vivacity" and "cordiality" of minds and manners. A certain number of Patriot writers follow Cérutti on this terrain of *seduction by decent laughter*. His friend Ginguené for instance, the collaborator closest to the *Feuille villageoise*, offers a civilized but at the same time very useful reading of the work of François Rabelais.[18]

Ginguené rehabilitates Rabelais with the same aim as the ex-Jesuit, to "speak seriously" of him only to retain what is suitable for "persuasion by the channels of the playful mind." Above all, Rabelais's is essentially a language of the body, for he "wrote at a time when one had very much to cover oneself with an allegorical veil, however transparent it may have been." He called on the narrative-bodies of allegory to balk censors and "feudal superstitions," setting a physiognomy to match each truth. Certainly, Ginguené continues, "today truth walks with its brow uncovered and raised," but the playful imagination that, before, gave a veiled and comic body to truth, can and must, with the Revolution, raise this veil, enlighten this body, and let persuasive laughter run a free course. It is through this demonstration of the usefulness of the comic allegory in Rabelais that Ginguené invites his readers to read "Master François."

But the reading is selective, for Rabelais continues to smack of heresy, even if he is rediscovered after the 1770's. His grotesquery, his farce, and his "obscene images" could threaten the propriety of French gaiety. It is a matter of keeping the work in the register of comic imagination, by refusing to retain in it whatever might stem from ludicrous exaggeration: "I take care to test everything in it and to reread everything: things that are exaggerated, extravagant, obscure on purpose, obscene without gaiety, ludicrous without beauty, trivial, insignificant and coarse, irritated me only once. But pleasing tales, the numerous qualities of an ingenious and delicate style, the images that paint philosophical ideas by delightful images, these things, bold for their time, were still so for our time only a few years ago, and they shine today with a straight meaning, a superior reason, a wisdom that charms me. Each time I took up my Rabelais, it was only after I had reread all those passages marked in my first copy that I could put it down. I thought that all the fair, pleasing, and imaginative ways they treat grandees, fantastic battles, the despoilings of parliaments, monks, nay even the Pope—that all that, I say, might indeed contain something piquant, perhaps useful, and could make an impression on minds by its comic authority." Ginguené draws a rule from his reading of the "marked passages," of Rabelaisian excerpts: the good use of laughter. He profits thus from a few Rabelaisian figures to laugh with reserve at the "grand gousier" king and at the "grande gamelle" queen, at the "seventeen thousand nine hundred and thirteen cows" necessary for the upkeep of the civil list, at the "noble *chats-fourrés*," at the farmer-general "Grippe-minaud," and at the prelates of the "island of Papimanie," rascals and drunkards venerating the "papagesse" that the "disguised sovereign" serves them.

Further, in several pamphlets we find stated intentions that demonstrate the hold that persuasion by proper laughter can have on the playful imaginations of the "people-child" of the Revolution, an entirely political influence: "Under a very gay and even somewhat smutty exterior, this work encloses a pure morality, philosophical ideas, some remarks whose fairness the present revolution proves. Young man, read and laugh; reread and reflect. You will perhaps not have wasted your time," writes, in his foreword, the author of a reprint of the saucy and lighthearted pamphlet *The life and work of the late Abbé Bazin, Bishop of Mizoura in Mizourie.*

An anticlerical pamphlet of January 1790, *The regiment of the cloth,* agrees with this, and, after an explicit epigraph ("Readers . . . Read and make fun of the aristocracy"), tries to lead the Frenchman of the Revolution, who has become "a little too serious, dreaming only of punishment

and vengeance," to a "calmer gaiety" no less patriotic: "We must particularly encourage public but honest amusements, and above all favor works
that, under the mask of laughter, give salutary advice. And I believe that
this gaiety, far from harming the activities that are meant to insure our liberty, would serve on the contrary to keep everyone close to his duty, divert
intrigues, avoid pride's pretensions, and especially chastise bad citizens by
denouncing their turpitude and their villainies in ironic fashion." [19] In like
manner, a few Patriot pamphlets from May 1789 try to promote the Third
Order by gaiety, contrasting it with the "scornful heads" of the nobility and
with the "hollow heads" of the clergy,[20] celebrating in this "Third Estate
that alone laughs to tears" the "best of the Orders," the one that manages
to make fun of the "ridiculous ceremony" imposed by the hierarchizing of
places and costumes during the procession and later the opening meeting
of the Estates General.

Taking up on its own account this "decent joyousness," counterrevolutionary satire quickly finds its place opposite Patriot laughter. It is a kind
of renaissance: the literary movement born in the beginning of the 1780's,
depending on the ironic and virtuoso pens of Rivarol, Campcenetz, Palissot, Sabatier, and Dorat, is perpetuated in the beginning of the Revolution,
arraying itself against Cérutti, Ginguené, and Grouvelle, who were rivals
in the ancien régime republic of letters before remaining so on the scene
of revolutionary writing. The "Patriot laughers" attack their opponents by
referring to them as "oversubtle minds," and portray them in these words:
"Rivarol convinced the bookseller Le Jay that satire is literature's first
genre. Two whole centuries have been spent instructing the world; now the
time has come to amuse it, to make it forget everything and force it to become fierce." [21]

The weapon of these "laughers at tradition" is the decomposition by
satire of the body of their victims. The art of caricature unique to the group
of satirists, whose scathing sharpness is best illustrated by Rivarol in his
Little Almanac of Our Great Men in 1788, then in *Little Dictionary of Great
Men of the Revolution* in 1790, aims exactly at breaking up the body: from
one detail, a subtle imagination makes an acerbic stroke that serves to "cut
up the body of innocent victims of the satirist's pen," and from one stroke,
the whole expression, the result is a wounding portrait. Subtle minds find
in these galleries of characters an opportunity to exercise the virtuosity of
their writing, "the corruption and decadence of laughter," to use Cérutti's
words.[22] Cérutti himself is not spared by the barbs and earns the nickname

of "Des Superficies" in *Library of the Court and the Town*, provoking this
sentence from Rivarol: "Nothing indifferent comes from the hand of such
a great writer, since even boredom [*ennui*] has such beautiful results."[23]

It is to struggle against this "ennui" that the group of satirists formed,
and it is to subject to derision the claims of the revolutionaries that it
enters into politics. In the beginning of November 1789, the *Acts of the
Apostles* [*Actes des apôtres*], the newspaper that the satirists create, manages
to stir considerable repercussions by their caustic writing. Creating a caricature of the Jacobin, ridiculing the reformist claims of the Constituent
Assembly, yet without surpassing the limits of propriety, the paper defines
the framework in which it plans to position itself, one between "the sweet
enjoyments of beautiful language" and "the witticisms of a cruel gaiety":
"Our Post will be one of the monuments of this elegant and delicate language, transmitted by Carriage to Abbé Sabathier. The beautiful language
of our times will be conserved in it, mixed however with a few aristocratic
vapors that the people of satiric art alone can distinguish. We are honored
to offer our readers these witticisms of cruel gaiety that we fearlessly direct
at the raving apostles who claim to regenerate our morals."[24]

Thus, as its title indicates, the paper reports the "acts" of the "apostles
of the Revolution," making a pastiche of religious language to "brighten
the heroic deeds of our great civil servants," turning traditional writing
upside down to comment with irony on the deeds and gestures of the deputies of the Constituent Assembly: "We were planning, when we began our
Acts, on directing toward each of our apostles, one by one, the artillery of
our praises. An inconceivable fate thwarts at each instant, and turns us
away from our progress. For we cannot fire the battery of praises without
denouncing to our readers the stupid puns, the gibes, and epigrams on the
most distinguished members of the Assembly that have been addressed to
us from all sides. They claimed thus that M. Duport had had placed above
the door to his house, a sumptuous marble with the popular inscription
Hôtel du Port; and that at night they had substituted this oligarchic inscription: *Hôtel du Port frais*. Those of our readers who know the physical
constitution of M. Duport are capable of judging that this sign was not at
all suitable for him."[25] [Duport, in writing his name "du Port," is affecting an aristocratic title. He wants to imply "The Du Port Mansion," but in
fact the phrase *hôtel du port* more calls to mind a sailors' bar. The nocturnal "editor," in turn, transforms the harborside dive into what sounds like
porc frais, or fresh pork, evidently alluding to the bodily form of M. Duport. Trans.]

Royalist satire thus fights Patriot gaiety on its own terrain, by "mock-ery" and perverting praise by ridicule. Brissot, when offering his readers a pamphlet of February 1791, *The golden legend, or the acts of the martyrs to serve as counterpart to the acts of the apostles*, designates this under the phrase "war of the epigrams": "This patriotic legend at least balances the success of the *Acts of the Apostles*, and we can apply to it these verses that I read in the second issue: With what cruel art, this bitter irony / Causes Paris, and all France, to laugh at our expense."[26] The revolutionary scene, from Cérutti to the *Acts of the Apostles*, from the thoroughly moderate re-reading of Rabelais to satiric irony, from the "Picrocoline wars" to the "war of the epigrams," uses here a fresh form of laughter to try to persuade French gaiety.

A second scene opens out quickly for revolutionary laughter: raree-shows at the fair, introducing an entire series of ludicrous characters. Since the middle of the eighteenth century, a "stove merchant" has intervened among the characters of the parades of the Saint-Germain fair: Father Duchesne. Pipe in mouth, standing apart, he takes charge of short, fast "dialogues in jargon" played by one or two actors. In these, he comments on the news and lavishes his advice. Sometimes he translates fairground words into "Parisian language" and reads the texts written on posters for the benefit of the spectators. He is, in a way, an intermediary offered to the public to help them understand the spectacle better or to facilitate easier dialogues with the other actors.[27]

Soon, beginning in 1788, Father Duchesne enters politics: the news that he commented on before, the posters that he deciphered, from now on bear specifically political events and words. *The voyage of Father Duchesne to Versailles*, in the fall of 1788, ends with a conversation between the king and the stove merchant concerning "current affairs." Duchesne maintains his role as literary intermediary: he speaks directly to high-ranking people and reports his conversations to the inhabitants of his neighborhood, for he "takes pleasure in going every day to certain nightclubs, of which he is the oracle, and where he brings together members of the public, like Savoy-ards, chimney sweeps, ragmen, bakers with their big wooden peels, etc." Even more, Duchesne is an intermediary of laughter. Not only does he re-gale the "public" with his direct language, plunging the slang of Parisian professions into political commentary, but his body too forces laughter: his "bad manners," the way he uses his pipe, his cries, his oaths, his "great anger" and his "great joy." Soon a theatrical play, no longer fairground but fully staged (*Father Duchesne, or The Bad Habit*), is played at the end of 1788. These parodies of "the talk of the people" and "the body of the people" now enjoy an unparalleled vogue.

In this sense, Duchesne joins two other "popular types" of prerevolutionary literature: Ramponeau, the innkeeper of Basse Courtille, and the fishwives of the market and the Place Maubert (Mmes Salmon, Margot the darner, or Mère Simon). The first comes from a real enough person, "Cabartié-z-à-la-mode," who left his inn, the Royal Drum, in 1760 to try to make his success as a comic drunk pay on the stage of the *Amusing Varieties*. Since "his face cheers up the brain" and "all Paris runs in a crowd, foreigners and onlookers alike, to sing of Ramponeau and drink a wine that's new," the character survives his actual death, in 1765, to attain the perennialism of the folkloric type. Incarnated by "a bellowing and drinking actor," he too peoples the scene of fairground spectacles and theatrical shows. The narrative of the Revolution does not forget him and at times makes him converse with Duchesne. Thus, in July 1791, in the *Letters from Ramponeau to the Brave Father Duchesne*: "Come to my aid, Father Duchêne, excellent Patriot, help me to reduce to powder all these knaves, traitors to the country . . . Know that Ramponeau is brought back to life to defend his Country alongside you. The wine merchants in Paris made me sleep a very long nap because they were jealous that I sold more wine than all of them together; but love of the Country has woken me up, and I have come back to Earth to poison all these blackguards who want to betray it."[28]

As for the fishwives, these fictional characters enter politics on Shrove Tuesday of February 1789, when several pamphlets written in the "idiom of the gossips of La Halle"[29] are printed to comment on "current affairs." The fishwives "drink to the health of the Third Estate"[30] and pay homage to the Duc d'Orléans. It is from this camp, one of the most organized in the art of pamphleteers, and which occupied a good part of the Palais Royal, that the first writings of *poissard* [literally, "fishmonger"] politics are issued, using "low" language, expletives, and phonetic spelling.

The riposte is not long in coming. In August and September 1789, the "ragladies of La Halle"[31] line up in the camp of General La Fayette against the Orléans party, and are joined in February 1790 by "Jean Bart," an old seaman settled in Paris to transcribe, in a comic and direct language, his thoughts on the "affairs of state." This paper, *I don't give a f——, or the thoughts of Jean Bart on the affairs of state*, meets with a great success, and is the first to introduce the multiple use of "fuck" and "bugger," oaths with a sexual overtone, into his articles, a prelude to numerous imitations in the spring of 1790.

All these characters, then, make up a folklore of grotesque travesty whose roles are fixed and who get taken in hand by political polemics. Drinking bouts, expletives, rages, scatology and sexual allusion, cabaret patter, and the trade talk of minor professions are the common basis for a humor on which all camps quickly draw.

This political competition of burlesques culminates early in 1791. I will stress here the most representative case, that of Father Duchesne. On one side, three Patriot papers, *The Downright Patriotic Letter of Father Duchesne* written by the Fayettist Antoine Lemaire, *Father Duchesne of the Rue du Vieux-Colombier* by Abbé Jumel, who was involved in the Jacobin camp, and *Father Duchesne* by Hébert, of Constitutionalist tendency, are all born in the fall of 1790. Opposed to these, between November 1790 and February–March 1791, an intense Royalist campaign gets under way, circulating a "false" Father Duchesne "distributed gratis at the Place Saint-Michel and Rue Saint-Andre-des-Arts," along with a "true" *Mother Duchesne*.[32] Abbé Adrien Buée invents this last one to be able to reply better to the three Patriot *Duchesnes*. He uses the same procedures, "laughing with those who laugh, swearing with those who swear, with the intention of enlightening that interesting portion of the people that Messrs Fine Wits have always disdained and to which they have never written,"[33] but tries to turn them back against revolutionary laughter. Hébert's *Father Duchesne* had, for instance, insulted and whipped Abbé Maury; Buée's *Mother Duchesne*, in mid-November 1790, takes up the same words and the same implements to "correct her husband for having spoken badly of Monsieur the Abbé Maury, his confessor."[34] A second series of Buée's *Mother Duchesne* appears at the beginning of 1791, in four issues, portraying the ensemble of characters of ludicrous folklore, the title couple surrounded by ladies of La Halle, neighbors, and "nightclub habitués."[35] Mother Duchesne lectures her husband and makes him understand, with help, the necessity of supporting the clergy who refuse to serve the Constitution, launching her "very energetic curses against the oath-takers."

The battle gets going again at the end of February 1791, when the Patriots integrate Mother Duchesne into their own texts, investing the character created by the Royalist camp with the militant values of Jacobin discourse. This intense struggle between the Patriot Duchesnes, "mouthpiece" of the Assembly, and the Royalist Duchesnes, "devil's backside" of the monarchic club, outlines the boundaries of a second form of laughter of the Revolution, that of the grotesque travesty of the political scene.

Through these first two forms of political gaiety, it is a body that the laughers attack, and it is also a body that they assume for themselves. On both sides of the epigrammatic campaign, one finds bodies: the bodies are cognate but distributed according to a Manichean division of roles. The attacker confers upon himself a smile, a "charming air," and a "vivacity of physiognomy only equalled by the vivacity of wit,"[36] while the victim is deformed by the art of caricature, reduced to organic details and exaggerated appendages, overemphasized physical contrasts, overworked facial features. Revolutionary laughter in this way continues the rich gallery both of court portrayal and of the physiognomy of the salon.

Comic travesty offers an alternative body: the "lower body," with its inversion of forms and hierarchies, dominates description and spectacle. Manifesting both anger and joy, the emotions of Hébert's Father Duchesne make the ever-present corporeal punishments alternate with the common persiflage of laughter and wine. Thus, the positive comic character imprints on his body the organic concerns of farce: the "muzzle," the "fuck," and the "shits." His emotions follow direct paths. He drinks, he smokes, he swears, he shouts and vomits his rages, he doesn't give a "f——" for any of his enemies; his is a role often understood from a literary point of view through the licentious literature where Father Duchesne is a "first-rate imbecile [*fameux fourneau*]."[37] Finally he doesn't hesitate to make his opponents, whether bodies or effigies, undergo the outrage of the patriot "ass-torch." The attacks of laughter against the negative comic body follow, paradoxically, the same itinerary of organic analogy. The mouth receives the first blows, teeth pulled out of the clergy, emetic forced on the aristocrats who are too fat, screams let out by the whipped and the tortured. Sex organs are similarly mistreated by comic attack, generally linked with impotence and venereal disease or else wasted by orgies and obscene excesses. Finally the buttocks and the anus remain the target of all affronts, public whippings and bootings for the former, organ of scandalous speech for the latter, or passage for emotions (from fear to laughter)—the words offered and the emotions experienced belong to excremental evacuations. Thanks to these forms of "revolutionary gaiety," the body inherits two rich traditions, the ironic and the grotesque, and makes them cover the whole breadth of the scene of political spectacle.

After the spring of 1791 the third form of "French gaiety" takes place, more violent but not less joyful: blasphemous laughter. Until then, in fact, the outbursts had touched, on the political scene, not minor figures but prominent characters: deputies of the Assembly, men of the municipality, members affiliated with different political clubs. From then on, two long-protected values, two taboos, are broken by laughter: the religious monarchy and the Bourbon monarchy, that is, the pope and the king. The former is certainly not a new target for French mockers, who are of course Gallican, but, more than the papal figure itself, what is called into question is deeper: the place of France in the spiritual hierarchy of the states. The "Most Christian" kingdom is emancipated from religious legitimacy. As for the royal figure, I have already emphasized his ludicrous fate. The image of the pig linked to the portrayal of the king takes on an openly blasphemous quality, as much with regard to monarchic tradition as to the constitutional events of the fall of 1791; it reaches the point where an actual crackdown on the bestial representation of Louis XVI is organized by the municipality of Paris, which firmly orders the police superintendents of the Palais Royal to make every trace of such engravings disappear: "One can still see on display, at the print sellers', engravings that recall the moment of return of the king [from Varennes], and prints even more offensive still to his person, when the king has requested we forget all that has happened. Charged, as we are, with maintaining order, we request you to make the rounds as promptly as possible of your whole precinct; to make all the prints and engravings of this genre that you find displayed vanish, to draw up a report, and to send us a dispatch of it. You will at the same time alert all sellers of engravings that if they persist in allowing them to be displayed for sale, they will be denounced to the police tribunal." [38]

This insult to traditional bodies had been launched a few months before by Parisian anticlerical agitation. In the beginning of April 1791, when the contents of the papal brief of 10 March 1791 become known, the first manhunts for nonjuring priests and the first forays into the capital's convents are gotten under way. Though violent, these assaults against the clerical body also have an openly joyous character, a way of "embodying" the carnival masquerade using religious figures themselves. Some nuns are publicly whipped, a "patriotic discipline" that is notably exercised in Saint-Roch, at the convent of the Ladies of Providence, and then at Saint-Sulpice, Saint-Nicolas-des-Champs, and Saint-Paul, against the Trinitarians of La Roquette, between 6 and 10 April 1791. In this atmosphere of anticlerical fever, multiple pamphlets are printed, furnishing, for instance, a *List of aristocratic and anticonstitutional backsides that have been whipped*, then a *List of all the nuns and pious ladies who have been whipped by the market ladies of Paris, with their names and those of their parish, along with a very true to life, detailed account of all their affairs with the curates, vicars, and habitués of said parishes*, an enumeration peppered with grotesque and ribald allusions.

Political cartoons are not to be outdone, since five different versions of *Patriotic Discipline* were engraved, all taking up the same scene of comic flagellation: a nun, her posterior laid bare, being corrected by "patriotic ladies." Only the captions change from one piece to the other, illustrating the different forms of revolutionary laughter. There is Voltairean irony in one of these engravings, *Miraculous deed that happened in Paris in the year of salvation 1791, on 6 April*, which uses eight verses imitated from *La Pucelle*. Farce piled on farce, imitating the blows of the whip regularly inflicted by the Hébertist Father Duchesne on his clerical adversaries: "According to a very exact list, there were found to be 621 buttocks whipped; a total of 310 and a half asses, seeing that the lady treasurer of Miramiones had only one single buttock." [39] All these engravings, however, are joined together in a single pedagogical wish, a common crucible of forms of revolutionary laughter: "The grey sisters of Saint-Roch, seconded by the little Jesuits, have given birth to a little catechism for the use of children of the parish. The poor little ones and little Patriots who were made to swallow all these drugs have suffered indigestion of conscience. So the citizen mothers have run to their aid armed with rods." [40]

Patriot laughter next specifically attacks the person of the pope through more and more exact likenesses. First, the image of Pius VI is "sent down into hell" by cartoons and pamphlets, a pope who, "for having trampled underfoot all the most sacred duties," must "be well grilled." Then the papal brief itself, published in French on the press of Abbé Royou, editor of *L'Ami du roi*, is "put on the Index" by laughter. The brief is thus shamefully dismantled with the traditional technique of the bodily grotesque: scatology. Rabelais himself, reincarnated for the occasion into a good mirthful Patriot (see Figure 15), gives advice on this: "You know that I was very fastidious about my choice of bum-wipers; it was my only luxury. Certain events of our revolution have put me back into the state of abundance on this fundamental softness of my life. The documents of the Palais Royal, especially of Gattey's place [a Royalist bookseller], have made for me in less than three weeks, twenty-five very handsome bum-wipers; calumnious lampoons have also procured for me sixty or so; certain printed sermons also came to my aid, as did some acts of the apostles and issues of the *Journal de Paris*. I must confirm that my anus was very satisfied with them. But the true bum-wiper, Gentlemen, the bum-wiper above all others, the fellow-citizen bum-wiper of the universe, is the brief of our Holy Father the Pope."[41] That is when Brissot, in his *Patriote français*, can assert without fear of being contradicted: "The blue tales of the Pope and of the ex-archbishops are nothing but lost faith, *bullatas nugas*. The reign of these follies is past; the people laugh at them."[42]

This laughter, in the beginning of May 1791, finds a new victim, an ingeniously reconstituted likeness in the effigy of the pope, and another ceremonial form, the auto-da-fé. On 4 May, a procession forms at the Palais Royal, a procession organized around the "burning" of the papal effigy. This blasphemy finds its pretext in the second publication of the papal brief, on 2 May, by the presses of Abbé Royou's *L'Ami du roi*. Gorsas, party leader of Patriot laughter, leads the antipapal demonstration and utters, on 2 May, in the pages of his paper *Le Courrier des 83 départements*, the indictment and then the sentence: "That an effigy representing the hideous traits of fanaticism, holding a sword in one hand, and the lampoon in the other, be cast on the pyre . . . That this useful execution teach that France of the eighteenth century no longer wants to be the slave of Ultramontane despotism; that it has torn off forever the blindfold of prejudices, and that by keeping the deepest respect for the Catholic religion that was its cradle, it can give over to the flames the image of an insolent Mufti who calls himself vicar of a God of peace, and who sharpens the swords of fury."

On the following day, the fraternal society of Minims, under the direction of Tallien, takes over and decides to put into effect Gorsas's journalistic indictment. To carry out this political masquerade, Tallien profits from the anticlerical context, but also from the "general gaiety" of Paris in this beginning of May. A few days before, in fact, on the first of the month, Parisians had a "great binge" on the occasion of the opening of the tollgates [*Barrières*] at the entries to the capital. Tallien calls for prolonging the drunken laughter of former days, so decried by philosophy, into the new politics: the pope offers the Patriots the occasion of "celebrating carnival until St. James' Day [July 25]"; a month and a half later, the king will prolong the festival "until St. John's Day [June 24]." "The days of cessation of the entry fee to the city were marked by numerous expressions of public joy," writes Tallien. "All the carriages came into Paris yesterday crowned with laurel and oak branches; Bacchus smiled at entering the city without obstacle; there was not a family that did not repeat with pleasure these famous verses:

The first day of the month of May
Was the happiest of my life.

Tomorrow we will celebrate this joyous time in our turn by proceeding in splendid array to the Place Royale and joyfully burning the long-awaited brief. Ridicule is the true means of destroying the baleful influence of the enemies of the new order of things."[43]

On the morning of 4 May, an effigy eight feet tall, the wicker pope, clothed in all the "pontifical adornments," is led from the Porte Saint-Bernard to the Palais Royal in a tipcart. Then, around 10:30, before a "rather considerable group," an orator (Gorsas himself) reads the sentence: the pope will be burned and his ashes thrown to the wind in an auto-da-fé, after having been "soaked in mud." The effigy figure is paraded in the Palais Royal, from the Passage Radziwill to the Café de Foy, then is cast on the pyre in the center of the garden, after having been manhandled, since a sign had been tacked on its chest "on which was marked in characters of blood: Civil War and Fanaticism."[44]

The ceremony, burlesque as it is, is nevertheless conducted calmly. An "amendment" was even rejected, for "the people could have been carried away toward scandalous outrages"; it would have included leading the pope to the fire with boos and "kicks in the ass." This show of restraint indicates that the festival of laughter is not exempt from political and civic ritual. The victim was carefully chosen, an old enemy indeed, yet one singularly significant in the conjuncture of events in spring 1791. The place itself is precisely symbolic: the Palais Royal, center of Parisian laughter at political commentary, whether it be Royalist or Patriot. But, even more accurately, the surroundings of the Café de Foy are chosen for the ceremony, "for it has been, for some time, the meeting-place of aristocrats." The setting for the scene was "remarkable," Gorsas notes. "The wind beat on the aristocrats, the sparks, and the ashes. They preserved the most mournful silence during the execution." A joyful round, "a danced pantomime whose actors expressed by their gestures the feelings that animated them, and with their indignant feet trampled the burning cinders of the effigy of Pius," completes the ceremony, a full-fledged political educational method of Patriot laughter. This festival, moreover, was neither forbidden nor condemned by the municipal or national authorities, who were passive and apathetic, it seems, when faced with the sudden outpourings of political emotions, and conceded these four hours of festive uproar to the habitués

of the Palais Royal. Faced with this permissiveness, the victim of the blasphemous laughter, the papal nuncio, Dugnani, decides to leave Paris.

The Battle of the Carnival

The attitude of the political authorities faced with the sometimes sudden outbreak of ceremonies of laughter is not devoid of ambiguity. The
municipality of Paris, though itself the great organizer of the joyous spectacles of July 1790 celebrating the Federative oath, is afraid of the festivities
of May 1791 organized for the abolition of the tolls levied at the gates of
the city, undoubtedly because these festivities have so many similarities to
carnival processions. The music of the detachments of the National Guard
accompanies the festival and drinking bouts of the first of May, marking
the rejoicings from gate to gate, but Bailly repeatedly puts the Marquis de
La Fayette on guard against "disorderly processions." On 27 April 1791, the
mayor of Paris warns the commander of the National Guard,[45] then renews
this warning on the twenty-ninth and the thirtieth of the same month:[46]
the academician begs La Fayette to "put considerable forces on the alert, to
obviate the disorders that ill-intentioned people threaten to provoke by getting the people drunk." The festival of laughter threatens at every moment
to escape from the control of the political authorities, since the people is
itself threatened, tricked by wine or manipulations, with loss of its own control. The fears linked with these successive torrents of disturbances all join
in the obsession with the carnival, the traditional "procession of masks"
drawing spectators into illusion, depriving them of the weapon of their reason, alienating them by plunging them into artifice and false values. For
such reasons, at the end of January 1790 the municipality of Paris forbids
carnival processions in every area of the district. The order of the committee of police of the Hôtel de Ville, dated 31 January 1790, is explicit: "Every
private individual is expressly forbidden to disguise himself, dress up, or
wear a mask, in whatever manner it may be, under penalty that those who
are met in the streets, public squares, or gardens will be arrested, immediately unmasked, and led to the closest precinct; it is likewise forbidden to
give any masked ball, public or private, under penalty of imprisonment
for the offenders."[47] The revolutionary authorities do not like the carnival
and its masks. In the great traditional mock-combat of Mardi Gras against
Lent, the men of 1789, paradoxically taking the side of the church, award

the victory to a newly rebaptized and unusual Lent: the supervision of public order.

This official fear of mask and disguise, somewhat understandable in these days of 1790 when denunciation of the "aristocratic conspiracy" runs wild in the Patriot press (the Marquis de Favras, convicted of having tried to rescue the king, is hanged on 19 February 1790), finds numerous echoes. Marat, in *L'Ami du peuple*, recalls to his readers on 21 December 1789 that "the carnival is a good festival for slave peoples," a festival denounced by most of the members of the fraternity of Patriot journalists. Desmoulins mocks the "old-fashioned procession" in the tenth issue of his *Révolutions de France et de Brabant*, yet is skeptical of any real dangers of "disguises of the traitor" since "faults are not disguisable." Brissot, the "lifter of masks,"[48] carries on in *Le Patriote français* of 2 July 1790 against "dissimulated faces" and "passions over which reason has not taken hold," just as the authors of *La Lanterne de Diogène* or the *Petit Journal du Palais-Royal*, officiously prescriptive, order the municipal police to maintain "virtue in the streets and in physiognomies."

The effects of these denunciations are not delayed. On 25 December 1789, a correspondent of Marat approves the condemnations of the journalist and offers to destroy "all the aristocrat masks taken in the carnival." The General Assemblies of Parisian districts in January 1790 have the same wish for "unmasking." While they did not yet know of the municipal decision to forbid the procession, they demand active supervision of the carnival, "to see the faces of the enemies of the Revolution who are concealing themselves." In the assembly of the Saint-Dominique district, it is even a question of preventing the "sale of all masks and disguises," the "wandering about in the streets of Paris of any citizen masked or disguised in whatever way, on foot, on horse or in a carriage," and the "masked balls of the Opera and other public places."[49] Similar suspicions motivate two later symbolic decisions, taken during the winter of 1793–94: the condemnation to death of any individual "disguised as a woman"[50] and the prohibition of anti-Christian masquerades. Robespierre carried on with virulence against the latter at the Jacobins on 21 November 1793, when Gobel, ex-Archbishop of Paris, came solemnly to recant at the head of an anticlerical procession: "With what right would they debase solemn homages made to pure truth in such endless and ridiculous farces! Why permit them to play thus with the dignity of the people, and to attach the bells of madness to the very scepter of philosophy?"

We notice, though, in all these condemnations, that it is more the masked body than laughter itself that is taken to task. It is rather a definition of "bad laughter" that the censors propose: farce, disguise, the grotesque always threaten to degenerate into a confusion of values. The forbidding of the carnival is more a matter of establishing a space of political transparency unique to the revolutionary ideal than it is an excommunication of laughter. For if the troubling of the hierarchy of social and political roles induced by laughter represents a possible disorder when disturbances take hold of them, they are also, *a contrario*, a designated way toward the "perfect equality" so sought after. Between the lowering of hierarchical barriers bringing the free circulation of words or bodies, and the drunken, violent, and grotesque bacchanals, the festivals of laughter keep an ambivalent status that wins them ardent defenders and redoubtable adversaries at the time of their entry into politics under the Revolution.

Whatever the case may be, on 22, 23, and 24 February 1789 the last Parisian carnival of the ancien régime takes place. The "Lord Bacchus" and the "masquerading poissards" follow the Rue Saint-Honoré for the last time, preceded by a drum. It is moreover a splendid carnival, lively and spirited, despite the severity of the circumstances, if we can believe the meticulous report of the bookseller Hardy, dated 23 February: "That day, notwithstanding the multiplied calamities that have devastated our capital and its environs for a year, notwithstanding the costliness of bread and of almost all other comestibles, the madnesses, the annual extravagances of the carnival lose nothing of their noisy brilliance: in the old Rue Saint-Honoré, from the Rue de la Ferronnerie to the end of the Faubourg, we saw a prodigious quantity of masquerades, as many on foot as on horse, even on donkey or in carriages, in the most grotesque costumes, some in indecent costumes. It seemed that every year they wanted to go further in the revolting hideousness of the faces given to the different masks destined to cover and disguise faces that no longer had any human quality. Such a continuity of delirium drew to that place a huge crowd of curious people and spectators, and fortunately nothing was heard spoken of any kind of incident occurring. . . . No other noticeable accident was reported than that of a mask unfortunately falling from the upper deck of a carriage and immediately being crushed on the pavement."[51]

After February 1789, however, the carnival is marked by politics, three months before the meeting of the Estates General. The most typical politicized procession takes place in Angers, in a context of grave troubles, when the nobility and the urban Breton bourgeoisie confront each other, often violently: "The young people of Angers, on Monday the twenty-third, produced a festival as brilliant as it was praiseworthy in its aim. At six o'clock in the evening, almost six hundred people of both sexes and every condition were gathered together in the hall of spectacles and in themselves constituted quite a brilliant and interesting spectacle. All ranks were mixed together without any of those humiliating distinctions. The richest bourgeois gave the example, council members danced with craftsmen; and in this alliance of pleasure and patriotism, everything took place with as much decency as gaiety. . . . The next day, Mardi Gras, a party of the same young people, mounted on horses and numbering sixty, presented a masked pantomime in the city, the subject of which was the reception of Voltaire and Rousseau in the Elysian Fields; black Pluto and his wife Persephone, the Furies, the Fates, the dog Cerberus, the skiff of Charon, choruses of legislators, kings, princesses, and finally Henri IV and Sully; all brilliantly costumed, and preceded by twenty musicians, formed a very entertaining spectacle for the people, and a very titillating one for the thinkers who observed the motto of the skiff of the dead, *here all are equal*, and the epigraph written on the sail, *toll abolished*. These two festivals prove better than any other thing, the spirit of patriotism and peace that reigns in Anjou, and suffice to refute the deplorable rumors formed by ill-intentioned people."[52]

If we are to believe this precise description, the carnival could occupy a political function in the new society, just as it had its place in the good ordering of life during the ancien régime. By laying politics bare, miming the Estates General, and using the imagination that already surrounds the hall of the Menus-Plaisirs of Versailles (the "legislators," Henri IV and Sully, an ideal couple with whom we connect Louis XVI and Necker—the burial of abuses—*toll abolished*—and the presence of philosophical values —the *here all are equal* born from the glory of Voltaire and Rousseau), the procession calms passions. The pantomime marks the reconciliation of political extremes, rejecting the "distinctions that humiliate," and calls for moderation by giving over to the public gaze the very divisions it exorcises by laughter and derision.

This ceremony of political catharsis, however, will not be put to use. Very quickly, in fact, public denunciation begins to play the role of purification, returning the carnival to the troubled space of dissimulation and disorder, even though, as the account of the Angers procession emphasizes, it could just as well have been to the space of revelation and catharsis. For the mask hides as much as it reveals. In February 1789, the political judgments on the carnival are not yet determined: Mardi Gras can lean to one side or the other of political space, toward revelation and pacification, or toward being prohibited for troubling the public order. The pamphlets of conspiracy and the activity of the denunciatory practice will decide its fate, along with the pressure of the press on the municipal authorities, who, as guarantors of public order, are receptive to all the fears about blameworthy travesty of public values. Though nothing is decided in February 1789, the fishwives who "drink to the health of the Third Estate on the occasion of Mardi-Gras" have a presentiment (unlucky in their case, but beneficial for the "verry patriotic country"): that they, who "were counting on swallowing some wine," are now living through their last carnival. And they cry out in a chorus: "Let us always sing of the carnival, and hope for better; maybe this year's will be the last. This Mardi Gras, let's go with the flow." [53]

If the Patriots quickly reject the revealing, or even equalizing, function of the mask, counterrevolutionary language takes hold of this body of "talking disguise." [54] Starting in January 1790, in fact, Royalist pamphlets play on the literary scene of the carnival forbidden from the street. The *Acts of the Apostles*, as we might expect, launches the laughter, offering, in the chapter dated on the "day of the kings," a description of the opening of the "Club of the Revolution" worthy of a masked carnival ball. "Ill-intentioned people spread the rumor that the present revolution might not be lasting because it had changed the nature of the French character, and because the pleasure that made up the essence of it seemed banished forever from the capital. We can triumphantly answer the objections of these rebels. We venture to say that the severe, somber revolution has today been consummated; now France, having given Europe the example of courage and rigor, after having given it models for all the constitutions already born and still to come, France, we say, will continue to be the center of the arts of mime and dance [*mimodrame*], of the taste for masquerade, and of joyous diversions," [55] write the satirists, insinuating themselves cleverly inside the very language of defenders of the Revolution. The description spares neither Condorcet (elevated, in reference to the Venetian carnival, to "Most Serene Mask") nor the Constituent Assembly, which is turned into the "Circus of National Disguise."

This carnival tale ricochets quickly, since the Royalist paper, acting the good false "true Patriot" that it claims to be, reveals to its readers a few weeks later a "masked conspiracy": the brave Furetin, "former police spy," outlines on paper the "hideous" (and absurd) "features" of this conspiracy in the course of which, taking advantage of "these days of pleasure and laughter when the Parisian forgets his interests to hand himself over to the saturnalias of the carnival," masked aristocrats aided by the "corporation of wigmakers" could easily have concealed themselves to "disembowel all good Patriots."[56]

Turned back by counterrevolutionary irony and satire, the burlesque procession leaves the pavement to inscribe itself instead in the words of pamphlets. Two great "political carnivals" are published on the occasion of Mardi Gras, 9 February 1790. Satire proceeds to apply itself to making a pastiche of the language of denunciation, not by lifting masks as the Patriot journalists wear themselves out doing, but by describing them in detail in order to reveal better the "true nature" of the political figures of the Revolution. *The great patriotic masked ball* makes use of these denunciatory signs, shielding its narrative under a convenient slogan ("Publicity is the safeguard of the people"), and then introduces the masquerade and "disguised members" of this patriotic carnival led by the Jacobins: Le Chapelier as "valet," Guillotin as "knife-maker carrying his new machine," Théroigne de Méricourt as "Flora," Talleyrand as "penny-pincher," the Duc d'Orléans "disguised as a prince of the blood," Aiguillon as "hermaphrodite," Mirabeau as "honest man," and the Abbé Grégoire as "rabbi."

This art of "revelatory disguise," as this pamphlet calls it, is continued by *The political carnival of 1790, or the exile of Mardi Gras to the National Assembly*. Since Mardi Gras, embodied in a ludicrous character with a "round and bloated body," is hunted from the street, it decides to take refuge in the Assembly: "The carnival is prohibited for the people; but since the very moment of the revolution you have had one permanently going on in your midst, and you take pleasure in it without shame or reserve. You prohibit, under penalty of fine, the right of merchants to display in their shops masks and costumes of characters, and you do not blush at clothing yourselves again with them on the most serious and important occasions. . . . Now, since you strive hard to unmask others, I want to mask you as close to your true physiognomy as possible." The gaze of Mardi Gras travels over the hall of the Assembly and sees everyone, particularly the Patriot heralds, "each in his own proper mask," which he hastens to retranscribe "with the most ample and amusing details." The "war of epigrams" led by Royalist satire was of a great literary virtuosity: it succeeded in reinvesting the carnival with its subversive function to turn it against the new revolutionary powers—the municipality of Paris and the National Assembly revealed through some of its "hideous masks."

The carnival of 1791 seems involved in the same auspices: Bailly, mayor of Paris, has not rescinded his prohibition of the preceding year, and Royalist satire has not disarmed, always trying to "attribute to everyone his just disguise" and thus to tell him the truth. Counting on the "gay nature" of the Frenchman, which the municipality "scorns" and the Jacobins "are unaware of," Royalist satire expects to renew its success of 1790. "As long as France is France, the French will be French; that is to say, we will have our days of carnival and we will adapt them to our customs. The madness of peoples can change name and face, but it always resumes the character that is suitable to it," explains *The Jacobite carnival or patriotic ball, banquet, and masquerade*. Royalist laughter naturally takes hold of this "joyous spirit of the French," defined as eternal, forged over the course of centuries by the "just monarchy," and tries to turn it against innovation, ridiculing the "happiness decreed by our new sovereigns, I mean the Directory of the Jacobins." Laughter is supposed to be the property of the Royalist writer, in accord with the "most accurate truth of French gaiety." Again, comic parades on paper besiege revolutionary assemblies to daub and disguise their members. *The carnival of 1791*, a pamphlet using again a title of the preceding year without any real change, describes the "list of masks that will show themselves at the Jacobins club, on three days of Gras," introducing a few new detailed figures such as a Robespierre "ghost, long white dress, veil on his head," of whom "they forewarn to have no fear." Similarly, *La Jacobinière, parade like none other*, making the Royalist tale of Mardi Gras more complex, invents the meeting and combat of "two masquerades," each masked and each equally ridiculous: that of Santerre, the "Jacobinière of the Faubourg Saint-Antoine," against that of La Fayette, the "municipal acrobat." After clashes and mixtures of disguises, the fight ends in a "fine revolutionary mess." [In French, *cacarde*, playing on *cocarde*, the revolutionary's cockade, and *caca*. Trans.]

Patriot camps surely understood the danger of leaving games of laughter only to Royalist satire, for, on the occasion of the carnival of 1791, they reply sharply. They also end up making a masked body serve to reveal the adversary. Paradoxically, the Fayettists, the very ones who are in charge of supervising the prohibition of street carnivals, answer first. *La Jacobinière, parade like none other*, of municipal origin, advances masked under the same name as the Royalist satire in order to challenge it better.[57]

The counterrevolutionary version described the fight of the municipal and Jacobin parades; the Fayettist rewriting substitutes for the first a "monarchic parade," an "infernal parade with thousands of heads" that it has warring against an identical Jacobin parade, one that the municipals are happy to see bogged down in the "fine revolutionary mess" that concludes this paper Mardi Gras as well.

In another pamphlet, the Fayettists are even more explicit, using not only the same Royalist words and inventions but also putting all the pieces together to make a "Counter-revolution by carnival." The scene, described by *The carnival of the aristocrats*, takes place "at the monarchic club," "at eight o'clock in the evening," where "a great speech uttered on 3 March 1791" sets out the conditions of the conspiracy. The text skillfully pastiches traditional language, vouching "on its honor" for the veracity of the deeds reported, justifying this "despotic carnival" in the name of the "illustrious ancestors of all the masks of pantomime." The conspirators, meeting after the failure of the Conspiracy of Knights of the Sword that disturbed Parisian thoughts on the night of 28 February 1791, decided to strike a great blow, constructing an immense chariot destined to gather together, "despite the prohibitions," more than six hundred masks. But that is only a diversion: "While the people, the general, and his soldiers rush up to the carnival, we will not miss the occasion that we missed on 28 February; we will set fires in all the neighborhoods of Paris, while they are rejoicing at the Barrier. The entire National Guard being thus occupied, we will have a great success at the castle of the Tuileries, and will make it seen that the courage of the French knights has not degenerated, by giving such a carnival to the Parisians." The Fayettist writing finally comes out into the open in the conclusion of this tale in which Monarchists have reclothed the revelatory and terrible corporeal mask of the "knights of the sword": "M. de la Fayette being forewarned of the plan of the Monarchists, consequently gave orders to the National Guard, which, no doubt, will once again cause their plans to misfire. The cavalry has been ordered to be armed with muskets; to keep itself ready to fire, and to run through with a saber all aristocrats it finds masked, along with their partisans who dare to attempt a Counter-revolution by carnival."

Having become a literary figure, cleansed of the violence of corporeal inversion and grotesquery of the street procession, the Mardi Gras on paper is now suitable for polemics. Not very alarming, and even playful, words endlessly pastiche the discourse of the opponent, words dress themselves

up, words transfer the real affronts and accidents of the street into virtuoso jousts of rhetoric. Bailly and La Fayette certainly prefer these fights *in
octavo* to the processions to the barriers organized for 1 May 1791 or, all
the more so, the anticlerical ceremony of the burning of the pope in effigy.
The cohort of Fayettist writers tried to inflate the carnival battle held in
pamphlets in order to spare the general the disorders of the street. In this
spring of 1791, certainly the most agitated of the entire revolutionary decade, this precaution will turn out to be insufficient, but it represents at
least the indisputable tactic of transferring political polemics from the dangerous terrain of the street toward the better-policed one of the printed
word. The spectacle of the Revolution, then, is to be seen as much in the
bodies of ideas and figures embodied by metaphors as in the ceremonies of
the public square. The carnival of pamphlets is the most expressive illustration of this, giving a travestied body to men on the political scene by
means of the language of laughter.

A long pamphlet (almost seventy pages) dated 18 February 1791 gives a
brilliant example of this spectacle of laughter played in a more and more
elaborate manner by the pamphlets of February–March 1791, marrying the
"war of epigrams" to the "ludicrous masquerades," summoning more and
more numerous characters, with more and more complex masks: *The shade
of Mardi Gras, or the masquerades of the court joined with those of the legislative body, of the municipality, and of some titled women.* This work "written
to replace the carnival of 1791," "laughing at all tyrants," strives to turn
the Revolution itself into an immense carnival, using all of its components,
friends and enemies alike. The trap of mockery ends up by snapping closed
on all of politics; the least corners of the revolutionary scene are explored,
and the least characters integrated into the different masquerades staged.
The Revolution, after the ancien régime, became a carnival spectacle: "In
the time when Louis XVI ate like an ogre and drank like a Templar—
and that time still lasts, it is in the juice of the vine that the French monarch drowns his decadence—when Marie-Antoinette gave herself over to
all the excesses of prostitution, when the dissolution of the Court knew no
limits, Mardi Gras played a great role in the Palace of our Kings and in the
heart of the Capital. The scepter of royalty was nothing other then than the
bauble of madness, and Parisians were at once drunk with pleasures and
bent under the weight of servitude and poverty. Today, the name of Mardi
Gras is uselessly placed on the calendar; it no longer presides over foolish-
ness and stupidity. Yet France has never been so disguised as it is at the

present time; it is a general masquerade. What presides now over these new costumes, clothes, hearts, and physiognomies? It is the Revolution, yes, the Revolution that has taken hold of the rights of Mardi Gras, and, since 13 July 1789, we see a perpetual carnival reign."

Everyone, then, wears the mask. The court has resumed those of the ancien régime, the municipality has seized "the bonnet of Midas, with ass's ears," while the Jacobins have invented the Patriot disguise: "When at the beginning of 1790, they proved, by means of pompously annoying phrases empty of all sense, that Mardi Gras had to be exiled from France, on the very day of that magnificent peroration, they clothed themselves in the paraphernalia of a Patriot masquerade; a popular cloak, the hypocritical forehead of a Tartuffe, the staring eyes of the waiting vulture, the nose of an ambitious man, the mouth of a vampire, the teeth of a cannibal, body clothed in a sepulchral wrap, and fingers terminating in the talons of a Kite." The "shade" of Mardi Gras, "ghost furious at its exile," in this way returns to Paris to "costume" politics and describe the masks: "I want to costume people in accord with their own inclinations; in a word, to give each person a suit of clothes to his size, decorated with the emblems that signify his passions, his vices and his virtues . . . Any one of us, or anyone else, will then think himself perfectly disguised, when in fact he will only be more recognizable."

This speech on disguise joins the one on surveillance and the one on unmasking that, almost simultaneously, denounce the bad electorate in the pages of Patriot papers. But where Brissot, Marat, or Desmoulins erect a moral hierarchy among the true and false friends of the people, *The shade of Mardi Gras* integrates *all* the Revolution into its masquerades. Thus, the "royal masquerade" opens the procession, behind a king "dressed in his fashion in carnival dress that suits him, since the attributes of royalty are vain and useless in his hands": the carriage, "built in the Chinese style, announcing by the jingle of little bells where all this royal family is being led," supports a "bacchante and naked" queen, a gentleman dressed as "Sancho Panza," a dauphin as "bastard Cupid," and a Louis XVI "installed on horseback on a barrel decorated with vine branches and grapes, crowned with vine leaves, a glass in one hand and a bottle in the other." Then comes the "legislative masquerade," guided by the "General Shit-a-bed," La Fayette as an Amazon, followed by the principal deputies, on the right and left, indiscriminately mingled, where Mirabeau as the "enchanter Merlin" is spotted, along with Lameth as "the Grand Turk," or Cazalès as "wild

child." Finally, at the end of the march occurs the "municipal masquerade," set in "an amphitheater decorated by ineptitude." Upon the passage
of this triple procession, "the people laughs, sings, and makes puns on the
functions of all these men revealed by ingenious disguises." This "day of
Ashes" [Ash Wednesday] completes the narrative-spectacle by proposing a
roaring fire in which all the masks of politics, that is to say all the powers of
the Revolution—the royal executive power, the legislative power, and the
municipal power—are burned together.

From the rebirth of the political carnival in the pamphlets of Mardi Gras
1790 to this ceremony of ashes of February 1791 in which all the masks
of the revolutionary powers burn, the writing of laughter served all sides
and integrated all the public figures into its game. But these, *The shade of
Mardi Gras* emphasizes, do not come out unscathed from this battle fought
over two years. Even if the combat was often transported from the actuality
of the street to the imagination in pamphlets and engravings, the carnival acted out offers nonetheless a burlesque and parodistic version of the
dispute, one that ends up transforming all the powers into a ridiculous
spectacle: these, in their royal, legislative, or bourgeois versions, are nothing more than absurd bodies (although only of paper), burnt, drifting away
in smoke.

In this way, by the uses and subterfuges of laughter, the Revolution
politically takes leave of the old world. Between February and June 1791,
this brutal caesura is again accentuated. Bursts of laughter accuse and attack the old bodies. The pope baited and burned in effigy, the king transformed into a pig, the powers of the new notables scorched in the masquerade of ludicrous disguise—all these outbursts of laughter are transformed
into attacks. They will leave profound traces in the memory of the belliger-
ents of this paper war, especially when, a few months later, after the very
real deaths of the summer of 1791 (the repression of the Champ de Mars on
17 July), after the violence of 10 August 1792, after the bloody massacres of
September 1792, the actors return to take their places in these fights, but
this time dressed for tragedy.

8. The Offertory of the Martyrs

The Wounded Body of the Revolution

Funeral rites were ordered in honor of Michel Lepeletier: this ceremony had an extraordinary character; the corpse was placed on the ruined base of the equestrian statue of Louis XIV in the middle of the Place Vendôme. His funeral oration was proclaimed by a voice that made itself heard over all the roofs. It was very cold. The body of Lepeletier, naked, livid, and bloody, showing the wide wound that had killed him, was carried slowly on a catafalque along a lengthy parade route, accompanied by the Convention along with the Society of Jacobins. The Society had its banner, and just beside it one could see another of its invention: it carried as its pennant the shirt, vest, and above all the breeches of Lepeletier still revolting with blood."[1] (See Figure 16.)

Through these ceremonies, the Revolution always wanted to impress minds and senses strongly, always sought to mobilize energies. It is this "terrible spectacle" that so fascinated Louis-Sébastien Mercier in the funeral ceremony of Louis Lepeletier of Saint-Fargeau, murdered by a Royalist on 20 January 1793, an emotion that he emphasizes: "It was a spectacle to produce profound impressions; and indeed it did. What had seemed hideous in the ceremony paled before the terrible images that it offered . . . All the women had terrifying dreams, and never was a dead man saluted by so many gazes, or accompanied by so many reflections." Between 1792 and 1794, when the tragic genre occupies the stage of the Revolution, peopled with Republican martyrs returning from the foreign front or fallen under the blows of domestic conspiracy, the mark of the wounded body means to be indelible, a visual pedagogy of sure efficacy that allows the political message to be written in wounds, during artfully prepared scenes.

This didactic of the wounded body is referred to explicitly by David in the course of his *Report on the heroic festival for the honors of the Pantheon to be awarded to the youths Bara and Viala*, who were young Republicans slain under the blows of the Vendéeans, the "Federates of the Midi": "You, incorruptible Marat, show the passage that the murderous steel opened to your soul. You, Lepeletier, uncover your side torn open by a minion of the last of our tyrants. You, Beauvais, the lacerations that with slow steps opened the doors of the tomb to you."[2]

The emotion felt at the sight of "holy wounds" opens up the path of political awareness. These ceremonies seem directly linked to the revolutionary moment and even more to the moment of the Terror. On one hand, they go against the development of the century, a slow evolution that little by little came to abstain from the public display of corpses during funeral rites. As Michel Vovelle writes: "We can measure the stages of a collective evolution, which progressively passed from the almost-nudity of the shroud of the baroque era to the custom of being buried clothed, then of being placed in a coffin."[3] Accordingly, these funeral rituals will soon enough be called into question. Beginning in Year VIII, the National Institute subjects to examination the question of the "good funeral rites" suitable for a "free people."[4] The answers, massively and without exception, condemn the "incongruous exhibitions" of wounded bodies that were offered for view between 1792 and 1794. It would seem almost that the conventional republic, during the time of the Terror, had instigated a "baroque revival" in its funeral ceremonies. As if, again, the terrible spectacle of a death exposed, laid bare, had to travel through the eyes of the community; as if, then, this transparency of the gaze to wounded bodies had to produce effects on the public imagination that the discourse of power would be able to contain, or even more importantly, direct.

Louis-Sébastien Mercier, for instance, vouches for his "political emotion" when he evokes invalids met on his path, around the streets of Paris, "those honorable wounded who recall to memory the terrible battles in which they had been involved": "One meets on the faces of these young mutilated heroes, the imprint of the courage that animated them in combat; and if our eye could penetrate their clothes, how many other glorious wounds would it discover there! How many men without arms, without legs! How many men without a nose, without a chin, without a mouth! O detestable kings who are in league against our newborn Republic, thinking to annihilate it, you are the authors of these sad mutilations. What Republican does not feed his patriotism with a new degree of strength and courage, when he sees these deplorable victims of the blind vindictive powers united against a generous people?"[5] The hero who lets his wounds be seen performs a political act: incarnating the wounded body of the Revolution, he offers a tragic, glorious, and avenging identity.

The Ceremony of Wounds

These funeral ceremonies that for several months punctuated the advance of the Revolution—the victims of 10 August, the funeral rites of Lepeletier, Lazowski, Marat, Chalier, Beauvais, Gasparin—are very much linked to the political conjuncture. This exhibition of bodies becomes established in the two-year period from summer 1792 to summer 1794. Of course, before that there had been the funeral rites of Mirabeau or of the soldiers of Châteauvieux, and afterward there were to be the funeral ceremonies in honor of Hoche, or Joubert, or those, especially expressive, that commemorated the Rastadt assassination, when, in April 1799, two French envoys, Bonnier and Robersjot, returning from their mission, were killed by Austrian hussars. However, the exhibition of the wounded body acquires its most pathetic ceremonial form between 1792 and 1794. The presentation of the wounds and injuries of martyrs is not part of a slow evolution of a collective mentality, but reflects the urgency of a precise historic moment. The link between political discourse and the portrayal of bodies is obvious here: the main function of the wounded body is to present to the eyes of all the bloody evidence of the counterrevolutionary plot.

The martyr bears the signs of conspiracy on him; he indicates by his mere suffering presence the guilt of the enemy just as he bears witness to its inescapable omnipresence. Thus, with the emotional logic introduced in midsummer 1792, Bourdon de l'Oise proposes to the National Assembly that the wounded of 10 August should have a conspicuous place on the rostrum during the judgment of Louis XVI: "It is customary, in matters of criminal justice, to confront the accused with the exhibits."[6] "Louis must be shown the bleeding wounds of the citizens whose massacre he had ordered," Philippeaux then stresses. This proposition is finally effectively refuted by Masuyer: "Judges do not cause the bleeding bodies that have been deprived of life to be brought before the eye of their murderers, whose fate they are going to decide."

Yet it is just this accusatory function that the wounded body of the martyr will most often fulfill: the oath of revenge sworn on the very wounds quickly becomes one of the commonplaces of revolutionary rhetoric. Let us listen, for instance, to Ronsin, on the occasion of the funeral ceremony in honor of the victims of 10 August: "The murderers of the people have received the just wages of their assassinations: they are no more; and their corpses, naked and bleeding, are dragged in the dust, while the People gathers, with sacred respect, the precious remains of the citizens who have perished for the defense of liberty. Let us all swear, on the coffin that encloses their wounded bodies, let us swear never to put down the sword with which we have armed ourselves, until we have purged the capital of France of all the oppressors of the people."[7]

This oath will come to its apogee a year later, with the numerous inaugural ceremonies of portrait busts dedicated to the martyrs of liberty: "Your precious blood," an orator addressing the martyr cries, "spread on the earth, has become the seed of patriotic virtues; each drop has produced a hundredfold. This dear blood that drenches the soil of liberty cries justice to the heavens. We will not delay full vengeance."[8]

This wounded body accuses and points out the enemy of the country; this last thus becomes, legitimately in the mind of every Republican, an assassin, indeed a "drinker of blood." Louis XVI, until then made ridiculous by the ludicrous association with the bestiary of laughter, or by the rumors concerning the impotence of his "imbecile body," metamorphoses into a monster after 10 August under the effects of this eloquence of blood: "I have seen this thirsty brigand drink in vermilion goblets the sweat and blood of the Frenchman, while this same Frenchman, a soldier crippled for the country, begged for alms," the citizen Dorfeuille cries out a few days after the execution of the king.[9] François Gamain, locksmith at the Tuileries who accuses Louis XVI of having poisoned him, also sees his words relayed in a very meaningful way by Peyssard to the Convention, in the name of the Committee of Public Safety: "It is at the tribune of liberty that the crimes of the oppressors of the human race must ring out. . . . Scarcely had he [the king] come out of childhood when the germ of that ferocious perversity that characterizes a despot developed in him. His first games were games of blood, and his brutality increased with age, and he reveled in indulging it on all the animals that came his way."[10]

Under the pressure of events, the image of the king has been turned up-side down in revolutionary propaganda: his history is rewritten according to the terrible body, the despot "drinker of blood," whereas the narrative hostile to the king had previously stressed his indecision and weakness. After 1791, corporeal metaphors and ceremonies massively changed reg-ister: the tragic has taken hold of them. This same genre of accusation pursued the murderers of all revolutionary heroes and martyrs: "Go forth, cowardly assassins who feed on human flesh and who are revolting with the blood of Marat; his body calls out to you: Monsters, you seem a thousand times more hideous than those kept in hell. Your hands and lips are still covered with blood . . . May your body dry up, may it never die, and find food only in the blood of those whom you have had slain and in the corpse flesh that thousands of worms will fight for with you." [11]

Visions of horror like this can of course be found in the pamphlets and papers at the beginning of the Revolution, but from now on they occupy official discourse and animate public rituals, becoming worthy counter-parts of the Republican pomp surrounding the bodies of martyrs. These visions culminate in the dissolute portrayal of the irreducible enemy: the English.[12] The speeches at the Convention during Prairial Year II abound with horrified descriptions of massacres perpetrated by the "English race." Barère thus describes, at the tribune, in a "profound silence" followed by "reactions of horror through all the Convention," a masked ball that was supposed to have been held in London: "In the festivals of the English, in the midst of their games, during their very meals, all they think about is killing the members of our two committees; the assassin is honored in their public games. In these masked balls, these unspeakable orgies, they assign to Robespierre above all a horrible priority. One of the maskers was a 'Charlotte Corday come from the tomb,' brandishing her bloody dagger all night in pursuit of a 'Robespierre.' . . . Such are the festivals of this can-nibal people." [13]

The visual pedagogy constructed around the body of the revolutionary martyr of course reflects a wave of assassination attempts very disturbing to Republican power. In the fifteen months from January 1793 to March 1794, six representatives of the people, not including those condemned to death by the revolutionary tribunal, were killed in the exercise of their duties: Lepeletier and Marat assassinated in Paris, Chalier guillotined by the Lyon-nais counterrevolutionaries, then Baille who chose suicide over serving the English at Toulon, and finally Beauvais and Gasparin dead of exhaustion following the siege of Toulon. Moreover, Robespierre and Collot d'Herbois both escaped assassination attempts in the beginning of Prairial Year II. But the wounded body is more than a circumstantial response to an isolated threat: it itself must terrify the assassins, against whom the wounds of the martyrs have turned. The threatened republic demands both "great victims" and "vile conspirators whose favorite pastime is to get drunk on our blood." [14] The exhibition of wounded bodies is one of the ceremonies necessary to the radical nature of the political discourse of the Terrorist period: the radical suffering of the victims, radical vice of the enemies, and radical vengeance of the Republic. Of these three summonings to tragic discourse, the ritual of wounded bodies reverberates loudest, like a snare drum of political resonance.

Many are the hero-martyrs whose wounds are unveiled. Famous heroes, including the trio of the "martyrs for Liberty" (Lepeletier, Marat, and Chalier), are side by side with anonymous heroes, volunteers returning from the front who present themselves, wounded and requesting help, before the different revolutionary assemblies. Diverse bodies, different stories, multiple scars, from the fatal wound to the most trifling cut, but always the same presentation: first to make compassion arise, the emotion of the spectator before the corpse; then to point out the enemy; then to fan the flame of revenge by exalting the glory of the martyr.

The obsequies of Lazowski, a hero of 10 August who died of "exhaustion" in the spring of 1793, held in the hall of the general council of the Commune de Paris on 28 April 1793, can serve as an example.[15] The body is present, on display, clearly visible, "naked on a sheet." This furnishes the funeral oration with a solemnity, a tragic actuality that touches sensibilities. The orator, Destournelles, retraces the career and then the death of the hero: "You see in this enclosure the remains of Lazowski. The revolution committee [*section*] of Finistère entrusted them to us at your request; it gave them up only with grief. Is there a Patriot who can see them without profound emotion?" On the occasion of this ceremony, the whole Republican community is gathered around the wounded body of the hero, a body whose very essence will be preserved by the revolutionary group that the Paris committee has become. "Good Sans-Culottes of the Finistère *section*, you wanted to have the heart of Lazowski . . . You will guard with care such a precious deposit; may it be placed religiously in the seat of your assemblies. Inspired by it . . . you will continue to accord to your deliberations the vigor that hitherto has characterized them." The "holy relics" of the martyr are the symbol of revolutionary continuity: under their auspices, the political community is united, comforted, and pursues the work to which the martyr has sacrificed himself.

The real presence of the body also allows them to discuss the virtuous actions of the dead man in the eulogy (a genre so prized by the eighteenth century that it became a hackneyed academic art[16]), thus instilling it with a new political urgency whose lyricism is justified by the wound itself: "Through a deluge of fire, on thousands of corpses of Royalist brigands, on the heaped-up debris and bodies, he displayed that liberty cap so dear to the free man . . . It was not in bed, worn down by illness and surrounded by grieving friends, that Lazowski came to die; it was on a battlefield, at the head of his brothers in arms, pierced by innumerable blows."[17] The revolutionary spirit and heroic glory displayed around the exposed body are then proffered by the *section* members to other citizens: "Come with us to shed tears that will proclaim to the tyrants that Lazowski lives again in us . . . Come, brave defenders of the Republic, come be joined around the body of the glorious Lazowski."[18]

The presentation of the wounded body permits this compassionate spirit and the glory of shed blood to be turned against the enemies: "Another of his attributes is no less honorable: it is the fierce hatred of the aristocracy. Just like him, present as he is to our eyes through his martyred body, we must hate," Destournelles cries out during the funeral eulogy.[19] The body of the hero appears, in Republican ritual, as the setting for a tragic dramaturgy perfectly composed: the community, gathered together, is grouped around the body, and finds cohesion and certainty in it, celebrating the glory of its funeral spectacle, before transforming this cohesion into a hatred of the Other, outside the group even if it had at times come from within it. The ceremony of wounds is a metamorphosis of pity for a wound into hatred for a foreign body.

This ritual implies two processes that form of the community: the identification of all Republicans with the wounded bodies of the martyrs, and a particular sensitivity to the tale of wounds of heroic bodies. Multiple traces of this double incorporation can be found in revolutionary discourse; in the case of identification, we find: "It is we who have been wounded; his wounded body is ours too. Citizens, don't you feel it, it is we who have been struck . . . The vile Pâris has wounded in Lepeletier all the friends of freedom, all true Frenchmen," the mayor of Amiens cries out in the course of his funeral eulogy for Lepeletier.[20] Innumerable instances of such tragic identification could be found.[21]

Sensitivity to the story of the wounds is the second way toward the martyred body, as attested, for example, by the works of the Committee of Public Instruction of the Convention on the presentation of heroic acts.[22] Charged with the publication of the *Collection of the Heroic Deeds of the French Republicans*, this committee tries, through the intermediary of Léonard Bourdon de La Crosnière and Antoine-Claire Thibaudeau, to erect a precise framework in which short accounts are published, intended to be morally edifying to children and *section* members: "One must shed tears on the bodies of generals killed in combat, . . . but one must also regret not having marched along with them from the instant that the army set off, until the glorious moment when they found immortality in death."[23] Similarly, the death of the young Bara, "immolated by the brigands of the Vendée," "touches all souls, but it pierces them with horror at the assassins of the young hero."

Here we find again, in these pedagogical precepts, the same preoccupations that surrounded the presentation of the body of Lazowski: emotion and tears at the description of the wounds, revolutionary glory and continuity portended by the heroic act, pointing-out of the enemies, and desire for community revenge. The Republic wanted to understand and control the emotions linked to the exhibition of wounded bodies: it is the work of the pedagogues to channel such a sensibility into a coherent political discourse. Presentations of wounded bodies are thus arranged around three privileged "moments," three successive phases ritually respected — a practice inherited from ancient, then from Christian, traditions that also had reason to exhibit, at certain moments, the corpses of their own martyrs. These three moments are the narrative of the wound, the display of the wounded body, and the substitution of a simulacrum of the body to assure the spread of the martyr's glory.

Narrative, Exhibition, and Simulacrum of the Tragic Body

Three main sources retrace the tale of the wound: the account of the last moments of the martyr presented by the orator to the assembled community; this same account distributed by pamphlets and journals; and then by anthologies collecting together "heroic acts" for the use of schools, local committees, and revolutionary clubs. The same constant recurs in whatever form the tale may employ: the extreme precision devoted to the description of the wounded or suffering body, an anatomical precision that guarantees the veracity of the wounds. "Félix Cabanes, grenadier in the Third Battalion of Gers, hit with a bullet in the thigh, at the camp in Sarre, fires twenty cartridges, and sustains the shock of the enemy cavalry. Taken to the hospital, he pulls out the bullet with his corkscrew, and the healing involves loss of bone. On 23 July, he receives a bullet wound on the back of the head that makes a cut an inch long in the nape, but fires two hundred cartridges, and kills six Catalans with a knife. On 23 August, a cannonball falls at his knees and buries him with earth, while another carries away half his cartridge pouch and makes a deep gash in his right side; at the same instant a poisoned bullet penetrates his hat, gouges out an eye, and remains lodged in the right eyesocket. Carried to the hospital, he falls into a state of asphyxia that makes him seem dead. They are ready to bury him when suddenly he cries out: 'Wretch, you want to bury me alive? I still have some blood left to shed for my country!' " [24]

This striking example is drawn from the *Collection of the Heroic Deeds*, in which the particularity of the description guarantees the belief of the community. Detailing the wounds, far from shaking listeners or readers, helps to strengthen their Republican faith. That such a description can be integrated into a book especially designed for schools emphasizes the confidence felt by Republican pedagogues in the emotional link leading from the wound to mobilization.

This same transparency of the martyred body to the political act animates another variety of tales about the death of the hero, namely, the numerous "autopsy reports" that make public the dissection and the description of the corpses of great revolutionaries. This narrative is reserved for nonviolent but nonetheless glorious deaths. Here it is a question of an essential stage in the progress of the ceremony of the wounded body, a harrowing tale: Loustallot, Mirabeau, Cérutti, Lazowski, Gasparin, Beauvais—all died of "exhaustion" for the country. The first function of these morbid narratives consists in establishing the possible presence of conspiracy, an unveiling that confirms it or rejects it. The autopsy report is the only way (since it is both medical and public) for the transparency of gaze to visit the body sacrificed in the revolutionary cause.

In this sense, during the Convention, the most exemplary tale of wounding is linked to the death of Gasparin, a representative who died of illness on assignment, following the siege of Toulon. The Convention, having had the martyr's heart brought back, silently listens to the reading of the autopsy report before ordering the honors of the Pantheon: "The putrefaction of the body was such that one could not approach it without precaution. However, to calm the anxieties of the people on the causes of death of Citizen Gasparin, we proceeded, in the presence of a number of citizens, to open the chest, and, after having removed the sternum, we found the left lobe of the lung gangrened, while the rest of this viscera, along with the heart, was in an ordinary state; the heart was extracted in order to be embalmed." [25] The description continues like that for several minutes, the doctors Arnous and Fabre going into detail, before the deputies, on the "state of the lower abdomen," then of the head.

This anatomical precision seems indispensable to the recognition of the martyr: the corpse becomes a community affair, and the fellow citizens must be confronted with the reality of the wounded body—this is the necessary condition for emotion, for the political gesture (here, the enshrining of Gasparin's heart in the Pantheon), and for terrible revenge. We find this anatomical precision again in other types of stories about wounds—at the bar of the Convention, for instance, during the presentations of soldiers returning from the front, or during the accounts of the most edifying deaths. The actual presence of the wounded body, or of a relic in the case of the deceased (clothes of the dead soldier, medals, bullets extracted from the wounds, weapons, crutches), is always accompanied by a detailed narrative of the circumstances of the act and of the wounds received. There again, it is a question of exciting pity: emotion is built up on the anatomy of the wounds. The abundant applause that punctuates these narratives at the National Assembly testifies to this. For example, on 10 June 1793, as reported by Lakanal: "Joseph Sauveur . . . falls into the hands of rebels; they want to force him to blaspheme against freedom [indignation in the hall, note the secretaries]; in order to do so, they make him experience all that the aristocracy can conceive of that is cruel; they cut fingers off his hands and toes off his feet; they drag him in the streets; they fire several rounds of pistols loaded with lead into his eyes and mouth [horrified reactions]; finally, they throw him in a roaring fire, where he expires, pressing to his lips the civic medal that we have here [applause, all the representatives stand up and continue to applaud at the sight of the medal shown by Lakanal]." [26]

Thus the sacrifice of his body becomes an edifying lesson: the tales of wounds always establish a direct relationship between the precise description of physical pain and the spiritual satisfaction of the hero. This is the role attributed, by these tales, to the last words of the martyrs, words that will often be engraved and paraded at the funeral festivals of the Revolution, the last words painstakingly collected. In the case of the death of Chalier, for instance, the report read before the Convention on 26 Brumaire Year II links terminal agony with the last words: "They [the 'rebels of Lyon'] had carried barbarism to the point of arranging the guillotine so that each blow would mutilate without killing him. Five times the fatal iron descends to make five new wounds in him; imagine it! Insensible to the pain and thinking only of his country, Chalier shakes his dying head and cries to the executioner of the rebels: 'Pin a cockade on me—I die for liberty.'"[27] The detail of injuries put to the service of emotion and moral edification—such is the narrative of the wound.

In the matter of displaying bodies, the first Republican reference—this will scarcely be surprising—is to Antiquity. At a time when the deportment of the body is supposed to be directly inherited from the deeds of the ancient hero, the exhibition of the "sacred remains," around which the revolutionary community gathers and bonds, finds historic references. "In the centuries of Antiquity, . . . when war had deprived the State of some of its citizens, public gratitude was expressed by funeral eulogies. First the eyes were impressed by an imposing and august apparatus: a tent was set up to which the bones of the warriors were carried; there they would remain for three days, displayed for public veneration. The populace crowded in . . . Can you not hear the blood of our martyrs who cry to us: 'We have shown you your duty; we have opened to you the road along which you all must march!'"[28]

Revolutionaries allow the same importance to the exhibition and funerals of the bodies of their heroes as Homer or Sophocles did to the dead of the Trojan War. The gathering of the remains of the martyr is the very condition of its cult. No ceremony without a body, or without some relic to impress people's minds—that is the first stage of the ritual. This absolutely necessary collecting of the remains is not without its dangers, as in Sophocles' *Ajax*. Couthon, for instance, declares before the Convention, on the first of Nivôse Year II, that the funeral ceremonies of Chalier were only made possible thanks to the devotion of Citizen Padovani who, at the risk of her life, "the night following the execution," "gathered the precious remains of the martyr": "She unearthed the head that the putrefaction had spared, then guarded it reverently before delivering it to the legitimate authorities."[29] This wounded body, object of all cares and all gazes, is then exhibited, watched over, and paraded, during a ritual arranged and recomposed afresh each time. Mercier described Lepeletier's ceremony, but each martyr had his own. Chalier, whose remains were first paraded in the streets of "the Liberated City" [*Ville-Affranchie*—Lyon] retaken by the armies of the Convention, has his apotheosis in Paris during a procession in which, behind "three banners bearing his prophecies," a triumphal chariot is driven surmounted by an altar "on which will be placed the head of Chalier covered over with a crêpe, adorned with a crown."[30]

Beauvais was given this honor too. His naked corpse, "carried by eight members of popular society," was brought to the Champ de Mars from the city of Montpellier, where the representative had died from the consequences of sufferings during a long stay in the prisons of the "rebels of Toulon." There, he was placed on a pyre and burned "in the presence of the people" who "sang the patriotic hymn."[31]

The most remarkable exhibition, however, remains that of the body of Jean-Paul Marat.[32] From the evening of 15 July 1793 (Marat was assassinated on the thirteenth), the embalmed body of the martyr is exhibited in the church of the Cordeliers: "We decided," David states at the Convention, "to place him on a bed, like Lepeletier, covered with a simple sheet, which would bring to mind rather well the idea of the bath."[33] Intention to reconstruct and expiate is affirmed at once by the organizer of the funeral ceremony. This wish for "expressiveness" will dominate the entire ceremony. In the church of the Cordeliers, Marat's corpse is exhibited half uncovered, "so that everyone can see the wound."[34] A towel stained with blood is there also, exhibited below the body set on a platform. The funeral bed on which the body lies is covered with flowers, and Marat's head is surrounded with a crown of oak leaves. A text is inscribed beneath the bed: "Marat, Friend of the People, assassinated by the enemies of the people. Enemies of the people, temper your joy, there will be avengers." The crowd presses in next to this *doubly* wounded body—by the wound, marked out for public view, but also by the martyr's skin disease, also "exhibited" since it altered the corpse very quickly. Thus, in the eyes of Parisians panic-stricken by the omnipresent threat of conspiracy, this twice-wounded body perfectly symbolizes the state of their besieged republic: the body itself is this republic, eaten away from within by disease (conspiracy), finished off by external aggression.

On 16 July the funeral ceremony takes place. The mortal remains are carried through the streets to the garden of the Cordeliers. Here again, the body is exhibited in its double woundedness, the chest laid bare to show the wound caused by the "fatal knife of criminal counterrevolution," the face decomposed by the attacks of the disease: putrefaction, as it advanced, had in fact given it a green tint, easily decipherable since we know that this color, taken from the livery of the Comte d'Artois, has been associated with conspiracy since the beginning of the Revolution. The blood on the chest is the mark of the knife, the green of the corpse is that of conspiracy: on the wounded body of Marat the appeal to turn terror against enemies and traitors is sketched out in the eyes of everyone. After mid-July 1793, in fact, the most radical Parisian district committees, those that surrounded Marat during the funeral procession, call for "terrible" measures in the name of the martyr to frighten conspirators and money-grabbers. The exhibition of the body seems one of the most effective political ways to mobilize the people of Paris.

Just like the tale of wounds, the exhibition of the body has its rules. Attention first centers around the preparation and presentation of the corpse (bodies are embalmed, powdered, sprinkled with perfume, covered with flowers): bodies are stretched out on a funeral bed, heads placed on an altar, wounds laid bare or carefully dressed, bodies carried on a stretcher, accompanied by the elements of ceremony (last words engraved or printed, symbols of their martyrdom—shirt or linens stained with blood, knives). This ceremonial dramatizes the funeral moment, elicits the identification of everyone with the tragedy of the body, and vigorously reinforces the narrative of wounds. But the exhibition, a privileged moment, remains ephemeral. In one sense it does persist, engraved in memories, related in the papers. But its time and space are limited, quickly circumscribed by the destruction or burial of the body. The ashes gathered into funeral urns that mount in numbers from the départements toward the Convention, the Pantheon, or the Archives of France, the embalmed and preserved hearts (Lazowski, Marat, Gasparin) then become the chief signs recalling the sacrifice of the martyr, chief symbols of a wider distribution of the tragic and glorious image of the wounded body of the Revolution. The tale of wounds is a call to civic mourning addressed to the community. The time of the actual display of the body corresponds to the paroxysm of emotion. But this moment is not enough: it calls for diffusion in space and time of the message carried by the open wounds, a pedagogical work that only the simulacrum of the martyr's body can ensure.

Busts seem the best guarantee of memory. Because of their almost perfect resemblance to the model, and the tragic identification that they evoke, they overcome any obstacle to mediation, such as a mere relic would present. Republicans demand perfection of the simulacrum of the body. Often they describe it as a real body, passing beyond imitation, and find again in its perfection the transparency of view to the body: "Seeing him here everywhere, we will all know how to die like him," the president of the Convention declares when welcoming a bust of Lepeletier sculpted by Desenne, on 11 April 1793, almost three months after the death of the actual body. Busts of great martyrs were moreoover often molded directly on the face of the dead man, and were always reproduced with "the greatest severity and the greatest exactitude."

The reminder is tragic, not nostalgic. The bust of the martyr designates a wounded body; it is not the celebration of the beauty or greatness of a man. It is almost a question of "conceptual art," in the sense that the spectator sees in the traits of the exhibited face as much a wounded republic as a personal face. But both are indissociable: one recognizes the republic because one sees, conscientiously imitated, the features of Marat. The busts of martyrs for liberty are massively distributed during the de-Christianization of fall-winter 1793–94 in Paris,[35] a distribution that calls for new funeral festivals at which eulogies and tales of heroic acts are uttered. The body and the discourse of its replica together weave the endlessly repeated history of the wounded and threatened Republic. For these busts all accompany the processions, "carried on stretchers" by young volunteers, surrounded by women "in Classical garb" or by adolescents "holding an oak branch in their hand." The busts represent the central element of the procession, and during halts marked by civic oaths, orators apostrophize them directly. It is the body of the martyr that is addressed; it is to him that they swear fidelity: "His features are not lost to Patriots; we will send you his bust along with his ashes," write the citizens of Montpellier, certain of being heard, when announcing the death of Beauvais to the Convention.[36]

Paintings and prints also have a role to play in the memory of the wounded body. The most famous example is of course David's tragic trilogy, *Lepeletier-Marat-Bara*, three naked and wounded bodies, three perfect expressions of the suffering, fragile, threatened, but glorious Revolution. "Come running, all of you! mother, widow, orphan, oppressed soldier; all you whom he defended at the peril of his life, come close and contemplate your friend, the one who was vigilant is no more; his pen, the terror of traitors, his pen falls from his hands. O despair! Our indefatigable friend is dead . . . It is to you, my colleagues, that I offer the homage of my brushes; your gazes, traveling over the livid and bloody traits of Marat, will recall to you the virtues that must never cease being yours,"[37] David cries out when presenting his *Marat Assassinated* to the Convention on 24 Brumaire Year II. The great painting is accompanied by a massive distribution of prints, a circulation of images that creates an echo in speeches and at festivals.[38] More than a hundred different prints representing Marat after his death have been counted.

These "eulogy images" of the wounded body, these "body slogans," are, moreover, reinforced by an intense propaganda involving many other "portrait objects": portraits on lockets often grouping together the three principal martyrs, wall calendars, almanacs, medals, dishes, fans, brooches, box lids. All these images elaborate an endlessly reproduced emblematic. What is fascinating in these reproductions is the constant play between glorious idealization and macabre realism, as if the simulacrum of the wounded body could only be located in this troubling equilibrium. David's *Marat Assassinated* is, from this point of view, particularly illuminating: the painting is realist, since the body and wound are painted in a *lifelike* manner; the painting is ideal, since this body and this wound are also painted *perfectly*. This balance seems necessary in a pedagogical perspective that insists as much on tragedy as on glory. But the simulacrum of the wounded body, neglecting the perfect balance of the neoclassical body, most often makes this relationship lean to the actual presence of the corpse, to the side of dramatization.

Symbols of this provoked dramatization: Marat's bath and nightdress, for instance, were carried during his funeral rites, then used expressively again by some Parisian local committees during funeral festivals, such as that of 8 August 1793, more than three weeks after the assassination, in the church of Saint-Eustache, on the initiative of the committee on the Social Contract: "The simulacrum of this representative of the people stretched out on his death bed, the bath where he lay during his detestable assassination, will be offered all day to the view of the citizens . . . Come, Parisian citizens, come, our brothers from the *départements*, come see this frightful spectacle of pain; come see the mortal wound that was the work of the knife driven in by the crime; come with us to pour forth your heart; come, come hear the unfortunate life of this martyr for liberty, you will tremble at his tale, you will shed tears, and Marat will be, for you as for us, the immortal man that posterity will crown with glory." [39]

Simulacra, in this perspective of absolute dramatization, could take very diverse forms: orphans adopted by the Nation, like Lepeletier's daughter, or Caroline, Beauvais' daughter, fifteen years old, adopted by a deputy, adolescents endlessly paraded from ceremony to ceremony like the symbolic figure of their fathers; clothes full of holes and blood, carried during tragic ceremonies, as on 16 September 1792 when a widow presents herself to the Assembly, demanding, in the name of the macabre relic, the relief needed for her survival; even bullets pulled out of wounds, as the parcel of Michel Berruyer, volunteer from the Eure, reveals, when he sends to the Convention, on 22 Germinal Year II, a "big bullet from my wounds . . . The proof of my public-spiritedness" — as many tokens as possible to recall to the gazes of the citizens the suffering of a wounded body.

Amidst this heterogeneity, however, and alongside the references to Antiquity, the undeniable filiation from religious tradition, the Catholic inheritance, must be emphasized. One finds this inheritance in the draperies, the candelabra, the sarcophagi surrounding the "instruments of the Passion" (Marat's bath, for example) and the "Holy Relics," a tradition that assimilates the martyred body with the body of Christ, and calls for a regrouping of citizens into a "body politic" mapped from the "Mystical Body" of the Catholic community. The body of the martyr, like a host of flesh, is offered as a sacrifice to the Republic and is reborn in each of its members as an appeal to protect it. It is, however, a political body, for a good number of Republican elements (such as the patriotic colors replacing black, civic proclamations displacing biblical quotations, and hymns taking the place of religious songs) are directly linked to the revolutionary context. The message of this cult of the wounded body is above all political, even if the process of identification of the community with the martyred body stems from Catholic tradition: the incorporation follows in fact the rite of a sort of Republican Eucharist. In effect, this cult of the suffering body is a ritualized call to political action.

The Republican wound is not, as one might think and as it is sometimes presented, an immoderate excitation of the senses, an unthinking appeal to violence and revenge. On the contrary, it rests, like the ritual of the Eucharist in the Catholic Mass, on a strict ceremonial norm, and on the repeated and recognized gestures of a controlled initiation. It even tends to establish an interdiction. Thus there is, in the use of the ceremony of wounds by Republican power, a taboo that is sometimes severely enforced. When on 10 September 1793 the Citizen Béranger sends to the Convention, as a proof of his "merciless public-spiritedness," a handkerchief "tainted with the impure blood of the scoundrel I killed, an émigré who dared to carry iron into the heart of my mother Country,"[40] that is to say a token of the body of the enemy, the Assembly protests with murmurs of indignation and, despite the justifications of the citizen ("May this bloody cloth teach crowned traitors and tyrants that their reign will pass and that national revenge will not pass"), orders that the reading be interrupted and "that the letter be solemnly torn up." It is not the bleeding body of its enemies that the Revolution wants to present to its children, but its own. The ceremony of Terror has this mission: to give some order to revenge and to forbid the anarchic excesses of the massacres at the beginning of the Revolution, when the mangled bodies of aristocrats had been carried in triumph by the people of Paris. From now on, triumph is reserved by the political ceremony of the Terror only for the wounded body of its own heroes. Wounds thus allow the two faces of the threatened country to be seen: here is suffering, but here also is an implacable and organized force.

It is symptomatic that the presentation of the wounded at the National Assembly is most often combined with the introduction of volunteers leaving for combat: the wounded body is inseparable from the vigorous body. On 3 February 1794, Citizen Bethisy, a farmer disabled ever since being wounded eighteen months before, comes to offer his eldest son to the Convention: "The blood from which he comes is a sure guarantor of his gallantry. His two cousins and myself . . . have covered our wounds with glory on many occasions."[41] Similarly, on 7 Floréal Year II, after hearing the report of the funeral ceremony of the deputy Beauvais in Montpellier, the representatives receive three cavalrymen equipped by a Parisian *section* and ready to leave for combat. These two dimensions — the wound calls for ordered vengeance just as it evokes vigor — are intimately linked: macabre realism, emphasizing the gaping and bleeding wound, cannot be read without the ideal citation of promised glory. The Revolution is fascinated by the bodies that sacrifice themselves for it: the wound ceaselessly calls for vigor, weakness calls for strength, the wounded Republic will be merciless.

From the Cult of the Great Martyrs to Everyday Wounds: The Bodily Makeup of Terrorist Discourse

The exhibition of the wounded body is not reserved just for famous martyrs; it extends to a much more everyday level, thanks to the many celebrations to mark the homecomings of wounded soldiers from the front. Great funeral ceremonies punctuated discourse during the Terror, but the continued exhibition of the wounds of soldier-citizens embodied it. Alongside illustrious corpses, there is a proliferation of anonymous bodies: I counted almost a hundred presentations of the wounded to the National Assembly between spring 1792 and summer 1794 alone, a continual flow that extends uniformly over legislative and convention periods without any clear division between busy season and slack season. I will simply point out that the moments following the great internal or foreign battles (10 August, Jemmapes, the war of the Vendée, Fleurus) are the most favorable to these presentations, as is the period in which the Great Terror was inaugurated in Floréal–Prairial Year II.

This continual flux contributes to establishing a permanent climate of tension in the Assembly, but the deputies observed certain ceremonies with special emphasis. On 20 March 1793, for instance, the Minister of War, Beurnonville, presents to the National Assembly the seventeen-year-old Lavigne, a volunteer whose arms were blown off by a cannonball. He mounts next to the president to accept a civic crown. The emotion that all the representatives felt at the sight of this poor mutilated body falling into the arms of their president is noted by the journalists on hand: "His presence and the tears that run abundantly from his eyes excite the greatest emotion; they inspire feelings of tenderness, of love for the country and hatred for the enemies of our freedom." [42] Such presentations multiply and hold a prominent place in the civic pedagogy of the National Assembly.

How do these anonymous martyrs come before the deputies? Some are in the care of the Minister of War, who presents them himself to the Assembly; that is the case with Beurnonville, who introduces the young Lavigne. Bouchotte also will have his protégés, like Bedel, dragoon of the thirteenth regiment "who was struck with seven blows of the saber." [43] Others are presented to the National Assembly by the Parisian local committees [sections], witnesses of their patriotism. On 17 December 1792, Gonchon, orator of the deputation of the section of the Quinze-Vingts, introduces a soldier whose arms are in a sling: "Long ago, courtiers and their wives presented for the curiosity of kings men whom the crimes of their fathers had ennobled; today the sansculottes of the faubourgs present to the representatives of the Republic one of the heroes of the battle of Jemmapes: Jean-Jacques-Louis Vien. There he is [he points him out; lively applause]. He received seven wounds, and all in the front of the body [repeated applause]."[44]

Another case, just as telling, is that of the young Pajot, fifteen and a half, seriously wounded by a bullet in the leg, who appears at the bar with his drum in the middle of the deputation of the *section* of sansculottes: "There he is, legislators, this nascent and perfect model of valor and generosity; there he is, as the Austrians saw him; you see him in his battle clothes; he would be marred if he had any adornments other than his wounds."[45] Sometimes administrative organizations and institutions present their wounded, directories of departments, tribunals, or even, more often, deputations from the Invalides. One such deputation, on 24 February 1793, at the same time that it transmits a patriotic gift of 6,251 livres, introduces two wounded soldiers: Denis Bosquet, blinded, his face "wrapped in bandages," and Jean-Jacques Juffre, both arms blown off by a cannonball.[46] But most of these martyrs come on their own initiative, motivated no doubt by patriotism but even more certainly by their need for help. They are then taken care of by the Committee of Public Help, which draws a few examples from among the most edifying cases to offer to this continual ceremony of wounds.

All these wounded are pensioned by the state.[47] Charles-Albert Pottier, in the name of the Committee of Public Help, presents for instance the blind captain Nicolas Passepont in these words: "He was fighting with dedication, when he was wounded in the head in May 1792, by an enemy bullet that hit the sinus. He lost the left eye and the right was badly injured . . . On 10 August following, though a patient at the Invalides, he nevertheless drags himself to the Carrousel, hurls himself in the midst of the Sans-Culottes, does combat and flies with them to victory; but a rifle shot deprives him of his right eye, and he remains blind and stricken with deafness."[48] Passepont obtains a pension of three thousand livres. The Republic takes charge of its wounded, and the men who sacrificed themselves receive equitable recompense in the name of their wounds: they are pensioned *and* martyrs, taken care of by the state *and* presented before the Assembly. The Republic shows its wounded body along with its generosity.

In a long report on the retirement pensions to be granted to wounded soldiers, presented on 6 June 1793, Pottier specifies the function of these numerous presentations: "Every day we have before our eyes these exhibitions of pain, and we tremble because of them. At each step we meet citizens clothed again in the national uniform, whose artificial legs and bandaged and paralyzed arms summon our attention; often we have seen in the heart of the Assembly brave soldiers exhibiting to us their honorable wounds, because for them they are acts of glory; they do not deplore their condition except because they have no other arms to offer to the Republic. Who could recall without the tenderest emotion the scene of pity that the presence in our midst of the young Lavigne, deprived of both his arms because of murderous shots, caused to arise? The tears that flowed from his eyes while he received the civic crown so justly deserved, those tears became the tears of each one of us . . . The presence of battalions marching to the frontiers, and taking their oath before the nation and before that admirable wounded man, to die or to return triumphant, reinforced even more our sublime sentiments." [49]

Another question is posed to these martyrs: how should they express themselves? In general, discretion and modesty rule during these ceremonies. The wounded, their injuries carefully bandaged, speak little: the orators take it upon themselves to express suffering and glory. Wounds, however, remain quite present to the minds of the deputies, and the discourse is always constructed in reference to them: "You received 26 wounds on the head and arms, the country has counted them. The National Convention has contemplated with tenderness a Republican having all his veins cut yet always preserving fortitude, an unchangeable courage, and the sentiment of liberty," declares the president to the Citizen Rouvert on 1 Prairial Year II. Sometimes the wounded themselves take the stand, always to express loyalty to the patriotic cause: great shivers of emotion travel through the hall. On 25 Floréal Year II, a soldier presents to the bar his battle comrade, seriously wounded: "Citizen Fort had his upper jaw, the bones of his nose, the globes of his eyes, and part of the frontal bone forming the sockets, blown off by a single blast of the cannon." The volunteer Fort, horribly disfigured, then takes the stand. He hesitates ["the liveliest emotion reigns in the Assembly," notes *Le Moniteur*]: "I request . . . the honorable testimony of your satisfaction in favor of the generous citizen . . . who has been a second father to me, and who has led me to your bar." [50] The hall resounds with the most enthusiastic applause, and Carnot, then president of the Assembly, answers him: "Citizen, your presence and your aspect excite the liveliest emotions in the breast of the representatives of the people. None of us would refuse glory at the price that it cost you. It is not in vain that blood has run for the Republic." The action of these two citizens, like so many acts to which the wounded testify, will then be inserted into the "Republican annals" by the Committee of Public Instruction: their stories will be included in the *Collection of the Heroic Deeds of the French Republicans* edited by Bourdon and Thibaudeau.

Who are these glorious wounded? Most, it seems obvious in the military presentation of events, are soldiers returning from the front. The wounds here accuse the foreign enemy, principally the Austrians, then the English, whose baleful presence they imagine behind every belligerent event. Another type is a different kind of military victim: the ones who come back from *départements* in rebellion—from the west, bringing back on their bodies the testimony of the "atrocities of the rebels of the Vendée," or from the southeast, carrying back, engraved in their flesh, the proof of the "vices of Federalism." The last sort of case forms a far from negligible group: the civilian victims of the "aristocratic conspiracy" that afflicts the simple citizens in the interior of the Republic. Thus on 16 August, there is a procession of Parisians burned in the face and arms during the assault of the Tuileries; on 10 Messidor Year II, the savior of Collot d'Herbois presents himself, the "brave locksmith Geffroy," whose medical bulletin is read daily before the deputies as a symbol of sacrifice to the nation. Martyrs, coming from various horizons, thus effectively recall the two conspiracies that threaten the Republic: external danger and internal danger. The wounded body designates all enemies; it speaks the universal, but very precise, language of sacrifice and revenge.

The last question is no less pressing: what are the criteria according to which these wounded are chosen for presentation? We can determine the criteria by examining the characteristics of the martyrs actually designated by authority (minister, Committee of the Assembly) or by a political group (committee, club). These wounded are, in general, "traps for emotions," because they are very young (from thirteen to eighteen years old) or old veterans; or especially because they are damaged in some spectacular way (blind, disfigured, amputated); finally, because they come with a moral, a legend, an edifying anecdote. The sacrifice must be, in some way, clearly legible on the wounded body. These phenomena can be combined, and the greatest moments of emotion that the Legislative Assembly and the Convention felt when faced with the wounded bodies of its children were those occasions when young amputees or cruelly mutilated old soldiers were presented.

Certain cases are thus particularly revealing of this pathetic inflation, whereby the number of wounds received is equivalent to the moral and civic worth of the martyr. Jean-Thibault Gechter, from the Scevola *section*, an adolescent whose hands had been amputated from the right wrist and from the left forearm, was "accompanied by all the tears" of the deputies when he stepped up to the president to receive his civic crown after having said, "What saddens me is that I can no longer fight the enemies of my country."[51]

The emotional charge depends on the very form of the wounded body and on the appropriateness of this appearance with the discourse that the martyr sustains. In this respect, two presentations seem quite exemplary. First, the grenadier Pie, the first true martyr of this type, whom the Legislative Assembly does not see but whose detailed narrative of sacrifices it hears in May 1792. One month after the beginning of the hostilities, following the first failures at the frontiers, and the first rebellions, the Assembly looks for a "great example to offer to the army" to calm lack of discipline. The cult of the martyrs is, most often, a discourse of order, given impetus from above by a power seeking to avert any unrest among the populace. The occasion presents itself on 11 May 1792, with Pie, the "brave grenadier of the seventy-fourth regiment": "Hear his sublime groans and the accent of despair and of honor. This grenadier, seriously wounded, calls for the Adjutant-General Beauharnais, and tells him: 'General, finish me off, so I don't see the shame of this day of defeat. You see that I die beside my rifle; my only regret is that I can't carry it any longer.' [Repeated applause]."[52]

The celebration of suffering is here put to the service of respect for military discipline, and integrates itself perfectly into the political context of May 1792. The grenadier Pie, saved from death, is honored by the Assembly. On his hospital bed he is presented with a "civic saber" delivered by Marshal Rochambeau and Marshal Luckner. For a time he becomes the national example of public-spiritedness, receiving an abundance of patriotic gifts, among them a cane with a golden grip "for his recovery" and a gold medal awarded by the Society of Friends of the Constitution. An engraver will even offer the Assembly six portraits of the brave Pie "whose courage and suffering cannot be forgotten."

Another "brave of the brave" whose wounded body was celebrated, a striking illustration of a certain pathetic excess, is Bertèche. Fighting at

Jemmapes, he received 41 saber cuts and one pistol shot, all numbered and bandaged. His eulogy is given by Marie-Joseph Chénier in the name of the committees of Public Instruction and of War, on 5 March 1793. "Citizens," begins the deputy, "it seemed difficult that among all the conquerors of Jemmapes, in the midst of that multitude of intrepid men who sealed with their blood the liberty of France and the conquest of Belgium, one could find one citizen placed in such a position that the gazes of the National Convention were naturally fixed on him. Bertèche is this man. Lieutenant for fourteen years in the French army, at this memorable battle, at the peril of his life, he saves a man, a French citizen, a general. . . . After having received 41 saber cuts, he escapes an almost certain death. You have seen him among you, citizens, you have counted his wounds; you have been touched; and the patriotic enthusiasm with which he has penetrated your souls has poured a salutary balm on his wounds. Let him present himself again at the bar of the Convention . . . let him show again his forty wounds to your eyes; let the crown of oak, the prize for public-spiritedness and courage, be placed by the president of the National Convention on that head covered with scars. Since he was attacked so many times by the enemy saber, let the national saber be placed in his hands, and, armed with this sacred sword, let him plunge again into the midst of the ranks of our adversaries . . . that the name of the French Republic engraved on the saber's blade gleam in the tumult of battle, to inflame and rally our warriors. Have no doubt, representatives of France, it is by such means that a nation of heroes is made." [53]

These exhibitions of wounded bodies are not restricted to the National Assembly alone. Just as simulacra spread the image of the bodies of martyrs for liberty, there is a genuine dissemination of bodies of the unknown wounded in all the levels of revolutionary political society. Images represent the great martyr, but the bodies of the wounded walk among us. Follow the soldier Duplessis: wounded at Sierck by "sixty enemy fusiliers waiting only for his death," he is honored by the *section* of 10-Août, which hands over to him a saber of honor and plants a tree of liberty bearing his name in homage; he is then presented to the Convention by a deputation of the *section* on 21 March 1793; then marches "in full view" in the procession of the festival of Regeneration on 10 August 1793. At each stage of the route, his wounds are honored, counted, and commented on, vectors of political discourse.

Popular clubs and societies sometimes welcome martyrs, as on 20 January 1793 at the Jacobins Club, where Berruyer, the "oldest soldier of the Republic present at the meeting," introduces a young wounded man "to the gaze of society, and to tender sentiments, offering a child who lost an arm at the siege of Lille."[54] However, it is above all civic festivals that, with a steady need for expressiveness, demand the wounded. Often these wounded march in a special corps associated with the most illustrious martyrs, as in the procession of Chalier's ceremony, in which the "defenders of the country wounded in combat" carry a banner with this inscription: "Like Chalier, we offered to give our life,"[55] or, later on, in the course of a festival in honor of Lepeletier and Marat in Nantes, which Carrier describes in a letter to the Convention: "Opening the march, the veterans and wounded carry on stretchers the busts of Lepeletier and Marat."[56] In another example, the procession of the festival of 30 Nivôse Year II in Fréjus in honor of Marat, Lepeletier, Chalier, and the Toulon martyrs, we can make out a young drummer, his hand lost in battle, accompanied by a sign: "I still have another one to beat back attackers," beside a wounded lieutenant-colonel of the hussars, with a banner bearing these words: "I would rather die than see the impure hand of an émigré bandage my wounds." Finally, in the same procession, we see the brave Bertèche, the hero singled out by Marie-Joseph Chénier at the Convention, proudly displaying his national saber and showing his scars. Bertèche becomes a striking symbol of this "circulation" of wounded bodies, used at all levels of political society as effective vectors of propaganda.[57]

The ceremony of wounds takes place in a very particular political context. Its message is that of an organized appeal for revenge: in the name of the wounded body, citizens demand "terrible measures" to struggle against the "aristocratic conspiracy." These measures are to be granted by the power that focused political discourse on the wounds of the Republican body, that caused the desire for vengeance to be born, and that appropriated it in the name of that body, trying to purge from public life the sudden and spontaneous revenges of popular massacres. The wound thus becomes, almost naturally, a vector of discourse during the Terror. This is a "psychopathological" explanation of the Terror that can be elaborated through this approach of numerous exhibitions of wounded bodies. I would like to illustrate this idea by focusing on the genesis of the great law of the Terror of Prairial Year II.

Georges Lefebvre[58] has described the tensions that surrounded the issu-

ing of the orders for the Reign of Terror and the adoption of the law of 22
Prairial, "terribly" enlarging the meaning of suspects and accelerating the
judicial procedure of the revolutionary tribunal. And Mona Ozouf[59] has
emphasized that this law is not the strict reflection of the political and military context, since the Prairial laws do not trace exactly the severity of the
punishment on the dangers threatening the republic: external pressures
have in fact lessened, and French armies are victorious at the frontiers. The
Terror is no longer a reflection of the "conjuncture," but is conditioned by
the more diffuse and obsessive fear of conspiracy from within.

This fear of conspiracy, this fear that is so dreaded *and* so desired,
is supported precisely by the ceremonial of the wounded body, which is
quickly arranged around the martyr Geffroy, the "brave locksmith." On
the night of 3 to 4 Prairial, he thrust himself in front of the murderer during L'Admirat's assassination attempt on Collot d'Herbois.[60] The spectacle
of the wound calls for new measures of terror, as if, by a phenomenon of
self-persuasion in the face of the wounds of the Republic, the Convention
let the legal revenge demanded by the martyred body get inflated out of all
proportion. On the morning of 4 Prairial, the assassination attempt is announced at the Convention: "The aristocrats feel that they will never conquer us, so they want to assassinate the national representation,"[61] cries the
president, while a letter from the Lepeletier *section* promotes Geffroy, one
of its members, to the rank of martyr for the Republic, citing the "moving
display of courage" in that citizen, who, after having intervened, wounded
with a bullet, between the assassin and the victim, nevertheless seized the
murderer and had him arrested.

This letter serves as "tale of the wound." It is applauded by the deputies
on 4 Prairial, then recalled to mind by the *sections* that parade before the
Convention on the following days to announce their indignation at the assassination attempt and their admiration for the body that, literally, placed
itself *between* conspiracy and the state, thus marvelously embodying the
organic metaphor of the great citizen body. The ceremony of wounds is
thus launched again, calling for the discourse on the state's need for intran-
sigence and revenge. The exhibition of the wound, "a very serious wound"
specifies Barère, takes place in the Assembly moved by the means of Geffroy's medical bulletin, read daily before the representatives who insist on
rising in homage: "The National Convention wishes . . . to be informed
of the condition of the wounds of this good citizen. There was a period of

degradation and shame in the Constituent Assembly, when insigificant and revolting bulletins about the health of a faithless king were read in the presence of the citizens. Well, we will make a civic expiation by reading in the midst of the National Convention, in the presence of the people, the bulletin on the condition of the wounds of a citizen who has devoted himself to the country. . . . A curse on those cold souls that do not feel the value of such arrangements in a decree! They are neither citizens, nor children of the Republic!" The reference to the royal illness of March 1791 is not ingenuous: the Convention, through the voice of Barère, is anxious to give itself a supreme martyr, a simple citizen who sacrificed himself to protect the body of the representatives. All this is accompanied by direct threats against the internal enemy: the person who refuses to see this martyred body is "neither a citizen, nor a child of the Republic." Anyone blind to the sufferings of the Republican body is suspect.

The deputies listen religiously for almost three weeks, an essential period in the decision to reactivate the laws of the Terror, and then unanimously applaud the readings that two doctors perform of Geffroy's bulletin of health. From 5 Prairial ("The initial fever was high all day yesterday, but the two blood-lettings calmed it and elicited a good sweating that kept up all night; the urines are good; there was no sleep") to 26 Prairial ("The state of the wounds making rapid progress for the better, suppuration and other symptoms continuing favorable, we will not give the bulletin until the day after tomorrow"), 22 daily bulletins keep the deputies very precisely up to date on all the "swellings," "blood-lettings," "suppurations," "oozings," "pricklings," "falling off of scabs," and various "hemorrhages."

Then, in the name of this wound so much described, the *sections* launch their calls for revenge: "The death of Lepeletier gave a wholesome impetus to the cause of liberty. The death of Marat made a great stride toward equality. May this new crime not be wasted. May it serve to affirm and complete our great Revolution. Turn against their own perfidies our enemies; may our national vigilance become stricter as our enemies become crueler. From now on, may a great terror turn against the authors of these crimes,"[62] proclaims the orator of the Brutus *section* to the sound of the drum.

Calls for ultimate revenge are taken up by the principal Montagnard deputies, haunted as they are by the "assassination that is still on all lips." On 5 Prairial, Cécile Regnault's murder attempt against Robespierre is announced to the Assembly. Robespierre becomes the first, in a context of tragedy, to prophesy his coming death under the dagger blows: "Calumnies, treasons, fires, poisonings, atheism, corruption, famine, assassinations, have all lavished their crimes; there still remain assassination, and then assassination, and then again assassination. In saying these things, I sharpen daggers against me, and it is for that very reason that I say it. . . . When we have fallen under their blows, you will have to finish your sublime enterprise, or else share our fate."[63]

In this climate of extreme tension the great Terror law of 22 Prairial is passed. The climate of the Terror—turmoil, violent emotions tinged with panic, calls for justice—is well illustrated by the arrival, this time in person, of the martyr Geffroy at the Convention on 10 Messidor Year II. Presented by his *section*, Geffroy comes in together with his family and his doctors, to the "redoubled applause" of the deputies. "The villains are at the scaffold, Geffroy is saved. . . . The most festering wounds will heal, the people will be strong, vigorous and invincible, while traitors will be forced to rot,"[64] Collot declares, triumphant. It is in the name of its own wounds that the Republic demanded and obtained the Reign of Terror, just as, ten months before, the wounded body of Marat had sublimated and conveyed the radical demands of the Parisian *sections*.

The story of the wounded body of the Republic is a drama, played by revolutionaries themselves, renewed perpetually and every day, a tragedy on the theme of the glory of a fragile, wounded body that nevertheless transforms its pain into a merciless strength. So the wounded body of the martyr, exposed to the eyes of all between 1792 and 1794, possesses two appearances. In the first, it embodies the *unbearable contemplation*; it manifests as a macabre, frightful horror that everyone must look upon. In the second, it takes the form of *glory*, it shines as the ideal to which the hero-martyr has consecrated his sacrifice, and that everyone must imitate. The complementarity of these two figures of the wounded body is inscribed in a supreme political ceremony: illustrating suffering and pain, emphasizing tragic glory, the martyr and his body point out the guilty and cry out for revenge. The presentation of the wounded body, of the mutilated corpse, is thus a way of creating fear, a visualization of the "terrifying" that must endlessly put the Republic in danger so that it can better defend itself. But unlike Christian tradition, in which the body remains despised, the corpse also takes on the appearance of glory: the wounds are the sign of patriotism. For that very reason, they become political discourse: the Republic recognizes itself in this body and stands united in the language of vengeful terror. The two appearances of the Republican body, the appalling wounded and the glorious wounded, are like the existential affirmation of the Terrorist state: the wound becomes a "summons to exist," and those who refuse to see it are threatened with disappearance.

A Few Bodies to End
(the Revolution)

The organicist image forged by Emmanuel Sieyès of the great sovereign citizen body did not survive the event of the Revolution without some difficulty. First of the Jacobins, Sieyès had conceived the citizen body to rival the traditional royal body: joined into one single national body without any division into orders of society, represented by a legislative organ comparable to the head of such a body, assigning the executive organ to a functionary monarch somewhat like the "arm of the Constitution," the French have found a sovereign organization. First of the liberals, Sieyès had not forgotten to set the principle of freedom in the very interior of this sovereign body. The concept of "adunation" in fact allowed the philosopher priest to conceive simultaneously the link (a single body) and the unlinking (the division of France into *départements*, for instance), the state (legislative centralization and the organization of the government) and civil society (the competition of individual desires). In like manner, the concept of "representation" regulated the all-powerful but also sudden and violent impulses of popular sovereignty: the giant forged by Sieyès had its strength softened, contained, and directed by the many intermediate levels of representative government. This balance was to be challenged by the Revolution itself a few years later.

The Terror, or The Club of Hercules

When he presents the report before the Convention on a mode of revolutionary government, Billaud-Varenne, on 28 Brumaire Year II, proposes a new organization of the state and of society: from now on the two are to be governed together, with the intention of regenerating both. Speaking in the name of the Committee of Public Safety, Billaud-Varenne describes this French body that is to be reformed. He says it is inherited from the monarchy, is "apathetic and in rags"; he thinks of it as an immense metaphor in which images of the organic come to balance and complete mechanical or vegetable registers: "Fix your eyes on all the parts of France, and everywhere you will see laws without vigor; you will see that many laws do not even reach the local governments, and that the remainder reaches them so late that often their purpose is diminished. You will see a general apathy among all government officials. In a word, you will be frightened. . . . We have decreed the Republic, and we are still organized as a monarchy. The head of the monster is defeated, but the trunk still survives with its defective forms. So many authorities who were the perennial vampires of liberty have lost nothing of their despotism, of their corrosive imposts, or of their all-consuming domination. With a king, they represented that giant of the fable, who, with a hundred vigorous arms, dared to invade the Empyrean. . . . The people, forgetting their vigor before coming to know it, has permitted their energy to rust. And that is the propitious moment for the colossal usurper who still knows very well how to base his power on the laziness and apathy of the citizen. Do not conceal it from yourselves: that is the danger that most imminently threatens the Republic."[1]

Billaud-Varenne thus introduces the regenerative task of the Committee of Public Safety. It is a matter of establishing a revolutionary government that will awaken the citizen populace from its apathy and will fight the royal monster with blazing intensity: "The French people will take up Hercules' posture. It was waiting for this robust government to strengthen all its parts, spread revolutionary vitality through its veins, immerse it in energy and complete its strength by the lightning of action. Laws, which are the soul of the national body, are immediately transmitted, and travel through it, circulating swiftly through all its veins, reaching from the heart to the extremities in an instant,"[2] writes the Committee of Public Safety to the national district agents on 10 Nivôse Year II, following Billaud's report.

Through this struggle of titans that is also an implacable rivalry between two organicist systems—Hercules faced with the royal monster—Billaud-Varenne outlines the corporeal metaphor that guides the "revolutionary government" in its organization of the Terror: to create a colossal body that can legitimately fight and succeed the monarchical giant.

This colossus, this "Hercules of the people," is the symbol of Republican France. Erected during the festival of regeneration of 10 August 1793, represented by numerous artists of the Terror, Hercules seems on the way to making himself known.[3] The engraver Dupré contemplates representing him on the new seal of the nation, and David had proposed, ten days before Billaud-Varenne's speech, to consecrate a colossal sculpture to him erected atop the rubble of the statues of the kings torn off Notre-Dame. From this gallery of the kings of the Bible and of France formed into an incoherent heap, "truncated allegorical debris," David makes the pedestal of an immense body, with the values of the new people inscribed on it.

The speech that David delivers on this subject before the deputies of the Convention, on 17 Brumaire Year II, is a version of the terrible embodiment dreamed of by Billaud-Varenne: "Kings, not being able entirely to usurp the place of divinity in the temples, occupied the porticoes; they had their proud effigies placed there, no doubt so that the adoration of the people would linger with them before reaching the sanctuary. Accustomed to invading everything, they dared to dispute vows and incense with God Himself. You have turned upside down these insolent usurpers; they lie at this instant stretched out on the earth that they befouled with their crimes, objects of derision now to the populace finally cured of long superstition. Citizens, let us perpetuate this triumph of reason over prejudice; let a monument be raised in the heart of the commune of Paris, not far from that very church they made their pantheon! Let us transmit to our descendants the first trophy raised by the sovereign people to mark its immortal victory over the tyrants; may the truncated debris of their faces, confusedly heaped together, form a lasting monument to the glory of the people, and to the downfall of tyrants. May the traveler who journeys through this new land, reporting lessons useful to the people in his own country, say: 'In Paris I had seen kings, objects of a degrading idolatry: I went there again, and they were no longer there.' What I propose is to place this monument, assembled from the piled-up rubble of those figures, on the square of Pont-Neuf, and to mount above it the image of the giant people, of the French people. May this image, so imposing in its strength and simplicity, bear written in large letters on its forehead, 'light'; on its chest, 'nature and truth'; on its arms, 'strength'; on its hands, 'work.' On one of its hands, may the figures of Liberty and Equality, clasping each other, and ready to pass through the whole world, show to all that they rest exclusively on the genius and virtue of the people. May this image of the people upright hold in its other hand that terrible and genuine club, of which Hercules' old one was just the symbol." [4]

Sieyès too had evoked this gigantic image in his writings after 1789, but his body was made of a multitude of little individual and sometimes contradictory wills, and the great whole was the intimate union of divisions, powerful but balanced, held up by a chain of intermediaries. The body dreamt of by Billaud and David, however, is absolutely transparent, held, under pain of inertia and death, by a single and unique will, animated by a single action from head to foot. According to the legislator, this body is the "nervous system and blood vessels by which the government communicates with the nation," the "enigmatic sign" conjured up by the painter thanks to a sublime vision of transparency—the value-words [mots-valeurs] inscribed right on the body. It is as if there were no room for a single instant of hesitation between order and action, between looking at the body and understanding it, between the vision and the regeneration of citizens, between the vision and the punishment of traitors.

Here is a body in fusion: "The best constitution," Billaud-Varenne proclaims, "is that which is closest to the processes of the natural body, which accommodates only three principles in its movements: the motive will, the entity that will brings to life, and the action of that body on the surrounding objects. Thus every good government should have a center of will, levers that are directly attached to it, and secondary bodies that these levers activate in order to extend movement in a lightning flash out to the last extremities of the national body. By this physical precision, action loses nothing of its force or its direction in a communication that is more rapid and better regulated. Everything that falls short of that becomes overgrown, parasitic, lacking vigor and unity. . . . A disastrous result is always to be feared if ever the organic complication of the government should relax the controlling sinew that, if it is to avail, must, without interruption and with a single common support, proceed from the center to connect with the periphery.

"It is an old mistake to believe that it becomes necessary in a vast state to double its strength by multiplying instruments of control. On the contrary, it has been demonstrated that, since each level brings it to a stop, the initial impetus decreases in proportion to the number of stations that it meets in its journey. . . . It is time to return the body politic to robust health through dispensing with gangrenous limbs. Note that everything around you is ob- structed, or engulfed by distance, since that time when in every region we cared more about ourselves than about our country. . . . That makes a dan- gerous alliance, since it inevitably produces the habit of ignoring the center of action. That is, limbs want to act without the direction of the head. That is how anarchy of laws is created, and how the political chaos is produced that provokes secessionist rifts and exhausts the whole of the body politic by movement that is either incomplete or that ceaselessly contradicts itself. Any legislation without compulsion is like those beautiful statues that seem lifelike even though they have no vital spark: it is a mechanism without a mainspring, a corpse deprived of nervous impulse. . . . We want to shape with the reformer's hand a government completely organized and formed according to the true laws of bodily motion: will, impetus, and action. . . . It is thus that all your decrees, all your laws in the future will have no other effect but vivifying general prosperity, preserving all the strength of the Convention, and in a word: giving energy to the great body politic."

This absolute fusion, a distinct refutation of the theory of "intermediary controls" so dear to Sieyès, is the very condition of a transparent corporeal organization: a legislating committee at the head or heart of the Republic, a taut sinew that propagates each decision toward the circumference, and citizen hands that immediately materialize the action. This transparency must confer an absolute efficiency on the government but, at the same time, strike terrible blows, using the fearful club of Hercules, on all the obstacles, "overgrowths," and "parasites," the intermediaries thought of as cells for- eign to the national body. Quickness of execution implies that the state and society are integral parts of the same and unique body, as well as an aboli- tion of individual fate in the common will, a sacrifice of all the pullulating lives of the multitude to the perfect corporation. Where Sieyès could still distinguish two separate corporeal entities—the body of citizens and the body of deputies—connected to each other by an indirect and contradic- tory representation (the primary assemblies and the "shock of opinions"), Billaud dreams of total fusion, and David sculpts it: all citizens, without exception, are directly incorporated into the "image of the giant people"; they read the words inscribed on the colossus without an intermediary, and live in and by its laws.

The experiment of the Terror, a political arrangement calqued on the corporeal metaphor of Billaud-Varenne, quickly leads the French colossus to an impasse, however: it is no longer apathy or anarchy that are frightening in the eyes of the deputies, it is the sacrifices demanded to feed the energy of the great national body. The colossus could no longer function without making a void in its own body, endlessly struggling against those parts of itself, more and more numerous, that it judged excessive or parasitic. The fusion so ardently wished for threatened to turn into fragmentation and dispersal of the organs—indeed to anthropophagy, as *Bitter Forms* [*Les Formes acerbes*], the most famous of the Thermidor engravings, illustrates: the "giant of the Terror" collects the blood of the decomposed bodies of the torture victims, a blood that he guzzles ecstatically. (See Figure 17.) After Thermidor, once again the insistent question is asked: what corporeal metaphor ought to be proposed for the legislators and their political organization? What symbol should be offered to painters and sculptors to represent the embodiment of citizen sovereignty?

Leaving the Terror: Can the French Colossus Be Pacified?

Physicians are the first to try to answer these questions. A controversy agitates the scientific community about the true relationship of the human body to the decisive and symbolic instrument of the Terror, the guillotine.[5] On 20 May 1795, Dr. Soemmering, a scholar of international repute, writes from Frankfurt to his friend and colleague Œlsner, who transmits the letter to the *Encyclopedic Magazine* [*Magasin encyclopédique*]: "They do not seem to have reflected on the suffering of sensation that still continues in the head after execution by guillotine, or to have calculated the duration of this state, or done anything to shorten it. It is however easy to demonstrate to anyone who possesses even a slight knowledge of the composition of the vital forces of our body, that feeling is not completely destroyed by this execution. What we advance is founded, not on suppositions or hypotheses, but on facts."[6] Less than a year after the end of the Reign of Terror, a doctor reviews a tragedy that leaves "haunting memories," and questions the role assigned to the guillotine as the "surest, quickest, and least painful" form of death, the "gentle execution" that followed as close as possible the three principles of ideal temporal sequence dreamt of by Billaud-Varenne: decision, impetus, and action all grouped together in a single, almost imperceptible, but all-powerful instant.

Dr. Soemmering offers a demonstration in three points. First: the seat of feeling and its "apperception" is established in the brain alone, the organ immediately adjacent to the "neck of the executed victims." Second: the operations of the awareness of feelings can occur "even if the circulation of the blood through the brain is suspended, or weak, or partial." Finally: the point of impact of the blade causes a great pain, for "the guillotine strikes on that part of our body that is the most sensitive to pain, because of the nerves that spread from and join together there." Soemmering's conclusion falls with the same resolution as the blade: "In the head, separated from the body by the torture of the guillotine, the ego remains alive for some time and feels the after-pain that the neck suffers."

A few weeks later, Jean-Joseph Sue, professor of medicine in Paris, known and respected for his experiments on the nervous system, takes up Soemmering's thesis and turns it into a nationwide controversy.[7] Sue explains the pain of the victim by the existence in the human body of "two characteristics of sensitivity": that which perceives sensation in the actual place where one suffers and that which, in the brain, comprises the awareness of this sensation. Thus, according to Sue, a guillotined person suffers twice: the back of the neck feels the sensation of pain while the brain possesses the awareness of this pain. He summarizes his position in these horrifying sentences: "The more swiftness and precision the murdering action has, the longer those who are exposed to it keep the awareness of the frightful torment that they experience: the local pain, it is true, is less long, but the recognition of torture has a longer duration, since, with the rapidity of lightning, the impression of pain warns the center of thought about what is happening." What more horrible situation than that of having the perception of one's execution and then, after that, the afterthought of one's agony?

The key to this exposition is a "localist" philosophy of the human body, a belief in the notion of "concentration of energy" in certain particularly sensitive organs: "In man, several different kinds of lives are gathered together, yet joined in a wonderful way to form only one single whole. These kinds of lives can be reduced to three: the moral life, intellectual life, and animal life. Each species of vital force has a particular seat in the human body where it typically manifests itself; thus we can place intellectual life in the head, and the eye as its focus; moral life in the chest, and the heart as its center; and animal life, which is a kind of vegetation, extends to the organs of reproduction, which then must be considered as the focus or center of that life. . . . We can summarize then that intellectual life is the sanctuary of the soul: for it is from the soul that the lightning of thought shoots. Moral life is the center of feeling: from it all the emotions are born. Animal life is the seat from which all automatic movements come. According to this distinction, it is easy to observe that intellectual life can be separated for some time by the decapitation of moral life, and still enjoy its action. The two other lives can likewise be isolated from each other, and keep their effects for some minutes." Leading this localist logic to its end, Sue tries to demonstrate that each "center of vitality" can have, after a separation from the organic whole, its own distinct life and movement.

These positions swiftly elicit energetic response from the scholarly community. First, two Parisian doctors, Lepelletier and Wedekind, are thoroughly amazed "in the name of Republican science" in the pages of the *Moniteur*,[8] and, on 7 Frimaire Year IV, Sédillot junior, doctor of medicine, utters, before the Republican Directory of the Lycée des Arts in Paris, a violent indictment against Soemmering and Sue, whose "purely metaphysical ideas" are nothing but "the fruit of imagination."[9] More calmly, he tries to demonstrate that "the faculty of thought, like that of feeling, is suddenly extinguished at the time of decapitation." For Sédillot, the vital functions share "relationships so direct and of such a connectedness that one cannot be damaged, suspended, or annihilated, without instantly causing the damage, suspension, and annihilation of the others." If some movements or grimaces are seen in a head decapitated by execution, there is no suffering or even awareness, just "automatic irritability." For the victim is dead, struck down, "already at that perhaps incalculable instant when the falling knife strikes the medulla oblongata before cutting it."

What Sédillot advances here is a "totalist" conception of the division of life in the human body: "We will not approach that famous question, What is the seat of the soul? We will place it neither in the pineal gland, which is often just a stone, nor in the corpus callosum that can sustain major lesions without harm, nor in any point of the brain or cerebellum, from which considerable portions can be removed without causing death and that are sometimes entirely lacking, nor in the spinal marrow, nor in the cardiac plexus, nor in the pylorus, nor even in the medulla oblongata, even though injuries to it are always fatal. It seems to us reasonable to think that the soul or life exists and is spread throughout the entire machine like the matter of fire, and is the combined result of the vital organs in their state of integrity."

Sédillot is immediately supported by other doctors, both unknown, like René Georges Gatsellier,[10] who denounces the "paralogisms of Citizen Sue," and famous, like Cabanis.[11] The intervention of Mirabeau's former

doctor, soon to be a deputy at the Council of the Five Hundred, is important: it closes the debate, awards the victory to the "totalist" or "globalist"
concept, and ends up politicizing the controversy. For even if the controversy is specifically scientific, the visions of the body lead to very different political philosophies. The papers, too, quickly seized hold of it. Like
their old Spanish colleagues, the French doctors of the end of the eighteenth century allow themselves a few crossings-over between science and
politics: "I know too well," begins Cabanis, the Republican doctor, "with
what ease marvels are seen in times of agitation and misfortune. When the
public intelligence no longer allows us to see miracles, we at least want to
find new phenomena in nature." Then the doctor, after having countered
Soemmering's metaphysics, which "locates sentience in the brain alone,"
concentrates his attacks on the localist theses of Sue, who "proposes to iso-
late a center of energy in each major organ."

Why discuss this debate at such length? Because this argument, in its
specialist jargon, is an important political battle. How can we fail to see,
in the choice of the brain as the seat of feeling with Soemmering, and in
the autonomization of centers of vitality with Sue, a metaphor for political
organization? Soemmering's brain is a king's head; Sue's centers of energy
along with the three "lives" that he distinguishes in the human body make
up a discourse of orders. Faced with this return of tradition, Cabanis defends both Republican regime and national sovereignty, embodied in one
single, unique body, all of whose organs are vitally linked. But this defense
nevertheless is concerned to propose a political organization freed of certain Jacobin demands. Conservative doctors, in fact, tried to give life back
to the old corporeal images of monarchical politics. The colossus of the
powerful national body, victorious as a result of those same organicist metaphors in 1789, then fell back to earth, knocked down by the excesses of the
Terror, by the impossible total fusion demanded in a community rejecting
all elements foreign to it.

Cabanis wishes to raise up this colossus again, but without making it
terrible. He must, in some way, *civilize* it, sweeten its manners, train its gestures, limit its sovereignty, in order once again, following the example of
Sieyès in 1789, to try to impose it as the quintessential metaphor of the sovereignty of the people. Above all, it is a question of giving this colossus not
the desire to punish all traitors instantly, but to restrain its arm: to make
opaque that which was immediate fusion with Billaud-Varenne, to separate
more precisely in its body, even at the risk of a certain slowing down, the

function of governance from the function of activity, and to balance the impulses of the latter by the wise decisions of the former. To rid the national body in some way of the despotic characteristics it had borrowed from the old monarchy, that "absolute democracy" devouring its own excesses just as "absolute royalty" persecuted those who went against it. Sieyès analyzes this at the time with much lucidity: "The sovereignty of the people seemed so colossal to the imagination only because the mind of the French, still full of royal superstitions, made it its duty to endow it with all the inheritance of pompous attributes and absolute powers that once gave usurped sovereignties such luster. . . . They even seemed to say to themselves, with a kind of patriotic pride, that if the sovereignty of the great kings is so powerful, so terrible, then the sovereignty of a great people, an even more colossal body, ought to be even more imposing." [12]

In thus attacking royal despotism, Sieyès tries in fact to dissociate the metaphor of the citizen body from the terrible images that have accompanied it since the Terror. Dr. Cabanis, physician of the new medicine, defines himself explicitly as an emulator of Sieyès, physician of the social body. All the more so since the old priest is, for Cabanis, an illustrious respected contemporary and soon a partner in politics. Sieyès claimed that the 18 and 19 Brumaire Year VIII were the very soul of Bonaparte. Cabanis is an adherent of that coup d'état, and defends with conviction the Constitution that results from it, on 25 Frimaire, before the Constitutional commission of the Council of the Five Hundred. Several times in his speech Cabanis quotes Sieyès — more than even Bonaparte, which will soon enough succeed in irritating the general. Each time, the image of the great body of citizens returns, that colossus, the only organic foundation of sovereignty, the one that cracked open the revolutionary fracture and the one that, paradoxically, in Year VIII, once its "excited passions" are calmed, must heal it up again. With Cabanis, then, this great body is that of a "confident colossus," twin brother (but civilized and educated) of the giant Strong-arm of the 1789 fable, the giant who propagated the thinking of the philosopher priest Sieyès. The doctor openly expresses this derivation in his speech of 25 Frimaire Year VIII, when he proposes to join into one single whole both the sovereignty of the people and its own limits: "The colossal strength of the people animates all the parts of political organization. While its sovereignty, the true source, the unique source of all its powers, imprints on their various acts a solemn, sacred character, it lives tranquilly under the protection and conduct of the law. In a word, it enjoys all its strength, but also the sweet fruits of an actual liberty guaranteed by a government powerful enough to be always a protector."[13] What this government protects, quite obviously, is first of all the colossus of the people from their outbursts of passion.

Only this wise conduct can keep the good order and efficiency of the government, and allow the feared colossus to become once again an image of unity—not the sacrificial fusion required by Billaud-Varenne, but the receptacle of all the corporeal metaphors that have succeeded each other since the end of the ancien régime. Thus the colossus must welcome in itself, in a balanced and not absolutist manner, the virtues lauded by yesterday's adversaries. Cabanis says this on 3 Nivôse Year VIII, promising the fortunate conclusion of the revolutionary path: "A revolution is not truly ended until the traces of its various commotions, and even the names of the different parties, no longer exist: it is ended only when all those who have taken part in its successive movements, joined at last by the feelings common to them, now form only one single band of brothers, and swear, on the book of the new alliance, to forget their mistakes and their mutual resentments. The spirit of exclusion, agitation, and reaction is found in all the parties: yet from now on the Republic must no longer be prey to that. It must be, if I may say so, the domain, the refuge, the body of all the French. . . . Legislators, you have rid democracy of the agitations and disorder that have characterized it up to this day; you have borrowed from aristocracy all that it can offer that is useful for the emulation of virtues. You have even enriched your work with the only thing that was able to make the monarchy worthy of respect for such a long time: I mean the impetus, energy, and harmony of its movements. Finally, referring all the needs of the people to a small number of offices thanks to national representation, you organize a genuine representative system, while placing everywhere authorities who ceaselessly act for the people. You have done more: all the useful passions are stimulated, all the harmful passions are restrained. You have found the harmony of the social body while being inspired by the nature of the physical body: complete regeneration joins all the most varied organs into one identical and harmonious physiognomy, just as you make all Frenchmen, torn asunder for more than a decade between rival factions, taste the fraternity of the beautiful name of Republicans."[14]

The colossus born of the metaphorical diffusion of the principles made clear by Sieyès in 1789 has arrived at the end of its journey. From now on, purged of the passions engendered by too sudden and too demanding

a growth, restored to order and to the reasoned knowledge of its old excesses, rid of any wish to regulate the private lives of all the members of
civil society, the body should be happy, modest, and supremely aware of
its own limits. As Cabanis says, everywhere the authority of the government acts for the colossus of the people; it is a way of providing this great
convalescent body with the guardians who can keep it civil and restrained,
educated according to the codes of propriety. It remains to be seen if the
body of the colossus, by dint of being "restrained," of having aristocratic
"virtues," monarchic "energy," and republican "vigor" all integrated into
it, and through the perfection of the harmony that governs its organs and
limits its urges, has not lost the simple vigor of its origins.

The Body of Liberty: Prophecy of a Completed Revolution

It seems that the Revolution did not really want to choose between the
terrible organic images associated with the colossus of the Terror and the
polite education that Cabanis and Sieyès later propose for it. Or rather:
it found another corporeal representation. Not the Herculean body, but a
wiser image, of a woman. What in fact is the embodiment of the Revolution, of the Republic? The image of Liberty. It is she who, even today, best
"represents" that period in the minds of the French, while Hercules did
not have any true descendants in France, no doubt because his message
was mixed, drawn toward too many contradictory possibilities. Revolutionary discourse took over the old corporeal metaphor of the monarchy in
order to modify it profoundly: the body of the king has become a colossus
of the people. But in the course of this transfer, the Revolution killed this
image, at least for itself, lost in the excesses of the Terror. Rather than the
Herculean metaphor of a political system, the Revolution came to prefer
the easily controllable, reassuring representation of a principle: the gentle
figure of Liberty. It is no longer a question of lodging a government and an
entire nation in this body of Liberty, or of metaphorically dividing up the
functions and tasks of the different organs, but simply of seeing it, of recognizing it. The revolutionaries have gone from the position of members
of the great organic whole, attached to each other by ties of blood, actors
of the narrative-body [corps-récit] of their own adventure, to that of spectators of a value-body [corps-valeur] to be contemplated. The allegorization,
much more than the metaphorization, of the body of the Republic tells of
this upheaval from a point of view that is also a way of distancing passions,

of leaving behind the revolutionary event. How can the Republic best be symbolized in the majesty of its sovereign body while still respecting the tranquillity of appearance dreamt of by Cabanis? By taking up the classical body of positive traditional allegory while at the same time dressing it in symbols of the Revolution. This is the positive body whose typified portrait is easy to draw up from the iconological inheritance carefully respected by revolutionary artists and engravers:[15] a chastely clothed woman, standing at ease, facing the spectator, each hand holding an emblem. These are the symbols of the Revolution: the liberty cap, the pikestaff, and the bound fasces of the sovereignty of the people. Thus, the allegory of Liberty, as it is represented on the seal of the national archives proposed by Camus on 22 September 1792, becomes the actual value-body of the Republic, replacing the problematic colossus, the ambiguous Hercules: "I ask the Convention to decree that the seal of the Archives be changed, and henceforth bear as a model a standing woman leaning with one hand on a fasces, holding in the other hand a spear surmounted by a liberty cap, with these words as the legend: 'Archives of the French Republic.' "

In fact, the revolutionary imagery so often linked with the cliché of the naked and disheveled allegory leading men into battle is a myth. The French Revolution prefers, on the contrary, to entrust its virtues to prudent goddesses. The immense majority of naked women running in the wind in the allegorical engravings of the era are connected with vice; they look more toward fury than toward sublime enthusiasm. Allegory must no longer tell of a tormented history, like the colossus of the people born in 1789 and handled roughly by all the political systems, but must offer instead a representation of poise and serenity that can be recognized and loved. The same Revolution that in 1789 describes itself as ceaselessly threatened, first by inner conspiracy and then by foreign armies, that regularly welcomes to the bar of the National Assembly discourse about struggle to the death against united kings and émigrés, now chooses, after some hesitations, an official representation that shows the opposite of this discourse. The representation emphasizes the yearning for security, the dream of a Revolution finally at peace, unchanging, having arrived at its state of serenity; words, on the other hand, while not neglecting that register of assurance, must still and always serve as supports of conflict and as arguments in struggle. The revolutionary engraving is precisely dual: the illustration of conflicts returns to the political cartoon, while to allegory returns the power to calm them, or at least to keep them quiet. Political allegory, then, is allied most often to the prophecy of a completed revolution. It is allegory, much more than the colossus, that ends up supporting that dignified, polite body that Cabanis had proposed as a final image for the story of the Revolution.

Where can this prophecy best be read? I have chosen a corpus that will conclude this interdisciplinary book: the engraved letterheads of the official letters of the first French Republic,[16] totaling almost four hundred emblems engraved on the stationery of the nation's administrators. Here we encounter a self-representation of the Republic in its most official character, and the stereotypes drawn from the emblems appear with much force, intended to distribute the representation of the Revolution to the whole network of the French administration, as well as to those it administers. The 383 human bodies appearing on these letterheads can be grouped into no more than 11 possible allegorical emblems. We can assess the quite intentional restriction of allegorical choice. Uniformity is pushed to its outcome: a regime is identified with the body of a value, the immediate and instantaneous embodiment of sovereignty. What David had proposed without success in the value-words inscribed on the body of Hercules, the allegory of letterheads makes evident: the transparency of the corporeal symbol to the political regime. This happens with all the more force since one single, unique figure, that of Liberty, comprises 90 percent of the personages illustrated. On the official papers of the Republic, from now on, nine allegories out of ten are of Liberty. Moreover, the body and gestures of this allegory are themselves made uniform. For all 348 Liberties counted, 3 positions are offered, which, from a certain point of view, still leaves some latitude in the choice: one unique seal was never imposed on the French administration under the Revolution. Almost two-thirds of the Liberties stem, however, from the classical representation of the seal of the Archives, that of a woman standing at ease, presented from the front, chastely clothed and obviously mature. It is also the simplest, most immediately recognizable figure. Pacification is decreed by the uniformity of bodies and gestures.

Alongside this ideal body, there are also Liberties on the march, striding, breast bared, hair flowing. They number 37, or 10 percent of the category we are studying. Small in number, but still steadily present, the "Liberty in movement" animates both the letters and the aspirations of one administrator out of ten, no doubt the most radical of them.

Finally, how can we interpret the presence, not at all negligible when all is said and done, of 80 seated Liberties, a little more than 20 percent of the corpus? It is difficult not to think that this shaping of an allegorical symbol of order, indeed of inertia, determinedly poised, often next to the tablets of the law, sometimes wearing the helmet of Minerva, is a normative counterpart to the overanimated figure of the Liberty of the radicals.

A stereotype of Liberty is thus imposed, with the wide distribution of the 1792 seal showing the serene woman of allegorical tradition, selected by the political determination to display the confidence of the Republican regime. But two Liberties, competing in body as well as in politics, appear at the margins: the tousled, precipitate, naked radical, carrying the flame of revenge, and the seated woman of the notables, presiding over the tablets of a perfected law, helmeted to defend a society closed to all movement.

The Revolution, through its official self-representation, in this way offers the nineteenth century three bodies of Liberty to match three conceptions of political sovereignty. The long history of the spread of "Republican sentiment" through the successes of its representation by the body of a woman will from now on sustain the embodiment fashioned by the first Republicans of France.[17] That is the legacy of the French Revolution: abandoning the terrible colossus to totalitarian regimes, it has raised up the body of a woman to tell of Liberty.

Reference Matter

Notes

Introduction

1. Serge Daney, *Devant la recrudescence des vols de sac à main*, Lyon: Editions Aléa, 1991, p. 122.

2. Paul Ricœur, *La Métaphore vive*, Paris: Le Seuil, 1975, p. 313 [translated as *The Rule of Metaphor: Multi-Disciplinary Studies of the Creation of Meaning in Language*].

3. Judith Schlanger, *Les Métaphores de l'organisme*, Paris: Vrin, 1971, pp. 42–45.

4. It is on the critical gaze directed at cinema that I will base my approach. This gaze has not, I think, been addressed with enough curiosity by researchers in the social sciences. In two texts, Eric Rohmer's "L'Hélice et l'Idée" [The helix and the idea] (on Hitchcock's *Vertigo*, *Cahiers du cinéma*, no. 93, March 1959) and "Le cercle brisé" [The broken circle] by Jean Douchet (on Lang's *Moonfleet*, *Cahiers du cinéma*, no. 107, May 1960), film criticism can offer a model for an approach to metaphoric representation. For Rohmer and Douchet, it is a question of extracting, starting from the vision of the film, an "organizing shape of the fiction" (the helical form with Hitchcock, the "broken circle" with Lang) that allows one to "interpret the work intimately." The helix accordingly would guide all Hitchcock esthetics and allow the critic to go back to the very "idea" of the film's auteur, back to the working outline of his artistic awareness. Similarly, the metaphor of the body politic, as it was converted from the "body of the king" into the "great citizen body," seems to me a "configuration" (from the Latin *figura*, "form") allowing one to grasp the very idea of the revolution, the transition from

royal sovereignty to national sovereignty. To represent these "forms of history," historians can perhaps sharpen their gazes, just as film critics try to discern a film's form of organization (its mise-en-scène). This history as "description of discursive forms" was proposed and discussed by A. Boureau, "Propositions for a Limited History of Mentalities" [Propositions pour une histoire restreinte des mentalités], *Annales E.S.C.*, November–December 1989, pp. 1491–1504.

5. On this concept of "representation": R. Chartier, "The World as Representation" [Le monde comme représentation], *Annales E.S.C.*, November–December 1989, pp. 1505–20; L. Hunt (ed.), *The New Cultural History*, Berkeley: University of California Press, 1989; A. Corbin, " 'The Vertigo of Proliferations': Panoramic Sketch of a History Without a Name" ['Le vertige des foisonnements.' Esquisse panoramique d'une histoire sans nom], *Revue d'histoire moderne et contemporaine*, January–March 1992, pp. 103–26.

6. Robert Darnton, *The Great Cat Massacre and Other Episodes in French Cultural History*, New York: Vintage Books, p. 5.

7. Hans Georg Gadamer, *Truth and Method*, Paris: Le Seuil, 1976, p. 183.

8. Antoine Compagnon, *La Seconde Main, ou le travail de la citation*, Paris: Le Seuil, 1979, pp. 42–43.

9. See M. de Certeau, "Reading: A Pilfering" [Lire: un braconnage], in *L'Invention du quotidien. 1. arts de faire*, Paris: Gallimard, 1990, pp. 239–55.

10. This "return to narrative" was initiated by L. Stone in an article that marked a breakthrough and was published in French as "Retour au récit ou réflexion sur une nouvelle vieille histoire," in *Le Débat*, no. 4, 1980, pp. 116–42. Aside from the reflections of M. de Certeau (*L'Ecriture de l'histoire*, Paris: Gallimard, 1975) and P. Ricœur (*Temps et récit*, Vol. 3, *Le Temps raconté*, Paris: Le Seuil, 1985), cf. the works of Hayden White on this subject, notably *The Content of the Form: Narrative Discourse and Historical Representation*, Baltimore: Johns Hopkins University Press, 1987; Natalie Z. Davis, *Fiction in the Archives*, Stanford: Stanford University Press, 1987; or Jacques Rancière, *Les mots de l'histoire. Essai de poétique du savoir*, Paris: Le Seuil, 1992. See too Peter Gay's essay, *Style in History*, New York: Norton Paperback, 1988 (the first edition was 1974), reprinted in the symposium *Fictions of the French Revolution* edited by B. Fort, Evanston: Northwestern University Press, 1991; and the issue of *Espaces/Temps* dedicated to "The Fabric of Social Sciences" [La fabrique des sciences sociales], no. 47/48, 1991.

11. Jean Starobinski, *L'Œil vivant*, Paris: Gallimard, 1961, pp. 24–28. In English: *The Living Eye*, trans. Arthur Goldhammer, Cambridge: Harvard University Press, 1989, p. 12.

12. Walter Benjamin, *The Origin of German Tragic Drama*, trans. John Osborne, London: NLB, 1977. The passages quoted are on pages 38, 43, and 56. [The first passage is in fact by Max Scheler; Benjamin is citing from Scheler's "On the Phe-

nomenon of the Tragic," from *Vom Umsturz der Werte*, Der Abhandlungen und Aufsätze 2., durchgs. Aufl., I, Leipzig: 1919, p. 241. Trans.]

Chapter 1

1. E. Raunié, *Chansonnier historique du XVIIIe siècle*, Vol. 8, Paris, 1884, pp. 205–6.

2. *Letter from the King to His Grace the Archbishop of Paris*, 19 December 1778. Bibliothèque Nationale: Inv 2,400 Paris, item 453.

3. *Journal de Louis XVI*, ed. L. Nicolardot, Paris, 1873, entry for the date 19 December 1778.

4. *Speech uttered in the parish church of Coueron*, 1 November 1778, on the occasion of the queen's pregnancy, Nantes. Bibliothèque Nationale: Lb39 6260.

5. *Speech uttered in the provinces on 12 June 1770 on the occasion of the wedding of His Royal Highness the Dauphin*, n.p. Bibliothèque Nationale: Lb39 109.

6. E. Raunié, *Chansonnier historique*, Vol. 9, pp. 17–21. Madame Campan tells us: "The King and Queen were very pleased with this couplet, and sang it several times during the lying-in period."

7. The details come from the *Description of festivals prepared by the city of Paris, on 21 and 23 January 1782*, Paris. Bibliothèque Nationale: Lb39 310.

8. *Plan or rather festival ideas to be carried out for the coming wedding of His Royal Highness the Dauphin, and for the births to come*, Paris, 1770. Bibliothèque Nationale: Lb39 106.

9. *Song on the wedding of His Royal Highness the Dauphin, by an invalid of the Hôtel-Dieu*, recorded in manuscript form on the flyleaves of the pamphlet class mark Ye 20763 at the Bibliothèque Nationale.

10. *Song on the wedding of His Royal Highness the Dauphin*, n.p., 1770. Bibliothèque Nationale: Ye 20763.

11. *Sermon on the wedding of His Royal Highness the Dauphin*, n.p., 1770. Bibliothèque Nationale: Lb39 119 A.

12. *Dream or horoscope of the future childbirth of Marie-Antoinette of Lorraine, Archduchess of Austria, Queen of France*, Paris, 1781. Bibliothèque Nationale: Lb39 297.

13. *Epistle to a foreign friend on the marriage of His Royal Highness the Dauphin*, Paris, 1770. Bibliothèque Nationale: Ye 21474.

14. *Ode on the wedding of His Royal Highness the Dauphin*, by the Abbé du Rouzeau, Paris, 1770. Bibliothèque Nationale: Ye 35443.

15. *Mars deceived. Ode presented to Their Majesties on the birth of a princess*, by M. A. F. Chivot, n.p., 1778. Bibliothèque Nationale: Ye 2321.

16. *The vows of France and of the empire: allegorical medallions*, by the Abbé Petity, n.p., 1770. Bibliothèque Nationale: Lb39 107 (the second medallion).

17. *Honeymoon bouquets, or The two flower sellers. Conversation on the wedding of His Royal Highness Louis-Auguste, Dauphin of France, with Her Royal Highness Marie-Antoinette, Archduchess of Austria*, n.p., 1770. Bibliothèque Nationale: Yf 7052.

18. *Festival at the Place Louis XV for the wedding of His Royal Highness the Dauphin*, n.p., 1770. Bibliothèque Nationale: Lb39 108.

19. *Speech on the occasion of the wedding of His Royal Highness the Dauphin*, Collège royal de la Flèche, 1770. Bibliothèque Nationale: Lb39 6232.

20. All the details of these ceremonies are given in *Letter on the wedding of His Royal Highness Louis-Auguste of Bourbon, Dauphin of France*, Amsterdam, 1770. Bibliothèque Nationale: Lb39 6229.

21. *Correspondence of foreign diplomatic agents in France before the Revolution*, ed. J. Flammermont, Paris, 1896, p. 475.

22. Ibid., p. 350.

23. *Marie-Antoinette: Secret Correspondence between Maria Theresa and the Comte de Mercy-Argenteau (1770–1780)*, ed. A. d'Arneth and A. Geffroy, Paris, 1874, 3 vol., letter of 12 June 1772.

24. Ibid., p. 99.

25. Quoted by Evelyne Lever, *Louis XVI*, Paris: Fayard, 1985, p. 68.

26. *Marie-Antoinette: Secret Correspondence*, letters of 15 June 1770, 20 October 1770, 1 August 1770, 6 June 1771, 25 February 1771, 16 December 1772.

27. Quoted by Evelyne Lever, *Louis XVI*, pp. 70–72.

28. *Marie-Antoinette: Secret Correspondence*, letter of 3 January 1774.

29. *Correspondence of foreign diplomatic agents*, p. 103.

30. Ibid., pp. 476–78. I thank Pierre Serna for the translation of these letters from the Spanish, the original language in which they are published in the collection edited by J. Flammermont.

31. *Marie-Antoinette: Secret Correspondence*, letter of 3 January 1774 (Joseph II had planned a first trip in 1774, which he had to postpone); letter of 15 June 1777.

32. A. d'Arneth, *Marie-Antoinette, Joseph II und Leopold II, ihr Briefwechsel*, Leipzig, 1866, letter of 16 June 1777.

33. *Louis XVI, Marie-Antoinette, and Mme Elisabeth: Unpublished letters and documents*, ed. F. Feuillet de Conches, 6 vol., Paris, 1873, letter of 21 December 1777.

34. *Correspondence of foreign diplomatic agents*, pp. 477–78, letter of 27 September 1777.

35. The cause of the consummation remains somewhat mysterious. Operation on the king's phimosis? No source has been adduced to prove it; even more tellingly, Louis XVI and his chief surgeon Lassone had always declined it. Or was it just the effect of Joseph II's advice, and the king's emphatic insistence, as the letters of Louis XVI and Marie-Antoinette seem to indicate? Perhaps. But I incline,

with Jean-Claude Laburthe, to a third hypothesis: the operation, very slight, was not performed on the sex of the king but on that of the queen. A simple incision of the hymen, an operation that was in no way unusual, would have allowed the piercing of the obstacle that until then had been impenetrable because of the pain in the king's prepuce, thus leaving him free passage.

36. *Correspondence of foreign diplomatic agents*, p. 349, letter of 3 November 1777; p. 350, letter of 3 January 1778; p. 436.

37. The Comte de Provence, as Mercy reports to Maria-Theresa (letter of 24 December 1778), had made some offensive remarks about the king and queen at the time of the baptism in 1778, reflections that lampoonists lose no time in putting into verse, as the ambassador Luigi Pio indicates: "They made room for Madame / Right next to the babe. / Monsieur cried out: 'Madame / Already has some suspicions.' / Each looked at the other / And made a face" (*Correspondence of foreign diplomatic agents*, p. 435).

38. Théveneau de Morande, *The Cuirassed Gazetteer, printed a hundred leagues from the Bastille under the sign of liberty*, 1771. Bibliothèque Nationale: Lb38 1270, p. 141.

39. Quoted in Grimm's *Literary Correspondence*, January 1771, Vol. 9, p. 225.

40. Pidansat de Mairobert, *The English Observer, correspondence between Milord all'eye and Milord all'ear*, London, 1776–80, 10 vol. The dialogue quoted was written in 1773 and is published in Vol. 1, p. 36.

41. J. Revel described this "mechanics of scandal" in his portrayal of Marie-Antoinette for the *Critical Dictionary of the French Revolution*, ed. F. Furet and M. Ozouf, Paris: Flammarion, 1988, pp. 286–98. Cf. C. Thomas's essay, *The Villain Queen: Marie-Antoinette in Pamphlets*, Paris: Le Seuil, 1989.

42. Allusion to the "taste for puce" introduced to the court by the queen, and to the brown color of certain cloth, ribbons, or dresses that the sovereign wore by preference.

43. E. Raunié, *Chansonnier historique*, Vol. 9, pp. 77–82.

44. P. Manuel, *The Police of Paris Unmasked*, n.p., Year II. Bibliothèque Nationale: Lf34 39, Vol. 1, pp. 237–38.

45. A. de Baecque, "The 'Livres Remplis d'Horreur': Pornographic Literature and Politics at the Beginning of the French Revolution," in P. Wagner (ed.), *Erotica and the Enlightenment*, Frankfurt-New York: Peter Lang, 1990, pp. 123–65.

46. P. Manuel, *The Police of Paris Unmasked*, Vol. 1, p. 37.

47. *Historical Essays on the Life of Marie-Antoinette of Austria*, in London, 1789. Bibliothèque Nationale: Enfer 334.

48. *The Private, Libertine, and Scandalous Life of Marie-Antoinette of Austria*, to be bought at the Palais de l'Egalité, formerly the Palais Royal, at the newsagents, the first year of the republic. Bibliothèque Nationale: Enfer 790-91-92.

49. *The Uterine Furies of Marie-Antoinette, Wife of Louis XVI*, n.p., 1791. Bibliothèque Nationale: Enfer 654.

50. *The Day of Love or the Last Pleasures of Marie-Antoinette, comedy in three acts, in prose, presented for the first time at the Temple*, 20 August 1792. Bibliothèque Nationale: Enfer 685.

51. Frontispiece of the pamphlet *Marie-Antoinette in a predicament*, 1790.

52. *Portfolio of the patriot containing the Declaration of the Rights of Man, a great number of racy and little known anecdotes on the Court, the ministers, the clergy, the nobility, the parliaments, and on various other subjects that demonstrate how misjudged and despised the rights of man were until now, and how indispensable the present revolution was*, n.p., n.d. Bibliothèque Nationale: Lb39 7601.

53. *Petition and decree in favor of whores, fuckers, madams, and friggers, in Cocksuckerie, and can be obtained from all national fuckers, the second year of the fuckative regeneration*. Bibliothèque Nationale: Enfer 762.

54. M. Desmarest, *The Anecdote*, n.p., 1789. Bibliothèque Nationale: Lb39 1340.

55. *Advice to the King*, n.p., 1790. Bibliothèque Nationale: Lb39 3165.

56. *Contrition and confession of Louis XVI to the Pope*, n.p., 1790. Bibliothèque Nationale: Lb39 2775.

57. *Louis IX at Saint-Cloud or the apparition of Saint Louis to Louis XVI*, n.p., n.d.; *Louis XIV at Saint-Cloud at the bedside of Louis XVI*, n.p., n.d.; *Louis XIV finding Louis XVI forging chains*, n.p., n.d.; *Louis XIV finding Louis XVI in his study, glass of rum in hand*, n.p., n.d.; *Henri IV and Louis XIV at the royal going-to-bed ceremony of Louis XVI*, n.p., n.d.; *Louis XIV finding Louis XVI on the terrace of Saint-Cloud having a padded baby bonnet for a crown, a rattle for a scepter, and training leash for a sash*, n.p., n.d.; *The dream of Louis XVI and his conversation with Henri IV*, n.p., n.d.; *The discussions of the Bourbons*, n.p., n.d., pamphlets joined under the listing Bibliothèque Nationale: Lb39 4266-4267.

58. *The decline of the royal blood and the poisoning of Louis XVI*, Paris, 1791. Bibliothèque Nationale: Lb39 4722.

59. *Archives parlementaires*, meeting of 8 March 1791, Vol. 23, p. 785.

60. *Bulletins of the king, from 8 to 16 March 1791*, Paris, 1791. Bibliothèque Nationale: Res Lb39 4720.

61. J.-P. Brissot de Warville, *Le Patriote français*, no. 582.

62. C. Desmoulins, *Les Révolutions de France et de Brabant*, no. 69, p. 159.

63. *Le Patriote français*, no. 585, no. 591, no. 592.

64. *Les Révolutions de Paris*, no. 88, week of 12 to 19 March 1791.

65. A.-J. Gorsas, *Le Courrier des 83 départements*, no. 22, 22 June 1791.

66. *Le Patriote français*, no. 683.

67. *Pleasure outing of Louis XVI to the frontier, aborted at Varennes*, n.p., n.d. Bibliothèque Nationale: Lb39 5033.

68. *Le Patriote français*, no. 683.

69. *Le Courrier*, no. 22, 22 June 1791.

70. *Great Departure of the King to rejoin the army of the ci-devant Prince of Condé*, n.p., 21 June 1791. Bibliothèque Nationale: Lb39 5018.

71. *Les Révolutions de France et de Brabant*, no. 82, 27 June 1791.

72. *Louis XVI and Antoinette treated as they deserve*, n.p., 21 June 1791. Bibliothèque Nationale: Lb39 5080.

73. *Le Courrier*, no. 22, 22 June 1791 (the play on words is drawn from the *Great Response of the Parisians to M. de Bouillé*, Paris, n.d., Bibliothèque Nationale: Lb39 5069); no. 23, 23 June 1791; no. 24, 24 June 1791; no. 26, 26 June 1791; no. 27, 27 June 1791.

74. *Great festival given by the madams of Paris*, Paris, 1791. Bibliothèque Nationale: Enfer 1429.

75. *The Chatterbox*, 23 June 1791. Bibliothèque Nationale: Lc2 605.

76. *The Day of Love or the Last Pleasures of Marie-Antoinette.*

77. *Great Response of the Parisians to M. de Bouillé*, n.p., n.d. Bibliothèque Nationale: Lb39 5069 A.

78. J.-R. Hébert, *Le Père Duchesne*, no. 61.

79. *Les Révolutions de France et de Brabant*, no. 82, 27 June 1791. J.-C. Bonnet, "Boiled Chicken and Pig's Feet," *Le Monde de la Révolution française*, no. 2, February 1989, p. 14.

80. See A. de Baecque, *La Caricature révolutionnaire*, Paris: Presses du CNRS, 1988, pp. 177–85, and especially A. Duprat's dissertation, *Repique est Capet. Louis XVI dans la caricature: naissance d'un langage politique*, Université de Rouen, 1991, published by Editions du Cerf under the title *Le Roi décapité: essai sur les imaginaires politiques*, 1992. No less than sixteen cartoons play on this successful association.

81. *Response of the French to the King's manifesto to submit this people to his arbitrary authority*, n.p., n.d. Bibliothèque Nationale: Lb39 5020.

82. *Description of the royal zoo of live animals*, n.p., n.d. Bibliothèque Nationale: Lb39 6056. The word QUEUE [tail] is printed in capital letters in the pamphlet.

83. Romeau, *The head and ear of the pig*, Paris, n.d., Bibliothèque Nationale: Lb42 912. Quoted by A. Duprat in "From the Father-King to the Pig-King," documents from the colloquium *Saint-Denis or the Last Judgment of the Kings*, Editions de l'Espace européen, La Garenne-Colombes, 1992, pp. 81–90.

84. *Le Patriote français*, no. 692.

85. *Archives parlementaires*, meeting of 15 July 1791, Vol. 28, pp. 326–31.

86. *The Great Dénouement of the Constitution, politico-tragi-comic parody played at Brussels on the 1st of January 1791*, Brussels, 1791. Bibliothèque Nationale: Lb39 4487.

Chapter 2

1. E. Sieyès, *Plan for a law against the offenses that can be committed by printed matter and by the publication of writings and engravings, presented at the National Assembly on 20 January 1790*, pp. 5–6. References to the writings of Sieyès are given according to the facsimile reproduction of all his printed texts in the *Œuvres* of Sieyès, collected and annotated by M. Dorigny, Paris: Edhis, 1989, 3 vol.

2. E. Sieyès, *Opinion on several articles, Titles IV and V, of the plan for a constitution, pronounced at the Convention on 2 Thermidor of the Third Year of the Republic*, pp. 19–20.

3. E. Sieyès, *Views on the executive methods that could be used by the representatives of France in 1789*, n.p., 1789, pp. 29–30.

4. E. Sieyès, *What Is the Third Estate?*, n.p., 1789, p. 71.

5. E. Sieyès, *Views on the executive methods*, p. 129.

6. E. Sieyès, *What Is the Third Estate?*, p. 102.

7. *Responses to the alarms of good citizens*, n.p., 1789. Bibliothèque Nationale: Lb39 1199.

8. *Impartial glance*, n.p., n.d. Bibliothèque Nationale: Lb39 965.

9. *Ideas of an almost sexagenarian citizen on the present state of the kingdom of France, compared to those of his youth*, Paris, 1787. Bibliothèque Nationale: Lb39 354.

10. *The bread of the people*, n.p., 1789. Bibliothèque Nationale: Lb39 1852.

11. *The political painter, or the rate of present operations*, n.p., 1789. Bibliothèque Nationale: Lb39 2719.

12. Morainville, *The union of the three orders and boiled chicken*, n.p., 1789. Bibliothèque Nationale: Lb39 1324.

13. *The Restoration of France*, n.p., 1788. Bibliothèque Nationale: Lb39 754.

14. P. Le Maître, *The Most Original of Notebooks: Extract from that of a madman who has some moments of sanity, at Momus, printer of maniacs*, 1789. Bibliothèque Nationale: Lb39 1607.

15. *The head turns them*, n.p., 1788. Bibliothèque Nationale: Lb39 573.

16. Mossère, *At the deputies of the French nation and at the Estates General*, n.p., 1789. Bibliothèque Nationale: Lb39 1734.

17. *La Sentinelle du peuple*, n.p., 1788. Bibliothèque Nationale: Lb39 680.

18. E. Sieyès, *Essay on Privileges*, n.p., 1788, pp. 17–18.

19. E. Sieyès, *What Is the Third Estate?*, p. 127.

20. Ibid., p. 122.

21. B. Noillac, *The Strongest of Pamphlets*, n.p., 26 February 1789. Bibliothèque Nationale: Lb39 1235.

22. R. Giesey, *The Royal Funeral Ceremony in Renaissance France*, Geneva: E. Droz, 1960.

23. R. Descimon and A. Guéry, "The 'royal monarchy,'" A. Burguière and J. Revel (eds.), *Histoire de la France*, Vol. *L'État et les pouvoirs*, Paris: Le Seuil, 1989, p. 238.

24. P. Manent, "Thomas Hobbes: Leviathan," in *Dictionnaire des œuvres politiques*, ed. F. Chatelet, O. Duhamel, and E. Pisier, Paris: Presses Universitaires de France, 1986, pp. 417–29.

25. R. Descimon and A. Guéry, "The 'royal monarchy,'" p. 238; J.-M. Apostolidès, *Le Roi-machine: spectacle et politique au temps de Louis XIV* [The king-machine: spectacle and politics in the time of Louis XIV], Paris: Editions de Minuit, 1981, p. 13; R. Giesey, *Cérémonial et puissance souveraine. France, XV*e*–XVII*e* siècles*, Paris: A. Colin, 1987, p. 81.

26. M. Foucault, *The Birth of the Clinic: An Archaeology of Medical Perception*, Paris: Presses Universitaires de France, 1988, particularly Chapter 8, "Open Some Cadavers," pp. 125–49.

27. P.-J.-G. Cabanis, *Note touching on the torture of the guillotine*, reprinted in the *Œuvres complètes* of Cabanis, Paris, 1823, Vol. 2, pp. 161–83. Bibliothèque Nationale: Z 44547.

28. J.-A. Cérutti, *Letter to M. le Vicomte de Noailles*, n.p., n.d. Bibliothèque Nationale: Lb39 7560.

29. J.-A. Cérutti on Sieyès, ibid.

30. Œlsner, *On the political opinions of Citizen Sieyès and on his life as public figure*, Paris, Year VIII. Bibliothèque Nationale: Ln27 18957.

31. "However ardent, however rash individual opinions may seem, in any deliberative body, should we not pay attention to the fact that it is just those, like all the ideas and more or less fleeting impulses in the brain of the individual, that precede decision on any important matter? Well! this mass of impulses, as manifold as they are imperceptible, that agitate this way and that the fibers of the brain in a single individual, are the very image of individual opinions in a deliberative assembly. Both are the materials of deliberation, the elements of which it is made up, the preliminaries of judgment; they offer competing motives to determine the final combination of mind and will that make up what is called a *fixed opinion [parti pris]*" (E. Sieyès, *Views on the executive methods*, pp. 97–98).

32. *Instruction given by His Grace the Duke of Orléans to his representatives for the bailiwicks*, n.p., 1789, p. 53.

33. *Opinion of Sieyès on the attributions and organization of the constitutional jury proposed on 2 Thermidor Year III, uttered at the National Convention on the 18th of the same month*, p. 11.

34. E. Sieyès, *Views on the executive methods*, pp. 129–30.

35. R. Giesey, *Royal Funeral Ceremony*, p. 192.

36. M. Gauchet, *La Révolution des droits de l'homme*, Paris: Gallimard, 1989, pp. xviii, 23–28.

37. *Liberty or the advantages of the new French Constitution*, n.p., 1789. Bibliothèque Nationale: Lb39 2262.

38. *Margot, the good old lady of 102 years, sister of the curate of 97 years, to the gentlemen of the Estates General*, n.p., 1789. Bibliothèque Nationale: Lb39 1733.

39. *Celestial notebook*, n.p., 1789. Bibliothèque Nationale: Lb39 1603.

40. *Political madmen*, no. 1, n.p., 1789. Bibliothèque Nationale: Lc2 2230. Also, with the same image, *Advice to the assembled nation*.

41. *What is the nation and what is France?*, n.p., 1789. Bibliothèque Nationale: Lb39 1289.

42. *The Coalition, or the terrible adventures of Strong-arm the giant*, n.p., 23 April 9871 (1789). Bibliothèque Nationale: Lb39 1552.

43. *France compared to the human body*, Paris, 1790. Bibliothèque Nationale: Lb39 9823.

44. Marie-Vic Ozouf-Marignier, *La Formation des départements: La représentation du territoire français à la fin du 18e siècle* [The formation of the departments: representation of the French territory at the end of the eighteenth century], Paris: Editions de l'Ecole des Hautes Etudes en Sciences Sociales, 1989.

45. Mona Ozouf, *Festivals and the French Revolution*, Paris: Gallimard, 1976, pp. 44–74.

46. *Archives parlementaires. Complete collection of the legislative and political debates of the French chambers*, ed. J. Mavidal and E. Laurent, Paris, 1867–96, Vol. 8, p. 492.

47. Quoted by M.-V. Ozouf-Marignier, *La Formation des départements*, p. 40.

48. M. d'Argenson, *Considerations on the former and present government of France*, Amsterdam, 1764.

49. Le Trosne, *On provincial administration and tax reform*, Basel, 1779.

50. *Posthumous works of M. Turgot, or Memoirs of M. Turgot on the provincial administrations*, Lausanne, 1787.

51. E. Sieyès, *Statement of the Abbé Sieyès on the question of the royal veto*, Paris, 7 September 1789, p. 10; the system is repeated in E. Sieyès, *Observations on the report of the Constitution Committee concerning the new organization of France*, Paris, 2 October 1789, p. 2.

52. E. Sieyès, *Preliminary of the French Constitution: Survey and reasoned exposition of the rights of man and of the citizen*, Paris, 1789, p. 33.

53. E. Sieyès, *Observations on the report of the Constitution Committee*, p. 46.

54. Mona Ozouf, "The French Revolution and the Perception of National Space," in *L'Ecole de la France*, Paris: Gallimard, 1984, p. 27.

55. E. Sieyès, *Statement of the Abbé Sieyès on the question of the royal veto*, p. 18.

56. E. Sieyès, *Observations on the report of the Constitution Committee*, p. 13.

57. *Archives parlementaires*, Vol. 9, pp. 202–10.

58. Ibid., p. 441.   59. Ibid., p. 461.

60. Ibid., p. 462.   61. Ibid., p. 481.

62. Ibid., pp. 752–53.   63. Ibid., p. 658.

64. Ibid., p. 691.   65. Ibid., pp. 659–62, 731–36.

66. Ibid., pp. 654–59, 723–28, 755–59.

67. M.-V. Ozouf-Marignier, *La Formation des départements*, pp. 123–299.

68. *Free translation, or rather imitation of three odes of Horace applicable to the present time*, Paris, 1789. Bibliothèque Nationale: Ye 10135; *Miraculous harangue, or the mute turned orator*, n.p., n.d. Bibliothèque Nationale: Ye 10136; M. Dumolard, *Advantages of the new division of the kingdom*, Paris, 1790. Bibliothèque Nationale: Lb39 8278.

69. M. Mentelle, *Short and simple method to learn easily and retain without difficulty the new geography of France*, Paris, 1791. Bibliothèque Nationale: L8 12.

70. C. Desmoulins, *Les Révolutions de France et de Brabant*, no. 14, p. 25.

71. Ibid., no. 30, p. 280.

72. *Speech uttered at the bar of the National Assembly by M. de Cloots, orator of the committee of Foreigners*, at the meeting of 19 June 1790, in A. Cloots, *Ecrits révolutionnaires*, Paris: Editions Champ Libre, 1979, pp. 28–29.

73. *Plan for a federative pact, by the administrative council of the National Guard of Rennes*, n.p., April 1790. Bibliothèque Nationale: Lb39 8782.

74. *Le Moniteur*, Vol. 4, p. 559.

75. C. Desmoulins, *Les Révolutions de France et de Brabant*, no. 34, pp. 462–63.

76. Ibid., no. 35, pp. 510–11.   77. Ibid., no. 34, p. 467.

78. Ibid., no. 35, pp. 514–15.   79. Ibid., p. 517.

Chapter 3

1. M. Ozouf, "The French Revolution and the Formation of the New Man," in *L'Homme régénéré. Essais sur la Révolution française*, Paris: Gallimard, pp. 116–57 (taken from the contribution to the symposium *The Political Culture of the French Revolution: The French Revolution and the Creation of Modern Political Culture*, Vol. 2, C. Lucas, ed., Oxford: Pergamon Press, 1988, pp. 213–32).

2. Article entitled "Regeneration," *Encyclopédie*, Vol. 13, 1765, pp. 912–13.

3. Cf. the two decisive decrees of the summer of 1788 that both use the word "regeneration" in its political acceptation: *Decree of the Council of State of the King, concerning the convocation of the Estates General of the kingdom*, 5 July 1788, and *Decree of the Council of State of the King, which fixes the holding of the Estates General of the kingdom for the 1st of May next*, 8 August 1788.

4. Charles Duclos, *Voyage en Italie*, in his *Œuvres complètes*, Vol. 7, Paris, 1806, p. 52. Bibliothèque Nationale: Z 27 834.

5. F. Brunot, *Histoire de la langue française*, Vol. 9, Paris: A. Colin, 1937, pp. 226–27.

6. L. R. Caradeux de La Chalotais, Preface to the *Second Compte-rendu des constitutions des jésuites*, Rennes, 1762. Bibliothèque Nationale: Ld39 443.

7. J.-A. Cérutti, *Prospectus for a dictionary of exaggeration*, n.p., n.d. Bibliothèque Nationale: Lb39 910.

8. P.-L. Ginguené, *The Satire of Satires*, n.p., 1778. Bibliothèque Nationale: Ye 23 333.

9. See the reprint of Abbé Grégoire's *Essay on the physical, moral, and political regeneration of the Jews*, with a preface by R. Hermon-Belot, Paris: Flammarion, 1988, pp. 130–35, 144–60, 174.

10. *Interesting consultation on the nature of the people*, n.p., 1789. Bibliothèque Nationale: Lb39 3208.

11. *The political painter, or the rate of present operations*, n.p., 1789. Bibliothèque Nationale: Lb39 2719.

12. *Last sighs of a centenarian on the misfortunes of his country*, n.p., 1789. Bibliothèque Nationale: Lb39 1322.

13. *The eyeglasses of the zealous citizen*, n.p., 1789. Bibliothèque Nationale: Lb39 1189.

14. J. Pétion de Villeneuve, *Advice to the French on the salvation of the country*, n.p., 1789. Bibliothèque Nationale: Lb39 755.

15. *Memorandum on the regeneration of the public order*, n.p., n.d. Bibliothèque Nationale: Lb39 1305.

16. *Harangue of Fat Jean on the letters of the convocation of the Estates General*, n.p., 9 March 1789. Bibliothèque Nationale: Lb39 1386.

17. *The Estates General of the year 1999*, n.p., June 1789. Bibliothèque Nationale: Lb39 1736.

18. Cf. the works of H. J. Lüsebrink and R. Reichardt on the image of the Bastille: *Die "Bastille." Zur Symbolgeschichte von Herrschaft und Freiheit*, Frankfurt: S. Fischer, 1990, a summary of which can be found in M. Vovelle (ed.), *L'Image de la Révolution française*, actes du Congrès mondial du bicentenaire, Vol. 1, Oxford: Pergamon Press, 1990, pp. 315–24, "The Narratives of 14 July in France and Germany."

19. Le Tellier, *The triumph of the Parisians*, Paris, July 1789. Bibliothèque Nationale: Lb39 1952.

20. *The resurrection of the good French and the civil death of the aristocrats*, n.p., 1789. Bibliothèque Nationale: Lb39 2200.

21. Pithou, *The triumph of the Parisians*, n.p., 1789. Bibliothèque Nationale: Lb39 2214.

22. "The secret of Mme Cuntlicked," "historic" anecdote reported in *The fuckomanic echo, or collection of several lewd and libertine scenes*, A Démocratis, n.d. Bibliothèque Nationale: Enfer 70.

23. *The trumpet of judgment*, n.p., September 1789. Bibliothèque Nationale: Lb39 2752.

24. *French Citizens, or the triumph of the Revolution, by Pierre Vaqué, Colonel of the National Guard*, Paris, 1790. Bibliothèque Nationale: Lb39 4491.

25. *The tomb of ministerial despotism, or the dawn of happiness*, Paris, n.d. Bibliothèque Nationale: Lb39 1958.

26. *Parallel of the French hero with those of antiquity*, Paris, 1790. Bibliothèque Nationale: Lb39 8301.

27. *Essay on patriotism, dedicated, addressed, and presented to the nation assembled at Versailles*, n.p., n.d. Bibliothèque Nationale: Lb39 1747.

28. *The Dies irae, or the three orders at the Last Judgment*, n.p., 1789. Bibliothèque Nationale: Lb39 1132.

29. References to the parliamentary discussion on the Declaration of the Rights of Man are given according to *L'An I des droits de l'homme: Controverses et débats de 1789 autour de la Déclaration des droits de l'homme*, ed. A. de Baecque, Paris: Presses du CNRS, 1988. This is the complete edition of the debates of the months of July–August 1789, unlike the *Archives parlementaires*, Vol. 8, which only took into account the *Moniteur*.

30. *L'An I des droits de l'homme*, p. 103 (meeting of 1 August).

31. Ibid., p. 104.

32. *Examination of the Declaration of the Rights of Man and of the Citizen*, n.p., n.d. Bibliothèque Nationale: Lb39 2168.

33. Le Hodey, *The Logograph: National Journal*, Paris. Bibliothèque Nationale: Fol Lc2 140, Vol. 2, pp. 306-7.

34. *Conversation between a retired cobbler and a financier*, n.p., 1789. Bibliothèque Nationale: Lb39 7796.

35. Barère, *The point of the day*, Vol. 1, p. 381.

36. *L'An I des droits de l'homme*, p. 104.

37. Ibid., p. 101.

38. Ibid., p. 117.

39. Ibid., p. 94.

40. Ibid., p. 103 (intervention of Grandin on 1 August).

41. Ibid., p. 123.

42. Ibid., p. 138.

43. "One of those words that magic uses to change the scene of the world," Cérutti writes on the subject of the tale of origins forged by revolutionary writers, in J.-A. Cérutti, *Letter to M. le Vicomte de Noailles*, n.p., n.d. Bibliothèque Nationale: Lb39 7560.

44. *The destinies of France*, n.p., 1 January 1790. Bibliothèque Nationale: Lb39 2759.

45. *1789 in hell, political episode in one act*, n.p., n.d. Bibliothèque Nationale: Lb39 2751.

46. *The Misuse of Words*, n.p., n.d. Bibliothèque Nationale: Lb39 2724.

47. *Kingdom to be regenerated by enlisting*, n.p., April 1790. Bibliothèque Nationale: Lb39 3066.

48. *Sleep in peace, good people, the Friends of the Constitution are watching out for you*, n.p., January 1791. Bibliothèque Nationale: Lb39 4549.

49. *Necessity for a ballot against double despotism*, n.p., 1789. Bibliothèque Nationale: Lb39 7297.

Chapter 4

1. *The Giant Iscariot, Aristocrat*, n.p., n.d. Bibliothèque Nationale: Cabinet des estampes, coll. de Vinck 3659. This engraving is discussed by A. de Baecque, *La Caricature révolutionnaire*, Paris: Presses du CNRS, 1988, pp. 138–39.

2. *La Gazette de Paris* (by the Royalist journalist de Rozoi), Paris, 6 January 1792. Bibliothèque Nationale: Lc2 255.

3. *The last cry of the monster, an Indian tale*, n.p., n.d. Bibliothèque Nationale: Lb39 2097.

4. Cf. the following engravings entitled *Iscariot, aristocratic giant*: Bibliothèque Nationale, Cabinet des estampes, coll. Hennin, Vol. 129, f. 71; and Carnavalet, Cabinet des estampes, coll. Soulavie, Monuments de l'histoire en France en estampes et dessins, Vol. 43, f. 29. Another "Iscariot" free of direct reference to the taking of the Bastille appears in the political cartoon entitled *The Aristocratic Roman Lady* (Bibliothèque Nationale: Cabinet des estampes, coll. de Vinck 2749).

5. L. Réau, *Iconographie de l'art chrétien*, Paris: PUF, 1955–59, Vol. 2, *Iconographie de la bible: Le Nouveau testament*, pp. 432–43.

6. J.-L. Carra, *Patriotic and literary annals*, 15 January 1790.

7. D. Haugg, *Judas Ischariot in den Neutestamentlichen Berichten*, Fribourg, 1930, pp. 34–36. I thank Marielle Silhouette for her help in the translation of these few German expressions.

8. C. Thomas, "The Archtigress of Austria: Animal Metaphor in the Pamphlets Against Marie-Antoinette," in P. Rétat (ed.), *La Révolution du journal*, Paris: Editions du CNRS, 1989, pp. 229–34.

9. *Tractate on the History of France on 21 June 1791*, Paris, n.d. Bibliothèque Nationale: Cabinet des estampes, coll. de Vinck 3931.

10. Cf. A. Duprat's study, "The Royal Redhead," in *Annales historiques de la Révolution française*, no. 289, July–September 1992.

11. J. Guilhaumou, *La Langue politique et la Révolution française*, Paris: Méridien Klincksieck, 1989, pp. 52–68.

12. *The Misuse of Words*, n.p., n.d. Bibliothèque Nationale: Lb39 2724.

13. J. P. Gallais, *Extract from a useless dictionary*, 500 leagues from the National Assembly, 1790. Bibliothèque Nationale: Lb39 3901.

14. *Advice to the French on clubs*, n.p., 1791. Bibliothèque Nationale: Lb39 4559.

15. J. Guilhaumou, entry entitled "Aristocracy" of the *Dictionnaire des usages sociopolitiques*, Vol. 1, Saint-Cloud, 1985, pp. 9-38.

16. E. Loustallot, *Les Révolutions de Paris*, no. 18, 7-14 November 1789 (quoted by J. Guilhaumou, "Aristocracy," in *Dictionnaire des usages sociopolitiques*).

17. *New French dictionary*, n.p., 1790. Bibliothèque Nationale: Lb39 3976.

18. *Advice to my dear fellow citizens on quarrels over nothing, or dissertation on the party names we give each other, without wanting to agree*, n.p., 1790. Bibliothèque Nationale: Lb39 9323.

19. *Diogenes' barrel, or the revolutions of the clergy*, Paris, 1790. Bibliothèque Nationale: Lc2 311, no. 19; *The great menagerie, or posturing on the boulevards*, Paris, 1790. Bibliothèque Nationale: Lc2 2318, no. 1.

20. C.-C. and G. Ragache, *Les Loups en France: légendes et réalité*, Paris: Aubier, 1981; R.-F. Dubois, *Vie et mort de la bête du Gévaudan*, Liège: Ogam, 1988. The most suggestive text concerning the writings about the monstrosity of the beast of the Gévaudan is by Y. Séïté, "The Beast of the Gévaudan in Newspapers: From News Item to Legend," in *Les Gazettes de langue française en Europe, XVIIe-XVIIIe siècles*, Table Ronde de Saint-Etienne, May 1992.

21. J.-L. Desprez, *Chimeras*, Paris, 1774-76. Bibliothèque Nationale: Cabinet des estampes, Yb3 1444, quarto, original engravings. Reproduced in Werner Hofmann (ed.), *Europa 1789*, Cologne: DuMont, 1989, p. 189.

22. Descriptions of the different harpies linked to the figure of the queen are given in *Inventaire analytique de la collection de Vinck*, Vol. 1, pp. 533-38. Eight variants of this type are kept at the Cabinet des estampes of the Bibliothèque Nationale.

23. *Marie-Antoinette in the form of a harpy, trampling beneath her talons the Rights of Man and the Constitution of the French*, n.p., n.d. Bibliothèque Nationale: coll. de Vinck 1148. The description is drawn from the *Petit journal du Palais-Royal*, Paris. Bibliothèque Nationale: m. 4233(1), no. 4.

24. *The Club of Les Halles*, n.p., 1789. Bibliothèque Nationale: Lc2 696, no. 1.

25. *The National Pikestaff*, no. 2, 1789. Bibliothèque Nationale: Lc2 2293.

26. *The Echo of the Palais-Royal, or the courier of the cafés*, no. 2, 1789. Bibliothèque Nationale: Lc2 2409.

27. Fuller developments of this can be found in G. Chaussinand-Nogaret, "An Aspect of the Nobility's Way of Thinking in the Eighteenth Century: Antinobilism," *Revue d'histoire moderne et contemporaine*, 1982, pp. 442-52; and A. de Baecque, "Anti-noble Discourse (1787-1792). The Origins of a Slogan: 'The People Against the Fat,'" *Revue d'histoire moderne et contemporaine*, January-March 1989, pp. 3-28.

28. *The Comte d'Artois at death's door*, n.p., 1789. Bibliothèque Nationale: Lb39 2052 (*bis*) Réserve.

29. *Continuation of the delights of Coblentz, or the brilliant festival given by M. le Prince de Condé for the illustrious French émigrés*, Coblentz, 1791. Bibliothèque Nationale: Enfer 1428(2).

30. *Petition and decree in favor of whores, fuckers, madams, and friggers, in Cocksuckerie, and can be obtained from all national fuckers, the second year of the fuckative regeneration*. Bibliothèque Nationale: Enfer 762.

31. *The monster torn apart, prophetic vision of a Parisian who does not always sleep*, n.p., 1789. Bibliothèque Nationale: Lb39 2199.

32. *Exact narrative of the great fight waged at Nancy between the regiment of Châteauvieux and the traitor Bouillé*, n.p., n.d. Bibliothèque Nationale: Lb39 3991.

33. E. Sieyès, *Qu'est-ce que le tiers état?*, Paris: Ed. Presses Universitaires de France, 1982, pp. 32–33.

34. J.-P. Brissot de Warville, *Le Patriote français*, no. 330, 4 July 1790.

35. P. Tort, "The Logic of the Deviant: The Classifications of Monsters Between 1750 and 1850," *Revue des sciences humaines*, no. 188, 1982, pp. 7–32.

36. *The Spanish fly of the nation, or The operator-dentist-doctor of the clergy of France*, Paris, 2790 (1790). Bibliothèque Nationale: Lb39 8253.

37. *The Pope led to hell by Abbé Maury*, n.p., April 1791. Bibliothèque Nationale: Lb39 9922; or *Conveying the clergy to hell*, n.p., May 1791. Bibliothèque Nationale: Lb39 9867.

38. R. Darnton, "Peasants Tell Tales: The Meaning of Mother Goose," in *The Great Cat Massacre and Other Episodes in French Cultural History*, New York: Vintage Books, 1985, pp. 9–72.

39. *The flood, or the aristocrat carried off in the current*, n.p., 1789. Bibliothèque Nationale: Lb39 8190.

40. *The Club of Les Halles*, no. 1.

41. T. Todorov, *Introduction à la littérature fantastique*, Paris: Le Seuil, 1970, p. 165. In English: *The Fantastic: A Structural Approach to a Literary Genre*, trans. Richard Howard, Cleveland: Case Western, 1973.

42. M. Bakhtin, *Rabelais and His World*, French trans., Paris: Gallimard, 1970, pp. 69–148.

43. L. Hunt, *Politics, Culture, and Class in the French Revolution*, Berkeley: University of California Press, 1984, pp. 35–37.

44. For more details on Cérutti and revolutionary rhetoric, see A. de Baecque, "The War of Eloquence: Joseph-Antoine Cérutti and Revolutionary Pamphlets," in *History of European Ideas*, special issue devoted to revolutionary pamphlets, H. Chisick (ed.), nos. 2–3, pp. 191–214.

45. J.-A. Cérutti, *Prospectus for a dictionary of exaggeration*, published in *Christmas gifts to the public*, n.p., n.d. (January 1790), Bibliothèque Nationale: Lb39 910,

pp. 29–56. This "debate of exaggeration" under the Revolution continues the lively polemics that saturated the world of letters at the end of the eighteenth century. To grasp the meaning of it, see M. Delon, *L'Idée d'énergie au tournant des Lumières. 1770–1820*, Paris: Presses Universitaires de France, 1988, pp. 131–82.

Chapter 5

1. *Jacques-Louis David, 1748–1825*, catalogue of the Louvre exhibition (26 October 1989–12 February 1990), ed. A. Schnapper, Paris: Ed. de la Réunion des musées nationaux, 1989, pp. 92, 100–101, 102–3.

2. Ibid., p. 92.

3. "This composition occasioned some pleasure in Rome; they saw the classical intentions, but alas! they also saw certain French traces in it. I perceived them myself, and made the resolution to purge myself of them as soon as the opportunity presented itself" (concerning the *Funeral of Patroclus*, ibid., pp. 93–95).

4. Ibid., p. 102.

5. Johann J. Winckelmann, *Reflections on the Imitation of Greek Works in Painting and Sculpture*, ed. Jacqueline Chambon, Nîmes, 1991 edition, p. 38. Concerning the influence of Winckelmann: *Ecrits autour de Winckelmann: Goethe, Herder, Lessing*, texts collected and translated by M. Charrière, ed. Jacqueline Chambon, Nîmes, 1991; and E. Pommier (ed.), *Winckelmann: la naissance de l'histoire de l'art à l'époque des Lumières*, Paris: La Documentation française, 1991.

6. J. J. Winckelmann, *Geschichte der Kunst des Altertums*, Dresden, 1764; cited in E. Pommier's translation, in "Dreaming Before Antiquity, Winckelmann in Hand," catalogue *La Mort de Bara*, Avignon: Musée Calvet, 1989, pp. 78–81.

7. On the link between the nude *Patroclus* of David and the *Dying Gaul* of the Capitol: K. Holma, *David, son évolution et son style*, Paris: P. Lejay, 1940, pp. 32–33, as well as the contribution of S. Howard to the colloquium *David contre David*, Paris: La Documentation française, 1993.

8. J. J. Winckelmann, in his *Reflections on the Imitation of Greek Works*, severely condemns the grimace, which he qualifies as "insolent ardour accompanying the most extraordinary attitudes and actions," that "franchezza" (literally, "effrontery," "audacity" in Italian) that calls for "contrast," that "soul that, like a comet, deviates from its orbit" (pp. 36–37). On this mistrust the classic revival felt for bodily abnormality, cf. R. Michel, *Le Beau idéal, ou l'art du concept*, Paris: Ed. de la Réunion des musées nationaux, 1989, pp. 54–57.

9. On David as reader of Winckelmann, see E. Pommier's article, "Dreaming Before Antiquity, Winckelmann in Hand."

10. P. Bordes, *Le Serment du jeu de paume de Jacques-Louis David*, Paris: Ed. de la Réunion des musées nationaux, 1983, p. 29.

11. The phrase is R. Michel's in *Le Beau idéal, ou l'art du concept*.

12. On the problem of David and contemporary attire, see P. Bordes, *Le Ser-*

ment du jeu de paume, and R. Michel, "Bara, from Martyr to Ephebe," catalogue *La Mort de Bara*, p. 68 especially.

13. This expression is used by R. Michel, "Bara, from Martyr to Ephebe." Concerning the fascination for the beautiful body and for nudity, see T. Crow's article, "Revolutionary Activism and the Cult of Male Beauty in the Studio of David," in B. Fort (ed.), *Fictions of the French Revolution*, Evanston: Northwestern University Press, 1991, pp. 55–83.

14. J. J. Winckelmann, *Geschichte der Kunst des Altertums*, cited in E. Pommier, "Dreaming Before Antiquity, Winckelmann in Hand."

15. On the importance of line and contour in neoclassical drawing, see J. Starobinski, *1789, The Emblems of Reason*, Paris: Flammarion, 1979, pp. 75–87; R. Michel, *Le Beau idéal*, pp. 48–49.

16. P. Bordes, *Le Serment du jeu de paume*, p. 127.

17. E. Pommier, "Dreaming Before Antiquity, Winckelmann in Hand," p. 78.

18. P. Bordes, *Le Serment du jeu de paume*, p. 128.

19. *Supplément au Journal de Paris*, Paris, 1791. Bibliothèque Nationale: Lc2 80, 10 June 1791.

20. J. W. Lapierre, "Biological Body, Political Body in the Philosophy of Hobbes," *Revue européenne des sciences sociales/Cahiers Wilfredo Pareto*, no. 49, 1980, pp. 85–100.

21. J. J. Winckelmann, *Reflections on the Imitation of Greek Works*, p. 36: "The calmer the attitude of the body is, the more able it is to express the true nature of the soul: in all the positions that deviate too much from repose, the soul is not in the state that is the most suitable to it; it is in a state of violence and compulsion. It is in these states of violent passion that it is most easily recognized, but, on the other hand, it is in the state of repose and harmony that it is great and noble."

22. J. J. Winckelmann, *Reflections on the Imitation of Greek Works*, pp. 83, 117. The metaphor is discussed by R. Michel, *Le Beau idéal*, p. 47, and by the same author in *Aux armes et aux arts!*, Paris: Adam Biro, 1988, pp. 12–13.

23. E. Pommier, "Dreaming Before Antiquity, Winckelmann in Hand," p. 79.

24. All the notes and drawings from the painter's two notebooks having to do with *The Tennis Court Oath* were published by P. Bordes, *Le Serment du jeu de paume*, pp. 204–34.

25. C. Cosneau, "A Great Project of J.-L. David (1789–1790)," *Revue du Louvre*, 1983, Vol. 4, pp. 255–63.

26. Reprinted by P. Bordes, *Le Serment du jeu de paume*, p. 200.

27. J. J. Winckelmann, *Reflections on the Imitation of Greek Works*, pp. 34–36: "Just as the depths of the sea remain calm at all times, no matter how agitated the surface is, so does the expression in the faces of the Greeks reveal, even when they are prey to the most violent passions, a great soul always equal to itself. This soul is read on the face of Laocoön in the midst of the most violent sufferings. Pain,

which is revealed in all the muscles and tendons of the body, and that we think we ourselves can almost feel at the mere sight of the painfully contracted abdomen, this pain does not manifest with any fury either in the face or in the general attitude. Laocoön does not emit horrible cries, like the Laocoön that Vergil sings of; the mouth is not open enough to allow this. It is rather a question of an anguished, oppressed groan. . . . His distress penetrates us down to the depths of the soul; but we would wish to be able to bear the distress as this great man bears it. For the Laocoön to represent pain alone would have been *parenthyrsis* ["low pathos"]. It is for this reason that the artist, in order to fuse the character and the nobility of the soul into one whole, gave Laocoön the attitude that, in such pain, was closest to the state of repose."

28. P. Bordes, *Le Serment du jeu de paume*, pp. 82–83 and the chapter "The Abandoned Work," pp. 85–90.

29. Ibid., pp. 177–78.

Chapter 6

1. Hippolyte Taine, *Origins of Contemporary France*, reprinted in two volumes, Paris: Robert Laffont, Coll. "Bouquins," 1986 (references will be to this edition), pp. 218, 227–28, 244–45.

2. H. Taine, *On Intelligence*, Paris: Hachette, 1870, preface. See also his "On Method," preface to *Essais de critique et d'histoire*, Paris: Hachette, 1858.

3. C. Wolikov, "Centenary in the Bicentenary. 1891–1991: Aulard and the Transformation of the Course on the History of the French Revolution," *Annales historiques de la Révolution française*, October–December 1991, pp. 431–58.

4. Alphonse Aulard, *Taine, historien de la Révolution française*, Paris: Armand Colin, 1907, pp. 324–27.

5. The preface to Aulard's *Histoire politique de la Révolution française: Origines et développements de la démocratie et de la république (1789–1804)*, Paris: A. Colin, 1901, is exemplary of this psychological approach to the sources of revolutionary history.

6. Ibid., p. 409.

7. A. Mathiez, "Robespierre and Vergniaud," reprinted in *Girondins et Montagnards*, Paris: Firmin-Didot, 1930, p. 26.

8. A. Mathiez, *La Corruption parlementaire sous la Terreur*, Paris, 1912, pp. 5–13.

9. L. Hunt, *Politics, Culture, and Class in the French Revolution*, Berkeley: University of California Press, 1984, pp. 74–86; D. Roche, *The Culture of Clothing: Dress and Fashion in the Ancien Régime*, Paris: Fayard, 1989, pp. 485–94; N. Pellegrin, *Les vêtements de la liberté. Abécédaire des pratiques vestimentaires françaises de 1780 à 1800*, Aix-en-Provence: Alinéa, 1989.

10. D. Outram, *The Body and the French Revolution: Sex, Class, and Political Culture*, New Haven: Yale University Press, 1989; P. Brooks, "The Revolutionary

Body," in B. Fort (ed.), *Fictions of the Revolution*, Evanston: Northwestern University Press, 1991, pp. 35–54; A. de Baecque, "The Blood of Heroes: Figures of the Body in the Political Imagination of the French Revolution," *Revue d'histoire moderne et contemporaine*, October–December 1987, pp. 553–86.

11. On "suspicion" during the Revolution, see L. Jacob, *Les Suspects pendant la Révolution*, Paris: Hachette, 1952; A. Soboul, *The Sans-Culottes: The Popular Movement and Revolutionary Government, 1793–1794*, Paris: Clavreuil, 1958, pp. 549–60; and J.-L. Matharan, "Suspects/soupçon/suspicion: la désignation des ennemis," published in two parts in *Dictionnaire des usages sociopolitiques*, Paris: Institut National de la Langue Française, URL. 1789–1793, fascicle 1, 1985, p. 187; 1793– Year III, fascicle 4, 1989, pp. 167–85; J. Guilhaumou, "Denunciation," in the papers of the colloquium *The Terror in the French Revolution*, K. Baker, C. Lucas, and S. Kaplan (eds.), Stanford and Oxford: Pergamon Press, 1994.

12. R. Darnton, *Bohème littéraire et Révolution: Le monde des livres au XVIIIe siècle*, Paris: Seuil/EHESS, 1983 (see Darnton, *The Literary Underground of the Old Regime*, Cambridge: Harvard University Press, 1982); R. Chartier, "Frustrated Intellectuals and Political Radicalism," *Cultural Origins of the French Revolution*, Paris: Seuil, 1990, pp. 226–32.

13. R. Chartier, "Public Space and Public Opinion," in *Cultural Origins of the French Revolution*, pp. 32–52.

14. J. Habermas, *The Structural Transformation of the Public Sphere: An Inquiry into a Category of Bourgeois Society*, Paris: Payot, 1978.

15. O. Coquard, "Correspondence in the Journals of Marat," *Annales historiques de la Révolution française*, no. 267, 1987; and, by the same author, *Le Peuple et son ami. Étude de la correspondance publiée par Marat dans ses journaux*, master's thesis (under the direction of M. Vovelle), Université de Paris I, 1985.

16. These attention-getters are drawn, respectively, from the following pamphlets: *The Patriot Confidant, can be bought in the country of good patriots, under the sign of sincerity*, 1789, Bibliothèque Nationale: Lb39 2550; *List of all the nuns and pious ladies who have been whipped*, Paris, n.d., Bibliothèque Nationale: Lb398 5504; *Execrable conspiracy against the king*, Paris, 1789, Bibliothèque Nationale: Lb39 7402; *Great and horrible conspiracy against the Assembly of representatives of the nation*, Paris, n.d., Bibliothèque Nationale: Lb39 7677.

17. *The conspiracy of conspiracies*, Paris, n.d. Bibliothèque Nationale: Lb39 1007.

18. *Rougyff, or The Frank as Celebrity*, n.p., n.d. Bibliothèque Nationale: Lc2 795, no. 1.

19. *The Listener at Doors*, n.p., n.d. Bibliothèque Nationale: Lc2 256, no. 1.

20. *The Patriot Confidant.*

21. C. Desmoulins, *The speech of the lantern to the Parisians*, France, 1789. Bibliothèque Nationale: Lb39 2297, p. 33.

22. Ibid., p. 34.

23. H. G. Comte de Mirabeau, *Letter to the investigative committee*, Paris, 1789. Bibliothèque Nationale: LB39 2441.

24. S. Rials, in *La Déclaration des droits de l'homme et du citoyen*, Paris: Hachette (Coll. Pluriel), 1988, pp. 247–49, discusses the different positions advanced during the Assembly's debate on freedom of the press. On the debate of the usefulness of public denunciation, see also the chapter "The Observing and Censoring Journalist" in C. Labrosse and P. Rétat, *Naissance du journal révolutionnaire*, Lyon: Presses Universitaires de Lyon, 1989.

25. *The denouncers denounced*, Paris, 1790. Bibliothèque Nationale: Lb39 7518.

26. *Not all the absent ones are wrong*, n.p., October 1789. Bibliothèque Nationale: Lb39 2476.

27. *Christian France, really and truly free*, n.p., September 1789. Bibliothèque Nationale: Lb39 2299.

28. *The thousand and one abuses*, Paris, September 1789. Bibliothèque Nationale: Lb39 2393.

29. J.-P. Marat, *L'Ami du peuple*, no. 37, 13 November 1789.

30. C. Desmoulins, *Les Révolutions de France et de Brabant*, n.p., December 1789, no. 5.

31. *To all citizens and all districts: motion on the conspiracy uncovered*, n.p., July 1789. Bibliothèque Nationale: Lb39 7406.

32. Ibid.

33. *Three words to Parisians on the necessity of publishing the names of their candidates*, n.p., April 1789. Bibliothèque Nationale: Lb39 1522.

34. *Whom should we elect? or, Advice to the people on the choice of its deputies to the Estates General*, n.p., March 1789. Bibliothèque Nationale: Lb39 1351.

35. P. Gueniffey, *La Révolution française et les élections: Suffrage, participation et élection pendant la période constitutionnelle, 1789–1792* (thesis under direction of F. Furet), EHESS, 1991.

36. Cf. nos. 492, 494, and 496 of *L'Ami du peuple*.

37. Ibid., no. 244, 8 October 1790.

38. Ibid., no. 391, 6 March 1791.

39. J.-P. Marat, *Le Publiciste de la République française*, no. 220, 18 June 1793.

40. Ibid., no. 198, 21 May 1793.

41. C. Desmoulins, *The Miller's Insignia*, inscription.

42. C. Desmoulins, *Protests against new abuses, by the author of free France*, n.p., n.d. Bibliothèque Nationale: Lb39 2380.

43. N. de Bonneville, *The Iron Mouth*, Paris, imprimerie du Cercle social, April 1791. Bibliothèque Nationale: Lc2 317, no. 39.

44. Johann Caspar Lavater, *Essays on Physiognomy, Designed to Promote the Knowledge and the Love of Mankind*, The Hague, 1781–1803, 4 vols., Bibliothèque

Nationale: V 1915–1918; *On Physiognomic Signs Suitable for Allowing the Recognition of Great Men*, preceded by *Essay on Megalanthropogenesia by L. J. M. Robert*, Paris, Year X, Bibliothèque Nationale: Tb68 84; *The Art of Knowing Men by Physiology*, Paris, 1806, Bibliothèque Nationale: V44024. On Lavater: M. Dumont, "The Fashionable Success of a False Science: The Physiognomy of Johann Kaspar Lavater," *Actes de la recherche en sciences sociales*, no. 54, September 1984, pp. 2–30; J.-J. Courtine, *Histoire du visage: exprimer et taire ses émotions, XVIe–XIXe siècle*, Paris: Rivages, 1988; A.-M. Jaton, *Jean Gaspard Lavater*, Lausanne, 1988; and the first chapter of G. Tytler, *Physiognomy in the European Novel: Faces and Fortunes*, Princeton: Princeton University Press, 1982.

45. J. C. Lavater, *Physiognomy, or The Art of Knowing Men According to the Features of Their Physiognomy*, Lausanne: L'Age d'homme, reprinted in 1979, pp. 6–7, 100.

46. M. Dumont, "The Fashionable Success of a False Science," p. 5.

47. *The Physico-Economical Library*, Paris, 1786. Bibliothèque Nationale: S 18910, no. 34.

48. See R. Hennequin's study, *Edme Queneday des Riceys, portraitiste au physionotrace*, Troyes: Société Académique de l'Aube, 1926.

49. J. C. Lavater, *Physiognomy*, p. 127.

50. R. Darnton, *Mesmerism and the End of Enlightenment in France*, Cambridge: Harvard University Press, 1968.

51. *The first attack of the claw on the black foxes*, n.p., n.d. Bibliothèque Nationale: Lb39 1049. [*Renard* (fox) can refer to spies and informers. Trans.]

52. Klaus Herding, "Diogenes, Symbolic Hero of the French Revolution," in M. Vovelle (ed.), *L'Image de la Révolution française*, Oxford: Pergamon Press, 1989, Vol. 3, pp. 2259–71.

53. *Diogenes at the Estates General*, n.p., 1789. Bibliothèque Nationale: Lb39 1740.

54. C. Desmoulins, *Protests against new abuses*.

55. *Dialogue between Diogenes the cynic and d'Esp[préménil] the energumen*, n.p., May 1789. Bibliothèque Nationale: Lb39 1760.

56. *Diogenes at the Hôtel de Ville and in the sixty districts of Paris*, n.p., December 1789. Bibliothèque Nationale: Ln39 2703.

57. *L'Observateur Féminin pour Mme de Verte Allure*, n.p., n.d. Bibliothèque Nationale: Lc2 356, no. 3.

58. C. Desmoulins, *Les Révolutions de France et de Brabant*, no. 4.

59. Ibid., no. 28.

60. *Advice to the public, and chiefly to the Third Estate, in the name of the Commandant of the Château des Isles Sainte-Marguerite*, n.p., 1788. Bibliothèque Nationale: Lb39 685.

61. J.-P. Marat, *L'Ami du peuple*, 5 October 1789.

62. Ibid., 12 June 1791.

63. C. Desmoulins, *Les Révolutions de France et de Brabant*, no. 22.

64. *The patriot tailor, or the clothes of Tricky Dick [jean-foutre]*, n.p., n.d. Bibliothèque Nationale: Lc2 378 A, no. 1.

65. A. de Baecque, "Anti-noble Discourse (1787–1792). The Origins of a Slogan: 'The People Against the Fat,'" *Revue d'histoire moderne et contemporaine*, January–March 1989, pp. 3–28.

66. C. Desmoulins, *Les Révolutions de France et de Brabant*, no. 33.

67. *L'Ennemi des aristocrates*, n.p. Bibliothèque Nationale: Lc2 558, no. 6.

68. Ibid.

69. Ibid., no. 7.

70. J.-P. Marat, *L'Ami du peuple*, no. 306, 10 December 1790.

71. Ibid., no. 329, 3 January 1791.

72. *Opinion of Sieyès on several articles of the plan for the Constitution*, 2 Thermidor Year III, p. 7.

Chapter 7

1. M. Ozouf, *La Fête révolutionnaire*, Paris: Gallimard, 1976, p. 9. In English: *Festivals and the French Revolution*, trans. Alan Sheridan. Cambridge: Harvard University Press, 1988, p. 3.

2. C.-M. Bosséno, "Actors and Spectators in the Official Festivals of the Revolution," in B. de Andia, V. N. Jouffre, et al. (eds.), *Fêtes et Révolution*, Paris: Délégation à l'Action Artistique de la Ville de Paris (DAAVP), 1989, pp. 112–39.

3. *Aerostatic festival that will be celebrated today, 18 July 1790, at the Champ de Mars*, n.p., n.d. Bibliothèque Nationale: Lb39 3763.

4. *Faithful description of all that preceded, accompanied, and followed the ceremony of the National Confederation of 14 July 1790*, n.p., n.d. Bibliothèque Nationale: Lb39 3768.

5. Ibid.

6. *Aerostatic festival*.

7. *Faithful description*.

8. See "Receipts for the bottles provided for the banquets of 14 and 18 July 1790" in the manuscripts of the Bibliothèque Nationale, fonds français 7005, fol. 5.

9. *Aerostatic festival*.

10. *Faithful description*.

11. *The great Kindness of the National Assembly*, Paris, n.d. Bibliothèque Nationale: Lb39 9090.

12. *Faithful description*.

13. S. Robic, "An Excess of Salvation. Jean-Pierre Camus: A Baroque Practice of the Devout Novel," in the contributions to the colloquium *L'Homme baroque*, Prague, 12–17 March 1991, forthcoming from Editions de l'EHESS.

14. J.-P. Camus, *The Academic Conference*, Paris, 1630. Bibliothèque Nationale: Z 19919, p. 33.

15. Ibid., pp. 180–82.

16. Lequinio, *Prejudices destroyed*, Paris, 1792. Bibliothèque Nationale: R 25453.

17. J.-A. Cérutti, *Letter on the advantages and origins of French gaiety*, n.p., n.d. Bibliothèque Nationale: X 19198.

18. P.-L. Ginguené, *On the authority of Rabelais in the present Revolution*, In Utopia, at Paris, 1791. Bibliothèque Nationale: Lb39 4493.

19. *The regiment of the cloth: Patriotic Christmas presents offered to all the reformed religious orders*, Paris, 1790. Bibliothèque Nationale: Lb 39 2756.

20. *Quick sketch that can give an idea of a great painting, "At the bottom of the stairs of the Estates General,"* n.p., 1789. Bibliothèque Nationale: Lb 39 1764.

21. *The satire of satires*, n.p., 1778. Bibliothèque Nationale: Ye 23 333.

22. J.-A. Cérutti, *Universal satire: Leaflet dedicated to all the powers of the Earth*, Paris, 1788. Bibliothèque Nationale: Ln2 26.

23. A. Rivarol, *Little Dictionary of Great Men of the Revolution*, Paris, 1790. Bibliothèque Nationale: Lb39 3899.

24. *The Acts of the Apostles*, Paris, 2 November 1789. Bibliothèque Nationale: Lc2 273, chapter 16, pp. 3–4.

25. *The Acts of the Apostles*, chapter 1.

26. J.-P. Brissot, *Le Patriote français*, no. 602, 2 April 1791. *The golden legend* warns its readers in its leaflet of February 1791: "The purpose of this work, undertaken by a Society of Patriot writers, is to prove to the Aristocrats that all the laughers are not on their side, and that one can also laugh on the Revolutionary road."

27. J. Guilhaumou, "The Thousand Tongues of Father Duchesne: The Parade of Popular Culture during the Revolution," *Dix-Huitième Siècle*, no. 18, 1986, pp. 143–54; O. Elyada, "The Popular Parisian Press and Carnival Time, 1788–1791," in M. Vovelle (ed.), *L'Image de la Révolution française*, New York: Pergamon Press, 1990, Vol. 1, pp. 108–17.

28. *First letter from Ramponeau to the brave Father Duchesne*, Paris, 1791. Bibliothèque Nationale: Lb39 7717.

29. *First conversation between a fishwife and a market porter*, n.p., n.d. Bibliothèque Nationale: Lb39 7577. On the *poissard* genre, see P. Frantz, "Travestis poissards," *Revue des sciences humaines*, no. 190, 1982, pp. 7–20; and A. P. Moor, *The Genre Poissard and the French Stage of the Eighteenth Century*, New York: Columbia University Press, 1935.

30. *Three fishwives drinking to the health of the Third Estate at carnival time*, n.p., 1789. Bibliothèque Nationale: Lb39 1229.

31. *Solemn procession of the ragladies of La Halle*, n.p., n.d. Bibliothèque Nationale: Lb39 7705.

32. O. Elyada, "Mother Duchesne: Popular Masks and Pamphlet Wars, 1789–1791," *Annales historiques de la Révolution française*, no. 271, January–March 1988, pp. 1–16.

33. A. Buée, *Jacques-René Hébert to his fellow citizens*, Paris, 27 May 1793. Bibliothèque Nationale: Fol Lb41 4754.

34. A. Buée, *Mother Duchesne correcting her husband*, November 1790, Bibliothèque Nationale: Lc2 3884. This answers "Bend over and you'll have no war, or The Abbé Maury whipped by Father Duchesne," in Hébert's *Father Duchesne*, no. 5.

35. *In the name of Mother Duchesne. Very energetic anathema against the oath-swearers*, Bibliothèque Nationale: Lc2 586; *Great conversion of Father Duchesne by his wife*, Bibliothèque Nationale: Lc2 584; *Great wrath of Mother Duchesne*, Bibliothèque Nationale: Lc2 585; *Great judgment of Mother Duchesne*, Bibliothèque Nationale: Lc2 587.

36. J.-A. Cérutti, *Letter on the advantages and origins of French gaiety*.

37. *The labors of Hercules*, Paris, 1790. Bibliothèque Nationale: Res Enfer 332, p. 30.

38. *Archives of the Police of the Prefecture of Paris*, AA 86, item 53.

39. *Patriotic Discipline, or Fanaticism Corrected*, n.p., n.d. Bibliothèque Nationale: Cabinet des estampes, Coll. de Vinck 3495.

40. Ibid., n.p., 7 April 1791. Bibliothèque Nationale: Cabinet des estampes, Coll. de Vinck 3494.

41. *Letter from Rabelais, formerly parish priest of Meudon, to the 94 editors of the Acts of the Apostles*, Paris, 5 April 1791. Bibliothèque Nationale: Lb39 3250. A political cartoon illustrates this advice very explicitly: *The Papal Brief of 1791*, n.p., n.d. Bibliothèque Nationale: Cabinet des estampes, Coll. de Vinck 3452. (See Figure 15.)

42. J.-P. Brissot, *Le Patriote français*, no. 602, 2 April 1791.

43. J. L. Tallien, *Great arraignment of the burning of the Pope and his Brief*, n.p., n.d. Bibliothèque Nationale: Lb39 9921. See also Gorsas's *Courrier* of 3 May 1791.

44. Descriptions given by Gorsas's *Courrier*, 4 May 1791.

45. Bibliothèque Nationale: Cabinet des manuscrits, fonds français 11697, fol. 147.

46. Bibliothèque Nationale: Cabinet des manuscrits, fonds français 11697, fol. 151.

47. Bibliothèque Nationale: Cabinet des manuscrits, nouvelles acquisitions française 2671, fol. 142. (Edict reproduced in *L'Ami du peuple*, "false" Marat, no. 60, 3 February 1790. Bibliothèque Nationale: Lc2 232.)

48. C. Desmoulins, *Les Révolutions de France et de Brabant*, no. 10, Vol. 1, p. 494.

49. *Register of deliberations of the General Assembly of the Saint-Dominique district of Jacobins*, 1790. Bibliothèque Nationale: Lb40 1415.

50. Decree of 7 August 1793 bearing "Penalty of death against any citizen disguised as a woman in gatherings." One instance of the enforcement of this measure is known: on 11 Germinal Year II, the *Moniteur* mentions among the guillotined victims of that day a certain "individual who took part in a riot and presented himself disguised as a woman."

51. The "Journal of events as I learn of them" kept by the bookseller Siméon Prosper Hardy between 1764 and 1789 (Bibliothèque Nationale: Cabinet des manuscrits, manuscrits français 6680–6687) was published for the years 1764 to 1773 by M. Tourneux and M. Vitrac, *"Mes loisirs," par S. P. Hardy*, Paris: A. Picard, 1912. The rest remains unpublished. I thank Bernard Coppens and Daniel Roche for allowing me to read a photocopied version of the original manuscript.

52. *Account of a Patriotic festival given by the youth of Angers to the deputies of the youth of Nantes*, n.p., February 1789. Bibliothèque Nationale: Lb39 1228.

53. *Three fishwives drinking to the health of the Third Estate.*

54. *Great patriotic masked ball*, n.p., n.d. Bibliothèque Nationale: Lb39 2465.

55. *The Acts of the Apostles*, chapter 23, pp. 19–20.

56. Ibid., chapter 42, pp. 220–27.

57. *La Jacobinière, parade like none other*, n.p., n.d. Bibliothèque Nationale: Lb39 9776.

Chapter 8

1. L.-S. Mercier, *The New Paris*, Paris, 1798, pp. 175–76.

2. *Archives parlementaires from 1787 to 1860. Complete collection of the legislative and political debates of the French chambers, begun under the direction of Messrs. Mavidal and Laurent, continued by the Institut d'Histoire de la Révolution Française*, Vol. 93, pp. 77–78.

3. Michel Vovelle, *Piété baroque et déchristianisation en Provence au XVIIIe siècle*, Paris: Le Seuil, 1978, p. 84.

4. On this competition, see P. Hintermeyer, *Politiques de la mort: Le concours de l'Institut sur les funérailles convenant à un peuple libre, germinal an VIII*, Paris: Payot, 1981. On death during the Revolution: M. Vovelle, *La Mort et l'Occident de 1300 à nos jours*, Paris: Gallimard, 1983, pp. 489–503; E. Liris and J.-M. Bizière (eds.), *La Révolution et la mort*, Toulouse: Presses universitaires du Mirail, 1991.

5. L.-S. Mercier, *The New Paris*, Vol. 5, pp. 98, 103.

6. *Archives parlementaires*, meeting of 25 December 1792, Vol. 55, p. 434.

7. *Great speech made by C.-P. Ronsin, on the occasion of the funeral ceremony, performed on 26 August in the garden of the Tuileries, ordered in honor of our brothers-in-arms dead on the day of 10 August*, n.p., n.d. Bibliothèque Nationale: Lb39 10861.

8. *Oration pronounced by Puhlpin, magistrate of the section of Les Arcis, for the inauguration of the busts of Lepeletier and Marat*, n.p., n.d. Bibliothèque Nationale: Lb40 1698.

9. *Civic sermon to the soldiers of the Republic by Citizen Dorfeuille*, published in the *Archives parlementaires*, meeting of 23 January 1793, Vol. 57, p. 607.

10. *Archives parlementaires*, meeting of 28 Floréal Year II, Vol. 90, p. 413.

11. Citizen Guirault, *Funeral oration of the "Social Contract"* section, published in the *Archives parlementaires*, meeting of 1 September 1793, Vol. 73, p. 301.

12. On the portrayal of the English developed during the Terror, see S. Wahnich, "The English: Extraordinary Enemies (January–July 1794)," *Dictionnaire des usages sociopolitiques*, Paris: Institut National de la Langue Française, URL, Coll. "Saint-Cloud," 1989, Vol. 4, pp. 35–62.

13. *Archives parlementaires*, meeting of 24 Prairial Year II, Vol. 91, pp. 549–50.

14. *Speech uttered at the Champs-Elysées for the inauguration of the busts of Lepeletier and Marat, Décadi 10 of Brumaire Year II*. Bibliothèque Nationale: Lb40 1899.

15. The details of this ceremony can be found in the *Speech on the death of Lazowski, and great details of his funeral, by Destournelles*, Paris, 1793. Bibliothèque Historique de la Ville de Paris: 132769.

16. J.-C. Bonnet, "The Illustrious Dead: Funeral Oration, Academic Praise, Necrology," in P. Nora (ed.), *Les Lieux de mémoire*, Paris: Gallimard, 1984, II. *La Nation*, Vol. 3, pp. 217–41; M. Papenheim, *Erinnerung und Unsterblichkeit. Semantische Studien zum Totenkult in Frankreich*, Stuttgart: Klett-Cotta, 1992.

17. Lazowski, a mysterious individual and ephemeral hero, commanded the artillery of the Federates on 10 August during the assault on the Tuileries. Suspected by the Girondins of being one of the leaders during the September massacres, he was sharply taken to task as a symbol of political radicalism. Marat energetically defended him. Lazowski was then one of the stakes in the struggle between Montagnards and Girondins. His mysterious death (poisoning was mentioned in one camp, "debauchery" in the other) in April 1793 allows the Commune de Paris, politically arrayed on the side of the Cordeliers and the Montagnards, to make him into a martyr, and the ceremonies that surround his funeral rites (funeral in the Place du Carrousel, monument raised to his glory, adoption of his daughter by the Commune) play a role in the increase in intensity of the radical demands made by the Cordeliers, supported by the Parisian sansculottes.

18. *Notification to the Finistère* section *on 28 April 1793, on the burial of Lazowski*, n.p. Bibliothèque Nationale: m. 9441.

19. *Speech on the death of Lazowski*.

20. *Report on the funeral ceremony in Amiens in honor of Michel Lepeletier*, published in the *Archives parlementaires*, meeting of 6 March 1793, Vol. 59, p. 646.

21. Barère, for example, holds forth on 23 January 1793 before the Convention at the time of Lepeletier's death: "Citizens, it is not one man alone who was struck, it is you; it is not Michel Lepeletier who was basely assassinated, once more it is you. It is not a deputy against whose life the blows were struck; it is the life

of the nation, it is public freedom, it is the sovereignty of the people. Yes, your death will be useful to the Republic; your death is a victory over tyranny," *Archives parlementaires*, Vol. 57, p. 604.

22. On the *Collection of the Heroic Deeds of the French Republicans*, see Alphonse Aulard, *Etudes et leçons sur la Révolution française*, Vol. 8, Paris, 1921. This collection, published in Year II and many times reprinted (the Bibliothèque Nationale possesses nine different editions), is made up of five installments joined into one volume (Bibliothèque Nationale: 8e Ln2 39) including almost 150 "heroic deeds."

23. *Report in the name of the Committee of Public Instruction on the publication of the Collection of the Heroic Deeds of the French Republicans, by Thibaudeau, meeting of 13 Messidor Year II*. Bibliothèque Nationale: Le38 835.

24. *Collection of the Heroic Deeds of the French Republicans*, Vol. 4, Year II, presented at the bar of the Convention on 1st Prairial by Léonard Bourbon.

25. *Archives parlementaires*, Vol. 80, pp. 372–75.

26. Ibid., Vol. 66, p. 234. 27. Ibid., Vol. 79, p. 318.

28. Ibid., Vol. 48, p. 338. 29. Ibid., Vol. 82, p. 74.

30. *Civic festival in honor of Chalier, martyr for freedom, on 30 Frimaire Year II*. Bibliothèque Nationale: Lb40 1337.

31. *Archives parlementaires*, Vol. 88, pp. 255–58.

32. J. Guilhaumou, "The Death of Marat in Paris," in J.-C. Bonnet (ed.), *La Mort de Marat*, Paris: Flammarion, 1986.

33. *Archives parlementaires*, meeting of 15 July 1793, Vol. 69, p. 49.

34. M. Ozouf, "The Simulacrum and the Revolutionary Festival," in J. Ehrard and P. Vialleneix (eds.), *Les Fêtes de la Révolution*, Paris: Société des études robespierristes, 1977, pp. 323–53.

35. On the distribution of portrait busts, see A. Soboul, *The Sans-Culottes: The Popular Movement and Revolutionary Government, 1793–1794*, Paris: Clavreuil, 1958, pp. 299–309; and J.-C. Bonnet, "The forms of Celebration of the Cult of Marat," in *La Mort de Marat*, pp. 101–27.

36. *Archives parlementaires*, Vol. 88, p. 255.

37. Ibid., Vol. 79, p. 211.

38. Lise Andriès, "Prints of Marat During the Revolution: An Emblematics," in *La Mort de Marat*, pp. 187–201.

39. *Archives parlementaires*, Vol. 73, p. 301.

40. Ibid., Vol. 73, p. 643. 41. Ibid., Vol. 84, p. 249.

42. Ibid., Vol. 60, pp. 349–50. 43. Ibid., Vol. 86, pp. 382–83.

44. Ibid., Vol. 55, p. 124. 45. Ibid., Vol. 83, pp. 146–47.

46. Ibid., Vol. 59, p. 147.

47. As an example, see Isser Woloch's work, *The French Veteran from the Revolution to the Restoration*, Chapel Hill: University of North Carolina Press, 1979.

48. *Archives parlementaires*, Vol. 91, p. 64.

49. Ibid., Vol. 66, p. 105.

50. Ibid., Vol. 90, p. 323. The omissions in the speech are taken into account by the original in the *Moniteur*.

51. *Archives parlementaires*, Vol. 81, p. 331.

52. Ibid., Vol. 43, p. 249.

53. Ibid., Vol. 59, p. 634.

54. *The Society of the Jacobins: Collection of Documents Toward the History of the Jacobins Club of Paris*, ed. A. Aulard, Paris: Librairie Jouaust, 1889, Vol. 4, pp. 683–84.

55. *Civic festival in honor of Chalier, martyr for freedom, on 30 Frimaire Year II*.

56. *Archives parlementaires*, Vol. 80, p. 329.

57. *Festival given in Fréjus in honor of the martyrs for freedom, on 30 Nivôse Year II*, n.p. Bibliothèque Nationale: Lb40 1342.

58. Georges Lefebvre, "On the Law of 22 Prairial Year II," *Annales historiques de la Révolution française*, 1951; reprinted in *Etudes sur la Révolution française*, Paris: PUF, 1954.

59. M. Ozouf, "War and Terror in Revolutionary Discourse, 1792–1794," in *L'Ecole de la France: Essais sur la Révolution, l'utopie et l'enseignement*, Paris: Gallimard, 1984, pp. 109–27.

60. A. de Baecque, "The Course of a Wound: From Corruption to Regeneration. The Brave Locksmith Geffroy, Harbinger of the Great Terror," in the contributions to the colloquium *The Terror in the French Revolution*, K. Baker, C. Lucas, and S. Kaplan (eds.), Stanford and Oxford: Pergamon Press, 1994.

61. *Archives parlementaires*, Vol. 90, p. 577.

62. Ibid., Vol. 91, pp. 17–25.

63. Ibid., pp. 41–43.

64. Ibid., Vol. 92, pp. 247–48.

Conclusion

1. *Report made in the name of the Committee of Public Safety on a provisional and revolutionary form of government. Meeting of 28 Brumaire Year II*. Bibliothèque Nationale: Le38 2031. Concerning this corporeal metaphor in Jacobin discourse, see L. Jaume, *Echec au libéralisme: Les Jacobins et l'Etat*, Paris: Ed. Kimé, 1990, pp. 26–29, as well as the text edited by F. Brunel of the *Principes régénérateurs du système social*, Paris: Publications de la Sorbonne, 1992.

2. Reproduced in the *Patriotic and literary annals*, Vol. 16–17, p. 1641.

3. Concerning Hercules, symbol of the sovereignty of the Republican people, see the chapter entitled "The Imagery of Radicalism" in L. Hunt, *Politics, Culture, and Class in the French Revolution*, Berkeley: University of California Press,

1984, pp. 87–119; and J. Schlanger, "The People—with Forehead Inscribed," in J. Ehrard and P. Vialleneix (eds.), *Les Fêtes de la Révolution française*, Paris: Société des études robespierristes, 1977, pp. 387–95.

4. J.-L. David, *Speech before the National Convention, meeting of 17 Brumaire Year II*, Bibliothèque Nationale: Le 38 554. This speech is reported and discussed extensively by *Les Révolutions de Paris*, no. 217, pp. 288–90.

5. On this debate, see the works of D. Arasse, "The Guillotine, or The Unimaginable: The Result of Simple Mechanics," *Revue des sciences humaines*, nos. 186–87, April–October 1982, an article later developed and enlarged to the dimension of a book: *The Guillotine and the Terror*, Paris: Flammarion, 1987.

6. *On the torture of the guillotine, by Professor Soemmering*, n.p., Year III, Bibliothèque Nationale: Tb11 5, republished in *The Encyclopedic Magazine*, Thermidor Year III, no. 3, pp. 463–77, then in *Le Moniteur*, 9 November 1795.

7. *Opinion of Citizen Sue, professor of medicine and botany, on the torture of the guillotine*, Paris, Year III, Bibliothèque Nationale: Tb11 6, reprinted in *The Encyclopedic Magazine*, Year III, no. 14.

8. Dr. Wedekind's opinion was published in *Le Moniteur* of 11 November 1795, no. 26, p. 395, and that of Dr. Lepelletier in *Le Moniteur* of 15 November 1795, no. 26, p. 426.

9. Sédillot, *Historic and physiological reflections on the torture of the guillotine*, Paris, Year IV. Bibliothèque Nationale: Tb11 80.

10. *What, finally, should we think about the torture of the guillotine? New examination of this question*, Paris, Year IV. Bibliothèque Nationale: Tb11 7.

11. P.-J.-G. Cabanis, *Note on the opinion of M. Soemmering and of Citizen Sue concerning the torture of the guillotine*. Written in the first months of Year IV, this little book was reprinted in the *Œuvres complètes* of Cabanis, Paris, 1823, Vol. 2, pp. 161–83, Bibliothèque Nationale: Z 44547.

12. *Opinion of Citizen Sieyès. Meeting of 2 Thermidor Year III of the National Convention*. Bibliothèque Nationale: Le38 1551.

13. P.-J.-G. Cabanis, *Some considerations on the social organization in general and particularly on the new Constitution. Speech before the Commission of the Council of the Five Hundred*, 25 Frimaire Year VIII. Bibliothèque Nationale: Le44 35.

14. *Speech pronounced by Cabanis at the Commission of the Council of the Five Hundred, meeting of 3 Nivôse Year VIII*. Bibliothèque Nationale: Le44 48.

15. I have continued this research into the allegorical embodiment of the monarchy, and later of the Republic, in a study forthcoming in the journal *Representations*, to be published by the University of California Press (Berkeley) under the title "Power Incarnate. The Evolution of the Allegorical Mode Between 1750 and 1800: A Political Crisis of Representation." Concerning the rivalry between Hercules and feminine allegories, see L. Hunt, *Politics, Culture, and Class*, pp. 87–119.

16. *Collection of letterheads of the first French Republic*, Cabinet des manuscrits de la Bibliothèque Nationale, nouvelles acquisitions françaises 3568-3571.

17. Maurice Agulhon has written an account of this history, *Marianne into Battle: Republican Imagery and Symbolism in France, 1789–1880*, Paris: Flammarion, 1979, followed by *Marianne au pouvoir: L'imagerie et la symbolique républicaines de 1880 à 1914*, Paris: Flammarion, 1989. The third volume of this research was presented by the author during the "Images of the French Revolution" conference held at the Musée de Vizille in June 1991 under the sponsorship of the Institut d'Histoire de la Révolution Française. The text can be found in the *Annales historiques de la Révolution française*, no. 289, July–September 1992.

Index

In this index, "f" after a page number indicates a separate reference on the next page; "ff" indicates separate references on the next two pages. A continuous discussion over two or more pages is indicated by a span of page numbers (e.g., "57–59"); *passim* is used for a cluster of references in close but not consecutive sequence.

Addison, Joseph, 218
Alighieri, Dante. *See* Dante
Antraigues, Emmanuel-Louis d', 56
Aranda, Count d', 40–44 *passim*
Artois, Compte d', 46–53 *passim*, 162f, 169, 171, 243, 292
Aubry du Bochet, Pierre-François, 115f
Audoin, Pierre-Jean, 224
Aulard, Alphonse, 210–15 *passim*

Bailly, Jean-Sylvain, 125, 193–97 *passim*, 202, 238, 244, 269, 275, 277
Bakhtin, Mikhail, 179
Bara, François-Joseph, 287
Barère de Vieuzac, Bertrand, 118, 149, 186, 222, 284, 304f
Barnave, Antoine, 72ff, 150f, 156, 187–90 *passim*, 196f, 202
Bart, Jean (fictional character), 262
Basire, Claude, 215

Beauharnais, Alexandre-François-Marie de, 301
Beaumarchais, Pierre-Augustin, 49
Beauterne, Antoine de, 168
Benjamin, Walter, 23–25 *passim*
Bérenger, Laurent-Pierre, 92
Bergasse, Nicolas, 77
Bertillon, Alphonse, 216
Beurnonville, Pierre, 297
Bichat, Xavier, 5, 93
Billaud-Varenne, Jacques-Nicolas, 310–17 *passim*, 319
Bodin, Jean, 100
Bordes, Philippe, 193, 203
Bossuet, Jacques-Bénigne, 134, 255
Bouche, Charles-François, 115
Bouchotte, Jean-Baptiste, 297
Boufflers, Stanislas-Jean, 47
Boulainvilliers, Henri de, 173
Bouquier, Gabriel, 183

Bourdon de la Crosnière, Léonard, 287, 300

Bourdon de l'Oise, François-Louis, 282

Brialy, Jean-Claude, 21

Brillat-Savarin, Jean-Anthelme, 115

Brissot, Jacques-Pierre, 59–64 *passim*, 175, 220, 227–32 *passim*, 261, 267, 270, 278

Buée, Adrien-Quentin, 263

Buffon, Georges-Louis, 5, 176

Bureaux de Pusy, Jean-Xavier, 108

Burke, Edmund, 56, 154

Buzot, François-Nicolas, 72

Cabanis, Pierre-Jean-Georges, 93, 316–22 *passim*

Camus, Jean-Pierre, 151, 254f, 321

Carra, Jean-Louis, 160f, 224

Cato, 221f

Certeau, Michel de, 18, 22

Cérutti, Joseph-Antoine, 9, 80, 94, 96, 135, 181, 198, 255–61 *passim*, 288

Chabot, François, 215

Chalier, Marie-Joseph, 282, 284f, 290, 303

Champcenetz, Louis-Edmond, 259

Charles IX, 60

Chartier, Roger, 217

Chénier, André, 189f

Chénier, Marie-Joseph, 223f, 302f

Cicero, 221f

Cloots, Anacharsis, 124

Coigny, Duc de, 48, 50, 53

Collot d'Herbois, Jean-Marie, 285, 300, 304, 306

Condorcet, Marie-Jean-Antoine-Nicolas, 273

Coquille, Guy, 89

Corday, Charlotte, 192, 284

Courtois, Edme-Bonaventure, 215

Couthon, Georges-Auguste, 290

Daney, Serge, 5

Dante, 161, 163

Danton, Georges-Jacques, 212–15 *passim*

Darnton, Robert, 16, 177, 217

David, Jacques-Louis, 17, 183–205, 281, 291, 293f, 311ff, 322

Delandine, Antoine-François, 150f

Descimon, Robert, 89

Desmoulins, Camille, 59–70 *passim*, 122–27 *passim*, 141, 221–45 *passim*, 270, 278

Desprez, Jean-Louis, 167

Diderot, Denis, 135

Diogenes, 238f

Dorfeuille, Antoine, 283

Dominique, Antoine, 21

Douchet, Jean, 1

Drouet, Jean-Baptiste, 69

Dubois-Crancé, Edmond-Louis, 186, 197, 236

Duchesne, Father (fictional character), 261–66 *passim*

Duchesne, Mother (fictional character), 263

Duclos, Charles, 134

Dupont de Nemours, Pierre Samuel, 115

Duport-Dutertre, Marguerite-Louis-François, 117, 260

Durand de Maillane, Pierre-Toussaint, 151

Duval d'Epréménil, Jean-Jacques, 159

Fabre d'Eglantine, Philippe-François, 215

Fersen, Axel von, 48, 69

Francis de Sales, 254

Frederick II of Prussia, 40, 42, 47

Fréron, Louis-Marie-Stanislas, 223f

Frey, Junius, 215

Gadamer, Hans-Georg, 18

Gamain, François, 283

Garrau, Pierre-Anselme, 214

Gasparin, Thomas-Augustin, 282–92 *passim*

Gauchet, Marcel, 101f

Gaultier de Biauzat, Jean-François, 115, 118
Gérard, Michel, 195
Gerle, Christophe-Antoine, 127, 193
Giesey, Ralph, 89, 100
Ginguené, Pierre-Louis, 258f
Gobineau, Arthur de, 216
Godard, Jean-Luc, 5, 20–25 passim
Goltz, Baron de, 40, 42, 47
Gorsas, Antoine-Joseph, 59–69 passim, 160, 224, 227, 267f
Gouttes, Jean-Louis, 115
Gouy d'Arsy, Louis-Henry, 116
Grégoire, Baptiste-Henri, 72, 136f, 151ff, 193, 274
Grouvelle, Philippe-Antoine, 259
Guéry, Alain, 89
Guillotin, Joseph-Ignace, 274

Hammett, Dashiell, 21
Hautefort, Marie de, 31
Hébert, Jacques-René, 69, 263f
Hegel, Georg Wilhelm Friedrich, 187
Henri IV, 51, 58, 89, 138, 272
Henriot, Louis-François, 209
Hérault de Séchelles, Marie-Jean, 215
Hobbes, Thomas, 90, 196
Homer, 290
Huarte, Juan, 88
Hunt, Lynn, 180, 216

Jessé, Joseph-Henri, 115
Joseph II of Austria, 43f, 47
Julien de Toulouse, Jean, 215

Kant, Emmanuel, 233, 235
Kantorowicz, Ernst, 76
Karina, Anna, 21

La Bruyère, Jean de, 255
La Fayette, Gilbert de, 53, 57, 64, 238, 244, 269, 277
Lafayette, Louise de, 31
La Fontaine, Jean de, 91, 155
Laguna, Andrés de, 88

Lakanal, Joseph, 289
La Luzerne, César-Guillaume, 147, 150
Lamballe, Marie-Thérèse de, 32
Lambesc, Charles Eugène, 169, 199
La Rochefoucauld, François-Alexandre de, 222
Lassone, Joseph-Marie-François, 41f
Lavater, Johann Caspar, 233–39 passim
Lavicomterie, Louis, 59
Le Bon, Gustave, 216
Lebreton, Pierre-François, 214
Le Chapelier, Isaac-Pierre-Guy, 274
Lefebvre, Georges, 64, 303
Le Hodey, Pierre, 148
Lepeletier de Saint-Fargeau, Louis-Michel, 192, 280–95 passim, 305
Lequinio de Kerblay, Joseph-Marie, 255
Le Trosne, Guillaume-François, 109
Lévis, Gaston-Pierre de, 117, 147–50 passim
Linguet, Jean-Pierre, 249
Louis, Antoine, 133, 156
Louis IX, 58
Louis XII, 51
Louis XIII, 31, 100
Louis XIV, 30, 37, 58f, 90, 134, 138
Louis XV, 30–42 passim, 47, 53, 59f, 91, 135, 138, 172, 237, 243
Louis XVI, 8–19 passim, 29–39 passim, 46–96 passim, 134, 138, 180, 192, 265, 272, 277, 282f
Loustallot, Elysée, 138, 164, 223, 288
Luchet, Jean-Pierre-Louis, 236
Luckner, Nicolas, 301

Mairobert, Pidansat de, 48
Malouet, Louis-Antoine-Victor, 149
Manent, Pierre, 90
Marat, Jean-Paul, 11, 17, 146, 191f, 199, 215, 219–32 passim, 240, 244, 270, 278, 283ff, 291–95 passim, 305f
Maria-Theresa of Austria, 40–45 passim
Marie-Antoinette, 35–38 passim, 46–54 passim, 66–69 passim, 161, 169ff, 199, 243, 277

Marin, Louis, 8
Martin d'Auch, Joseph, 117, 196, 198, 202
Massieu, Jean-Baptiste, 60
Masuyer, Charles-Louis, 282
Mathiez, Albert, 212–16 *passim*
Maupetit de la Mayenne, Michel-
   René, 195
Mauriac, Claude, 21
Maury, Jean-Siffrein, 159, 170, 219, 222,
   243, 263
Mercier, Louis-Sébastien, 160, 280f
Mercy-Argenteau, Florimond-Claude
   de, 40
Mesmer, Franz Anton, 77
Michel, Régis, 187, 201
Mignet, François-Auguste, 108
Mirabeau, Honoré-Gabriel, Compte de,
   80, 116–21 *passim*, 147, 190, 195–98
   passim, 202ff, 212, 221f, 243, 248, 274,
   282, 288, 316
Mirabeau, Victor, Marquis de, 135
Montana de Monserrate, Bernardino, 88
Muguet de Nanthou, François-Félix, 73

Necker, Jacques, 83, 159, 236, 272
Neufchâteau, François, 204
Nodier, Charles, 178
Noillac, Benigne Victor Aimé, 86f, 92

Œlsner, Conrad Engelbert, 314
Orléans, Duc d', 32, 57, 159, 226,
   262, 274
Ozouf, Mona, 112, 125, 247, 304

Palissot de Montenoy, Charles, 259
Panckoucke, André-Joseph, 227
Paré, Ambroise, 43, 131f, 175
Pellerin, Joseph-Michel, 115
Pérez de Herrera, Cristóbal, 88
Pétion de Villeneuve, Jérôme, 72, 139
Philippeaux, Pierre, 282
Pio, Luigi, 46
Pison du Galand, Alexis-François,
   116, 118
Pithou, Ange, 199

Pius VI, 266ff
Polignac, Diane de, 32, 159, 162–63,
   169, 171
Pottier, Charles-Albert, 298f
Prieur de la Marne, Pierre-Louis,
   72, 196f
Provence, Comte de, 46, 47

Queneday des Riceys, Edme, 234

Rabaut Saint-Etienne, Jean-Paul, 94,
   152–56 *passim*, 193, 222
Rabelais, François, 91, 180, 257–66
   passim
Raffron du Trouillet, Nicolas, 213–14
Ramel-Nogaret, Dominique-Vincent, 115
Ramponeau (fictional character), 262
Reinhardt, Antoine-Pierre, 133f
Restif de la Bretonne, Nicolas-Edme,
   144, 218
Reubell, Jean-François, 64
Richelet, Pierre, 132
Ricoeur, Paul, 1
Rivarol, Antoine, 56, 135, 236, 259f
Robespierre, Maximilien, 60, 64,
   72, 195ff, 212–15 *passim*, 222, 270,
   284f, 306
Roederer, Pierre-Louis, 64
Rohan, Prince Edouard de, 48, 50
Roland de la Platière, Marie-Jeanne-
   Phlipon, 212
Ronsin, Charles-Philippe, 283
Rousseau, Jean-Jacques, 58, 272
Royou, Thomas-Marie, 266f

Sabatier de Castres, Antoine, 259
Saint-Just, Antoine-Louis, 60
Saint-Pierre, Bernardin de, 2
Saint-Priest, François-Emmanuel de, 221
Saint-Simon, Duc de, 46
Scarnafis, Count de, 40, 45
Schlanger, Judith, 6
Shakespeare, William, 91
Sieyès, Emmanuel, 2, 9, 12, 17, 63, 76–

128, 157, 174, 192–97 *passim*, 201, 203, 236, 245, 309, 312–20 *passim*
Soemmering, Samuel Thomas, 314–17 *passim*
Sophocles, 290
Sue, Jean-Joseph, 188, 315ff

Taine, Hippolyte, 209–17 *passim*
Target, Guy-Jean-Baptiste, 95f, 227
Théveneau de Morande, Charles, 172
Thibaudeau, Antoine-Claire, 287, 300
Thouret, Jacques-Guillaume, 110–20 *passim*
Todorov, Tzvetan, 179

Turgot, Anne-Robert, 109

Vadier, Marc-Guillaume, 72, 214
Verdet, Louis, 117
Vien, Joseph-Marie, 183f
Villette, Charles-Michel de, 124
Virieu, François-Henri de, 151
Voltaire (François-Marie Arouet), 134, 178, 180, 248, 272
Vovelle, Michel, 281

Winckelmann, Johann Joachim, 184–203 *passim*

Library of Congress Cataloging-in-Publication Data

Baecque, Antoine de.
[Corps de l'histoire. English]
The body politic : corporeal metaphor in revolutionary France,
1770-1800 / Antoine de Baecque : translated by Charlotte Mandell.
p.   cm. – (Mestizo spaces = Espaces métissés)
Includes bibliographical references and index.
ISBN 0-8047-2915-1 (cloth : alk. paper). – ISBN 0-8047-2817-8 (pbk : alk. paper)
1. France–Politics and government–18th century–Historiography.
2. Body, Human–Symbolic aspects–France.   3. Louis XVI, King of
France, 1754-1793–Death and burial–Symbolic aspects.   4. France–
History–Revolution, 1789-1799–Art and the revolution.   I. Title.
II. Series: Mestizo spaces.
DC136.5b3413   1997
944'.035–dc21   96-44516
                                                                       CIP

⊗ This book is printed on acid-free, recycled paper.

Original Printing 1997
Last figure below indicates year of this printing:
06   05   04   03   02   01   00   99   98   97